W9-CHS-925

A BOOK OF
SEA JOURNEYS

By the same author:

Naval
Sub-Lieutenant: A Personal Record of the War at Sea
Nelson's Captains
Pursuit: The Chase and Sinking of the *Bismarck*
Menace: The Life and Death of the *Tirpitz*

Crime and the Law
10 Rillington Place
The Trial of Stephen Ward
A Presumption of Innocence
The Portland Spy Case
Wicked Beyond Belief

Travel and Diaries
One Man's Meat
Very Lovely People

Play
Murder Story

Anthologies
A Book of Railway Journeys
A Book of Sea Journeys
(in preparation) A Book of Air Journeys

A ship of 1565

A BOOK OF
SEA
JOURNEYS

Compiled by
LUDOVIC KENNEDY

RAWSON, WADE PUBLISHERS, INC.
New York

Library of Congress Cataloging in Publication Data
Main entry under title:

A Book of sea journeys.

   1. Ocean travel—Literary collections. 2. English
literature. 3. American literature. 4. Ocean travel—
Collected works. I. Kennedy, Ludovic Henry Coverley.
PR1111. 025B6   820′.8′0355   81-40268
ISBN 0-89256-178-5   AACR2

Composition by American—Stratford Graphic Services, Inc.
  Brattleboro, Vermont
Printed and Bound by Halliday Lithograph Corp.
  West Hanover, Massachusetts
Designed by Jacques Chazaud
First Edition

"The Ship" by W. H. Auden. Copyright 1945, 1966 by W. H. Auden. Reprinted from
W. H. Auden: Collected Poems by W. H. Auden, edited by Edward Mendelson, by
permission of Random House, Inc. and Faber & Faber Ltd. Extract from *The Cruise
of the Nona* by Hilaire Belloc. Reprinted by permission of A. D. Peters & Co. Ltd. and
the Estate of Hilaire Belloc. Extract from *The Memoirs of Chateaubriand*, by Chateaubriand, selected and translated by Robert Baldick. Copyright © 1961 by Hamish
Hamilton Ltd. Reprinted by permission of Alfred A. Knopf, Inc. Extract from *The
Big Spenders* by Lucius Beebe published by the Hutchinson Publishing Group Ltd.
and Doubleday and Co., Inc. Copyright © 1966 by Doubleday & Company, Inc. Reprinted by permission of Doubleday & Company, Inc. and the Hutchinson Publishing
Group. Extract from *Surface at the Pole* by James Calvert, published by McGraw-
Hill Book Company. Copyright © 1960 by James Calvert. Reprinted by permission
of McGraw-Hill Book Company. Extract from *Point of Departure* by James Cameron,
published by Arthur Barker. Reprinted by permission of David Higham Associates
Ltd. Extract from *Pedro Vaz De Caminha's Report on the Discovery of Brazil* from
Portuguese Voyages translated by C. David Ley. Published by Everyman's Library
series. Copyright J. M. Dent & Sons Ltd. Extract from *The Life and Letters of David
Beatty* by Admiral Chalmers. Reprinted by permission of the Estate of Admiral Peter
Chalmers. Copyright A. P. Watt Ltd. Extract from *Man Overboard* by Winston
Churchill. Published in the Harmsworth Magazine, January 1899. Reprinted by per-
mission of the Executors of Lady Churchill. Extract from *The Liners* by Terry Cole-
man, published by Allen Lane The Penguin Press. Reprinted by permission of A. D.

For
Ailsa and Chris
and, in time, Saskia

ILLUSTRATIONS:

SOURCES AND ACKNOWLEDGMENTS

Jacket: The Guildhall Gallery, London; *Frontispiece:* (A ship of 1565) National Maritime Museum, London; 46. Mansell Collection; 56. Mary Evans Picture Library; 62. The British Library; 73. Mansell Collection; 79. Mary Evans Picture Library; 83. By courtesy of William Buchan; 86, 89, and 95. Mary Evans Picture Library; 109. Imperial War Museum; 111. (top) Mansell Collection (bottom) Mary Evans Picture Library; 133. National Maritime Museum, London; 137. Mary Evans Picture Library; 147 and 151. National Maritime Museum, London; 155. Mary Evans Picture Library; 161. National Maritime Museum, London; 165. Ajax News Photos; 170. Imperial War Museum; 173. Godfrey-Fausset Collection, Churchill College, Cambridge; 174. National Maritime Museum, London; 177. Imperial War Museum; 203. Associated Press, London; 235 and 241. Mary Evans Picture Library; 249. National Maritime Museum, London; 257. Mary Evans Picture Library; 263. The British Library; 269. Mary Evans Picture Library; 271. National Portrait Gallery, London; 275. Stewart Bale Ltd; 279. Mary Evans Picture Library; 281. Compagnie Générale Transatlantique; 287. Mary Evans Picture Library; 289 and 292. The Illustrated London News Picture Library; 298. Cooper-Bridgeman Library; 301. Compagnie Générale Transatlantique; 302, 303 and 305. Mary Evans Picture Library; 317. The Royal Geographical Society, London; 329. The Tate Gallery, London; 341. Sir Joseph Causton & Sons Ltd; 343. The Naval Library, London; 352. The British Library; 385. Mansell Collection; 393. Compagnie Générale Transatlantique.

CONTENTS

PART TWO: A Miscellany of Voyages

NAVAL OCCASIONS

CONTENTS

SMALL BOATS

WHEN THE GOING WAS ROUGH

VOYAGING IN STYLE

OPEN BOATS

FICTION

INTRODUCTION

My own love of the sea began with my father, a sailor dedicated to it, cruelly axed as a naval captain under the economy measures after World War I, but called back on his own request at the beginning of World War II to command the armed merchant cruiser *Rawalpindi*. On her second patrol off Iceland, the *Rawalpindi* met the German battle-cruisers *Scharnhorst* and *Gneisenau*, and after the briefest of engagements went down with colours flying. There were twenty-six survivors; my father was not among them.

I loved that man more than any other, and longed to follow in his steps. When I was a boy we holidayed at Nairn on Scotland's Moray Firth, and for me the most exciting day of the year was when the British Home Fleet sailed up the Firth to its summer base at Invergordon. It took all morning for those distant gray shapes, silhouetted against the cliffs of the further shore, to enter harbour; and as the long procession passed slowly by,—battleships, aircraft carriers, cruisers, destroyers—my father, beside me on the lawn that ran down to the seafront, pointed out each class of ship, explaining its armament and functions. One memorable summer we drove round to Invergordon to take tea on board the battleship *Nelson*, whose navigating officer was my cousin; to me it was like entering Valhalla.

I was unable to join the Navy as a boy, but, like my father, my time came with the last war, which I spent mostly in destroyers. We took convoys to Russia and Newfoundland, chased the *Bismarck*, raided German garrisons in Norway, crossed to France on D-Day. I loved every moment of it, sometimes fearing the enemy, never the sea, however turbulent its mood; for, as Hilaire Belloc says, the sea is in our blood, it is the matrix of creation, it was whence we came, and to which, I may add, when my time is up, I shall (if my executors obey me) be delivered.

Afterwards I took sea voyages whenever possible, and, before they all disappeared, sailed in the great liners—*Nieuw Amsterdam, Ile de France, America, Queen Mary*—to and from America. On three occasions, during the seventies, my wife and I were guest lecturers on part of the world cruises of the *Q.E.2*. During one of them, halfway between Japan and Hawaii, I was preparing to show a documentary film I had made for the BBC on the German battle-cruiser *Scharnhorst* (the ship that had sunk my father's) when I was told that the *Scharnhorst*'s former navigating officer was one of the passengers on board. Before the public performance (which he agreed to introduce with me), we had a private showing. In the huge empty theatre he saw once again his shipmates and friends of thirty years before, lived again those stirring and uncertain times; and when I turned to him as the lights went up to ask for his reactions, he was sitting like a statue in his seat, his eyes awash with tears.

And so to sea literature, almost as vast as the sea itself. It would be impossible for one man in a lifetime to discover all it contains, let alone find the time to read it. Unlike my *Book of Railway Journeys*, a large proportion of which would have been chosen by any other anthologist, this selection has been arbitrary and entirely subjective. The length of the average contribution is inevitably greater than those of the railway book, for sea journeys are in a different time-scale to railway journeys. Otherwise, my criteria for selection have been the same: lively and stylish writing and/or peculiar events. As with the railways, nothing is here because it ought to be; everything because I like it.

All the same, I have kept to certain self-imposed rules. Firstly, this is a book about sea *journeys*. It is not about the sea (if it were, I would have included something from Rachel Carson, and Matthew Arnold's *Dover Beach*, and that lovely sonnet of Keats's that begins: "It keeps eternal whisperings around/ Desolate shores . . ."). Nor is it about ships in harbour or sailors ashore. Nor, finally, does it embrace more than marginally the "Avast there, me hearties" school of writing, all creaking timbers and wind whistling in the rigging.

So the potential reader, browsing through the contents, will find nothing of Dana, Forester, Bartimeus, Taffrail, Shalimar, Kent. The sea stories of these authors are mostly about professional sailors; and admirable though many of them are, I propose here to let the amateurs, both passengers and sailors, have their say. Not that these last two should be linked too closely; for to many passengers the sea is uninteresting in itself, a tiresome impediment that lies between them and journey's end; while to today's small boat adventurers, the successors to Slocum, Chichester, Tabarly, etc., the sea is everything, a personal challenge, an Everest to be scaled, the means of grace and the hope of glory.

The factor common to all sections of the book is people—people as diverse as Noel Coward and Herman Melville, Lady Brassey and Ethel Mannin. People with a sharp eye for character and situation, like Anna Buchan and Harold Nicolson and Sophy Taylor. People with a nice edge of humour, especially about themselves, like Eugenio de Salazar and Robert Louis Stevenson. People of unusual courage like Ernest Shackleton and Ann Davison and Poon Lim. People who write about other people so felicitously that it is a joy to read whatever they write, like Hickey and Chateaubriand, Dickens and Conrad, Stephen Crane and Edgar Allan Poe, Somerset Maugham and Evelyn Waugh.

I decided at an early stage that I would avoid accounts of sea battles, for strictly speaking they are not journeys and, in any case, rarely make for entertaining reading. But should I include extracts from descriptions of life in warships, a field that could furnish the contents of several anthologies on its own? In the end, I decided to assemble a short collection of pieces about life in the Royal Navy and the U.S. Navy, which for one reason or another have taken my fancy over the years. I only wish I had had the space for more.

I am very grateful to all those who have helped me with the assembly of the material: Annabel Craig for her further untiring research work for text and illustrations; A. K. Astbury and Roy Fuller again for directing me, from· their wide knowledge of, respectively, sea prose and poetry, to items that would not otherwise have come my way; J. H. H. Gaute for putting me on to the Winston Churchill short story; and Peter Kemp, David James, Ann Monsarrat, Donald McCormick, Bruce Coward, Robin Acland, Commander Philip Aubrey, Leonard Coweill, H. Landless, Sir John Mallabar, Audrey Parry, Philip Stevens, Phyllis Garlick, and Geoffrey Taylor for their interesting and helpful suggestions. Joan Bailey has been an ever-ready guide to the darkest recesses of the London Library (as have all the staff there); and I also owe thanks to David Brown and the staff of the Naval Historical Library; my secretary Joyce Turnbull has skillfully coped with a mass of correspondence, including the obtaining of permissions; and the book's editors Hilary Davies in London and James Wade and Charles McCurdy in New York, have once again given me much valued advice and support.

The sea is the consolation of this our day, as it has been the consolation of the centuries. It is the companion and the receiver of men. It has moods for them to fill the storehouse of the mind, perils for trial, or even for an ending, and calms for the good emblem of death. There, on the sea, is a man nearest to his own making, and in communion with that from which he came, and to which he shall return. For the wise men of very long ago have said, and it is true, that out of the salt water all things came. The sea is the matrix of creation, and we have the memory of it in our blood.

HILAIRE BELLOC,
The Cruise of the Nona

The sea is there in order to be sailed over.
CAPTAIN JOSHUA SLOCUM

Part One

TRAVELLERS

AT LARGE

1500: Pedro Vaz de Caminha

Pedro Vaz de Caminha, secretary to the Portuguese admiral
Pedro Cabral, reports to the King of Portugal on the discovery
of Brazil.

SIRE,

The admiral of this fleet, besides the other captains, will write
to Your Majesty telling you the news of the finding of this new
territory of Your Majesty's which has just been discovered on
this voyage. But I, too, cannot but give my account of this matter
to Your Majesty, as well as I can, though I know that my powers
of telling and relating it are less than any man's. May it please
Your Majesty, however, to let my good faith serve as an excuse
for my ignorance, and to rest assured that·I shall not set down
anything beyond what I have seen and reflected on, either to add
beauty or ugliness to the narrative. I shall not give any account
of the crew or the ship's course, since that is the pilot's concern,
and I should not know how to do so. Therefore, Sire, I begin
what I have to tell thus:

And I say that our departure from Belém was, as Your Majesty knows, on Monday, 9th March. On Saturday, the 14th of the
same month, between eight and nine o'clock we sailed between
the Canary Islands, going in nearest to the Grand Canary. We
were becalmed in sight of them the whole day, for some three or
four leagues. On Sunday the 22nd of the same month, at about ten
o'clock, we came in sight of the Cape Verde Islands, or, to be
precise, St. Nicholas's Island, as the pilot, Pero Escobar, declared.

On the following night, the Monday, we discovered at dawn
that Vasca de Ataide and his ship had been lost, though there
was no strong or contrary wind to account for this. The admiral
sought him diligently in all directions, but he did not appear

again. So we continued on our way across the ocean until on the Tuesday of Easter week, which was 21st April, we came across some signs of being near land, at some 660 and 670 leagues from the aforesaid island, by the pilot's computation. These signs were a great quantity of those long seaweeds sailors call *botelho*, as well as others to which they give the name of "asses' tails." On the following morning, Wednesday, we came across the birds they call "belly-rippers."

This same day at the hour of vespers we sighted land, that is to say, first a very high rounded mountain, then other lower ranges of hills to the south of it, and a plain covered with large trees. The admiral named the mountain Easter Mount and the country the Land of the True Cross.

He ordered them to drop the plumb-line, and they measured twenty-five fathoms. At sunset, about six leagues from the shore, we dropped anchor in nineteen fathoms, and it was a good clean anchorage. There we lay all that night. On Thursday morning we set sail and made straight for land, with the smaller ships leading, the water being seventeen, sixteen, fifteen, fourteen, thirteen, twelve, ten and nine fathoms deep, until we were half a league from the shore. Here we all cast anchor opposite a river mouth. It must have been more or less ten o'clock when we reached this anchorage.

From there we caught sight of men walking on the beaches. The small ships which arrived first said that they had seen some seven or eight of them. We let down the longboats and the skiffs. The captains of the other ships came straight to this flagship, where they had speech with the admiral. He sent Nicolau Coelho on shore to examine the river. As soon as the latter began to approach it, men came out on to the beach in groups of twos and threes, so that, when the longboat reached the river mouth, there were eighteen or twenty waiting.

They were dark brown and naked, and had no covering for their private parts, and they carried bows and arrows in their hands. They all came determinedly towards the boat. Nicolau Coelho made a sign to them to put down their bows, and they put them down. But he could not speak to them or make himself understood in any other way because of the waves which were breaking on the shore. He merely threw them a red cap, and a

linen bonnet he had on his head, and a black hat. And one of them
threw him a hat of large feathers with a small crown of red and
grey feathers, like a parrot's. Another gave him a large bough
covered with little white beads which looked like seed-pearls. I
believe that the admiral is sending these articles to Your Majesty.
After this, as it was late, the expedition returned to the ships, without succeeding in having further communication with them, because of the sea.

Pôrto Seguro of Vera Cruz,
Pedro Vaz de Caminha, 1 May 1500

ed. CHARLES DAVID LEY,
Portuguese Voyages

1573: Eugenio de Salazar

There is no wittier or more revealing account of what it must
have been like crossing the Atlantic in a Spanish ship in the
sixteenth century than this, by Eugenio de Salazar. De Salazar
made the journey with his wife and family in 1573, just
eighty-one years after Columbus. He had a distinguished career
in the Spanish colonial service, as Governor of Tenerife in the
Canaries and judge in the courts of Guatemala and Mexico. On
this occasion he was travelling to take up a judicial appointment on the island of Hispaniola.

I was in the island of Tenerife when my new appointment came
through, and I had to make my own arrangements for getting to
Hispaniola. I inquired about sailings, and eventually booked passage, at great expense, in a ship called the *Nuestra Señora de los
Remedios*—better by name than by nature, as it turned out. Her
master assured me that she was a roomy ship, a good sailor, seaworthy, sound in frames and members, well rigged and well
manned. Accordingly, on the day we were to sail and at the hour
of embarkation, Doña Catalina and I, with all our household,
presented ourselves on the bank of the Styx. Charon, with his

skiff, met us there, ferried us out to the ship, and left us on board. We were given, as a great privilege, a tiny cabin, about two feet by three by three, and packed in there, the movement of the sea upset our heads and stomachs so horribly that we all turned white as ghosts and began to bring up our very souls. In plain words, we were seasick, we vomited, we gagged, we shot out of our mouths everything which had gone in during the last two days, we endured by turns cold depressing phlegm, bitter burning choler, thick and heavy melancholy. There we lay, without seeing the sun or the moon; we never opened our eyes, or changed our clothes, or moved, until the third day.

Then, lying in the darkness, I was startled by a voice nearby which cried out, "Blessed be the light of day, and the Holy True Cross, and the Lord of Truth, and the Holy Trinity; blessed be the day and the Lord who makes it, blessed be the day and the Lord who sends it," and then the voice recited the prayers Our Father and Hail Mary; and then said, "Amen. God give us good weather and a prosperous voyage, may the ship make a good passage, Sir Captain, and master, and all our good company, amen; so let us make, let us make a good voyage; God give your worships good day, gentlemen aft and forward." I was somewhat reassured when I heard this, and said to my wife, "Madam, though I fear we may be in the Devil's house, I still hear talk of God. I will get up and go out, and see what is happening—whether we are moving, or being carried away."

So I dressed as well as I could, and crawled out of the whale's belly or closet in which we lay. I discovered that we were riding on what some people call a wooden horse, or a timber nag, or a flying pig, though to me it looked more like a town, a city even. It was certainly not the city of God that the sainted Augustine talked about. I saw no churches, nor courts of justice: nobody says mass there, nor do the inhabitants live by the laws of reason. It is a long narrow city, sharp and pointed at one end, wider at the other, like the pier of a bridge; it has its streets, open spaces and dwellings; it is encircled by its walls—that is to say, its planking; at one end it has its forecastle, with more than ten thousand knights in barracks, and at the other its citadel, so strong and firmly built that a puff of wind could tear it from its foundations and tip it into the sea. It has its batteries, and a gunner to command them; it has chain-wales, foresail, fore topsail, main course, topsail and top-gallant, bonnet and second bonnet. It has a capstan, the bane of the sailors because of the labor of turning it, and of the passengers because of the noise it makes, one or two fountains, called pumps, the water from which is unfit for tongue and palate to taste, or nostrils to smell, or even eyes to see, for it comes out bubbling like Hell and stinking like the Devil. The dwellings are so closed in, dark and evil-smelling that they seem more like burial vaults or charnelhouses. The entrances to these dwellings are openings in the deck, which they call companionways or hatches, and anyone who goes through them can say goodbye to the order, the comfort and the pleasant smells of dwellings on the earth; since indeed, these lodgings seem to be the caves of Hell (even if they are not so in fact) it is only natural that those who enter them should do so through holes in the ground, as if they were being buried. There is such a complicated network of ropes and rigging on every side, that the men inside it are like hens or capons being carried to market in grass or netting coops.

There are trees in the city, not fragrant with gums and aromatic spices, but greased with fish oil and stinking tallow. There are running rivers, not of sweet, clear, flowing water, but of turbid filth, full not of grains of gold like the Cibao or the Tagus, but of grains of very singular pearl-enormous lice, so big that sometimes they are seasick and vomit bits of apprentice.

The ground of this city is such, that when it rains the soil is hard, but when the sun is hot the mud becomes soft and your feet stick to the ground so that you can hardly lift them. For game in the neighborhood, there are fine flights of cockroaches—they call them *curianas* here—and very good rat-hunting, the rats so fierce that when they are cornered they turn on the hunters like wild boars. The lamp and the *aguja* of the city are kept at night in the binnacle, which is a chest very like the commodes which some gentlemen keep in their bedrooms. The city is dark and gloomy, black without and pitch-black within, black ground and walls, dark inhabitants, swarthy officers. In sum, from bow-sprit to bonaventure, from stem to stern, from hawse-holes to oilerport, from the port chains to the starboard topgallant yardarms, from one side to the other, there is nothing for which a good word can be said, except indeed that, like women, it is a necessary evil.

I would pass the time listening to the master giving his orders and watching the sailors carrying them out, until the sun was high in the sky; and then I would see the ship's boys emerge from the half-deck with a bundle of what they called table cloths, but alas, not white or handsomely embroidered. They spread out these damp and dirty lengths of canvas in the waist of the ship, and on them piled little mounds of broken biscuit, as white and clean as the cloths, so that the general effect was that of a cultivated field covered with little heaps of manure. They would then place on the "table" three or four big wooden platters full of beefbones without their marrow, with bits of parboiled sinew clinging to them. They call the platters *saleres*, and so have no need of salt-cellars. When the meal is laid out, one of the boys sings out, "Table, table, Sir Captain and master and all the company, the table is set, the food is ready, the water is drawn for his honor the captain, the master and all our good company. Long live the King of Castile by land and by sea! Down with his enemies, cut off their heads! The man who won't say 'amen' shall have nothing to drink. All hands to dinner! If you don't come you won't eat."

In a twinkling, out come pouring all the ship's company saying "amen," and sit on the deck round the "table," the bo'sun at the head and the gunner on his right, some crosslegged, some with legs stretched out, others squatting or reclining, or in any posture they choose; and without pausing for grace these knights of the round table whip out their knives or daggers—all sorts of weapons, made for killing pigs or skinning sheep or cutting purses —and fall upon those poor bones, stripping off nerves and muscles as if they had been practicing anatomy at Guadalupe or Valencia all their lives, and before you can say a *credo*, they leave them as clean and smooth as ivory. On Fridays and vigils they have beans cooked in salt water, on fast days salt cod. One of the boys takes round the mess-kettle and ladles out the drink ration—a little wine, poor thin stuff, not improved by the baptism it receives. And so, dining as best they can, without ceremony or order, they get up from the table still hungry.

The captain, the master, the navigator and the ship's notary dine at the same time, but at their own mess, and the passengers also eat at the same time, including myself and my family, for in this city you have to cook and eat when your neighbors do, otherwise you find no fire in the galley, and no sympathy. I have a squeamish stomach, and I found these arrangements very trying, but I had no choice but to eat when the others were hungry, or else to dine by myself on cold scraps, and sup in darkness. The galley—"pot island" as they call it—is a great scene of bustle and activity at meal times, and it is amazing how many hooks and kettles are crowded on to it; there are so many messes to be supplied, so many diners and so many different dinners. They all talk about food. One will say, "Oh for a bunch of Guadalajara grapes!"; another, "What would I give for a dish of Illescas berries?"; somebody else, "I should prefer some turnips from Somo de Sierra"; or again, "For me, a lettuce and an artichoke head from Medina del Campo"; and so they all belch out their longings for things they can't get. The worst longing is for something to drink; you are in the middle of the sea, surrounded by water, but they dole out the water for drinking by ounces, like apothecaries, and all the time you are dying of thirst from eating dried beef and food pickled in brine, for My Lady Sea won't keep or tolerate meat or fish unless they have tasted her salt. Even so, most of what you eat is half rotten and stinking, like the disgusting fu-fu that the *bozal* negroes eat. Even the water, when you can get it, is so foul that you have to close your eyes and hold your nose before you can swallow it. So we eat and drink in this delectable city.

And if the food and drink are so exquisite, what of the social life? It is like an ant-heap, or, perhaps, a melting-pot. Men and women, young and old, clean and dirty, are all mixed up together, packed tight, cheek by jowl. The people around you will belch, or vomit, or break wind, or empty their bowels, while you are having your breakfast. You can't complain or accuse your neighbors of bad manners, because it is all allowed by the laws of the city. Whenever you stand on the open deck, a sea is sure to come aboard to visit and kiss your feet; it fills your boots with water, and when they dry they are caked with salt, so that the leather cracks and burns in the sun. If you want to walk the deck for exercise, you have to get two sailors to take your arms, like a village bride; if you don't, you will end up with your feet in the air and your head in the scuppers. If you want to relieve yourself, you have to hang out over the sea like a cat-burglar clinging to a wall. You have to placate the sun and its twelve signs, the moon and the other planets, commend yourself to all of them, and take a firm grip of the wooden horse's mane, for if you let go, he will throw you and you will never ride him again. The perilous perch and the splashing of the sea are both discouraging to your purpose, and your only hope is to dose yourself with purgatives.

There is always music in the city: the sighing of the wind and the roaring of the sea as the waves strike the ship.

If there are women on board (and no city is without them) what a caterwauling they make with every lurch of the ship! "Mother of God, put me back on shore!" but the shore is a thousand miles away. If it rains in torrents, there are, it is true, roofs and doorways for the people to shelter; if the sun beats down, enough to melt the masts, there are shady places where you can escape it, and food and drink (of sorts) to refresh you. But if you are becalmed in the midst of the sea, the victuals running out and no water left to drink, then indeed you have need of comfort; the ship rolling night and day; your seasickness, which you thought you had left behind, returning; your head swimming; then there is no recourse but prayer, till the wind gets up again. When the sails are filled, and drawing well, they are a beautiful sight, but when the wind draws ahead, and the canvas slats against the masts, and the ship can make no headway, then life in her becomes a misery. If the navigator is inexperienced, and does not know when to look out for the land, or how to avoid reefs and shoals, you may seem one minute to be sailing in open water, and the next be fast aground, filling with water and about to drown. If the ship is a sluggish sailer, as ours was, she will hardly move with the wind before the beam. The other ships in company must constantly haul their luff, lie to and wait for her, or else take her in tow. But when she has a fair wind on the beam she will forge ahead, heeling well over to the wind; and we are all seasick once again.

Everything in the city is dark by day and pitch-black by night; but in the first watch of the night, after supper (which is announced in the same way as dinner), the city is reminded of God by the voice of the boy who sets the lamp in the binnacle. He cries, "Amen, and God give us good-night, Sir Captain, master and all the company." After that, two boys come on deck and say prayers, *Pater Noster*, *Ave Maria* and *Salve Regina*. Then they take their places to watch the hour-glass, and chant, "Blessed was the hour when God was born, Saint Mary who bore him and Saint John who baptized him. The watch is set, the glass is running. We shall make a good passage, if God wills." When the sand has run through the glass, the boy on watch sings out, "That which is past was good, better is that which is to come. One glass is gone, the second is running, more will run, if God wills; keep a good count, for a prosperous voyage; up forward there, attention and keep a good watch." The look-outs in the bows reply with a shout, or rather a grunt, to show that they are awake. This is done for each glass, that is, every half-hour, until morning. At midnight the boy calls the men who are to keep the middle watch. He shouts, "Turn out, turn out, the watch; turn out, turn out, hurry along, the navigator's watch; time is up, show a leg, turn out, turn out." The rest of us sit up till then; but after midnight we can no longer keep our eyes open, and we all go off to the accommodation allotted to us. I creep into my little hutch with my family, and we doze fitfully, to the sound of the waves pounding the ship. All night we rock about as if we were sleeping in hammocks; for anyone who travels in a ship, even if he is a hundred years old, must go back to his cradle, and sometimes he is rocked so thoroughly that the cradle overturns and he ends up in a heap with cradles and sea chests on top of him.

We sailed on alone for the first six days; for the eight other ships which left Santa Cruz harbor in Tenerife in our company all disobeyed the instructions which the judge of the *Contratación de Indias* sent us, and each went off on his own during the first night. What pleasure can a man have on board a solitary ship at sea? No land in sight, nothing but lowering sky and heaving water, he travels in a blue-green world, the ground dark and deep and far below, without seeming to move, without seeing even the wake of another ship, always surrounded by the same horizon, the same at night as in the morning, the same today as yesterday, no change, no incident. What interest can such a journey hold? How can he escape the boredom and misery of such a journey and such a lodging?

It is pleasant to travel on land, well mounted and with money in your purse. You ride for a while on the flat, then climb a hill and go down into the valley on the other side, you ford a running river and cross a pasture full of cattle, you raise your eyes and watch the birds flying above you; you meet all kinds of people by the way and ask the news of the places they have come from. You overtake two Franciscan friars, staves in their hands, skirts tucked into their girdles, riding the donkeys of the seraphic tradition, and they give you "Good-day and thanks be to God." Then, here comes a Jeronymite father on a good trotting mule, his feet in wooden stirrups, a bottle of wine and a piece of good ham in his saddle-bag. There will be a pleasant encounter with some fresh village wench going to town scented with pennyroyal and marjoram, and you call out to her, "Would you like company, my dear?" Or you may meet a traveling whore wrapped up in a cloak, her little red shoes peeping below the hem, riding a hired mule, her pimp walking beside her. A peasant will sell you a fine hare to make a fricassee; or you may buy a brace of partridge from a hunter. You see in the distance the town where you intend to sleep or stop for a meal, and already feel rested and refreshed by the sight. If today you stay in some village where the food is scanty and bad, tomorrow you may be in a hospitable and well-provided city. One day you will dine at an inn kept by some knife-scarred ruffian, brought up to banditry and become a trooper of the *Santa Hermandad;* he will sell you cat for hare, billy-goat for mutton, old horse for beef and watered vinegar for wine; yet the same day you may sup with a host who gives you bread for bread and wine for wine. If, where you lodge, tonight, your hostess is old, dirty, quarrelsome, querulous and mean, tomorrow you will do better and find a younger one, clean, cheerful, gracious, liberal, pious and attractive, and you will forget the bad lodging of the previous day. But at sea there is no hope that the road, or the host, or the lodging will improve; everything grows steadily worse; the ship labors more and more and the food gets scantier and nastier every day.

On the first Saturday out, we were still alone, and on that day, at the usual time for prayers, we held a solemn service in the city, a *Salve* and sung litany with full choir. They put up an altar with images and lighted candles. First of all the master asked, "Are we all here?" and the company responded, "God be with us." Then the master: "Let us say the *Salve*, and pray for a good passage; we will say the *Salve* and our passage will be prosperous." So we begin the *Salve;* we all sing together, we all give tongue—no fancy harmonies, but all eight keys at once. Sailors are great dividers; just as they divide each wind into its eight points, so they break the eight notes of the scale into thirty-two, diverse and perverse, resonant and dissonant. Our *Salve* was a storm, a hurricane of music. If God and His Holy Mother, and the saints to whom we prayed, attended to our singing voices and not to our hearts and spirits, it would have done us no good to beg for mercies with such raucous bawling. After the *Salve* and the litany the master, who acts as priest, continues: "Let us say together the creed in honor of the holy apostles, and ask them to intercede with Our Lord Jesus Christ, to give us a safe passage," and all who believe the creed recite it. Then one of the boys, who acts as acolyte: "Let us say the Hail Mary for ship and company"; the other boys respond, "May our prayer be received," and we all recite the *Ave*. At the end the boys all stand and say, "Amen, God give us good-night, etc."; and so ends the celebration for the day. This takes place every Saturday.

The next day, Sunday, in the morning, we sighted our vice-commodore, and she saluted us (for we were the flagship of the convoy); and we sailed contentedly in company for the next fifteen days. Then one morning the look-out at the masthead called out "Sail ho!" This caused great excitement, for to merchantmen, sailing as we were without escorting warships, any stranger is an object of suspicion; even the smallest may turn out to be a pirate. "Two sail!" cried the look-out, and doubled our alarm; "three sail"; and by this time we were convinced that we had to deal with corsairs. You may imagine how I felt, with my wife and children all on board. The gunner began to give the orders to clear away for action; the ports were opened for the falcons and culverins; the guns were loaded and run out, and small arms were mustered. Women began to shriek, "Why did we come here, miserable wretches? Whatever possessed us to go to sea?" Those who had money or jewels ran to hide them in the dark corners of the frames and futtock-timbers. We all stood by with our weapons at the best points of vantage we could find—for the ship had no nettings—all ready to defend ourselves, and we could see the same preparations on board the vice-commodore. The three ships drew closer, on a course to intercept. One was a very big ship, and caused much ironical speculation among the sailors. Some said she must be the Florentine galleon. "More likely the *Bucentaur*," said others; "She's the English *Minion*"—"No, she looks like the *Cacafogo* out of Portugal." Although there were three of them, they approached us at first as cautiously as we them; but when they came near enough for recognition, they saw who we were, and we recognized them as friends. They were, in fact, three of the missing ships of our own convoy, and all our fears vanished in the pleasure of reunion.

Even so, the sea played us another trick. The big ship closed up to speak, and as she bore down on us her helmsman misjudged his distance, and put us all in fear of our lives. His beakhead collided with our poop and holed us on the quarter so that the water poured in. Our city might have been taken by the forces of the sea within the hour, but our people ran to work and soon repaired the damage. It was an alarming experience for Doña Catalina, whose cabin was in that part of the ship. When the volleys of abuse had died down (though not the pounding of hearts) our fears were washed away with the salt water, and we greeted one another with relief and joy. The three stragglers promised to keep in sight of the flagship in future. We hoisted our flag at the main-mast head, mounted a crossbow on the poop, and lit our stern lantern at night. The other ships, when they closed us to salute, took care to come up under our lee; and all our subsequent operations were carried out in good order. The form of greeting each morning is a call on the bosun's whistle and a shout, "Good passage to you!"—bellowed loud enough to frighten anyone out of their wits; to hear this "Good voyage" unexpectedly one day would be enough to give one a bad voyage for a year of days.

We ran with a stiff northeast wind for the next four days; and the navigator and the sailors began to sniff the land, like asses scenting fresh grass. It is like watching a play, at this time, to see the navigator taking his Pole Star sights; to see him level his cross-staff, adjust the transom, align it on the star, and produce an answer to the nearest three or four thousand leagues. He repeats the performance with the midday sun; takes his astrolabe, squints up at the sun, tries to catch the rays in the pinhole sight,

and fiddles about endlessly with the instrument; looks up his almanac; and finally makes his own guess at the sun's altitude.
Sometimes he overestimates by a thousand degrees or so, sometimes he puts his figure so low that it would take a thousand years
to complete the voyage. They always went to great pains to prevent the passengers knowing the observed position and the distance the ship had made good. I found this secretiveness very
irritating, until I discovered the reason for it; that they never really
knew the answer themselves, or understood the process. They
were very sensible, as I had to admit, in keeping the details of
this crazy guesswork to themselves. Their readings of altitudes
are rough approximations, give or take a degree or so, yet on the
scale of their instruments the difference of a pin's head can produce an error of five hundred miles in the observed position. It is
yet another demonstration of the inscrutable omnipotence of
God, that the vital and intricate art of navigation should be left
to the dull wits and ham fists of these tarpaulin louts. You hear
them discussing it among themselves: "How many degrees does
Your Honor make it?" and one says, "Sixteen," another, "Barely
twenty," and yet a third, "Thirteen and a half." Then somebody
will ask, "How far does Your Honor reckon we are from land?":
one answers, "I make it forty leagues," another, "A hundred and
fifty," and the third says, "This morning I reckoned ninety-two."
It may be three or it may be three hundred; they never agree,
either with one another or with the truth.

    In the middle of all these vain conflicting arguments among
masters, navigators, and sailors who claimed to be graduates in
the art, on the twenty-sixth day out, God be praised, we sighted
land, and how much lovelier the land appears from the sea than
the sea from the land! We saw Deseada—appropriately named—
and Antigua, and set our course between them, leaving Deseada
to the east. We ploughed on, Santa Cruz hove in sight to windward, and we passed it at a distance; we reached San Juan del
Puerto Rico and coasted along the shore some way, keeping a
careful watch on Cape Bermejo, which is a notorious haunt of
pirates. We recognized Mona and the Monitos—easy to identify,
even at a distance—looked for Santa Catalina but failed to see it;
and eventually came in sight of Saona, the land of the blessed
saint, and blessed sight to us. All this time we were repeatedly

soaked by downpours of rain; but we made light of them, and thought ourselves lucky to have been spared hurricanes.

In the general rejoicing at the sight of our destination, the navigator—the wind's lieutenant and deputy, who held the reins of the wooden horse—grew a little careless, and allowed the ship to fall away to leeward of the harbor so that we had to beat with short boards in order to regain lost ground, with the result that it was already dark when we arrived off the mouth of the Santo Domingo River. We had to feel our way in, sounding as we went, and find a sheltered place to anchor for the night. We should certainly have looked very foolish if we had allowed ourselves to drift into danger, and perhaps founder, so close to the shore. We let go two anchors and a good length of cable and (thanks be to God) rode safely through the night. I did not allow any of my people ashore, because the authorities had not yet been warned of my arrival. It was the most disagreeable night of the whole voyage, for the ship pitched abominably, and our stomachs rebelled as they had done on the first day out. But I will weary you no more with the perils and miseries of the sea, except to ask you to imagine, if life can be so uncomfortable with fair winds and a relatively calm sea, what it must be like to experience contrary winds, encounters with pirates, mountainous seas and howling gales. Let men stay on firm ground and leave the sea to the fishes, say I.

Next day at dawn our city came to life, with much opening of trunks and shaking out of clean shirts and fine clothes. All the people dressed in their best, especially the ladies, who came out on deck so pink and white, so neat, so crimped, curled and adorned, that they looked like the granddaughters of the women we had seen each day at sea.

The master went ashore, and I sent my servant with a message of greeting to the president of the court. Boats began to put out to the ship, and since there was a head wind and the ship had to be warped up the river, my family and I went ashore directly in a launch which they sent for us. So we reached the longed-for land, and the city of Santo Domingo. We were kindly welcomed; and after a few days' rest I took my seat on the Bench, and here I stay for as long as God wills, without any desire to cross the sea again. I hope soon to hear that you also have the appointment which you deserve. Doña Catalina and the children send their respects and best wishes.

> from *Cartas de Eugenio de Salazar*
> J. H. PARRY (trans. & ed.), *The European Reconnaissance*

———◆———

THE SHIP

A ship from Valparaiso came
And in the Bay her sails were furled,
She brought the wonder of her name
And tidings from a sunnier world.

O you must voyage far if you
Would sail away from gloom and wet
And see beneath the Andes blue
Our white, umbrageous city set.

But I was young and would not go;
For I believed when I was young,
That somehow life in time would show
All that was ever said or sung.

Over the golden pools of sleep
She went long since with gilded spars;
Into the nigh-empurpled deep
And traced her legend on the stars.

But she will come for me once more,
And I shall see that City set,
The mountainous, Pacific shore—
By God, I half believe it yet!

OLIVER ST. JOHN GOGARTY

———◆———

1782: William Hickey

Sea literature abounds in accounts of storms, and in very few
does the quality of the writing match the intensity of the experience. The great exception is Conrad; but another is the
eighteenth-century English lawyer and memoir writer William
Hickey. In 1782, he and his common-law wife Charlotte embarked at Lisbon in the ship *Raynha de Portugal*, owned by
Luis Barretto, a rich Portuguese Bombay merchant, and here
approaching the coast of Ceylon.

At daylight on Sunday the 17th of November (a memorable day
to me), finding as I lay in bed the motion of the ship particularly uneasy, I got up to look out, and never to the last day of my
existence shall I forget the shock I experienced at what I beheld.
The horizon all round was of a blackish purple, above which
rolled great masses of cloud of a deep copper colour, moving in
every direction with uncommon rapidity; vivid lightning in every
quarter, thunder awfully roaring at a distance, though evidently
approaching us; a short, irregular sea breaking with a tremendous
surf, as if blowing furiously hard though then but moderate, the
wind, however, whistling shrill as a boatswain's pipe through the
blocks and rigging. The scene altogether was such as to appal
the bravest men on board. Going upon deck I found a dead silence
prevailing, not a syllable uttered by anyone, all looking in stupid
amazement. Not a single precaution was taken, no dead lights to
the great cabin or quarter gallery windows, not even a top-gallant
yard down; on the contrary, every sail set, notwithstanding they
reckoned themselves within a few leagues of Ceylon, for which
they were standing direct, and all this strange neglect at a time
when a British vessel would have struck everything that could be
and made all snug as possible in order to be the better able to
receive the shock that was so perceptibly coming upon us.

In great tribulation I returned to my cabin, telling Mrs.
Hickey to secure anything she was particularly anxious about and
prepare herself to undergo severe trials. I had a small strong ma-

hogany escritoire in which I kept my letters, papers of consequence and a few trinkets and valuable articles I had. This I
jammed in between two of the projecting knees in my cabin in
such a manner that until the ship went to pieces it could not be
thrown out of its place. At seven we each of us swallowed a dish
of tea, being the last and only refreshment we had for many subsequent sorrowful hours.

Although all violent tempests are in a great measure alike, par-
taking of the same circumstances and consequences as those I
have already had occasion to attempt a description of, yet this was
so peculiarly dreadful, and our escape with life so wonderful, that
I am led to relate the melancholy particulars. At eight in the
morning it began to blow hard, torrents of rain pouring down,
rendering it almost dark as night. Then was an order first given
to take in top-gallant sails and reef topsails. The order was too
late; the instant the sails were lowered they were blown to atoms,
being torn from their respective yards in shreds. The sea suddenly increased to an inconceivable height, the wind roaring to
such a degree that the officers upon deck could not make themselves heard by the crew with the largest speaking-trumpets. Between nine and ten it blew an absolute hurricane, far surpassing
what I had any idea of. As it veered all round the compass so did
the sea increase infinitely beyond imagination, one wave encountering another from every direction, and by their mutual force
in thus meeting ran up apparently to a sharp point, there breaking
at a height that is actually incredible but to those who unhappily
saw it. The entire ocean was in a foam white as soap-suds. At a
quarter before eleven the fore-topmast, yard rigging and all went
over the side, the noise of it being imperceptible amidst the roaring of wind and sea. In a few minutes it was followed by the
mizzen-mast, which snapped like a walking-stick about eight feet
above the quarter-deck; part of the wreck of it unfortunately got
foul of the rudder chains and every moment struck the ship's bottom with excessive violence. At half-past eleven the fore-mast
went, being shivered into splinters quite down to the gun-deck.
The fall of it drew the main-mast forward, whereby the levers
upon which the pumps worked (as they do in all ships built in the
East Indies) were totally destroyed, putting an end to our pumping. Before noon the main-mast and bolt-sprit both went at the

same instant. Thus in the short space of four hours was this noble vessel reduced to such a state of distress as few have ever been in. Our situation seemed hopeless, not a creature on board but thought every minute would be the last of their lives. When the masts were gone she immediately began to roll with unparalleled velocity from side to side, each gunwale, with half the quarter-deck, being submerged in water each roll, so that we every moment expected she would be bottom uppermost or roll her sides out.

Thus buffeted about on the angry ocean, I told my poor Charlotte, whom I had secured in the best way I could and was endeavouring to support, that all must soon be over, it being quite impossible that wood and iron could long sustain such extraordinary and terrific motion, and such were my real sentiments. The dear woman, with a composure and serenity that struck me most forcibly, mildly replied, "God's will be done, to that I bend with humble resignation, blessing a benevolent providence for permitting me, my dearest William, to expire with you, whose fate I am content to share, but oh! my dearest love, let us in the agonies of death be not separated," and she clasped me in her arms.

Mr. Bateman, at the commencement of the gale, had gone upon deck, from whence he dared not again venture to stir, but was obliged to lay himself down under the wheel and there remain. Mr. Kemp and Mr. Brown had lashed themselves to the gun rings of the aftermost part in the great cabin to prevent their being dashed from side to side. Whilst thus situated, three out of the five stern windows, frames and all, suddenly burst inward from the mere force of the wind, the noise attending which was such that I conceived the last scene of the tragedy was arrived, but awful as that moment was, the recollection of the way in which Mr. Brown had doubted the facts stated in the *Directory* relative to the hurricanes at the breaking up of the monsoon recurred so forcibly that I could not help saying to him, "Now, Mr. Brown, I think you can no longer entertain a belief that the accounts in the *Directory* are fabricated or exaggerated." He made me no answer, but raising his hands clasped together looked the very image of despair.

The ship was apparently full of water, and seemed to be so completely overwhelmed that we all thought she was fast settling downward. Nevertheless the velocity and depth of her rolling abated nothing, tearing away every article that could be moved; not a bureau, chest or trunk but broke loose and was soon demolished, the contents, from the quickness and constant splashing from one side to the other of the ship, becoming a perfect paste, adhering to the deck between the beams, many inches in thickness, so as near the sides actually to fill up the space to the deck. Amongst the furniture destroyed was a large bureau with a bookcase top belonging to Mr. Barretto, in which were deposited the whole of his ship's papers and his own private ones, scarce a remnant of any one of which was saved.

During the severity of the hurricane about twenty noble fellows, such as would not have disgraced the British Navy, at the head of whom stood the boatswain, acted with the same determined spirit they had shown on the 9th of September, doing all that could be performed by men, while the rest of the crew gave themselves up to despair, clinging round their priest and screeching out prayers for pardon and mercy in such dismal and frantic yells as was horrible to hear. So eager were the miserable enthusiasts to embrace the image of Jesus Christ upon the Cross (which the priest held in his hand) in the instant of their dissolution that they in their endeavours so to do actually tore it to pieces.

By two in the afternoon every bulkhead between decks, except that of my cabin, had fallen from the violent labouring of the ship. The altar also being demolished, an end was thereby put to the functions of the despairing priest. The reason of my cabin standing when every other yielded was that being the state room it partook of the general strength of the vessel, being erected at the time of her building and as firmly fixed as her decks, but the folding door that opened into the great cabin was soon torn off its hinges and broken to pieces, exposing to our view the foaming surges through the great cabin's stern windows. My darling girl sat like patience itself, though drenched to the skin and covered with filth from the washings that burst into our cabin.

At this awful hour did it occur to me what I had somewhere read that death by shipwreck is the most terrible of deaths. The spectacle of a field of battle is lofty and imposing—its glittering apparel, its martial music, its waving banners and floating standards, its high chivalric air and character elevate the soul and conceal from us the dangers of our situation: stretched on our

death-bed, enfeebled by sickness, our sensibility becomes enfeebled also, and, while heavy shocks shake the body and make it to
the bystander seem to suffer, nature throws over the soul the
kindly shroud of a happy insensibility, while the closed shutter,
the tiptoe tread and whispered attendance shut out the world we
are so soon to leave. But in a storm at sea the scene is not more
terrible than disgusting, in a miserable cabin, on a filthy wet bed,
in a confined and putrid air, where it is as impossible to think as
to breathe freely, the fatigue, the motion, the want of rest and
food, give a kind of hysteric sensibility to the frame, which makes
it alive to the slightest danger. No wonder, therefore, it should be
so to the greatest of all. If we look round the miserable group that
surround us no eye beams comfort, no tongue speaks consolation,
and when we throw our imagination beyond—to the death-like
darkness, the howling blast, the raging and merciless element, expected every moment to become our horrid habitation—surely,
surely it is the most terrible of deaths!

It is a remarkable circumstance that upon the fore-mast's
going and the confusion and panic that ensued the captain, who
had for so many days been confined in a delirium and so reduced
that he could not without assistance turn in his bed, on being told
what had happened, and that the ship was sinking, instantaneously recovered vigour both of body and mind sufficient to allow
not only of his jumping from his cot but going upon deck, where
he issued his orders with as much, or perhaps more, precision and
skill than he had done during any part of the voyage. The first
order he gave was by every possible means to lighten the ship.
The sea indeed had already done much towards it for us by carrying off the whole of the masts, yards, rigging and everything that
was upon the upper deck. An attempt was therefore made to
throw the guns overboard, but only five were so disposed of, and
those at the imminent risk of the lives of the men from the excessive motion. An attempt was likewise made to start the madeira
wine. The two first men that went into the hold for that purpose
were immediately jammed in between two pipes and killed, after
which no other would try. After exerting himself in a wonderful
manner the captain, by one of the violent jerks from a tremendous
sea breaking on board, was thrown down with such force as to
break his right arm and receive a severe contusion on his head,

which rendered him insensible. The chief mate, an active, clever seaman, was early in the gale carried away by a sea, washed forward, but luckily brought up in the galley under the forecastle, where he remained covered with wounds and bruises. The second mate was not seen after eight o'clock, it was therefore concluded that he had been carried overboard and lost. It, however, did not turn out so. He, apprehending nothing could save the ship, had shut himself up in a small booby hutch, or cabin, just abaft the helm upon the upper deck, where he spent the day between the brandy bottle and prayer book. The third officer had throughout showed the utmost fortitude and energy, sinking at last completely overcome by fatigue, and remained secured by a rope on the spot where he fell.

Mr. Barretto, as I have already observed, was no seaman; he, however, much to his credit, resolved to set his people an example by exposing his person to the raging element. He therefore remained upon the quarter-deck, lashed to the side, endeavouring to cheer and encourage the few sailors that were ready to do all in their power to prevent the ship from foundering. Thus he remained until two in the afternoon, when he fainted away, whereupon the people cast off the rope with which he was secured and were about to convey him between decks when at the moment an enormous wave came over the stern, sweeping them all away. Two of the poor fellows were irrecoverably lost, and for some time everybody thought Mr. Barretto had shared the same fate. He was, however, found amongst part of the broken rigging upon the forecastle in a state of insensibility, from whence he was with extreme difficulty carried between decks. Thus hour after hour passed with us in utter despair, but still to our amazement we remained afloat, which seemed to us little short of a miracle for a ship in such a state as ours was, so tossed about at the mercy of such a sea as never was seen, so involved in ruin and desolation on every side, making too, as she did before the hurricane commenced, thirty inches of water every hour, and not a single stroke of a pump after half-past eleven in the morning; nor could anybody account for her not going to the bottom but by supposing she actually rolled the water out of her as fast as it came in.

At six in the evening the fury of the storm had somewhat abated, though not sufficiently to afford us a hope of ever seeing

another day; our surprise only was at surviving from hour to hour
without the least expectation of escaping finally from a watery
grave.

Memoirs of William Hickey

LINES TO MR. HODGSON

Written on board the Lisbon Packet

Huzza! Hodgson, we are going,
    Our embargo's off at last;
Favourable breezes blowing
    Bend the canvas o'er the mast.
From aloft the signal's streaming,
    Hark! the farewell gun is fired;
Women screeching, tars blaspheming,
    Tell us that our time's expired.
            Here's a rascal
            Come to task all,
Prying from the custom-house,
            Trunks unpacking,
            Cases cracking,
    Not a corner for a mouse
'Scapes unsearch'd amid the racket,
Ere we sail on board the Packet.

Now our boatmen quit their mooring,
    And all hands must ply the oar;
Baggage from the quay is lowering,
    We're impatient, push from shore.
"Have a care! that case holds liquor—
    Stop the boat—I'm sick—oh Lord!"
"Sick, ma'am, damme, you'll be sicker
Ere you've been an hour on board."
            Thus are screaming
            Men and women,
        Gemmen, ladies, servants, Jacks;

Here entangling,
All are wrangling,
Stuck together close as wax.—
Such the general noise and racket,
Ere we reach the Lisbon Packet.

Now we've reach'd her, lo! the captain,
Gallant Kidd, commands the crew;
Passengers their berths are clapt in,
Some to grumble, some to spew.
"Heyday! call you that a cabin?
Why 'tis hardly three feet square:
Not enough to stow Queen Mab in—
Who the deuce can harbour there?"
"Who, sir? plenty—
Nobles twenty
Did at once my vessel fill."—
"Did they? Jesus,
How you squeeze us!
Would to God they did so still:
Then I'd scape the heat and racket
Of the good ship, Lisbon Packet."

Fletcher! Murray! Bob! where are you?
Stretch'd along the deck like logs—
Bear a hand, you jolly tar, you!
Here's a rope's end for the dogs.
Hobhouse muttering fearful curses,
As the hatchway down he rolls,
Now his breakfast, now his verses,
Vomits forth—and damns our souls.
"Here's a stanza
On Braganza—
Help!"—"A couplet?"—"No, a cup
Of warm water—"
"What's the matter?"
"Zounds! my liver's coming up:
I shall not survive the racket
Of this brutal Lisbon Packet."

Now at length we're off for Turkey,
Lord knows when we shall come back!
Breezes foul and tempests murky

May unship us in a crack.
But, since life at most a jest is,
  As philosophers allow,
Still to laugh by far the best is
  Then laugh on—as I do now.
    Laugh at all things,
    Great and small things,
  Sick or well, at sea or shore;
    While we're quaffing,
    Let's have laughing—
Who the devil cares for more?—
Some good wine! and who would lack it,
Ev'n on board the Lisbon Packet?

GEORGE, LORD BYRON

Falmouth Roads, June 30, 1809

◆

1791: François René Chateaubriand

The great French writer and diplomat visits America, travelling by way of the French islands of Saint-Pierre and Miquelon,
which lie to the south of Newfoundland.

The boatswain of my ship was an old supercargo called Pierre
Villeneuve, whose very name appealed to me because of the kindly
Villeneuve of my childhood. He had served in India, under the
Bailli de Suffren, and in America under the Comte d'Estaing; he
had been involved in countless engagements. Leaning against the
bows of the ship, beside the bowsprit, like an army veteran sitting
under the pergola of his little garden in the moat of the Invalides,
Pierre, chewing a plug of tobacco which filled out his cheek like a
gumboil, described to me the clearing of the decks, the effect of
the gunfire below decks, and the havoc caused by cannon-balls
richocheting against the gun-carriages, the guns, and the timber-

work. I made him tell me about the Indians, the Negroes, and the planters. I asked him how the trees were shaped, what was the colour of earth and sky, the taste of the fruit; whether pineapples were better than peaches, palm-trees more impressive than oaks. He explained all this to me with the aid of comparisons taken from things I knew: the palm-tree was a big cabbage; an Indian's dress was like my grandmother's; camels looked like hunchbacked donkeys; all the peoples of the East, and especially the Chinese, were cowards and thieves. Villeneuve came from Brittany, and we never failed to end up by singing the praises of the incomparable beauty of our native land.

The bell interrupted our conversations; it struck the watches and the time for dressing, for the roll-call, and for meals. In the morning, at a given signal, the crew lined up on deck, stripped off their blue shirts, and put on others which were drying in the shrouds. The discarded shirts were promptly washed in tubs in which this school of seals also soaped their brown faces and their tarred paws.

At the midday and evening meals, the sailors, sitting in a circle round the mess-can, one after the other, in an orderly fashion and without any attempt at cheating, dipped their tin spoons into the soup which splashed about with the rolling of the ship. Those who were not hungry sold their ration of biscuit or salt meat to their messmates for a plug of tobacco or a glass of brandy. The passengers took their meals in the captain's cabin. In fine weather a sail was spread over the stern of the ship, and we dined with a view of a blue sea, flecked here and there with white marks where it was touched by the breeze.

Wrapped in my cloak, I stretched myself out at night on the deck. My eyes contemplated the stars above me. The swollen sail sent back to me the coolness of the breeze which rocked me beneath the dome of heaven: half-asleep and driven onwards by the wind, I was borne along to new skies and new dreams.

*   *   *

The wind forced us to bear north, and we arrived at the Banks of Newfoundland. Some floating icebergs were drifting around in the midst of a pale, cold mist.

The men of the trident have games which have been handed down to them by their predecessors: when you cross the Line, you must resign yourself to receiving *baptism;* it is the same ceremony in the tropics as on the Banks of Newfoundland, and wherever it is held, the leader of the masquerade is always called the Old Man of the Tropics. Tropical and dropsical are synonymous terms for the sailor, so that the Old Man of the Tropics has an enormous paunch. He is dressed, even when he is in his native tropics, in all the sheepskins and fur jackets the crew can muster between them; and he squats in the maintop, giving a roar every now and then. Everybody looks up at him: he starts clambering down the shrouds with all the clumsiness of a bear and stumbling like Silenus. As he sets foot on deck he utters fresh roars, gives a bound, seizes a pail, fills it with sea-water, and empties it over the heads of those who have never crossed the Equator or never reached the ice-line. You may flee below decks, jump on to the hatches, or climb up the masts: the Old Man of the Tropics comes after you. A generous tip marks the end of these games of Amphitrite, which Homer would have extolled, just as he sang of Proteus, if Old Oceanus had been known in his entirety in the days of Ulysses; but at that time, only his head could be seen at the Pillars of Hercules; his body lay hidden and covered the world.

*   *   *

After taking on stores and replacing the anchor lost at Graciosa, we left Saint-Pierre. Sailing south, we reached the latitude of 38°, and were becalmed a short distance from the coasts of Maryland and Virginia. The misty sky of the northern regions had been succeeded by a clear, cloudless sky; we could not see the land, but the scent of the pine forests was wafted to us. Daybreak and dawn, sunrise and sunset, dusk and nightfall were all admirable. I was never tired of gazing at Venus, whose rays seemed to envelop me like my sylph's tresses in the past.

One day an incident occurred which very nearly put an end to my plans and my dreams. The heat was overpowering; the ship, lying in a dead calm and weighted down by its masts, was rolling heavily: roasting on deck and wearied by the motion of the vessel, I decided to have a bathe, and although we had no boat out, I dived into the sea from the bowsprit. All went well to begin with, and several passengers followed my example. I swam about without looking at the ship; but when I happened to turn my head, I saw that the current had already carried her some distance away from me. The sailors, alarmed by the situation, had thrown a rope to the other swimmers. Sharks appeared in the wake of the ship, and shots were fired at them to drive them away. The swell was so heavy that it slowed me down and exhausted my strength. There was a whirlpool below me, and at any moment the sharks might make off with one of my arms or legs. On board, the boatswain was trying to lower a boat, but the tackle had to be fixed first, and all this took time.

By the greatest good fortune, an almost imperceptible breeze sprang up; the ship, answering to the helm a little, came nearer to me; I was just able to catch hold of the rope, but my companions in foolhardiness were already clinging to it; when we were pulled to the ship's side, I was at the end of the line, and they bore on me with their whole weight. In this way they fished us out one after another, an operation which lasted a long time. The rolling continued; at every roll, we either plunged six or seven feet into the water or else we were lifted as many feet up in the air, like fish at the end of a line; at the last immersion, I felt as if I were about to faint; one more roll, and it would have been all up with me. I was hoisted on deck half-dead; if I had been drowned, what a good riddance that would have been for me and the rest!

Two days after this incident, we came in sight of land. My heart beat wildly when the captain pointed it out to me: America! It was barely indicated by the tops of a few maple-trees above the horizon. The palm-trees at the mouth of the Nile have since indicated the coast of Egypt to me in the same way. A pilot came on board; we entered Chesapeake Bay. That same evening a boat was sent ashore to obtain fresh provisions. I joined the party, and soon I trod American soil.

Gazing around me, I remained motionless for a few moments. This continent; which had been unknown for possibly the whole of antiquity and many centuries in modern times; the first wild destiny of that continent and its second destiny after the arrival of Christopher Columbus; the supremacy of the European monarchies shaken in this new world; the old society ending in young America; a republic of an unfamiliar type foreshadowing a change in the human mind; the part which my country had played in these events; these seas and shores owing their independence in part to the French flag and French blood; a great man issuing from the midst of the discord and the wilderness; Washington living in a flourishing city on the same spot where William Penn had bought a patch of forest-land; the United States passing on to France the revolution which France had supported with her arms; lastly, my own fate, the virgin muse which I had come to abandon to the passion of a new variety of nature; the discoveries which I hoped to make in the deserts which still extended their broad kingdom behind the narrow domain of a foreign civilization: such were the thoughts that revolved in my mind.

We walked towards the nearest house. Woods of balsam-trees and Virginian cedars, mocking-birds, and cardinal tanagers proclaimed by their appearance and shade, their song and colour, that we were in a new clime. The house, which we reached after half an hour, was a cross between an English farm-house and a West Indian hut. Herds of European cows were grazing in pastures surrounded by fences, on which striped squirrels were playing. Blacks were sawing up logs of wood, whites tending tobacco-plants. A Negress of thirteen or fourteen, practically naked and singularly beautiful, opened the gate to us like a young Night. We bought some cakes of Indian corn, chickens, eggs, and milk, and returned to the ship with our demijohns and baskets. I gave my silk handkerchief to the little African girl: it was a slave who welcomed me to the soil of liberty.

ROBERT BALDWICK (trans.),
Memoirs of Chateaubriand

———◆———

from ULYSSES

There lies the port; the vessel puffs her sail:
There gloom the dark broad seas. My mariners,
Souls that have toil'd, and wrought, and thought with me—

That ever with a frolic welcome took
The thunder and the sunshine, and opposed
Free hearts, free foreheads—you and I are old;
Old age hath yet his honour and his toil;
Death closes all: but something ere the end,
Some work of noble note, may yet be done,

Not unbecoming men that strove with Gods.
The lights begin to twinkle from the rocks:
The long day wanes: the slow moon climbs: the deep
Moans round with many voices. Come, my friends.
'Tis not too late to seek a newer world.
Push off, and sitting well in order smite
The sounding furrows; for my purpose holds
To sail beyond the sunset, and the baths
Of all the western stars, until I die.
It may be that the gulfs will wash us down:
It may be we shall touch the Happy Isles,
And see the great Achilles, whom we knew.
Tho' much is taken, much abides; and tho'
We are not now that strength which in old days
Moved earth and heaven; that which we are, we are;
One equal temper of heroic hearts,
Made weak by time and fate, but strong in will
To strive, to seek, to find, and not to yield.

ALFRED, LORD TENNYSON

1842: Charles Dickens

At the age of thirty, and with *Pickwick Papers* and *Nicholas Nickleby* already behind him, Dickens accepts an invitation to visit America. He travels to Boston in the *Britannia* of 1,200 tons.

The passage out

We all dined together that day; and a rather formidable party we were: no fewer than eighty-six strong. The vessel being pretty deep in the water, with all her coals on board and so many pas-

sengers, and the weather being calm and quiet, there was but little
motion; so that before the dinner was half over, even those passengers who were most distrustful of themselves plucked up amaz-
ingly; and those who in the morning had returned to the universal
question, "Are you a good sailor?" a very decided negative, now
either parried the inquiry with the evasive reply, "Oh! I suppose
I'm no worse than anybody else"; or, reckless of all moral obliga-
tions, answered boldly, "Yes": and with some irritation too, as
though they would add, "I should like to know what you see in
me, sir, particularly, to justify suspicion!"

Notwithstanding this high tone of courage and confidence, I
could not but observe that very few remained long over their wine;
and that everybody had an unusual love of the open air; and that
the favourite and most coveted seats were invariably those nearest
to the door. The tea-table, too, was by no means as well attended
as the dinner-table; and there was less whist-playing than might
have been expected. Still, with the exception of one lady, who had
retired with some precipitation at dinner-time, immediately after
being assisted to the finest cut of a very yellow boiled leg of mutton with very green capers, there were no invalids as yet; and
walking, and smoking, and drinking of brandy and water (but
always in the open air), went on with unabated spirit until eleven
o'clock, or thereabouts, when "turning in"—no sailor of seven
hours' experience talks of going to bed—became the order of the
night. The perpetual tramp of boot-heels on the decks gave place
to a heavy silence, and the whole human freight was stowed away
below, excepting a very few stragglers like myself, who were
probably like me, afraid to go there.

To one unaccustomed to such scenes, this is a very striking
time on shipboard. Afterwards, and when its novelty had long
worn off, it never ceased to have a peculiar interest and charm for
me. The gloom through which the great black mass holds its
direct and certain course; the rushing water, plainly heard, but
dimly seen; the broad, white, glistening track that follows in the
vessel's wake; the men on the look-out forward, who would be
scarcely visible against the dark sky, but for their blotting out
some score of glistening stars; the helmsman at the wheel, with
the illuminated card before him, shining, a speck of light amidst
the darkness, like something sentient and of Divine intelligence;

the melancholy sighing of the wind through block, and rope, and chain; the gleaming forth of light from every crevice, nook, and tiny piece of glass about the decks, as though the ship were filled with fire in hiding, ready to burst through any outlet, wild with its resistless power of death and ruin. At first, too, and even when the hour, and all the objects it exalts, have come to be familiar, it is difficult, alone and thoughtful, to hold them to their proper shapes and forms. They change with the wandering fancy; assume the semblance of things left far away; put on the well-remembered aspect of favourite places dearly loved; and even people them with shadows. Streets, houses, rooms; figures so like their usual occupants, that they have startled me by their reality, which far exceeded, as it seemed to me, all power of mine to conjure up the absent; have, many and many a time, at such an hour, grown suddenly out of objects with whose real look, use, and purpose I was as well acquainted as with my own two hands.

My own two hands, and feet likewise, being very cold, however, on this particular occasion, I crept below at midnight. It was not exactly comfortable below. It was decidedly close; and it was impossible to be unconscious of the presence of that extraordinary compound of strange smells, which is to be found nowhere but on board ship, and which is such a subtle perfume that it seems to enter at every pore of the skin, and whisper of the hold. Two passengers' wives (one of them my own) lay already in silent agonies on the sofa; and one lady's maid (*my* lady's) was a mere bundle on the floor, execrating her destiny, and pounding her curl-papers among the stray boxes. Everything sloped the wrong way; which in itself was an aggravation scarcely to be borne. I had left the door open, a moment before, in the bosom of a gentle declivity, and, when I turned to shut it, it was on the summit of a lofty eminence. Now every plank and timber creaked, as if the ship were made of wicker-work; and now crackled like an enormous fire of the dryest possible twigs. There was nothing for it but bed; so I went to bed.

The weather worsened and Dickens was dreadfully seasick

Not sea-sick, be it understood, in the ordinary acceptation of the term: I wish I had been: but in a form which I have never seen or heard described, though I have no doubt it is very common.

I lay there, all the day long, quite coolly and contentedly; with no sense of weariness, with no desire to get up, or get better, or take the air; with no curiosity, or care, or regret, of any sort or degree, saving that I think I can remember, in this universal indifference, having a kind of lazy joy—of fiendish delight, if anything so lethargic can be dignified with the title—in the fact of my wife being too ill to talk to me. If I may be allowed to illustrate my state of mind by such an example, I should say that I was exactly in the condition of the elder Mr. Willet, after the incursion of the rioters

Dickens's stateroom in the *Britannia*, 1842.

into his bar at Chigwell. Nothing would have surprised me. If, in the momentary illumination of any ray of intelligence that may have come upon me in the way of thoughts of Home, a goblin postman, with a scarlet coat and bell, had come into that little kennel before me, broad awake, in broad day, and, apologizing for being damp through walking in the sea, had handed me a letter, directed to myself, in familiar characters, I am certain I should not have felt one atom of astonishment: I should have been perfectly satisfied. If Neptune himself had walked in, with a toasted shark on his trident, I should have looked upon the event as one of the very commonest every-day occurrences.

Once—once—I found myself on deck. I don't know how I got there, or what possessed me to go there, but there I was; and completely dressed too, with a huge pea-coat on, and a pair of boots such as no weak man in his senses could ever have got into. I found myself standing, when a gleam of consciousness came upon me, holding on to something. I don't know what. I think it was the boatswain: or it may have been the pump: or possibly the cow. I can't say how long I had been there; whether a day or a minute, I recollect trying to think about something (about anything in the whole wide world, I was not particular) without the smallest effect. I could not even make out which was the sea, and which the sky; for the horizon seemed drunk, and was flying wildly about in all directions. Even in that incapable state, however, I recognized the lazy gentleman standing before me: nautically clad in a suit of shaggy blue, with an oil-skin hat. But I was too imbecile, although I knew it to be he, to separate him from his dress; and tried to call him, I remember, *Pilot*. After another interval of total unconsciousness, I found he had gone, and recognized another figure in its place. It seemed to wave and fluctuate before me as though I saw it reflected in an unsteady looking-glass; but I knew it for the captain; and such was the cheerful influence of his face, that I tried to smile: yes, even then I tried to smile. I saw by his gestures that he addressed me; but it was a long time before I could make out that he remonstrated against my standing up to my knees in water—as I was; of course I don't know why. I tried to thank him, but couldn't. I could only point to my boots— or wherever I supposed my boots to be—and say in a plaintive voice, "Cork soles": at the same time endeavouring, I am told, to

sit down in the pool. Finding that I was quite insensible, and for
the time a maniac, he humanely conducted me below.

There I remained until I got better: suffering, whenever I was
recommended to eat anything, an amount of anguish only second
to that which is said to be endured by the apparently drowned in
the process of restoration to life. One gentleman on board had a
letter of introduction to me from a mutual friend in London. He
sent it below with his card, on the morning of the head wind; and
I was long troubled with the idea that he might be up, and well,
and a hundred times a day expecting me to call upon him in the
saloon. I imagined him one of those cast-iron images—I will not
call them men—who ask, with red faces and lusty voices, what
sea-sickness means, and whether it really is as bad as it is represented to be. This was very torturing indeed; and I don't think I
ever felt such perfect gratification and gratitude of heart as I did
when I heard from the ship's doctor that he had been obliged to
put a large mustard poultice on this very gentleman's stomach. I
date my recovery from the receipt of that intelligence.

*   *   *

About midnight we shipped a sea, which forced its way
through the skylights, burst open the doors above, and came raging and roaring down into the ladies' cabin, to the unspeakable
consternation of my wife and a little Scotch lady—who, by the
way, had previously sent a message to the captain by the stewardess, requesting him, with her compliments, to have a steel
conductor immediately attached to the top of every mast, and to
the chimney, in order that the ship might not be struck by lightning. They, and the handmaid before mentioned, being in such
ecstasies of fear that I scarcely knew what to do with them, I naturally bethought myself of some restorative or comfortable cordial;
and nothing better occurring to me, at the moment, than hot
brandy and water, I procured a tumblerful without delay. It being
impossible to stand or sit without holding on, they were all heaped
together in one corner of a long sofa—a fixture, extending entirely
across the cabin—where they clung to each other in momentary
expectation of being drowned. When I approached this place with
my specific, and was about to administer it, with many consolatory

expressions, to the nearest sufferer, what was my dismay to see them all roll slowly down to the other end! And when I staggered to that end, and held out the glass once more, how immensely baffled were my good intentions by the ship giving another lurch, and their all rolling back again! I suppose I dodged them up and down this sofa for at least a quarter of an hour, without reaching them once; and, by the time I did catch them, the brandy and water was diminished, by constant spilling, to a teaspoonful. To complete the group, it is necessary to recognize, in this disconcerted dodger, an individual very pale from sea-sickness, who had shaved his beard and brushed his hair last at Liverpool: and whose only articles of dress (linen not included) were a pair of dreadnaught trousers; a blue jacket, formerly admired upon the Thames at Richmond; no stockings; and one slipper.

*   *   *

I was now comfortably established by courtesy in the ladies' cabin, where, besides ourselves, there were only four other passengers. First, the little Scotch lady before mentioned, on her way to join her husband at New York, who had settled there three years before. Secondly and thirdly, an honest young Yorkshireman, connected with some American house; domiciled in that same city, and carrying thither his beautiful young wife, to whom he had been married but a fortnight, and who was the fairest specimen of a comely English country girl I have ever seen. Fourthly, fifthly, and lastly, another couple: newly married too, if one might judge from the endearments they frequently interchanged: of whom I know no more than that they were rather a mysterious, runaway kind of couple; that the lady had great personal attractions also; and that the gentleman carried more guns with him than Robinson Crusoe, wore a shooting coat, and had two great dogs on board. On further consideration, I remember that he tried hot roast pig and bottled ale as a cure for sea-sickness; and that he took these remedies (usually in bed) day after day, with astonishing perseverance. I may add, for the information of the curious, that they decidedly failed.

The weather continuing obstinately and almost unprecedentedly bad, we usually straggled into this cabin, more or less faint and miserable, about an hour before noon, and lay down on the sofas to recover; during which interval the captain would look in to communicate the state of the wind, the moral certainty of its changing tomorrow (the weather is always going to improve tomorrow at sea), the vessel's rate of sailing, and so forth. Observations there were none to tell us of, for there was no sun to take them by. But a description of one day will serve for all the rest. Here it is.

The captain being gone, we compose ourselves to read, if the place be light enough; and if not, we doze and talk alternately. At one a bell rings, and the stewardess comes down with a steaming dish of baked potatoes, and another of roasted apples; and plates of pig's face, cold ham, salt beef; or perhaps a smoking mess of rare hot collops. We fall to upon these dainties; eat as much as we can (we have great appetites now); and are as long as possible about it. If the fire will burn (it *will* sometimes), we are pretty cheerful. If it won't, we all remark to each other that it's very cold, rub our hands, cover ourselves with coats and cloaks, and lie down again to doze, talk, and read (provided as aforesaid), until dinner-time. At five another bell rings, and the stewardess reappears with another dish of potatoes—boiled this time—and store of hot meat of various kinds: not forgetting the roast pig, to be taken medicinally. We sit down at table again (rather more cheerfully than before); prolong the meal with a rather mouldy dessert of apples, grapes, and oranges; and drink our wine and brandy and water. The bottles and glasses are still upon the table, and the oranges and so forth are rolling about according to their fancy and the ship's way, when the doctor comes down, by special nightly invitation, to join our evening rubber: immediately on whose arrival we make a party at whist, and, as it is a rough night and the cards will not lie on the cloth, we put the tricks in our pockets as we take them. At whist we remain with exemplary gravity (deducting a short time for tea and toast) until eleven o'clock, or thereabouts; when the captain comes down again, in a sou'-wester hat tied under his chin, and a pilot coat: making the ground wet where he stands. By this time the card-playing is over, and the bottles and glasses are again upon the table; and after an hour's pleasant conversation about the ship, the passengers, and things in general, the captain (who never goes to bed, and is never out of humour) turns up his coat collar for the deck again; shakes hands all round; and goes laughing out into the weather as merrily as to a birthday party.

As to daily news, there is no dearth of that commodity. This passenger is reported to have lost fourteen pounds at Vingt-et-un in the saloon yesterday; and that passenger drinks his bottle of champagne every day, and how he does it (being only a clerk) nobody knows. The head engineer has distinctly said that there never was such times—meaning weather—and four good hands are ill, and have given in, dead beat. Several berths are full of water, and all the cabins are leaky. The ship's cook, secretly swigging damaged whiskey, has been found drunk; and has been played upon by the fire-engine until quite sober. All the stewards have fallen downstairs at various dinner-times, and go about with plasters in various places. The baker is ill, and so is the pastrycook. A new man, horribly indisposed, has been required to fill the place of the latter officer; and has been propped and jammed up with empty casks in a little house upon deck, and commanded to roll out pie-crusts, which he protests (being highly bilious) it is death to him to look at. News! A dozen murders on shore would lack the interest of these slight incidents at sea.

*   *   *

Encountering squally weather again in the Bay of Fundy, we tumbled and rolled about as usual all that night and all next day. On the next afternoon—that is to say, on Saturday, the twenty-second of January—an American pilot-boat came alongside, and soon afterwards the *Britannia* steam-packet from Liverpool, eighteen days out, was telegraphed at Boston.

The indescribable interest with which I strained my eyes, as the first patches of American soil peeped like molehills from the green sea, and followed them, as they swelled, by slow and almost imperceptible degrees, into a continuous line of coast, can hardly be exaggerated. A sharp keen wind blew dead against us; a hard frost prevailed on shore; and the cold was most severe. Yet the air was so intensely clear, and dry, and bright, that the temperature was not only endurable, but delicious.

How I remained on deck, staring about me, until we came alongside the dock, and how, though I had had as many eyes as Argus, I should have had them all wide open, and all employed on new objects—are topics which I will not prolong this chapter to discuss. Neither will I more than hint at my foreigner-like mistake, in supposing that a party of most active persons, who scrambled on board at the peril of their lives as we approached the wharf, were newsmen, answering to that industrious class at home; whereas, despite the leathern wallets of news slung about the necks of some, and the broad-sheets in the hands of all, they were Editors, who boarded ships in person (as one gentleman in a worsted comforter informed me), "because they like the excitement of it." Suffice it in this place to say, that one of these invaders, with a ready courtesy for which I thank him here most gratefully, went on before to order rooms at the hotel; and that when I followed, as I soon did, I found myself rolling through the long passages with an involuntary imitation of the gait of Mr. T. P. Cooke, in a new nautical melodrama.

"Dinner, if you please," said I to the waiter.

"When?" said the waiter.

"As quick as possible," said I.

"Right away?" said the waiter.

After a moment's hesitation, I answered, "No," at hazard.

"*Not* right away?" cried the waiter, with an amount of surprise that made me start.

I looked at him doubtfully, and returned, "No; I would rather have it in this private room. I like it very much."

At this I really thought the waiter must have gone out of his mind: as I believe he would have done, but for the interposition of another man, who whispered in his ear, "Directly."

"Well! and that's a fact!" said the waiter, looking helplessly at me. "Right away."

I saw now that "Right away" and "Directly" were one and the same thing. So I reversed my previous answer, and sat down to dinner in ten minutes afterwards; and a capital dinner it was.

The hotel (a very excellent one) is called the Tremont House. It has more galleries, colonnades, piazzas, and passages than I can remember, or the reader would believe.

CHARLES DICKENS,
American Notes

A few years later, Dickens's fellow novelist William Thackeray was returning from America in the *Europa*. One of the officers of this ship told Thackeray he had been on board Dickens's ship the *Britannia* at the time of the events related above. Thackeray, a doubting Thomas, asked the officer whether the passage had been as stormy as Dickens made out. The officer, according to Eyre Crowe, Thackeray's companion, "corroborated the Dickensian version in every particular."

HOW THE WHALE GOT HIS THROAT

When the cabin port-holes are dark and green
Because of the seas outside;
When the ship goes *wop* (with a wiggle between)
And the steward falls into the soup-tureen,
    And the trunks begin to slide;
When Nursey lies on the floor in a heap,
And Mummy tells you to let her sleep,
And you aren't waked or washed or dressed,
Why, then you will know (if you haven't guessed)
You're "Fifty North and Forty West!"

RUDYARD KIPLING

1851: Sophia Taylor

Many of the best accounts of journeys at sea have been written
by women. It is they rather than men (apart from professional
writers like Dickens and Stevenson) who observe so acutely the
minutiae of shipboard life, the variety of human relationships.

Sophia Taylor, aged twenty-five, was going out to Australia
to be married. Her letters give an excellent account of what
life at sea must have been like for middle-class emigrants to
that country in the mid-nineteenth century. Meals, and the
preparation of them, feature much in Sophy's writings. It is no
surprise to read that a Mrs. Hudson "is always on at me because I get so stout and says she cannot help looking at my
double chin."

Some of the passengers are very intelligent, respectable and agree-
able. Among my companions is a young lady Chick knows, Miss
Goode from Islington. She is accompanied by her father and
mother, a very nice old couple, something like Mr. and Mrs.
Blanche. Then there is a Miss Stone, a Baptist, from Bourton-on-
the-Water in Gloucestershire, also a lively girl from London who
I have just discovered to be an intimate friend of Mr. Bonner of
Brighton. He was at Gravesend on Thursday to take leave of her
and another friend from Croydon. One of the young men is from
Whites & Greenhill in the Blackfriars Road, son of a dissenting
minister. The gentlemen are well behaved and as one has a flute
and another an accordion we intend getting up some singing
classes to amuse us in the evenings. It is delightful at night on
the poop, little groups of us remain up there till 10 o'clock, then
the lights are put out except four which are allowed to burn in
the 'tween decks all night. I am so pleased at that as I thought
we should be in darkness all night.

We seem like a large family, all parcelled out in Messes and
in each Mess one is appointed captain of a Mess for a week, and
has everything to superintend. All take their turn to be captain,
make puddings, etc., gentlemen and all. It is really quite fun to
see the poor single men at the other end of the vessel for they have
everything to learn respecting the pudding business! Some amuse
themselves with chess, others are wishing to see some love
matches that they may amuse themselves by watching them. We

have plenty of children and infants who add no little to the confusion at meal times.

I have been very busy on deck, when well enough, working
at your slippers. I would give a trifle if you could see how comfortable we are just now. There is such a beautiful fresh breeze
blowing, we are just getting an appetite; old Mr. Goode has
brought up some bottled stout and good Gloucester cheese. Nine
of us have had a very good lunch together. We are all very ac-
commodating, many of us having brought different things, we all
share what we have. We hope to get some leaven at Plymouth
that we may make some home-made bread.

*   *   *

I am not able to write so much as I thought I should have
time for; it is rather difficult to write up on deck although I have
to do so. There are so many walking about and talking that it
takes the attention. Down below we feel the motion of the vessel
more; it is so confined that if we feel at all squeamish we are
obliged to go upstairs. It is only because I am obliged to be down
here now in order to write to you that I can at all manage. I fear
I am getting rather extravagant but I must not indulge in it long;
since the sickness came on we have all been very delicate in our
appetite; that was the beginning. We can buy bottled stout and
Bass Pale Ale on board at 1/- per bottle. Miss Goode is able to
make some very nice home-made bread from an artificial yeast
which she also makes from a little beer, so we all join together
now and then for lunch or supper and have some Pale Ale; with
our nice bread and some cheese which different generous creatures
give us we quite enjoy ourselves. We shall endeavour to make
bread in our mess all the voyage, for we can get anything we like
baked on board if we can only make it; that will be much better
than the biscuits. I can almost live on home-made bread. I shall
have to take my turn in making it when Miss Goode is tired.

*   *   *

We had one very rough night last week. I think it was Friday.
We were wakened by the Captain crying out to the sailors: "Look

smart, my lads," and calling for volunteers from below, meaning the male passengers who always seem to enjoy helping the sailors to pull the ropes. They make plenty of bustle over it. I can't forget it, the pots and pans were rolling and tumbling about, waves dashing against the ship and the ship heaving most beautifully. I am getting used to it, but at first I did not at all like the sensation at night of their turning the ship and sails; this frequently has to be done between the intervals of calm when the wind is changeable and contrary. When they do so of course the ship turns from one side to the other in going round, and the side which is highest out of the water becomes the lowest, so that if you happen to be lying as you ought with your head higher than your feet when the vessel turns, down goes your head where your feet should be and makes you fancy that you are almost going down into the water yourself! I am now getting used to everything of the kind in moderation.

*   *   *

I hope when the day comes that I see you all again I shall remember some of the comical things I see and hear. One young man must needs take his sheet to sling up to the ceiling for a hammock and only being made of loose unbleached calico it gave way in the night and let him down unhurt. This is a curious life, totally different to what I have been used to. Our company now are not quite so select as when we were in the channel, for we took a great many on board at Plymouth. We have three Irish and several Scotch families all of whom are respectable, but the loud broad talk of the Irish and the slow plaintive sound of the Scotch seems to contrast strangely when all are talking freely together.

We have one old Irish gentleman who has been a magistrate. He is very old and quaint. He said to me the other day dryly: "I declare in this house they seem always a doing and never done." We are a promiscuous lot. A great many are pleasant and obliging, respectable and pious people, in fact Captain says he never took out such a respectable lot of emigrants before, but of course among so many we have some disorderly characters. We had rules read on board the other day and Mr. Goode and two others appointed so laws must be obeyed and order preserved as far as possible. There is of course great diversity of tastes and habits, but we find that on board ship everyone follows out their own fancy independently of what others like or think, so that there is quite a mixture of pursuits going on all at one time and in the same place.

The only place where we have lights in the evening is the 'tween decks below, so there is only this one place at that time for supper and family worship, reading, writing, working, talking, chess and card playing, besides plenty of singing going on upon the upper decks. It is not easy to live like this without one's real character being known; there is no disguising for we are so thrown together and have to live in each other's society for so long a time that the character gets revealed. It reminds me of a little village; as you look night or morning down the long 'tween decks it is as if people were peeping out of their little cottages. On some mornings when certain days bring round their extra duties we have all the bustle of a little town. We had a newspaper started called the *Candahar Express*, but not being well supported it was too hard work for the editors alone, and has therefore been discontinued. Two amateur theatrical performances were well attended as I can testify, for the poop was so clear that I had a beautiful walk with three others who like myself felt no interest in the play.

I cannot tell you how many sales by auction we have had, for when some of the unsteady characters have spent their money in drink and want to raise more they have a public sale of whatever they can best spare. One young man sold a coat for 7/- which cost 24/- when he came on board.

*   *   *

August 30th

Very stormy. A dear little creature was taken ill in the morning and died by 7 in the evening. Her parents are drapers by the name of Pike from Bristol. The poor mother was carried on deck in hysterics; the cause of the child's death I do not know unless it was that she had eaten something that disagreed with her. She suffered much and the evening she died she was carried up on the poop and laid in one of the boats at the side. At 8 next morning (Sunday), during drenching rain, the burial service was read and I saw the body of the dear little girl placed in a canvas wrapper and lowered in the deep, there to rest "till the sea shall give up its dead." I was not aware of the fact before that when there is a corpse on board sharks will follow the vessel until the person is buried.

*   *   *

Our Mess is No. 1 and the only one entirely composed of females, so whenever our pots and bottles roll off the shelves with the motion of the ship they say "Oh, there's some more of the No. 1 things over," or whatever mischief is done it is said: "Oh that is No. 1 again," and speak as though we were always in a scrape just because we have not a gentleman among us, but we declare that

The Ladies' Cabin. Intimations of *mal de mer*

we are happier than if we had one. I am sure that the number *one* will always be associated in my mind with the *Candahar* for we are always being talked of all over the ship; No. 1 has become quite a bye-word. Captain often comes down and sits on the stairs at our end of the table to chat with us; he tells us that ours is the only Mess he takes a positive interest in and that he feels he ought to protect the unprotected. His advice to us at first was to "keep the men at arm's length," and Miss Stone and I have not failed to follow it.

There is one gentleman we often have a chat with and a bit of fun. He has travelled in the wine trade, his name is Hudson. The last time he was in Bath not long since, he lodged with Mrs. Hyde's sister in Queens Square. He is a gentlemanly man and very obliging to us. His wife is a very nice woman; they are newly married. She is always on at me because I get so stout and says she cannot help looking at my double chin; I look the most contented on board. I could have told her, Father, that my happiness does not lie entirely in the things that are above me but in something within and above. I often think of a true saying of Dr. Cummings that "it matters far less *where* we are than *what* we are"; the mind is not so dependent for happiness on outward circumstances as we are apt to imagine.

*   *   *

September 22nd

On the 17th we crossed the line at 3 A.M. Neptune came on board in the evening, came as you may suppose up the side of the vessel, drank the Captain's health and went away with a promise to call next morning. The barrel of fire, in which we were to suppose he went away, we saw for a long time on the water; sometimes it is to be seen at a distance of ten miles. About nine next morning Neptune and his wife came on board in a rough kind of carriage drawn by four sailors dressed in the most grotesque manner, with tin caps on their heads and their faces blackened; then came two more who acted as bodyguards, another dressed as a clown, and another disguised to look like a bear with one leading him by the chain which is attached according to custom. In fact they were all so frightfully disguised that they hardly looked human; the sailor dressed as Neptune's wife was attired in a cotton gown, night-cap and shawl belonging to one of the passengers, looking as you may be sure, quite interesting. After forming the procession, singing and making a speech, they beg leave to make use of "the *legal little drop* of water" which is not only a *drop* but full buckets thrown over the victims. They then call out for each one in his turn to come and be shaved—most of whom when the time came were out of the way.

A large sail is placed across the deck to form a screen, then when the poor man who is to be shaved is dragged round the quarter deck to the spot by five or six sailors, all of them several times falling down in the wet together owing to his resistance, and while there having showers of water thrown over them. When they reach the spot where the sail is the man is handed up and seated on the top. Then the barber, after he has replied to the usual questions from Neptune who sits on the side of the ship, shaves him by smothering his face with some nasty paste and scraping it off with an iron hoop, after which he is taken by the legs and sent backwards into the water which is placed in some large affair behind the sail. This time the second mate and others were sent over the sail into the water unawares, for sport; they then kept throwing pails of water over each other in all directions till about twenty of them were completely soused and looked like drowned rats tumbling over and throwing one another about.

About ten persons were shaved who had not crossed the line before. Some were sailors or those who were working their passage out, and others were passengers who chose to do so for the sport of the thing. *What taste!* It was quite sport for the two hours it lasted, but to tell you the truth I felt rather timid, they looked such hideous frights. I asked permission to sit in the Captain's cabin to look on, which I did. At half past 11 Captain came out and gave orders for all to be cleared up. The scene was immediately changed, and in a very short time all who had taken part appeared in a different costume looking so nice and clean. They told me they had enjoyed it very much and that they had to leave off too soon.

On the evening of the 17th we celebrated crossing the line by having a supper and ball. Most of the gentlemen on board took tickets, which were 5/- each, and the ladies went free. Miss Stone and I went in company with Mrs. Picton, the lady from Norton St.

Philip, and I did heartily enjoy my supper. Two pigs were killed and roasted, and at 6 o'clock the table was spread with roast pork, pork pies, damson and other fruit-pies, Wiltshire cheese, port and sherry and bottled ale, and Captain, who presented the latter, sat down with us. Not having room to accommodate all at one time, the ladies sat down first and the gentlemen stood behind and waited upon us, after which the former retired and the latter took their turn. Every one dressed as smartly as they could and all looked so clean and gay that the *Candahar* did not look like the same ship. Extra lamps were hung up, also lamps tied to the rigging on the poop for the dancing. Punch and cake were plentifully handed round between the dancing and singing, both of which were very nice. Being such a special occasion and under the circumstances, for I really felt the exercise would do me good, I yielded to the repeated request of the best among the gentlemen and stood up *once* in a country dance.

I believe the party was kept up till nearly 12, but retired myself at 11. Each person had to carry his own knife, fork, mug and plate. It did seem to me so comical to be going to a supper for which all were making such preparations in the shape of dress, etc., and yet to carry our own utensils in our hands. A subscription having been raised for the sailors, to which most gave 1/-, they also sat down to supper the following evening at 6, and it would have done you good to have seen them all with their rosy faces and everything on clean, and looking so happy seated each side of the table with our worthy Captain and chief mate at the head. They had three hams, pies, bottled ale, etc., all in fact as nice as we had. They seemed to enjoy it much. Some of the gentlemen acted in the capacity of stewards and waited on them. One of the toasts on both occasions was of course the Captain's health, and all joined heart and voice in saying "He is a jolly good fellow and so say all of us!"

So this is *crossing the line* and I don't think I shall forget it as long as I live. It may seem very tame stuff to occupy so much paper in writing about, but I thought I would like to tell you a little of what it is like and I hope it will interest you if you can manage to understand it as I have written it.

*   *   *

September 25th

Passed the island of Trinidad, not near enough to see land; it is
not now an inhabited island though it has been. This is Captain's
wedding day, he has been married twenty years. I like him much,
he is full of fun and good humour without any foolery or nonsense.
When he comes on the poop the first question he calls out to the
man at the wheel is "How's her head now?" If *wrong* he scratches
one whisker, if right he lifts his hat on one side, scratches his head
and says "beau-ti-ful." He is about the height of Mr. Woolley but
rather stouter, good features and brown curly hair. I should like
you to see his funny ways with us here, perhaps as some of us
are coming down the poop stairs he will come behind and take us
by the shoulders pretending to push us down, or when Miss Stone
and I are taking our evening walks together on the poop he will
walk softly behind us, close to our heels when we little suspect
him, so on turning round there he is in our path like a post, pretending we had startled him. One Sunday evening we were sitting
on the deck reading and some one came behind and placed a great
hand each side of our heads and there were we in a vice; we felt
the hands but could not tell who it could be until we were liberated
and then we found it was Captain!

I had not long left Plymouth before he found out the object
of my coming so of course I often have to put up with a joke about
it, but he commends me for doing so and says he shall always come
to see me whenever he is in Adelaide. He is too hard upon me for
getting so stout; he says "If any of the passengers at the end of
the voyage feel inclined to go before a magistrate to complain of
the ship's provisions, he has only to show *Miss Stone and me*,
himself and the First Mate, and they will immediately say to the
complainants 'be off.'" So Miss Stone told him it was our contented minds that make us get stout. "Oh no," said he, "it's that
awful pudding pan that's under my nose when I look downstairs
every morning," and this is the way he is always going on. I do
not say there is not some truth in it but it is slightly stretched.
When the waves are extra high I say to him: "It's rather rough,
Captain." "Rough?" he says, "you are never going to call such a
beautiful day as this rough." So as he never will allow it to be
rough when *I* ask him, Mrs. Cooke the other day added: "Will
you tell us, Captain, when you *do* call it rough?" "I call it rough,

ma'm, when you can't sleep in your beds." So you see he is a kind, jocular, good-tempered man, familiar and yet in a way that we cannot be offended, has plenty of good sense, has seen much of life and human nature, possesses great nautical experience and often entertains us with the tales he relates.

I had no thin writing paper of my own so he made me a present of this, for which I have mended one of his shirts and hemmed him a silk handkerchief. Nearly all his shirts he bought in China last voyage. I was surprised when he told me they were all made by men as the men do all the needlework in China, and the women, if they are seen at all, are doing men's work, but they are generally out of the way and very seldom to be seen in public. So much for the Captain.

*   *   *

November 6th

Had another terribly rough night and to make bad worse, some of the unsteady young men made several of the sailors intoxicated so that they were not fit when wanted to unreef the topsails. I am sorry to say that the chief mate was not much better, but our dear Captain is always the same and ever at his post so no harm came to us. He says he had not had his clothes off since we came round the Cape. I was on the sliding scale all night and could not keep myself on the bunk but awoke and found I was half-way down the berth. Since then I have obviated it by placing my desk under my head or feet as the case may be.

*   *   *

November 7th

Wind changed in our favour and the weather warm enough to have a walk on deck. Lost our nice currant pudding in the copper through the string not being properly tied.

*   *   *

November 18th

A lovely day, and the boxes taken up out of the hold for the third time since we left England. The first time this was done it was indeed a scene. I wish I could describe it as comically as it appeared, for it really amused me very much. Just fancy, on a hot sunny day—for the sailors can only do it in fine weather—four or five men below and the main hold surrounded with passengers all looking eagerly to catch a glimpse of their boxes; one giving a description, and another telling how they may be known, gentlemen finding out the ladies' names, and those whose boxes were at the bottom, having been sent up from the country, looking very anxious. Then there are the long tables lined on each side with other passengers who have opened their boxes and are turning out the contents, some to wear and some to eat. At the same time Papas and Mammas may be seen busily preparing the regular morning cooking, beds being carried up on deck as usual for airing; others running about with pots and pans, and when you add to this confusion thirty-three children playing under foot and screaming, you may perhaps be able to form an idea of the bustle we were in. I like these days for they make a change.

Today Miss Stone ventured to taste the salt beef. Some say it is horses' flesh and others that it is donkeys', and has been several voyages. To me, when it comes out of the boiler, it looks and feels very much like a piece of mahogany.

Miss Stone had some trouble in biting it; when once her teeth were in she found it hard to get them out. Captain says the beef has only been one voyage and he eats a great deal of it. We asked his cook to steam us a piece; this makes it tender and we ventured to taste it. We like a little for a relish and fancy it is bullock's tongue.

*   *   *

November 24th

A lovely day; we expect to reach Adelaide about the 28th. All in such spirits. Tomorrow the anchor is to be placed in readiness to be dropped as soon as we reach the bay for we do not go into port directly. We are all anxious to get there of course, but I think I shall feel sad leaving the *Candahar*. I have had so many happy hours on board. Sometimes we are merry as crickets, there is always something occurring to amuse us among so many. Miss Skinner, the sister of Mrs. Hudson whom I have mentioned, is a tall girl of five-and-twenty; she is subject to fits which affect her brain and although you would offend her mother very much to say it, she is not in her right senses. Poor Sarah Ann, she is certainly rather soft. She has a way of saying *dear*, no matter whether she is speaking to Captain, the sailors or anyone else, and really I was obliged to laugh last night and so would you. Mr. Goode, as usual after service, read a sermon. Sarah Ann placed herself beside him for the evening, and the moment he had finished the discourse she looked up and said very deliberately: "Have you quite done, *dear?*" She took me by surprise, I assure you, as it was before service was over, and we generally sing after the sermon.

*　　*　　*

Monday, December 1st

This morning we woke early and to our great joy found ourselves casting anchor; the pilot has just come on board and now all is confusion and preparation to go on shore, finishing letters, dressing, etc. A vessel which arrived in Adelaide a fortnight before us had eleven children die on board of whooping-cough. How melancholy it must have been! I am thankful we have only had one death; a child in the next cabin was ill last week, we believe with measles, and as we have so many children on board it was thought that others would catch it, so we had our fears lest we should have to be in quarantine for some weeks. But he is recovering and our fears are at an end.

Having now reached thus far I do not think I can add any more as in less than an hour we expect to be at the Port. And as you know *who* I hope and expect to meet, you will not marvel that I feel inclined to lay down my pen. I have told you some of the roughs as well as the smooths of a sea passage that you may know some of the vicissitudes that attend a sea life.

ed. IRENE C. TAYLOR,
Sophy Under Sail

Sophy married her fiancé Edward Cooke in Adelaide in January 1852. In May 1853, she gave birth to a daughter, Eva, who developed an ear infection and died within six weeks. Sophy herself died three weeks later, from what her death certificate described as "debility after childbirth." She was only twenty-seven.

1868: Edward Lear

The author of the *Nonsense Rhymes*, who spent much of the
latter part of his life travelling in the Mediterranean, passes a
sleepless night.

Would it not have been better to have remained at Cannes, where
I had not yet visited Theoule, the Saut de Loup, and other places?

Had I not said, scores of times, such and such a voyage was the
last I would make?

To-morrow, when "morn broadens on the borders of the dark,"
shall I see Corsica's "snowy mountain-tops fringing the (Eastern)
sky"?

Did the sentinels of lordly Volaterra see, as Lord Macaulay
says they did, "Sardinia's snowy mountain-tops," and not rather
these same Corsican tops, "fringing the southern sky"?

Did they see any tops at all, or if any, which tops?

Will the daybreak ever happen?

Will 2 o'clock ever arrive?

Will the two poodles above stairs ever cease to run about the
deck?

Is it not disagreeable to look forward to two or three months
of travelling quite alone?

Would it not be delightful to travel, as J.A.S. is about to do,
in company with a wife and child?

Does it not, as years advance, become clearer that it is very
odious to be alone?

Have not many very distinguished persons, Oenone among
others, arrived at this conclusion?

Did she not say, with evident displeasure—
        "And from that time to this I am alone,
            And I shall be alone until I die"?—

Will those poodles ever cease from trotting up and down the
deck?

Is it not unpleasant, at fifty-six years of age, to feel that it is
increasingly probable that a man can never hope to be otherwise
than alone, never, no, never more?

Did not Edgar Poe's raven distinctly say, "Nevermore"?

Will those poodles be quiet? "Quoth the raven, nevermore."

Will there be anything worth seeing in Corsica?

Is there any romance left in that island? is there any sublimity
or beauty in its scenery?

Have I taken too much baggage?
Have I not rather taken too little?
Am I not an idiot for coming at all?—
Thus, and in such a groove, did the machinery of thought go
on, gradually refusing to move otherwise than by jerky spasms,
after the fashion of mechanical Ollendorff exercises, or verb-
catechisms of familiar phrases—
Are there not Banditti?
Had there not been Vendetta?
Were there not Corsican brothers?
Should I not carry clothes for all sorts of weather?
Must THOU not have taken a dress coat?
Had HE not many letters of introduction?
Might WE not have taken extra pairs of spectacles?
Could YOU not have provided numerous walking
boots? . . .
May THEY not find cream cheeses?
Should there not be innumerable moufflons?
Ought not the cabin lamps and glasses to cease jin-
gling?
Might not the poodles stop worrying?—
thus and thus, till by reason of long hours and monotonous rolling
and shaking, a sort of comatose insensibility, miscalled sleep, takes
the place of all thought, and so the night passes.

EDWARD LEAR

———◆———

1876: Robert Baden-Powell

The future founder of the Boy Scout movement, then a newly
commissioned subaltern in the 13th Hussars, travels to India
in the troopship *Serapis*.

In the Red Sea we had it awfully warm for three days, the
thermometer registering 96° at dinner; this in damp air is equal
to ten degrees higher in a dry climate. Four of five children died
and several ladies were ill, continually fainting. Worst of all, all
the cooks got so ill that they had to go into hospital; one of them
went mad, jumped overboard and was never seen again. The
soldiers then took charge of the cooking under the direction of a

steward, and the feeding was not exactly luxurious in consequence. Below decks was unbearable at night, but a lot of us made our sleeping places in the stern-windows of the main deck. The iron ports of these windows were let down until they hung out horizontally from the ship's side with chains to support them. The windows were all close together, with only six or eight inches between, so that some fellows put their mattresses out across the ports and lay in the cool outside the ship. There was some little risk, for, if you were a restless sleeper, you might roll off your bed and overboard, and this actually happened to an officer of the 109th Regiment, whose mattress was found in the morning doubled down in the centre and empty, and the regiment had lost the number of its mess.

ROBERT BADEN-POWELL,
Indian Memories

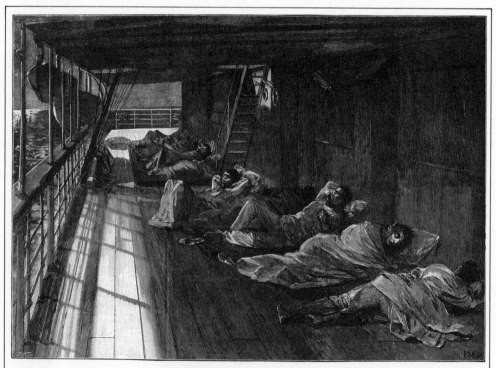

"A Hot Night in the Red Sea."
The saloon deck of the *Oceana*, 1895

1876–77: Anna Brassey

Anna Brassey was the wife of the English Member of Parliament Sir Thomas (later Lord) Brassey, son of the hugely successful railway contractor and himself the founder of *Brassey's Naval Annual*. Brassey was rich enough to run his own yacht, and in *A Voyage in the Sunbeam*, his wife chronicled their journey around the world in 1876–77. "There were forty-three of us on board," she wrote: they were her husband and herself, their four children (Thomas, Muriel, Mabelle, and Marie), four guests, a surgeon, twenty-three sailors and engineers, four stewards and a stewardess, two cooks, a nurse, and a lady's maid.

Mrs. Brassey was a lively, compassionate, and essentially practical woman; though with servants to hand and nightly dressing for dinner, her social outlook was inevitably somewhat different to that of Sophy Taylor.

February 28, 1876

We have now resumed our usual life-at-sea habits. In the morning we go on deck at a very early hour, to enjoy the exquisite freshness of the dawn of the tropical day. Tom and the Doctor help to man the pumps, sometimes assisted by the children, who appear to like the work of scrubbing decks as much as they did in the old days of our first long voyage round the world. Then we are most of us *hosed*. An open-air salt-water bath is a luxury not to be appreciated anywhere so thoroughly as in these tropical climates. After an early breakfast we settle down to our several occupations—the children to lessons, till it is time for sights to be taken and calculations made; Mr. Pritchett elaborates the sketches which he has made on shore during our recent wanderings; the Doctor makes himself generally useful, and has plenty of time to devote to this benevolent work, for at present he has hardly any patients. Later on he kindly gives the children a lesson in arithmetic, while Mr. des Graz, assisted by Prior, spends a considerable time in developing, printing, and toning the photographs which we have taken. I have always plenty to do in the way of writing, reading and general supervision. Often do I look wistfully at the many books which I long to read, and think regretfully of the letters and journal that ought to be written; but a good deal of time has to be spent in less interesting, and certainly more prosaic, work. In the afternoon there is more reading, writing, and lessons; and after tea there is a general taking off of coats by the gentlemen, a putting on of suitable costumes by the children, and a grand game of hide-and-seek and romps during the short twilights until the dressing-bell gives warning to prepare for dinner.

Landsmen can never know how delightful it is to be able to sit quietly on deck late in the evening, in the open air, without any tiresome wraps, and to enjoy the soft silvery light of the stars, scarcely dimmed by the brighter rays of the young moon. It is indeed a period of tranquil happiness. One is only agreeably fatigued by the exertions of the day; and one feels so soothed by the beauty and peacefulness of the scene as to be quite content to do absolutely nothing, and to rest satisfied with the mere pleasure of existence. Indeed it is only the recollection of the charms of early rising which induces any of us to leave the deck at last.

Thursday, July 13

When I went on deck, at half-past six, I found a grey, steamy, calm morning, promising a very hot day, without wind.

About 10.30 A.M. the cry of "Sail on the port beam!" caused general excitement, and in a few minutes every telescope and glass in the ship had been brought to bear upon the object which attracted our attention, and which was soon pronounced to be a wreck. Orders were given to starboard the helm, and to steer direct for the vessel; and many were the conjectures hazarded, and the questions asked of the fortunate holders of glasses. "What is she?" "Is there any one on board?" "Where does she come from?" "Can you read her name?" "Does she look as if she had been long abandoned?" Soon we were near enough to send a boat's crew on board, whilst we watched their movements anxiously from the bridge. We could now read her name—the *Carolina*—surmounted by a gorgeous yellow decoration on her stern. She was of between two and three hundred tons burden, and was painted a light blue, with a red streak. Beneath her white bowsprit the gaudy image of a woman served as a figure-head. The two masts had been snapped short off about three feet from the deck, and the bulwarks were gone, only the covering board and stanchions remaining, so that each wave washed over and through her. The roof and supports of the deck-house and the companions were still left standing, but the sides had disappeared, and the ship's deck was burst up in such a manner as to remind one of a quail's back.

We saw the men on board poking about, apparently very pleased with what they had found; and soon our boat returned to the yacht for some breakers,* as the *Carolina* had been laden with port wine and cork, and the men wished to bring some of the former on board. I changed my dress, and, putting on my sea boots, started for the wreck.

We found the men rather excited over their discovery. The wine must have been *very* new and *very* strong, for the smell from it, as it slopped about all over the deck, was almost enough to intoxicate anybody. One pipe had already been emptied into the breakers and barrels, and great efforts were made to get some of the casks out whole; but this was found to be impossible, without devoting more time to the operation than we chose to spare. The men managed to remove three half-empty casks with their heads stove in, which they threw overboard, but the full ones would have required special appliances to raise them through the hatches. It proved exceedingly difficult to get at the wine, which was stowed underneath the cork, and there was also a quantity of cabin bulkheads and fittings floating about, under the influence of the long swell of the Atlantic. It was a curious sight, standing on the roof of the deck-house, to look into the hold, full of floating bales of cork, barrels, and pieces of wood, and to watch the sea surging up in every direction, through and over the deck, which was level with the water's edge. I saw an excellent modern iron cooking-stove washing about from side to side; but almost every other moveable article, including spars and ropes, had apparently been removed by previous boarders.

It would have delayed us too long to tow the vessel into the nearest port, 375 miles distant, or we might have claimed the salvage money, estimated by the experts at 1,500*l*. She was too low in the water for it to be possible for us, with our limited appliances, to blow her up; so we were obliged to leave her floating about as a derelict, a fertile source of danger to all ships cross-

* Small casks, used for carrying water in boats, frequently spelt *barricos*, evidently from the time of the old Spanish navigators.

ing her track. With her buoyant cargo, and with the trade winds slowly wafting her to smoother seas, it may probably be some years before she breaks up. I only hope that no good ship may run full speed on to her, some dark night, for the *Carolina* would prove almost as formidable an obstacle as a sunken rock.

Tom was now signalling for us to go on board again, and for a few minutes I was rather afraid we should have had a little trouble in getting the men off, as their excitement had not decreased; but after a trifling delay and some rather rough play amongst themselves, they became steady again, and we returned to the yacht with our various prizes.

Friday, July 14

Our little party got on extremely well together, though a week ago they were strangers to each other. We are all so busy that we do not see much of one another except at meals, and then we have plenty to talk about. Captain Lecky imparts to us some of his valuable information about scientific navigation and the law of storms, and he and Tom and Captain Brown work hard at these subjects. Mr. Freer follows in the same path; Mr. Bingham draws and reads; Dr. Potter helps me to teach the children, who, I am happy to say, are as well as possible. I read and write a great deal, and learn Spanish, so that the days are all too short for what we have to do. The servants are settling down well for their places, and the commissariat department does great credit to the cooks and stewards. The maids get on satisfactorily, but are a little nervous on rough nights. We hope not to have many more just at present, for we are now approaching calmer latitudes.

In the course of the day, whilst Tom and I were sitting in the stern, the man at the wheel suddenly exclaimed, "There's land on the port bow." We knew, from the distance we had run, that this could not be the case, and after looking at it through the glasses, Tom pronounced the supposed land to be a thick wall of fog, advancing towards us *against* the wind. Captain Brown and Captain Lecky came from below, and hastened to get in the studding-sails, in anticipation of the coming squall. In a few minutes we had lost our fair breeze and brilliant sunshine, all our sails were taken flat aback, and we found ourselves enveloped in a dense fog, which made it impossible for us to see the length of the vessel. It was an extraordinary phenomenon. Captain Lecky, who, in the course of his many voyages, has passed within a few miles of this exact spot more than a hundred and fifty times, had never seen anything in the least like it. As night came on the fog increased, and the boats were prepared ready for lowering. Two men went to the wheel, and two to the bows to look out, while an officer was stationed on the bridge with steam-whistle and bell ready for an emergency; so that, in case we ran into anything, or anything ran into us, we should at least have the satisfaction of knowing that, so far as we were concerned, it had all been done strictly according to Act of Parliament.

Thursday, September 28

I was lying down, below, after breakfast, feeling very stupid, when Mabelle rushed into the cabin, saying, "Papa says you are to come up on deck at once, to see the ship on fire." I rushed up quickly, hardly knowing whether she referred to our own or some other vessel, and on reaching the deck I found everybody looking at a large barque, under full sail, flying the red union-jack upside down, and with signals in her rigging, which our signal-man read as "Ship on fire." These were lowered shortly afterwards, and the signals, "Come on board at once," hoisted in their place. Still we could see no appearance of smoke or flames, but we nevertheless hauled to the wind, tacked, hove to, and sent off a boat's crew, well armed, thinking it not impossible that a mutiny had taken place on board, and that the captain or officers, mistaking the yacht for a gunboat, had appealed to us for assistance. We were now near enough to the barque to make out her name through a glass—the *Monkshaven*, of Whitby—and we observed a puff of smoke issue from her deck simultaneously with the arrival of our boat alongside. In the course of a few minutes, the boat returned, bringing the mate of the *Monkshaven*, a fine-looking Norwegian, who spoke English perfectly, and who reported his ship to be sixty-eight days out from Swansea, bound for Valparaiso, with a cargo of smelting coal. The fire had first been discovered on the previous Sunday, and by 6 A.M. on Monday the crew had got up their clothes and provisions on deck, thrown overboard all articles of a combustible character, such as tar, oil, paint, spare spars and sails, planks, and rope, and battened down the hatches. Ever since then they had all been living on deck, with no protection from the wind and sea but a canvas screen. Tom and Captain Brown proceeded on board at once. They found the deck more than a foot deep in water, and all a-wash; when the hatches were opened for a moment dense clouds of hot suffocating yellow smoke immediately poured forth, driving back all who stood near. From the captain's cabin came volumes of poisonous gas, which had found its way in through the crevices, and one man, who tried to enter, was rendered insensible.

It was perfectly evident that it would be impossible to save the ship, and the captain therefore determined, after consultation with Tom and Captain Brown, to abandon her. Some of the crew were accordingly at once brought on board the *Sunbeam*, in our boat, which was then sent back to assist in removing the remainder, a portion of whom came in their own boat. The poor fellows were almost wild with joy at getting alongside another ship, after all the hardships they had gone through, and in their excitement they threw overboard many things which they might as well have kept,

Sunbeam passengers bartering with the
natives of Tierra del Fuego

as they had taken the trouble to bring them. Our boat made three trips altogether, and by half-past six we had them all safe on board, with most of their effects, and the ship's chronometers, charts, and papers.

The poor little dinghy, belonging to the *Monkshaven*, had been cast away as soon as the men had disembarked from her, and there was something melancholy in seeing her slowly drift away to leeward, followed by her oars and various small articles, as if to rejoin the noble ship she had so lately quitted. The latter was now hove-to, under full sail, an occasional puff of smoke alone betraying the presence of the demon of destruction within. The sky was dark and lowering, the sunset red and lurid in its grandeur, the clouds numerous and threatening, the sea high and dark, with occasional streaks of white foam. Not a breath of wind was stirring. Everything portended a gale. As we lay slowly rolling from side to side, both ship and boat were sometimes plainly visible, and then again both would disappear, for what seemed an age, in the deep trough of the South Atlantic rollers.

For two hours we could see the smoke pouring from various portions of the ill-fated barque. Our men, who had brought off the last of her crew, reported that, as they left her, flames were just beginning to burst from the fore-hatchway; and it was therefore certain that the rescue had not taken place an hour too soon. Whilst we were at dinner, Powell called us up on deck to look at her again, when we found that she was blazing like a tar-barrel. The captain was anxious to stay by and see the last of her, but Tom was unwilling to incur the delay which this would have involved. We accordingly got up steam, and at nine P.M. steamed round the *Monkshaven*, as close as it was deemed prudent to go. No flames were visible then; only dense volumes of smoke and sparks, issuing from the hatches. The heat, however, was intense, and could be plainly felt, even in the cold night air, as we passed some distance to leeward. All hands were clustered in our rigging, on the deck-house or on the bridge, to see the last of the poor *Monkshaven*, as she was slowly being burnt down to the water's edge.

Some account of the disaster, as gathered from the lips of various members of the crew at different times, may perhaps be interesting. It seems that, early on Monday morning, the day following that on which the fire was discovered, another barque, the *Robert Hinds*, of Liverpool, was spoken. The captain of that vessel offered to stand by them or do anything in his power to help them; but at that time they had a fair wind for Monte Video, only 120 miles distant, and they therefore determined to run for that port, and do their best to save the ship, and possibly some of the cargo. In the course of the night, however, a terrible gale sprang up, the same, no doubt, as the one of which we had felt the effects on first leaving the River Plate. They were driven hither and thither, the sea constantly breaking over them and sweeping the decks, though fortunately without washing any of them overboard. After forty-eight hours of this rough usage the men were all exhausted, while the fire was gradually increasing in strength beneath their feet, and they knew not at what moment it might burst through the decks and envelope the whole ship in flames. They were beginning to abandon all hope of a rescue, when a sail was suddenly discovered; and as soon as the necessary flags could be found, the same signal which attracted us was displayed. The vessel, now quite close to them, proved to be a large American steamer, but she merely hoisted her own ensign and code-pennant, and then coolly steamed away to the southward. "I think that captain deserved tarring and feathering, anyway," one of the men said to me. Another observed, "I wonder what will become of that man; for we had put all our lives in his hand by signalling as we did; and every seaman knows that right well." Another said, "When we saw that ship go away, we all gave in and lay down in despair to die. But our captain, who is very good to his crew, and a religious man too, said, 'There is One above who looks after us all.' That was true enough, for, about ten minutes afterwards, as I was talking to the cook, and telling him it was all over with us, I saw a sail to leeward, and informed the captain. We bore down a little, but did not like to go out of our course too much, fearing you might be a 'Portuguese,' and play us the same trick as the American." (They could not understand our white ensign; for, our funnel being stowed, we looked like a sailing vessel, while all gunboats of our size are steamers.) "When we saw it was an English vessel, and that you answered our signals and sent a boat off, we were indeed thankful; though that was nothing to what we feel now at once more having a really dry ship under our feet. Not that we have really suffered anything very terrible, for we had a bit of shelter, and plenty to eat, and the worst part was seeing our things washed overboard, and thinking perhaps we might go next. We have not had a dry deck since we left Swansea, and the pumps have been kept going most of the time. Why, with this sea, ma'am, our decks would be under water." (This surprised me; as, though low in the water, the *Monkshaven* did not appear to be overladen, and the Plimsoll mark was plainly visible.) "Our boats were all ready for launching, but we had no sails, and only one rudder for the three; so we should have had hard work to fetch anywhere if we had taken to them. We lashed the two boys—apprentices, fourteen and sixteen years old—in one of the boats, for fear they should be washed overboard. The youngest of them is the only son of his mother, a widow; and you could see how she loved him by the way she had made his clothes, and fitted him out all through. He was altogether too well found for a ship like ours, but now most of his things are lost. His chest could not be got up from below, and though I borrowed an old bread-bag from the steward, it was not half big enough, and his sea-boots and things his mother had given him to keep him dry and cover his bed— not oilskins, like ours."—"Mackintoshes," I suggested.—"Yes, that's the name—they were all lost. It did seem a pity. The boy never thought there was much danger till this morning, when I told him all hope was gone, as the American ship had sailed away from us. He said, 'Will the ship go to the bottom?' and I replied, 'I fear so; but we have good boats, so keep up your heart, little man.' He made no further remark, but laid down gently again, and cried a little."

This poor child was dreadfully frightened in the small boat coming alongside, and his look of joy and relief, when once he got safely on board, was a treat to me. Every one on board, including the captain, seems to have been very kind to him. One of the men had his foot broken by the sea, and the captain himself had his leg severely injured; so the Doctor has some cases at last.

Sunday, October 8: Tierra del Fuego

In the afternoon, when in English Reach, where many vessels have been lost, great excitement was caused on board by the appearance of a canoe on our port bow. She was stealing out from the Barbara Channel, and as she appeared to be making direct for us, Tom ordered the engines to be slowed. Her occupants thereupon redoubled their efforts, and came paddling towards us, shouting and making the most frantic gesticulations, one man waving a skin round his head with an amount of energy that threatened to upset the canoe. This frail craft, upon a nearer inspection, proved to be made only of rough planks, rudely tied together with the sinews of animals; in fact, one of the party had to bale constantly, in order to keep her afloat. We flung them a rope, and they came alongside, shouting "Tabáco, galléta" (biscuit), a supply of which we threw down to them, in exchange for the skins they had been waving; whereupon the two men stripped themselves of the skin mantles they were wearing, made of eight or ten sea-otter skins sewed together with finer sinews than those used for the boat, and handed them up, clamouring for more tobacco, which we gave them, together with some beads and knives. Finally, the woman, influenced by this example, parted with her sole garment, in return for a little more tobacco, some beads, and some looking-glasses I had thrown into the canoe.

The party consisted of a man, a woman, and a lad; and I think I never saw delight more strongly depicted than it was on the faces of the two latter, when they handled, for the first time in their lives probably, some strings of blue, red, and green glass beads. They had two rough pots, made of bark, in the boat, which they also sold, after which they reluctantly departed, quite naked but very happy, shouting and jabbering away in the most inarticulate language imaginable. It was with great difficulty we could make them let go the rope, when we went ahead, and I was quite afraid they would be upset. They were all fat and healthy-looking, and, though not handsome, their appearance was by no means repulsive; the countenance of the woman, especially, wore quite a pleasing expression, when lighted up with smiles at the sight of the beads and looking-glasses. The bottom of their canoe was covered with branches, amongst which the ashes of a recent fire were distinguishable. Their paddles were of the very roughest description, consisting simply of split branches of trees, with wider pieces tied on at one end with the sinews of birds or beasts.

Sunday, November 12

Another lovely day. We had the Litany and hymns at eleven, evening service and sermon at four.

Just before morning church someone turned on the water in the nursery bath, and forgot to turn it off again, so that when we came aft from the saloon we had the pleasure of finding everything in the children's cabins afloat, and that a good deal of water had got down into the hold. It was rather annoying at the time, but, I dare say, like many other present troubles, it was a good thing in the end. It obliged us, at any rate, to have all the stores brought up on deck, and led to our taking an inventory of our resources sooner than we should otherwise have done. I am sorry to say we found that, owing to the departure of our head steward and the illness of his successor, they have not been husbanded as carefully as they should have been, especially those provided for use forward. Sailors are more like children than grown-up men, and require as much looking after. While there is water in the tanks, for instance, they will use it in the most extravagant manner, without thought for the morrow; and they are quite as reckless with their other stores.

I find, however, that one of the drawbacks to taking a very close personal interest in the housekeeping arrangements on board is the too intimate acquaintance one makes with the various individuals composing the live stock, the result being that the private particular history of every chicken, duck, turkey, and joint of mutton is apt to be remembered with a damaging effect to appetite.

In the afternoon two boobies, the first birds we have seen for some days, paid us a visit. I suppose we are too far out to see anything more of our pretty little friends, the petrels.

Saturday, November 18

The two green paroquets, "Coco" and "Meta," given to me by Mr. Fisher at Rosario, have turned out dear little pets, with the most amusing ways. They are terrible thieves, especially of sugar, pencils, pens, and paper, and being nearly always at liberty, they follow me about just like dogs, and coax and caress me with great affection. They do not care much for anyone else, though they are civil to all and good-tempered even to the children, who, I am afraid, rather bore them with their attempts at petting. The other foreign birds, of which I have a large collection, are doing well, and I begin to hope I shall get them home safely after all. We had at one time about twenty parrots, belonging to the men, on board, all running about on deck forward, with their wings clipped, but about half of them have been lost overboard. The dogs keep their health and spirits wonderfully. Félise is quite young again, and she and Lulu have great games, tearing up and down and around the decks as hard as they can go.

Sunday, April 8, 1877

The two Chinese servants we shipped at Hongkong are a great success, as every one on board agrees. Even the old sailing master is obliged to confess that the two "heathen Chinee" keep the mess rooms, ships' officers' and servants' berths much cleaner and more comfortable than his own sailors ever succeeded in doing. At Galle we shipped three black firemen, two from Bombay and one from Mozambique, a regular nigger, with his black woolly hair clipped into the shape of Prince of Wales feathers. Their names are Mahomet, Abraham, and Tom Dollar. They live in a little tent we have had pitched for them on deck, cook their own food, and do their work in the engine-room exceedingly well. In the intervals they are highly amused with the children's picture books. The picture of the durbar at Delhi delighted them, especially as they recognised the figures, and learned a little English through them. They can say a few words already, and have told me all about their wives and children at Mozambique and Bombay, and have shown me the presents they are taking home to them. They have been nearly a year on board the P. and O. steamship *Poonah*, and appear to have saved nearly all their earnings. I do not suppose our own men could have stood the fearful heat below in the engine-room for many days together, so it was fortunate we met with these amiable salamanders.

Monday, April 9

No wind. We passed through a large shoal of porpoises, and at dusk we saw the light of a distant ship. At all the places we have recently visited we have found excellent ice-making machines, and have been able to get a sufficient supply to last us from port to port, which has been a great comfort. The machine at Colombo unfortunately broke down the day before we left, so that in the very hottest part of our voyage we have had to do without our accustomed luxury; and very much we miss it, not only for cooling our drinks, but for keeping provisions, &c. As it is, a sheep killed overnight is not good for dinner next day; butter is just like oil, and to-day in opening a drawer my fingers touched a sticky mess; I looked and discovered six sticks of sealing wax running slowly about in a state resembling treacle.

Friday, April 13

One of our large pigs took it into his head to jump overboard to-day. The helm was put round as quickly as possible, but the most anxious spying could not discover any trace of poor piggy's whereabouts; so we proceeded on our original course for a few minutes, when suddenly, to our great astonishment, we saw him alongside, having been nearly run down, but still gallantly swimming along. The dingy was lowered and two men sent in pursuit. They had, however, no easy task before them, for as soon as they approached, piggy swam away faster than they could row, and bit and fought most furiously when they tried to get him into the boat. It was a good half-hour's work before he was secured, yet when he arrived he did not appear to be in the least exhausted by his long swim, but bit and barked at everybody so furiously that he was condemned to death, to prevent the possibility of further accidents. It is quite clear from the foregoing incident that some pigs can swim, and swim very well too, without cutting their own throats in the process.

Sunday, April 22

While we were at lunch, the breeze freshened so much that we were all glad to add some wraps to our light and airy costumes. A little later, a summer gale was blowing ahead, making some of us feel very uncomfortable and long for the halcyon days of the past, even with the accompaniment of the inevitable heat. Such is mankind, and womankind too for that matter, "never blessed but always to be blessed." The gale freshened, the screw was raised, the yacht pitched and rolled, and we were obliged to put her off her course and under sail before night fell. The spray came over the decks, and there was a strong wind dead ahead. We all felt cold and miserable, though the thermometer still registered 75°. The poor monkeys and parrots looked most wretched and unhappy, and had to be packed away as speedily as possible. Nine monkeys in an empty wine case seemed very happy and cuddled together for warmth, but the two larger and more aristocratic members of the party required a box to themselves. The gazelle had a little tent pitched for him specially in a sheltered corner, and the birds were all stowed away and battened over in the smoking fiddle. Dinner was rather a lame pretence, and it was not long before we all retired, and certainly no one wished to take his or her mattress on deck to-night. It is the first night I have slept in a bed on board the yacht for many weeks, and a very disturbed night it was, for the waves ran high, and we have lately been sailing so steadily over smooth seas, that we did not know what to make of this.

Monday, May 14

About breakfast time to-day we crossed the meridian of Greenwich; and this virtually completed our voyage round the world, our original point of departure having really been Rochester, which is a few minutes to the east of Greenwich. The wind changed in the middle of the day, and we passed through a large fleet of merchantmen hove-to under shelter of Cape de Gat, where they had collected, I suppose, from various ports in Spain and Italy.

Tuesday, May 15

This was a somewhat sad day, many of our pets dying from the effects of the cold wind or from accidents. The steward's mocking-bird from Siam, which talked like a Christian and followed him about like a dog, died of acute bronchitis early this morning; and his monkey, the most weird little creature, with the affectionate ways of a human friend, died in the afternoon, of inflammation and congestion of the lungs. Two other monkeys and several birds also expired in the course of the day.

This evening "Beau Brummel," the little pig I brought from Bow Island, in the South Pacific, died of a broken spine, as the doctor, who made a post-mortem examination in each case, discovered. A spar must have dropped upon poor piggy accidentally whilst he was running about on deck, though of course no one knew anything about it. I am very sorry; for though I must confess he was somewhat greedy and pig-like in his habits, he was extremely amusing in his ways. He ran about and went to sleep with the pugs, just like one of themselves. Besides, I do not think any one else in England could have boasted of a pig given to them by a South-Sea-Island chief. Probably "Beau Brummel" was a lineal descendant of the pigs Captain Cook took out in the *Endeavour*.

The bodies were all placed together in a neat little box and committed to the deep at sunset, a few tears being shed over the departed pets, especially by the children.

ANNA BRASSEY,
A Voyage in the Sunbeam

THE AEGEAN

Chickens on board, eyes blinking, trussed alive,
The siren's tongue of steam, a restless night,
White columns in the moon's decaying light,
Travellers humped in bags, awake; at five
The sailors uncoil ropes and we arrive
At yet another island. People cough.
The sleeping harbour sends its small boats off.
The anchor does a belly-flopping dive.

O night! O moon! Staring and staring, we
Might lie forever on this parting wake:
Call up the waves and wind, stir us and make
Us crumble like those cities, stunned, until,
Another ruin on the endless sea
Our ship steams through, our love stands ever still.

JOHN FULLER

1879: Robert Louis Stevenson

In *A Book of Railway Journeys* we met Robert Louis Stevenson crossing America by emigrant train. Here he is on the first
part of his journey, from Glasgow to New York.

We steamed out of the Clyde on Thursday night, and early on the
Friday forenoon we took in our last batch of emigrants at Lough
Foyle, in Ireland, and said farewell to Europe. The company was
now complete, and began to draw together, by inscrutable mag-
netisms, upon the deck. There were Scots and Irish in plenty, a
few English, a few Americans, a good handful of Scandinavians,
a German or two, and one Russian, all now belonging for ten days
to one small iron country on the deep.

Our party in the second cabin was not perhaps the most interesting on board. Perhaps even in the saloon there was as much
good-will and character. Yet it had some elements of curiosity.
There was a mixed group of Swedes, Danes, and Norsemen, one
of whom, generally known by the name of "Johnny," in spite of
his own protests, greatly diverted us by his clever, cross-country
efforts to speak English, and became on the strength of that an
universal favourite—it takes so little in this world of shipboard to
create a popularity. There was, besides, a Scots mason, known
from his favourite dish as "Irish Stew," three or four nondescript
Scots, a fine young Irishman, O'Reilly, and a pair of young men
who deserve a special word of condemnation. One of them was
Scots: the other claimed to be American; admitted, after some
fencing, that he was born in England; and ultimately proved to
be an Irishman born and nurtured, but ashamed to own his country. He had a sister on board, whom he faithfully neglected
throughout the voyage, though she was not only sick but much
his senior, and had nursed and cared for him in childhood. In appearance he was like an imbecile Henry the Third of France. The
Scotsman, though perhaps as big an ass, was not so dead of heart;
and I have only bracketed them together because they were fast
friends, and disgraced themselves equally by their conduct at the
table.

Next, to turn to topics more agreeable, we had a newly married couple, devoted to each other, with a pleasant story of how they had first seen each other years ago at a preparatory school, and that very afternoon he had carried her books home for her. I do not know if this story will be plain to Southern readers; but to me it recalls many a school idyll, with wrathful swains of eight and nine confronting each other stride-legs, flushed with jealousy; for to carry home a young lady's books was both a delicate attention and a privilege.

Then there was an old lady, or indeed, I am not sure that she was as much old as antiquated and strangely out of place, who had left her husband, and was travelling all the way to Kansas by herself. We had to take her own word that she was married; for it was sorely contradicted by the testimony of her appearance.

The breakfast bell. An emigrant ship
leaving harbour, 1884

Nature seemed to have sanctified her for the single state; even the colour of her hair was incompatible with matrimony, and her husband, I thought, should be a man of saintly spirit and phantasmal bodily presence. She was ill, poor thing; her soul turned from the viands; the dirty table-cloth shocked her like an impropriety: and the whole strength of her endeavour was bent upon keeping her watch true to Glasgow time till she should reach New York. They had heard reports, her husband and she, of some unwarrantable disparity of hours between these two cities; and with a spirit commendably scientific, had seized on this occasion to put them to the proof. It was a good thing for the old lady; for she passed much leisure time in studying the watch. Once, when prostrated by sickness, she let it run down. It was inscribed on her harmless mind in letters of adamant that the hands of a watch must never be turned backwards; and so it behoved her to lie in wait for the exact moment ere she started it up again. When she imagined this was about due, she sought out one of the young second-cabin Scotsmen, who was embarked on the same experiment as herself and had hitherto been less neglectful. She was in quest of two o'clock; and when she learned it was already seven on the shores of Clyde, she lifted up her voice and cried "Gravy!" I had not heard this innocent expletive since I was a young child; and I suppose it must have been the same with the other Scotsmen present, for we all laughed our fill.

Travel is of two kinds; and this voyage of mine across the ocean combined both. "Out of my country and myself I go," sings the old poet: and I was not only travelling out of my country in latitude and longitude, but out of myself in diet, associates, and consideration. Part of the interest and a great deal of the amusement flowed, at least to me, from this novel situation in the world.

I found that I had what they call fallen in life with absolute success and verisimilitude. I was taken for a steerage passenger; no one seemed surprised that I should be so; and there was nothing but the brass plate between decks to remind me that I had once been a gentleman. In a former book, describing a former journey, I expressed some wonder that I could be readily and naturally taken for a pedlar, and explained the accident by the difference of language and manners between England and France. I must

now take a humbler view; for here I was among my own countrymen, somewhat roughly clad, to be sure, but with every advantage
of speech and manner; and I am bound to confess that I passed for
nearly anything you please except an educated gentleman. The
sailors called me "mate," the officers addressed me as "my man,"
my comrades accepted me without hesitation for a person of their
own character and experience, but with some curious information.
One, a mason himself, believed I was a mason; several, and among
these at least one of the seamen, judged me to be a petty officer in
the American navy; and I was so often set down for a practical
engineer that at last I had not the heart to deny it. From all these
guesses I drew one conclusion, which told against the insight of
my companions. They might be close observers in their own way,
and read the manners in the face; but it was plain that they did not
extend their observation to the hands. (There is nothing strange
in the omission: the only marvel being that, where we are all as
much interested about our neighbours, so few should have learned
to look critically at a part of the body, uncovered like the face and
nearly as eloquent and personal.)

To the saloon passengers also I sustained my part without a
hitch. It is true I came little in their way; but when we did encounter, there was no recognition in their eye, although I confess I
sometimes courted it in silence. All these, my inferiors and equals,
took me, like the transformed monarch in the story, for a mere
common, human man. They gave me a hard, dead look, with the
flesh about the eye kept unrelaxed.

With the women this surprised me less, as I had already ex-
perimented on the sex by going abroad through a suburban part
of London simply attired in a sleeve-waistcoat. The result was
curious. I then learned for the first time, and by the exhaustive
process, how much attention ladies are accustomed to bestow on
all male creatures of their own station; for, in my humble rig,
each one who went by me caused me a certain shock of surprise
and a sense of something wanting. In my normal circumstances, it
appeared, every young lady must have paid me some passing tribute of a glance; and though I had often been unconscious of it
when given, I was well aware of its absence when it was withheld.
My height seemed to decrease with every woman who passed me,
for she passed me like a dog. This is one of my grounds for sup-

posing that what are called the upper classes may sometimes produce a disagreeable impression in what are called the lower; and
I wish some one would continue my experiment, and find out exactly at what stage of toilette a man becomes invisible to the well-
regulated female eye.

Here on shipboard the matter was put to a more complete test;
for, even with the addition of speech and manner, I passed among
the ladies for precisely the average man of the steerage. It was
one afternoon that I saw this demonstrated. A very plainly dressed
woman was taken ill on deck. I think I had the luck to be present
at every sudden seizure during all the passage; and on this occasion found myself in the place of importance, supporting the sufferer. There was not only a large crowd immediately around us,
but a considerable knot of saloon passengers leaning over our
heads from the hurricane-deck. One of these, an elderly managing
woman, hailed me with counsels. Of course I had to reply; and as
the talk went on, I began to discover that the whole group took me
for the husband. I looked upon my new wife, poor creature, with
mingled feelings; and I must own she had not even the appearance
of the poorest class of city servant-maids, but looked more like a
country wench who should have been employed at a roadside inn.
(I confess openly, I was chagrined at this.) Now was the time
for me to go and study the brass plate.

To such of the officers as knew about me—the doctor, the
purser, and the stewards—I appeared in the light of a broad joke.
The fact that I spent the better part of my day in writing had gone
abroad over the ship and tickled them all prodigiously. Whenever
they met me they referred to my absurd occupation with familiarity and breadth of humorous intention. Their manner was well
calculated to remind me of my fallen fortunes. You may be sin-
cerely amused by the amateur literary efforts of a gentleman, but
you scarce publish the feeling to his face. "Well!" they would say:
"still writing?" And the smile would widen into a laugh. The
purser came one day into the cabin, and, touched to the heart by
my misguided industry, offered me some other kind of writing,
"for which," he added pointedly, "you will be paid." This was
nothing else than to copy out the list of passengers.

ROBERT LOUIS STEVENSON,
The Amateur Emigrant

1913: O. Douglas (Anna Buchan)

The third of these descriptions by women of life on board ocean-going ships is by John Buchan's sister, Anna, who wrote many successful novels under the name of O. Douglas. In *Olivia in India*, her letters home describe her journey out there in the steamship *Scotia* to visit another brother, William, nick-named Boggley.

Socially Anna Buchan is closer to Anna Brassey than Sophy Taylor, but without the former's manifold responsibilities. I find her enchanting; a delightful writer and the sort of woman one would like to have known.

S.S. Scotia, *Oct. 19, 19—*

. . . THIS is a line to send off with the pilot. There is nothing to say except "Good-bye" again.

We have had luncheon, and I have been poking things out of my cabin trunk, and furtively surveying one—there are two, but the other seems to be lost at present—of my cabin companions. She has fair hair and a blue motor veil, and looks quiet and subdued, but then, I dare say, so do I.

I hope you are thinking of your friend going down to the sea in a ship.

I feel, somehow, very small and lonely.

OLIVIA

S.S. Scotia, *Oct. 21*
(*In pencil*)

. . . WHATEVER you do, whatever folly you commit, never, never be tempted to take a sea voyage. It is quite the nastiest thing you can take—I have had three days of it now, so I know.

When I wrote to you on Saturday I had an uneasy feeling that in the near future all would not be well with me, but I went in to dinner and afterwards walked up and down the deck trying to feel brave. Sunday morning dawned rain-washed and tempestuous, and the way the ship heaved was not encouraging, but I rose, or rather I descended from my perch—did I tell you I had an upper berth? —and walked with an undulating motion towards my bath. Some people would have remained in bed, or at least gone unbathed, but, as I say, I rose—mark, please, the rugged grandeur of the Scot's character—and such is the force of example the fair-haired girl rose also. Before I go any further I must tell you about this

girl. Her name is Hilton, Geraldine Hilton, but as that is too long
a name and already we are great friends, I call her G. She is very
pretty, with the kind of prettiness that becomes more so the more
you look—and if you don't know what I mean I can't stop to explain—with masses of yellow hair, such blue eyes and pink cheeks
and white teeth that I am convinced I am sharing a cabin with
the original Hans Andersen's Snow Queen. She is very big and
most healthy, and delightful to look at; even sea-sickness does not
make her look plain, and that, you will admit, is a severe test; and
what is more, her nature is as healthy and sweet as her face. You
will laugh and say it is like me to know all about any one in three
days, but two sea-sick and home-sick people shut up in a tiny cabin
can exhibit quite a lot of traits, pleasant and otherwise, in three
days.

Well, we dressed, and reaching the saloon, sank into our seats
only to leave again hurriedly when a steward approached to know
if we would have porridge or kippered herring! I know you are
never sea-sick, unlovable creature that you are, so you won't
sympathize with us as we lay limp and wretched in our deck-chairs
on the damp and draughty deck. Even the fact that our deck-
chairs were brand new, and had our names boldly painted in
handsome black letters across the back, failed to give us a thrill
of pleasure. At last it became too utterly miserable to be borne.
The sight of the deck-steward bringing round cups of half-cold
beef tea with grease spots floating on the top, proved the last
straw, so, with a graceful wavering flight like a wood-cock, we
zigzagged to our bunks where we have remained ever since.

I don't know where we are. I expect Ushant has slammed the
door on us long ago. Our little world is bounded by the four
walls of the cabin. All day we lie and listen to the swish of the
waves as they tumble past, and watch our dressing-gowns hanging on the door swing backwards and forwards with the motion.
At intervals the stewardess comes in, a nice Scotswoman, Corrie,
she tells me, is her home-place, and brings the menu of breakfast—
luncheon—dinner, and we turn away our heads and say, "Nothing
—nothing!" Our steward is a funny little man, very small and thin
with pale yellow hair; he reminds me of a moulting canary and
his voice cheeps and is rather canary-like too. He is really a very
kind little steward and trots about most diligently on our errands,

and tries to cheer us by tales of the people he has known who have died of sea-sickness, "Strained their 'earts, Miss, that's wot they done!" It isn't very cheerful lying here, looking out through the port-hole, now at the sky, next at the sea, but what it would have been without G. I dare not think. We have certainly helped each other through this time of trial. It is a wonderful blessing, a companion in misfortune.

But where, you may ask, is the third occupant of the cabin? Would it not have been fearful if she, too, had been stretched on a couch of languishing? Happily she is a good sailor, though she doesn't look it. She is a little woman with a pale green complexion and a lot of sleek black hair, and somehow gives one the impression of having a great many more teeth than is usual. Her name is Mrs. Murray, and she is going to India to rejoin her husband who rejoices in the name of Albert. Sometimes I feel a little sorry for Albert, but perhaps, after all, he deserves what he has got. She

Children's playtime: the hazards of
travelling in India, 1880

has very assertive manners. I think she regards G. and me as two young women who want keeping in their places, though I am sure we are humble enough now whatever we may be in a state of rude health. Happily she has friends on board, so she rarely comes to the cabin except to tidy up before meals, and afterwards to tell us exactly everything she has eaten. She seems to have a good appetite and to choose the things that sound nastiest when one is seedy.

No—I don't like Mrs. Murray much: but I dislike her hat-box more. It is large and square and black, and it has no business in the cabin, it ought to be in the baggage-room. Lying up here I am freed from its tyranny, but on Saturday, when I was unpacking, it made my life a burden. It blocks up the floor under my hooks, and when I hang things up I fall over it backwards, when I sit on the floor which I have to do every time I pull out my trunk, it hits me savagely on the spine, and once, when I tried balancing it on a small chest of drawers it promptly fell down on my head and I have still a large and painful bump as a memento.

I wonder if you will be able to make this letter out. I am writing it a little bit at a time, to keep myself from getting too dreadfully down-hearted. G. and I have both very damp handkerchiefs under our pillows to testify to the depressed state of our minds. "When I was at home I was in a better place, but travellers must be content."

I don't even care to read any of the books I brought with me, except now and then a page or two of *Memories and Portraits*. It comforts me to read of such steady, quiet places as the Pentland Hills and of the decent men who do their herding there.

Is it really only three days since I left you all, and you envied me going out into the sunshine? Oh! you warm, comfortable people, how I, in this heaving, uncertain horror of a ship, envy you!

Oct. 25
(*Still in pencil*)

You mustn't think I have been lying here all the time. On Tuesday we managed to get on deck, and on Wednesday it was warm and sunny, and we began to enjoy life again and to congratulate ourselves on having got our sea-legs. But we got them only to lose them, for yesterday the wind got up, the ship rolled, we became every minute more thoughtful, until about tea-time we retired in disorder. It didn't need the little steward's shocked remark, "Oh my! You never 'ave gone back to bed again!" to make us feel ashamed.

However, we reach Marseilles to-day at noon, and, glorious thought, the ship will stand still for twenty-four hours. Also there will be letters!

This isn't a letter so much as a wail.

Don't scoff. I know I'm a coward.   OLIVIA

                                                S.S. Scotia, *Oct. 27*

. . . A FOUNTAIN-PEN is really a great comfort. I am writing with my new one, so this letter won't, I hope, be such a puzzle to decipher as my pencil scrawl.

We are off again, but now the sun shines from a cloudless sky on a sea of sapphire, and the passengers are sunning themselves on deck like snails after a shower. I'm glad after all I didn't go back from Marseilles by train.

When we reached Marseilles the rain was pouring, but that didn't prevent us ("us" means G. and myself) from bounding on shore. We found a dilapidated *fiacre* driven by a still more dilapidated *cocher*, who, for the sum of six francs, drove us to the town. I don't know whether, ordinarily, Marseilles is a beautiful town or an ugly one. Few people, I expect, would have seen anything attractive in it this dark, rainy October afternoon, but to us it was a sort of Paradise regained. We had tea at a *café*, real French tea tasting of hay-seed and lukewarm water, and real French cakes; we wandered through the streets, stopping to stare in at every shop window; we bought violets to adorn ourselves, and picture postcards, and sheets of foreign stamps for Peter, and all the time the rain poured and the street lamps were cheerily reflected in the wet pavements, and it was so damp and dark, and dirty, and home-like, we sloppered joyfully through the mud and were happy for the first time for a whole week. The thought of letters was the only thing that tempted us back to the ship.

                        *   *   *

How good of you to write such a long letter. Of course I shall write often and at length, but you must promise not to be bored, or expect too much. I fear you won't get anything very wise or

witty from me. You know how limited I am. The fairies, when
they came to my christening, might have come better provided
with gifts. But then, I expect they have only a certain number of
gifts for each family, so I don't in the least blame them for giving
the boys the brains and giving me—what? At the moment I
can't think of anything they did give me except a heart that keeps
on the windy side of care, as Beatrice puts it; and hair that curls
naturally. I have no grudge against the fairies. If they had given
me straight hair and brains I might have been a Suffragist and
shamed my kin by biting a policeman; and *that* would have been
a pity.

Later.

G. and I are crouched in a corner, very awed and sad. A poor
man died suddenly yesterday from heart failure, and the funeral
is just over. I do hope I shall never again see a burial at sea. It
was terrible. The bell tolled and the ship slowed down and almost
stopped, while the body, wrapped in a Union Jack, was slipped
into the water, committed to the deep in sure and certain hope of
a blessed Resurrection. In a minute it was all over.

The people are laughing and talking again: the dressing-bugle
has sounded; things go on as if nothing had happened. We are
steaming ahead, leaving the body—such a little speck it looked
on the great water—far behind.

It is the utter loneliness of it that makes me cry!   o.

S.S. Scotia, *Oct. 29*

. . . THIS won't be a tidy letter, for I am sitting close beside
the rail—has it a nautical name? I don't know—and every few
minutes the spray comes over and wets the paper and incidentally
myself. *And* the fountain-pen! I greatly fear it leaks, for my middle
finger is blackened beyond hope of cleansing, and though not ten
minutes ago Mr. Brand inked himself very comprehensively filling
it for me, already it requires frequent shakings to make it write
at all. I thought it would be a blessing, it threatens to become a
curse. I foresee that very shortly I shall descend again to a pencil,
or write my letters with the aid of scratchy pens and fat, respectable ink-pots in the stuffy music-room.

You will have two letters from Port Said. The one I wrote
you two days ago finished in deep melancholy, but to-day it is

so good to be alive I could shout with joy. I woke this morning
with a jump of delight, and even Mrs. Albert Murray—she of
the hat-box and the many teeth—could not irritate me, and you
can't think how many irritating ways the woman has. It is 10 A.M.
and we have just come up from breakfast, and have got our deck-
chairs placed where they will catch every breeze (and some salt-
water) and, with a pile of books and two boxes of chocolate, are
comfortably settled for the day.

You ask about the passengers.

We have all sorts and conditions. Quiet people who read and
work all day; rowdy people who never seem happy unless they
are throwing cushions or pulling one another down-stairs by the
feet; painfully enterprising people who get up sports, sweeps,

Anna Buchan at the age of about nineteen,
with her youngest brother, Alastair

concerts and dances, and are full of a tiresome, misplaced energy; bridge-loving people who play from morning till night; flirtatious people who frequent dark corners; happy people who laugh; sad people who sniff; and one man who can't be classed with any one else, a sad gentleman, his hair standing fiercely on end, a Greek Testament his constant and only companion. We pine to know who and what he is and where he is going. Yesterday I found myself beside him at tea. I might not have existed for all the notice he took of me. "Speak to him," said G. in my ear, "you don't dare!"

Of course after that I had to, so pinching G.'s arm to give myself courage, I said in a small voice, "Are you enjoying the voyage?"

He turned, regarded me with his sad prominent eyes. "Do I look as if I enjoyed it?" asked this Monsieur Melancholy, and went back to his bread-and-butter. G. choked, and I finished my tea hurriedly and in silence.

Nearly every one on board seems nice and willing to be pleasant. I am on smiling terms with most and speaking terms with many, but one really sees very little of the people outside one's own little set. It is odd how people drift together and make cliques. There are eight in our particular set. Colonel and Mrs. Crawley, Major and Mrs. Wilmot; Captain Gordon, Mr. Brand, G. and myself. The Crawleys, the Wilmots and Captain Gordon are going back after furlough; Mr. Brand and G. and I are going only for pleasure and the cold weather. Our table is much the merriest in the saloon. Mrs. Crawley is a fascinating woman; I never tire watching her. Very pretty, very smart with a pretty wit, she has the most delightfully gay, infectious laugh, which contrasts oddly with her curiously sad, unsmiling eyes. Mrs. Wilmot has a Madonna face. I don't mean one of those silly, fat-faced Madonnas one sees in the Louvre and elsewhere, but one's own idea of the Madonna; the kind of face as someone puts it, that God must love. She isn't pretty and she isn't in the least smart, but she is just a kind, sweet, wise woman. Her husband is a cheery soul, very big and boyish and always in uproarious spirits. Captain Gordon makes a good listener. Mr. Brand, although he must have left school quite ten years ago is still very reminiscent of Eton and has a school-boyish taste in silly rhymes and riddles. Colonel Crawley, a stern and somewhat awe-inspiring man, a distinguished soldier, I am told, hates *passionately* being asked riddles, and we make him frantic at table repeating Mr. Brand's witticisms. He sits with a patient, disgusted face while we repeat—

> Owen More had run away
> Owin' more than he could pay;
> Owen More came back one day
> Owin' more;

and when he can bear it no longer leaves the table remarking *Titbits*. He had his revenge the other day when the ship was rolling more than a little. We had ventured to the saloon for tea and were surveying uncertainly some dry toast, when Colonel Crawley came in. "Ah!" he said, "Steward! Pork chops for these ladies." The mere thought proved the thing too much, we fled to the fresh air—tealess.

I meant this to be a very long letter, but this pen, faint yet pursuing, shows signs of giving out. I have to shake it every second word now.

The bugle has gone for lunch, and G., who has been sound asleep for the last hour, is uncoiling herself preparatory to going down.

So good-bye.

OLIVIA

S.S. Scotia, *Nov. 1*

. . . ALL day we have glided through the Canal. Imagine a shining band of silver water, a band of deepest blue sky, and in between a bar of fine gold which is the desert—and you have some idea of what I am looking at. Sometimes an Arab passes riding on a camel, and I can't get away from the feeling that I am a child again looking at a highly coloured Bible picture-book on Sabbath afternoons.

We landed at Port Said yesterday morning. People told us it was a dirty place, an uninteresting place, a horribly dull place, not worth leaving the ship to see, but it was our first glimpse of the East and we were enchanted. The narrow streets, the white domes and minarets against the blue sky, the flat roofs of the houses, the queer shops with the Arabs shouting to draw attention to their wares, and, above all, the new strange smell of the East, were, to us, wonderful and fascinating.

When we got ashore the sun was shining with a directness hitherto unknown to us, making the backs of our unprotected heads feel somewhat insecure, so we went first to a shop where we spied exposed to sale a rich profusion of topis. In case you don't know, a topi is a sun-hat, a white thing, large and saucer-like, lined with green, with cork about it somewhere, rather suggestive of a lifebelt; horribly unbecoming but quite necessary.

A very polite man bowed us inside and we proceeded on our quixotic search for a topi not entirely hideous. Half an hour later we came out of the shop, the shopman more obsequious than ever, not only wearing topis, but laden with boxes of Turkish Delight, ostrich-feather fans, tinsel scarves and a string of pink beads which he swore were coral, but I greatly doubt it. We had an uneasy feeling as we bought the things that perhaps we were foolish virgins, but before the afternoon was very old we were sure of it. You wouldn't believe how heavy Turkish Delight becomes when you carry half-a-dozen boxes for some hours under a blazing sun, and I had a carved book-rest under one arm and G. had four parcels and a green umbrella. To complete our disgust, after weltering under our purchases for some time we saw

P & O passengers at dinner, c. 1880

in a shop exactly the same things much cheaper. G. pointed a wrathful finger, letting two parcels fall to do it. "Look at that," she said, "I'm going straight back to tell the man he's cheated us." With difficulty I persuaded her it wasn't worth while and tired and dusty we sank—no, we didn't sink, they were iron chairs—we sat down hard on chairs outside a big hotel and demanded tea immediately. Some of the ship people were also having tea at little tables, and a party of evil-looking Frenchmen were twanging guitars and singing sentimental songs for pennies. While we were waiting a man—an Arab I think—crouched beside us and begged us to let him read our hands for half-a-crown, and we were weak enough to permit it. You may be interested to know that I am to be married "soon already" to a high official with gold in his teeth. It sounds ideal. G. was rather awed by the varied career he sketched for her. After tea, which was long in coming and when it came disappointing, we had still some time, so we hailed a man driving a depressed-looking horse attached to a carriage of sorts, and told him to drive us all round. He looked a very wicked man, but it may have been the effect of his only having one eye, for he certainly had a refined taste in sights. When we suggested that we would like to see the Arab bazaar he shook his head violently and instead drove us along dull roads, stopping now and again to wave a vague whip towards some building, remarking in most melancholy tones as he did so, "The English Church"—"The American Mission."

Back on the ship again, sitting on deck in the soft darkness, watching the lights of the town and hearing a faint echo of the life there, I realized with something of a shock that it was Hallow e'en. Does that convey nothing to your mind? To me it brings back memories of cold, fast-shortening days, and myself jumping long-legged over cabbage-stalks in the kitchen-garden chanting—

This is the nicht o' Hallow e'en
When a' the witches will be seen—

in fearful hope of seeing a witch, not mounted on a broom-stick, but on the respectable household cat, changed for that night into a flying fury; finally along with my brothers, being captured, washed and dressed to join with other spirits worse than ourselves

in "dooking" for apples and eating mashed potatoes in momentary
expectation of swallowing a threepenny bit or a thimble. To-night,
far from the other spirits, far from the chill winds and the cabbage-
stalks, I have been watching the sunset on the desert making the
world a glory of rose and gold and amethyst. Now it is dark; the
lights are lit all over the ship; the floor of Heaven is thick inlaid
with patines of bright gold . . .

In such a night did young Lorenzo . . .

Nov. 2, 11.30 a.m.

Our fellow passengers derive much amusement from the way
we sit and scribble, and one man asked me if I were writing a
book! All this time I haven't mentioned the Port Said letters. We
got them before we left the ship, and, determined for once to show
myself a well-balanced, sensible young person, I took mine to the
cabin and locked them firmly in a trunk telling myself how nice it
would be to read them in peace on my return. The spirit was willing, but—I found I must rush down to take just a peep to see if
every one was well, and the game ended with me sitting uncomfortably on the knobby edge of Mrs. Albert Murray's bunk,
breathlessly tearing open envelopes.

They were all delightful and I have read them many times. I
have yours beside me now and to make it like a real talk, I shall
answer each point as it comes.

You say the sun hasn't shone since I left.

Are you by any chance paying me a compliment? Or are you
merely stating a fact? As Pet Marjorie would say I am primmed
up with majestic pride because of the compliments I receive. One
lady, whose baby I held for a little this morning, told me I had
such a sweet, unspoiled disposition! But what really pleased me
and made me feel inches taller was that Captain Gordon told someone who told me that he thought I had great stability of character.
It is odd how one loves to be told one has what one hasn't! I, who
have no more stability of character than a pussy-cat, felt warm
with gratitude. Only—I should like to make my exit now before
he discovers how mistaken he is!

*   *   *

All things considered you are a young man greatly to be envied, also at the present moment to be scolded. How can you possibly allow yourself to think such silly things? You must have a most exaggerated idea of my charms if you think every man on board must be in love with me. Men aren't so impressionable. Did you think that when my well-nigh unearthly beauty burst on them they would fall on their knees and with one voice exclaim—"Be mine!" I assure you no one has ever even thought of doing anything of the kind, and if they had *I wouldn't tell you.* I know you are only chaffing, but I do so hate all that sort of thing and to hear people talk of their "conquests" is revolting. One of the nicest things about G. is that she doesn't care a bit to philander about with men. She and I are much happier talking to each other, a fact which people seem to find hard to believe.

My attention is being diverted from my writing by a lady sitting a few yards away, the Candle we call her because so many silly young moths hover round. She is a buxom person with very golden hair growing darker towards the roots, hard blue eyes and a powdery white face. G. and I are intensely interested to know what is the attraction about her, for no one can deny there is one.

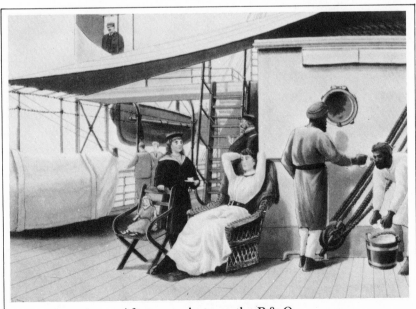

Afternoon siesta on the P & O

She isn't young; the gods have not made her fair, and I doubt of her honesty; yet from the first she has been surrounded by men, most of them, I grant you, unfinished youths bound to offices in Calcutta, but still men. I thought it might be her brilliant conversation, but for the last half-hour I have listened—indeed we have no choice but to listen, the voices are so strident—and it can't be that, because it isn't brilliant or even amusing unless to call men names like Pyjamas, or Fatty, or Tubby, and slap them playfully at intervals is amusing. A few minutes ago Mrs. Crawley came to sit with us looking so fresh in a white linen dress. I don't know why it is, she wears the simplest clothes and yet she manages to make all the other women look dowdy. She has the gift, too, of knowing the right thing to wear on every occasion. At Port Said, for instance, the costumes were varied. The Candle flopped on shore in a trailing white lace dress and an enormous hat; some broiled in serge coats and skirts; Mrs. Crawley in a soft green muslin and rose-wreathed hat was a cool and dainty vision. Well, to return, as Mrs. Crawley shook up her chintz cushions, she looked across at the Candle, a long look that took in the elaborate golden hair, the much-too-smart blouse, the abbreviated skirt showing the high-heeled slippers, the crowd of callow youths, and then, smiling slightly to herself, settled down in her chair. I grew hot all over for the Candle. I don't suppose I need trouble myself. I expect she is used to having women look at her like that, and doesn't mind. Does she really like silly boys so much and other women so little, I wonder! There is generally something rather nasty about a woman who declares she can't get on with other women and whom other women don't like. Men have an absurd notion that we can't admire another woman or admit her good points. It isn't so. We admire a pretty woman just as much as you do. The only difference is you men think that if a woman has a lovely face it follows, as the night the day, that she must have a lovely disposition. We know better, that's all.

The poor Candle! I feel so mean and guilty writing about her under her very eyes, so to speak. She looked at me just now quite kindly. I have a good mind to tear this up, but after all what does it matter? My silly little observations won't make any impression on your masculine mind. Only don't say "spiteful little cat" because I don't mean to be, really.

This is much the longest letter I ever wrote. You will have to read a page at a time and then take a long breath and try again.

Mr. Brand has just come up to ask us why a sculptor dies a horrible death? Do you know?

OLIVIA

S.S. Scotia, *Nov. 6*

No one unendowed with the temper of an angel and the patience of a Job should attempt the voyage to India. Mrs. Albert Murray has neither of these qualifications any more than I have, and for two days she hasn't deigned to address a remark to G. or me, all because of a lost pair of stockings; a loss which we treated with unseemly levity. However, the chill haughtiness of our cabin companion is something of a relief in this terrible heat. For it *is* hot. I am writing in the cabin, and in spite of the fact that there are two electric fans buzzing on either side of me, I am hotter than I can say, and deplorably ill-tempered. Four times this morning, trying to keep out of Mrs. Albert Murray's way, I have fallen over that wretched hat-box, still here despite our hints about the baggage-room, and now in revenge I am sitting on it, though what the owner would say, if she came in suddenly and found to what base uses I had put her treasure, I dare not let myself think. G. has a bad headache, and it is dull for her to be alone, so that is the reason why I am in the cabin at all. To be honest, it is most unpleasant on deck, rainy with a damp, hot wind blowing, and the music-room is crowded and stuffy beyond words, or I might not be unselfish enough to remain with G. I did go up, and a fat person, whose nurse was ill, gave me her baby to hold, a poor white-faced fretful baby, who pulled down all my hair, and I have had the unpleasant task of doing it up again. If you have ever stood in a very hot greenhouse with the door shut, and wrestled with something about your head you will know what I felt.

We passed Aden yesterday and stopped for a few hours to coal. That was the limit. The sun beating down on the deck, the absence of the slightest breeze, coal-dust sifting into everything—ouf! Aden's barren rocks reminded me rather of the Skye Coolin. I wonder if they are climbable. I haven't troubled you much, have I, with accounts of the entertainments on board? but I think I must tell you about a whistling competition we had the other day. You must know that we had each a partner, and the women sat at one end of the deck and the men stood at the other and were told the tune they had to whistle, when they rushed to us and each whistled his tune to his partner, who had to write the name on a piece of paper and hand it back, and the man who got back to the umpire first won—at least his partner did. Do you understand? Well, as you know, I haven't much ear for music, and I hoped I would get an easy tune, but when my partner, a long, thin, earnest man, with a stutter, burst on me and whistled wildly in my face, I had the hopeless feeling that I had never heard the tune before. In his earnestness he came nearer and nearer, his contortions every moment becoming more extraordinary, his whistling more piercing, and I, by this time convulsed by awful, helpless laughter, could only shrink further back in my seat and gasp feebly, "Please don't."

Mrs. Crawley was not much better. In my own misery I was aware of her voice saying politely: "I have no idea what the tune is, but you whistle beautifully—quite like a gramophone."

When my disgusted and exhausted partner ceased trying to emulate a steam-engine and began to look human again, I timidly inquired what he had been whistling. "The tune," he replied very stiffly, "was 'Rule, Britannia!'"

"Dear me," I replied meekly, "I thought at least it was something from *Die Meistersinger*," but he deigned no reply and walked away evidently hating me quite bitterly. I shan't play that game again, and I can't believe the silly man really whistled "Rule, Britannia," for it is a simple tune and one with which I am entirely at home, whereas—but no matter!

G. won by guessing "Annie Laurie." She is splendid at all games, and did I tell you how well she sings? In the cabin, when we are alone, she sings to me snatches of all sorts of songs, grave and gay, but she won't sing in the saloon where every other woman on board with the smallest pretensions to a voice carols nightly. She is a most attractive person this G., with quaint little whimsical ways that make her very lovable. We are together every minute of the day and yet we never tire of one another's company. I rather think I do most of the talking. If it is true that to be slow in words is a woman's only virtue, then, indeed is my state pitiable, for talk

I must, and G. is a delightful person to talk to. She listens to my
tales of Peter and the others, and asks for more and shouts with
laughter at the smallest joke. I pass as a wit with G., and have
a great success. She is going to stay with a married sister for the
cold weather. Quite like me, only I'm going to an unmarried
brother. I think we are both getting slightly impertinent to our
elders. They tease us so at meals in the saloon we have to answer
back in self-defence, and it is very difficult to help trying to be
smart; sometimes, at least with me, it degenerates into rudeness.
I told you about all the people at our table but I forgot one—a
very aged man with a long white beard, rather like the evil magi-
cian in the fairy tales, but most harmless. "Old Sir Thomas Er-
pingham," I call him, for I am sure, a good soft pillow for that
good grey head were better than the churlish turf of India. He is
very kind and calls us Sunshine and Brightness, and pays us the
most involved Early Victorian compliments which we, talking and
laughing all the time, seldom ever hear, and it is left to kind Mrs.
Wilmot to respond.

Nov. 7

Last night we had an excitement. We got into a thick fog and
had to stand still and hoot, while something—a homeward-bound
steamer they say—nearly ran us down. The people sleeping on
deck said it was most awesome, but I slept peacefully through it
until awakened by an American female running down the corridor
and remarking at the top of a singularly piercing voice, "Wal, I
am scared!"

To-day it is beautifully calm and bright; the nasty, hot, damp
wind has gone; and we are sitting in our own little corner of the
deck, Mrs. Crawley, Mrs. Wilmot, G. and I, sometimes reading,
sometimes writing, very often talking. It is luck for us to have
two such charming women to talk to. Mrs. Crawley is supposed
to be my chaperone, I believe I forgot to tell you that. Boggley,
who is a great friend of hers, wrote and asked her to look after
me. How clever of him to fix on one in every way so desirable!
Suppose he had asked the Candle!

We have such splendid talks about books. Mrs. Wilmot has,
I think, read everything that has been written, also she is very
keen on poetry and has my gift—or is it a vice?—of being able

to say great pieces by heart, so between us G. is sometimes just a little bored. You see, G. hasn't been brought up in a bookish atmosphere and that makes such a difference. The other night she was brushing her hair, unusually silent and evidently thinking deeply. At last she looked up at me in my bunk, with the brush in her hand and all her hair swept over one shoulder, and said in the most puzzled way: "What was that nasty thing Mrs. Wilmot was saying all about dead women?" and do you know what she objected to?

> Dear dead women, with such hair, too—
> What's become of all the gold
> Used to hang and brush their bosoms? I
> Feel chilly and grown old.

We are very much worried by people planting themselves beside us and favouring us with their views on life in general. One woman—rather a tiresome person, a spinster with a curiously horse-like face and large teeth—sometimes stays for hours at a time and leaves us limp. Even gentle Mrs. Wilmot approaches, as nearly as it is possible for her to approach, unkindness in her comments on her. She has such playful, girlish manners and an irritating way of giving vent to the most utter platitudes with the air of having just discovered a new truth. She has been with us this morning and mentioned that her father was four times removed from a peerage. I stifled a childish desire to ask who had removed him, while Mrs. Wilmot murmured, "How interesting!" As she minced away Mrs. Crawley said meditatively, "The Rocking Horse Fly," and with a squeal of delight I realized that that was what she had always vaguely reminded me of. You remember the insect, don't you, in *Through the Looking-Glass?* It lived on sawdust. One lesson one has every opportunity of learning on board ship is to suffer fools, if not gladly, at least with patience. The curious people who stray across one's path! One woman came on at Port Said—a globe-trotter, globe-trotting alone. Can you imagine anything more ghastly? She is very tall, dark and mysterious-looking, and last night when G. and I were in the music saloon before dinner, she sat down beside us and began to talk of spiritualism and other weird things. To bring her to homelier subjects I asked if she liked games. "Games," she said, "what sort of games? I can ride anything that has four legs and I can hold my own with a sword." She looked so fierce that if the bugle hadn't sounded at that moment I think I should have crept under a table.

"Quite mad," said G. placidly as we left her.

We are going to have a dance to-night.

OLIVIA

S.S. Scotia, Nov. 11

. . . Now we approach a conclusion. We have passed Colombo, and in three or four days ought to reach Calcutta.

Colombo was rather nice, warm and green and moist; but I failed to detect the spicy breezes blowing soft o'er Ceylon's isle, that the hymn led me to expect. The shops are good and full of interesting things like small ivory elephants, silver ornaments, bangles, kimonos and moonstones. We bought various things and as we staggered with our purchases into the cabin, which now resembles nothing so much as an over-crowded pawnshop, Mrs.

A soirée on board the *Cathay*
in the Red Sea, 1883

Murray remarked (we are on speaking terms again), "I suppose you thought the cabin looked rather empty that you bought so much rubbish to fill it up."

We were dumb under the deserved rebuke. We had bought her a fan as a peace-offering, rather a pretty one too, but she thanked us with no enthusiasm.

In Colombo we got rickshaws and drove out to the Galle Face Hotel, a beautiful place with the surf thundering on the beach outside. If I were rich I would always ride in a rickshaw. It is a delightful way of getting about, and as we were trotted along a fine, broad road, small brown boys ran alongside and pelted us with big waxy, sweet-smelling blossoms. We did enjoy it so. At the Galle Face in a cool and lofty dining-hall we had an excellent and varied breakfast, and ate real proper Eastern curry for the first time. Another new experience! I don't like curry at home, curry as English cooks know it—a greasy make-up of cold joint served with sodden rice, but this was different. First, rice was handed around, every particle firm and separate and white, and then a rich brown mixture with prawns and other interesting ingredients, which was the curry. You mix the curry with the rice when a whole trayful of condiments is offered to eat with it, things like very thin water biscuits, Bombay duck—all sorts of chutney, and when you have mixed everything up together the result is one of the nicest dishes it has been my lot to taste. Note also, you eat it with a fork and spoon, not with a fork alone as mere provincials do!

I begin to feel so excited about seeing Boggley. It is two years since he was home last. Will he have changed much, I wonder. There was a letter from him at Colombo and he hadn't left Darjeeling and had no house to take me to in Calcutta, so it would appear that when I do land my lodging will be the old ground. It sounds as if he were still the same casual old Boggley. Who began that name? John, I think. He had two names for him, "Lo-the-poor-Indian" and "Boggley-Wallah," and in time we all slipped into calling him Boggley. I like to think you two men were such friends at Oxford. Long before I knew you I had heard many tales of your doings, and I think that was one reason why, when we did meet, we liked each other and became friends, because we were both so fond of Boggley. I am filled with qualms as to whether he will be glad to see me. It must be rather a nuisance in lots of ways to have a sister to look after, but he was so keen that I should come that surely he won't think me a bother. Besides, when you think of it, it was really very good of me to leave my home and all my friends and brave the perils of the deep, to visit a brother in exile.

I wish I knew exactly when we shall arrive; this suspense is wearing. One man told me we would be in on Wednesday, another said we would miss the tide and not be in till Saturday. I asked the Captain, but he directed me to the barber who, he said, knew everything, and indeed there are very few things he doesn't know. He is a dignified figure with a shiny curl on his forehead, and a rich Cockney accent, full of information, generally, I must admit, strikingly inaccurate, but bestowed with such an air. "I do believe him though I know he lies."

Oct. 13

We are in the Hooghly and shall be in Kidderpore Dock to-morrow morning early. Actually the voyage is at an end. I may as well finish this letter and send it with the mail which leaves Calcutta to-morrow. We can't pack because Mrs. Albert Murray is occupying all the cabin and most of the passage. We shall creep down when she is quite done and put our belongings together.

Every one is flying about writing luggage labels, and getting their boxes up from the hold and counting things. Curiously enough I am feeling rather depressed; the end of anything is horrid, even a loathed sea-voyage. After all it isn't a bad old ship and people have been nice. To-night I am filled with kindness to every one. Even Mrs. Albert Murray seems to swim in a rosy and golden haze, and I am conscious of quite an affection for her, though I expect, when in a little I go down to the cabin and find her fussing and accusing us of losing her things, I shall dislike her again with some intensity. We have all laughed and played and groaned together, and now we part. No, I *shan't* say "Ships that pass in the night." Several people—mothers whose babies I have held and others—have given me their cards and a cordial invitation to go and stay with them for as long as I like. They mean it now, I know, but in a month's time shall we even remember each other's names?

It will be a real grief to part to-morrow from Mrs. Crawley and Mrs. Wilmot. The dear women! I wish they had been going to stay in Calcutta, but they go straight away up country. Are there, I wonder, many such charming women in India? It seems improbable. I shall miss all the people at our table: we have been such a gay company. Major Wilmot says G. and I have kept them all amused and made the voyage pleasant, but that is only his kind way. It is quite true, though, what Mrs. Crawley says of G. She is like a great rosy apple, refreshing and sweet and wholesome.

What is really depressing me is the thought that wherever I am to-morrow night there will be no G. to say—

"Good-night, my dear, sleep well."

And I shan't be able to drop my head over my bunk and reply—

"Good-night, my dear old G."

It will seem so odd and lonely without her.

The ship has stopped—we are to anchor here till daylight. Good-night, my friend.

OLIVIA

O. DOUGLAS,
Olivia in India

Anna's father died in 1911, and she spent the rest of her life looking after her mother, who died in 1937. She herself died, unmarried, in 1948.

———◆———

CARGOES

Quinquireme of Nineveh from distant Ophir
Rowing home to haven in sunny Palestine,
With a cargo of ivory,
And apes and peacocks,
Sandalwood, cedarwood, and sweet white wine.

Stately Spanish galleon coming from the Isthmus,
Dipping through the Tropics by the palm-green shores,
With a cargo of diamonds,
Emeralds, amethysts,
Topazes, and cinnamon, and gold moidores.

Dirty British coaster with a salt-caked smoke-stack,
Butting through the Channel in the mad March days,
With a cargo of Tyne coal,
Road-rails, pig-lead,
Firewood, iron-ware, and cheap tin trays.

JOHN MASEFIELD

1935: Ethel Mannin

The novelist Ethel Mannin embarks for Leningrad in a Soviet
ship—in the days before such a trip was fashionable.

At the docks she is referred to as "the Bolshy boat." There are
the inevitable jokes about her name—"No use trying to read it.
Nothing for it but to take it to the chemist's and have it made up."
And the no-less inevitable jokes about Keating's. The tourist
season is over, so there are no Bloomsbury Communists in dirty
flannels and high-necked sweaters—self-consciously "Bohemian"
to prove there is no taint of the bourgeoisie in them—to sing the
Internationale as the ship moves out. Which is a relief. I had
dreaded this ship. I had feared that its passengers might consist
of the friends of the more tiresome breed of Communist—such as
abound in Bloomsbury, Greenwich Village, Montparnasse—and
the more earnest kind of tourist who would take one aside and ask
what did one Really Think of Russia, and did one consider it
Really Worked, and was it true that You Only Saw What They
Wanted You to See. . . . I was some years ago invited to conduct a party of twenty-five people to Leningrad and Moscow in
return for three weeks' expenses paid. Though I had not then
been to the U.S.S.R. and very much wanted to do so when both

time and money should be available at the same time, I declined this offer simply because I felt that these questions would be inevitable, and that by the time the twenty-fifth person had asked me I should have gone melancholy-mad.

But on this my first journey to Russia by sea—the previous year I had gone by air—the ship is blessedly empty. There are several English engineers who have been home from Moscow on holiday. There is an American cartoonist going out with his wife to a job. There is an English designer going out to a job in a textile factory some miles outside of Moscow. There is a young Negro going out to study music. There is a party of representatives from various travel agencies going over to see how "Intourist" run things. There are a few Americans who are "taking in" Leningrad and Moscow in the same easy manner that they have just "taken in" London and the Shakespeare country, Paris, Rome, and the rest of it. But the tourist element is negligible; not much seeing-off is being done, and that unostentatiously.

The *Daily Worker*, and a selection of Communist booklets are for sale on the covered hatch of the ship, in charge of a Negro. An excellent supper is being served in the pleasant and airy dining salon. Flags of all nations decorate the tables.

A preliminary tour of the ship discovers the Red Corner in the crew's quarters. We examine it with interest, for we are not to know that before many weeks have passed the sight of one more red-draped picture of Lenin or Stalin is like to give us hysterics. . . . We decide that the Red Corner is Nothing Much. There are the usual framed photographs of dead and gone revolutionaries, and a small bronze statuette of Lenin. In the adjoining room members of the crew play a kind of billiards with flat discs like draughts which they push across the table with cues. There is a wall-newspaper, to the new edition of which I later contribute fine revolutionary sentiments which win the approval of the party-members amongst the officers and crew, and which Donia amusingly illustrates. A very loud-speaking gramophone playing Russian songs makes sleep impossible till midnight. There is a loudspeaking apparatus in each first-class cabin for those who want the music blared even more loudly into their ears.

Inescapable as the loud-speaker is the American accent, which I abominate equally. It pursues one everywhere, penetrates one's cabin, and follows one on deck. It accompanies one's meals, one's attempts at reading in the most secluded corners of the ship, breaks through one's shipboard dozes. It rides above the sound of the sea and of the engines. And how offensive is the American Child. There is one aboard, a typically precocious brat, grown old out of its due time. No wonder America is the home of that monstrosity the child film-star. Donia and I develop a phobia concerning this child. Donia draws it, maliciously, standing in its chair, waving its spoon above its head, yelling its wants and its don't-wants. After a few days we grind our teeth when it comes into the room, and reach the pitch at which we honestly believe that if it were washed overboard we should laugh. It refuses all the food offered it. Its bewildered parents speak no Russian, and the stewards speak no English. The most unkind cut of all is that Donia is called upon to translate the brat's requirements to the stewards. She is very gracious about it. Quite early on I decide that Donia is too nice. Too polite. Later in Moscow when I am storming against Russian bureaucracy I heap scorn upon her for this. She tells me, mildly, that it is as well she has this gift of inveterate courtesy, to counter-balance my own irascibility.

I am dreading Moscow. People ask me how long we are to be there, and I tell them: "Only as long as it takes to get out of it." By which I mean as long as it takes to get permits for Turkestan. We have been warned, and are prepared for, exhausting delays, infuriating frustrations, but I know myself well enough to dread the effects of such thwartings of my will. An "act of God" I can accept philosophically, but man-made frustrations, particularly of the bureaucratic kind, drive me crazy. My passion for personal liberty amounts almost to mania. I tell myself, endlessly, repeating it over like a lesson I must learn within a limited time, that in Moscow I must be patient, that no good purpose will be served by hurling myself angrily against bureaucracy, that those who have the gift of patience go farther and fare better. I dread, too, the exhausting tempo of the life there, the days spent rushing round and achieving nothing, the extraordinary amount of time even the simplest things take, the inability to get to bed any night before the small hours, the meal-times at fantastic hours, one's own degeneration into complete disregard for time, the sleeplessness, the excitement, the living on one's nerves. . . .

I have, as it is, immense arrears of sleep to make up. I spend a good deal of the time sleeping, in the determination to get properly rested in preparation for Moscow, but there seems no end to the unslept sleep in me. Between bouts of sleeping it occurs to me that a ship's cabin might be a good place in which to work if one could escape the sound of voices outside. I do work a little. I re-write the last chapter of *The Pure Flame*, and keep some sort of diary. As always in ships, I find concentration difficult. Perhaps in bad weather, when everyone is confined to cabin, and there are no intruding voices, it is easier; but an American voice, particularly a female one, I tell myself bitterly, would penetrate anywhere.

I lie about in low chairs on sheltered parts of the deck and read at, rather than read, Ella Maillart's *Turkestan Solo*, Anna Louise Strong's *Red Star in Samarkand*, and *From Moscow to Samarkand* by an anonymous Russian author. I dream endlessly of Bokhara and the storks' nests crowning the minarets, of Samarkand the Golden. I tell myself that if we do not get there I shall be too humiliated to return to England. Such humiliation is unthinkable. I hear Donia telling people, when they ask where we are going, that we are going to the Caucasus. Something hardens and tightens in me. A kind of anger. I don't give a dam' for the Caucasus. *We are going to Samarkand.*

"Why don't you tell them we are going to Turkestan?" I ask her roughly.

She answers patiently: "We don't know that we will get there—"

"Nothing can stop us!"

"We may not get permits."

"Then we'll go without!"

She is silent.

"Those other two got there without permits," I insist.

"They were turned out."

"We won't be!" I am burning with defiance.

She inquires with maddening coolness: "How do you propose we should manage, then?"

"I don't know!" I could weep with a curious combination of anger and helplessness. I don't know at all how we shall manage. I only know that the idea of not getting there is unthinkable. And

They—the all-powerful They—shall not turn us out, shall not discover us. I don't know at all how it will be, I know only that it must be, shall be.

By an unspoken mutual consent we speak no more of Samarkand, and the days at sea pass over us amiably enough, filled with the busyness of doing nothing very much. One spends so much time at sea merely gossiping. It is astonishing the amount of time one can spend in this pleasant pastime. The ship's doctor likes to talk of Life and Love—spelt in majuscules, like that. Glancing through a copy of my *Commonsense and the Child*, which I am taking to Moscow in the forlorn hope of getting it published there —for it seems absurd that it should be translated into Danish, Swedish, and Dutch, and not yet into Russian, Russia being the very centre of modern child education and upbringing today—he asks if I believe in God. When I assure him No, he comments that that is good. In Russia, he says, God, King, Imperialism, Marriage, they are all *Kapoot*. Donia takes him away to make a sketch of him, to give him English lessons, and no doubt to continue the discussion on that perennially interesting subject, Love. It is the first of many such discussions. The Russians like to talk of love. Throughout our journey we are continually being asked four leading questions: Do we believe in God, Are we Communists, Is England going to make war on Russia, What are the conditions of the working-classes in England? (Except during that part of the journey when we assumed Belgian nationality, when we were asked what were the conditions of the working-classes in Belgium.) And eventually we are asked if we are married. And so by easy stages we arrive at the inevitable discussion of Love.

But it is pleasant to lie in a deck-chair without some obsequious steward fussing round one as in capitalist ships, tucking one up, kow-towing to one in expectation of a tip, bringing one cups of Bovril as they do in trans-Atlantic liners and pleasure-cruises. And it gives the more revolutionary minded of us a "kick" to see the red flag flying at the ship's bows. When I express this sentiment an English lady and a pugnacious little Scotsman want to know what is wrong with the British flag. I feel that it would be difficult to say what is right with it, but I dislike arguments. Except on paper, where you have the advantage of being able to state your most vehement and controversial ideas and convictions without having anyone tiresomely—and usually irritably—answering back. I content myself with writing for the wall-newspaper that those who are living in a revolutionised society cannot realise what it means to us who are working for a revolution to be going to a country where all that we are working for is a living reality. . . .

After which, with the pettiness of which one is all too easily capable aboard ship, I write in my diary that "The Awful American Child grows daily worse. It is a Compleat Exhibitionist, shows off the whole time, and is all eyes to see what attention it is attracting. The doctor has been called upon to prescribe for it because it won't eat. Why don't they let the little horror starve?"

It is an extraordinarily "matey" ship. The passengers, including the second and third class, have the entire run of the ship. They are not even forbidden that holy of holies on all other ships, the Bridge. We spend a good deal of time leaning about on the bridge, discussing Communism, and, of course, Love; staring through binoculars, having compasses and charts explained to us, and mildly philandering. As an illustration of the liberty, equality, and fraternity of the Soviet ship—one day on deck a random remark that I wished I had a footstool sent Donia in search of one for me. She secured it, eventually, from the second-mate. He blew a whistle to call a sailor—a whistle is always blown when anything is wanted, it seems—and when he had blown it three times and nothing had happened, he left the watch in charge of a subordinate and went himself in search of the stool. Similarly, when the clasp of Donia's handbag breaks, nothing will do but that the chief engineer himself must be called in to mend it.

When we decide to send a radio message on one occasion, we cannot get hold of the radio-officer because he is attending a political meeting in the crew's quarters, and the radio-office is shut up. The crew—including stewards and stewardesses—all attend political study meetings. We glimpse them through portholes, sitting on benches, in rows, very solemn, like good schoolchildren. There is no uniform for the sailors. We chat to them and learn that a number of them study in the evenings, from a syllabus, to become captains. They are intelligent lads, and want to know about working-class conditions in England, how strong is the Communist Party, who is its leader, whether we are party members, and whether England is going to war with Russia. . . .

We try to organise a dance for passengers and crew, but run into bad weather before evening, and the crew is vastly amused at our suggestion that since dancing on deck is impossible they should come up into the salon. They will have nothing to do with so bourgeois an idea, it seems, so we have the dance without the crew, but the selection of dance-records is poor and limited, and we are thinking of retiring to bed when the second-mate brings a message inviting Donia Gregorevna, and Ethel Robertevna— for it is the pleasant Russian custom to compromise between formality and familiarity by the use of the patronymic—to a party in the captain's cabin.

Here we find the table set with a coffee-percolator, a large bowl of fruit, and a bowl of sweet biscuits. The ship's doctor is there, and a Russian passenger. We drink coffee and numerous vodkas. The conversation which begins flippantly turns to Russian writers in general and Chekhov in particular. Chekhov, it seems, is at a discount. He is charged with depicting humanity's sufferings without offering a solution. That is to say, he is a defeatist, which is counter-revolutionary. Gorki, now. . . . I want to make the point that surely art need not necessarily drag a burden of propaganda with it all the time, but it is difficult to make any point when one does not speak the language and must rely on translation of statement and counter-statement all the time. . . . It doesn't matter. There is curiously no feeling of being out of things because one does not speak the language—one does, of course, many, many times bitterly regret that one does not; but on an occasion like this the flow of reason and communion of soul is untrammelled by any barrier of language, and after a time one gets the drift of a language one does not know. Later I developed a technique which reminds me of a story I read a long time ago— it may have been by Paul Morand—about a man on a train who listened to a long and dramatic story from the guard in a language of which he understood not one word, though of the story itself he missed no nuance, and was able to express his sympathy and interest to the entire satisfaction of the narrator, who left him on the completion of the story convinced that the listener had understood every word . . . a story I could not understand at the time, but which I now comprehend perfectly.

We turn in very late after the party. The engines break down again. They have been breaking down all day. We shall arrive a day late in Leningrad. It is the first of a series of exasperations.

In the morning the sea is oilily flat. Donia and the second-mate organise a conducted tour of the ship, Donia translating for the second-mate, whose English is inadequate. Some of the men from the second and third class ask intelligent questions. The Scotsman is facetious and tiresome. He and the Negro sit opposite each other at meal-times in a stony silence, each despising the other. Only it can obviously never occur to the Scotsman that anyone can despise him; certainly not a "nigger."

We have no news of Geneva, which, after talking and thinking about Sanctions for weeks before sailing is, in spite of our continual wondering and anxiety, a relief.

We enter the Kiel Canal under a grey sky after a rough second night at sea, and a choppy sea on waking, with cabin-trouble in the form of things sliding about in what is perhaps best described as a sickening fashion. . . . As we enter the first lock men come alongside selling eau-de-Cologne, chocolates, cigarettes. All the morning there have been ships passing, flying the Nazi flag. In the first lock there is a French ship, and an English ship, the *Baron Pentland*. All day there has been a feverish writing of post-cards for posting at Kiel.

The country on the Danish side of the canal is brown and green, with red-roofed, neat-looking little houses, and farms set amidst trees, and a great melancholy holding everything.

We stand about on the deck whilst the dusk deepens and the lights come out along the tow-path. There is a great bridge like the Fourth Bridge, and a landing-stage labelled Ostermoor. It is all grey and monotonous and sad. We were promised news of Geneva today, but none comes through. The ship's company seems infected with a general melancholy. I could weep with a nameless sadness myself. Donia is vaguely homesick. The Negro confesses, with a far-away look in his mournful eyes, that he is lonely in the ship. A Russian is moved to confide to us that he is dissatisfied with his life, but has not the will to end it. He needs love, he declares. These Russians and their souls, what egotists they are! We talk of love till the canal is swallowed up in inky blackness. Even then we linger watching the lights and the emergence of the stars.

We dance that night, and I discover that one of the English engineers is a friend of someone I knew in Paris. We are as delighted over the smallness of the world as though we had realised it for the first time.

On the morning of the fourth day at sea a thin blue line that is Gotland is visible. The sea is flat and grey, the colour of the sky. There is a porpoise leaping, and a few small brown birds are flying about the deck, exciting the Scotsman to the point of going in search of crumbs for them.

We should have had news of Geneva by now, but nothing, we are told, has come through on the wireless owing to the bad weather. (The day before we could get nothing because the radio is shut down by international law in the Kiel Canal.) For all we know, Europe may have gone up in a blaze of war.

The fifth day breaks cold and grey and blustering, with a choppy sea. In the afternoon the sky breaks, and the sea goes down somewhat and the ship rolls less. But she is, all things considered, a steady ship. One cannot justly complain of her. She carries a cargo of rubber, tea, coffee, tin. Some of the rubber she was due to carry was destroyed in the Wapping fire.

We pass Tallinn, the capital of Estonia. Viewed from the bridge through binoculars, it emerges as a grey huddle of towers and chimneys and wooded cliffs. There are spirals of smoke, and a lighthouse on a point. I tell myself that one of these days I must have a look at the cobbled streets of Tallinn. Before the war, Reval, as it was then called, was one of the chief sources of food supply for St. Petersburg, and one of Russia's most important outlets to the sea. Is it a case of fox and the sour grapes which today causes Russia to refer to Estonia contemptuously as "the potato republic"? For Estonia resisted Russian domination in 1919 and regained her independence, together with fifteen million gold roubles in 1920, in return for which Russia got free transit to Estonian ports. For all that, the Communist Party was not made illegal until 1923 and even so there was a minor Communist revolution the following year, directed by Reval transport workers supported by Red guards against the government, and backed, of course, by "Moscow gold." This was suppressed, all Communist organisations officially closed, 30,000 men were enrolled as civil guards, and the revolutionary movement was down for the count, as the workers' movement was in Austria under Dollfuss. Today, Estonia is politically respectable, and, like Russia itself, a member of the League of Nations, and Tallinn, like Moscow, is developing as a tourist centre.

A number of cargo boats laden with timber pass, outward bound from Leningrad, and dipping their red flags to us in salute.

The following day, in the damp, penetrating, positively English cold of a drizzling grey morning, very early, we put into Leningrad, twenty-four hours late.

ETHEL MANNIN,
South to Samarkand

---◆---

1941: H. V. Morton

The "Atlantic Charter" meeting between President Roosevelt and Winston Churchill in 1941 was regarded at the time as highly significant—though few people remember it today. The travel writer H. V. Morton was one of a small number of journalists invited to accompany the Prime Minister and his staff in the battleship *Prince of Wales*.

We met after dinner for the nightly film in a mood of great cheerfulness. Firstly, we were all excited by the thought of what the morrow held for us; secondly, the film was *Lady Hamilton*, which we had been told was so good that Mr. Churchill had already seen it four times.

The lights went out and the story of Nelson and Emma Hamilton was unfolded in a manner that might not perhaps have satisfied an historian, but was satisfying to the emotions. Imagine the scene. We were in the ward-room of a battleship at sea and the audience was composed of officers who had recently taken the ship into action. As in Nelson's day, England was again at war, fighting for her life. Sitting in the front row in the light of the screen was a man no longer young in years whose worst enemy has never been able to say that he has ever faltered in his love for England, a man who, after a life of violent political hostility, has come at last, without rancour for prophesies unheeded or advice despised, to lead England to victory. The story he watched was one that touched his heart: the story of a man who gave everything he had to give so that England might live in freedom and in peace.

Winston Churchill was completely absorbed in the story, and for the first time spoke no longer to those near him, but seemed to retreat into himself, as if he were sitting alone in the dark, his face, his body even, expressing an attention so complete that it seemed one might look and find him no longer there, but taken up, merged and absorbed by the screen. Children wish themselves into picture-books and go riding with Red Cross knights, fighting dragons and blowing horns at castle gates, with that same passionate intensity of feeling and imagination. But it is rare to encounter it in disenchanted men. Then, as the last scene came, and

Winston Churchill on board the *Prince of Wales*

Nelson lay dying in the cock-pit of the *Victory*, and they bent above him and told him that the day was his, the man who was watching so intently took a handkerchief from his pocket and wiped his eyes without shame.

It is only within the last two hundred years that Englishmen have become ashamed of tears. Our forefathers were not ashamed to weep openly, and the references to tears in the literature of England prove to us that, to the men of other days, a man incapable of tears was believed to be a man hard, inhuman and inaccessible to mercy. Looking at Winston Churchill at that revealing moment, I thought that in some extraordinary way he belongs definitely to an older England, to the England of the Tudors, a violent swashbuckling England perhaps, but a warm and emotional England too, an England as yet untouched by the hardness of an age of steel.

H. V. MORTON,
Atlantic Meeting

———◆———

1943: Noel Coward

It feels strange to be starting off again and leaving England behind. I hope I shall get through these various journeyings safely because I do so much want to see the end of the war. The familiar Naval magic has already taken charge of me, I wander about, clamber up on to the Bridge whenever I feel like it, stamp up and down the Quarter Deck, have drinks in the Wardroom and make jokes and feel most serenely at home. This is unquestionably a happy ship, I felt it immediately when I came on board with the Captain this afternoon. He is a nice man, and has the usual perfect manners of the Navy. He has turned his cabin over to me as he will of course be using his sea cabin during the voyage. I am looked after by his Steward who is also typical, having been in the Service most of his life except for a few years before the war when he retired. Now he has been yanked back again and seems, on the whole, to be more pleased than not. He has what we would describe in the theatre as a "dead pan" but there is a glint of humour in his eye.

Cricket
at sea

Halfway across:
deck of a liner,
1926

I am an honorary member of the Wardroom and am to take my meals there which will be gayer than sitting in lonely state in the Captain's cabin. The ship's officers seem to be a good lot, mostly quite young and a lot of R.N.V.R.s among them. Just before dinner the Commander gave me a few casual instructions: (*a*) To wear my "Mae West" all the time (I pointed out that he wasn't wearing his and he laughed gaily), (*b*) That in the event of any submarine alarums and excursions the best place to make for was the Bridge where there is more to be seen, and (*c*) That if there should be a sudden loud bang and a violent list either to port or starboard I must pop out on to the Quarter Deck immediately and make for the nearest Carley Float of which I am also an honorary member, there, he added, I had better wait until the order came to abandon ship.

After dinner I went on to the Quarter Deck for a little and watched the sea swishing by, it was quite calm and there was still twilight but the land had disappeared. In all my travels there have always been certain moments which stick in my memory and this, I am sure, will be one of them. I have sailed away so many times from so many different lands nearly always with a slight feeling of regret mixed with exhilaration. This time there was a subtle difference. I had been in England for over two years, a long while for me ever to stay in one place, and except for a brief trip to Iceland with Joe Vian* in August 1941, and a few days in Destroyers here and there I have been with the Navy very little since the war. I felt aware, strongly aware, of the change in atmosphere, the switch over from peace-time, show-the-flag, spit-and-splendour efficiency, to this much grimmer, alert feeling of preparedness permeating the whole ship. The engines were throbbing, we were doing about twenty-two knots, and the wake churned away into the gathering darkness and I had a sudden impulse to shout very loudly with sheer pride and pleasure and excitement.

NOEL COWARD,
Middle East Diary

————◆————

* Later Admiral of the Fleet Sir Philip Vian.

ON BOARD A JERSEY STEAMER

A Midsummer Sunrise

Long had I watch'd, and, summon'd by the ray
From those small window-lights, that dipt and bow'd
Down to the glimpsing waters, made my way
On deck, while the sun rose without a cloud;
The brazen plates upon the steerage-wheel
Flash'd forth; the steersman's face came full in view;
Found at his post, he met the bright appeal
Of morning-tide, and answer'd "I am true!"
Then back again into my berth I crept,
And lay awhile, at gaze, with upward eye,
Where gleams and shadows from the ocean swept,
And flicker'd wildly o'er the dreaming fly,
That clung to the low ceiling. Then I slept
And woke, and sought once more the sea and sky.

CHARLES TENNYSON TURNER

1946: James Cameron

The distinguished British journalist has embarked in the
U.S.S. *Appalachian* to witness the fourth explosion of an
atomic bomb.

So we came to Bikini: a typical Pacific coral atoll, several tiny
islands surrounding a lagoon twenty miles long by ten miles wide.
The main island, drawing close on the starboard bow, was so precisely the conventional picture of a South Sea Island that it might
have been the jacket of a very old novel. Inside the lagoon, as far
as one could see, were the seventy-three largest vessels disposed in
an intricate pattern to achieve every degree of damage: the American battleships *Arkansas*, *Pennsylvania*, *New York*, and the Japanese *Nagato*. A barracks-barge like an iron Noah's Ark lay alongside. The carriers *Independence* and *Saratoga*, aircraft marshalled

tightly on the flight decks. The cruisers *Pensacola*, *Salt Lake City*, the Japanese *Sakawa*, and the German *Prinz Eugen*, and around and amongst them ranks of destroyers, submarines, auxiliaries, transports, landing craft, barges, and a floating dry-dock—an enormous naval condemned cell.

In the centre, standing out among the warship grey like a bloodspot on a monk's robe, was the battleship *Nevada*, painted from masthead to waterline a hard, hot red. She was dressed in this brutal colour to make her a clear and vivid mark on the lagoon; she was the bull's eye. Aboard the *Nevada* it was like some great forlorn house just before moving day. Here, however, as the tenants moved out the luggage moved in. All over the red decks lay the secondary sacrifices—a 30-ton tank, a heavy field-gun, rows of the newest and smartest automatic weapons, delicate electrical and photographic gear, an aircraft or two. Down on the boat-deck, under a tarpaulin awning stretched from an aircraft wing, waited the little company of flesh and blood, standing reflectively in pens for their most abrupt and instructive dissolution. There were a few goats, with pale and cynical eyes, one or two brown spotted pigs.

A scientist beside me said: "I feel a little like apologizing to those pigs. They belong to a reasonable and uncomplicated people, not without a certain grace. At least," he said, "they aren't crazy."

On that last night life went on; skeleton crews continued to work, sleep, brew coffee on the messdecks. On Bikini Island, among the reaching palms and the stark steel instrumentation towers, they had run up clubs and offices and canteens and softball diamonds in the clearings where, not too long ago, a hundred and eighty-odd Bikini Micronesians dawdled away a placid and uncomplicated life, until they awoke one day and found themselves transplanted, not without protest, to the island of Rongerik. Now already Bikini had that improvised, tawdry, squalid look of anywhere taken over by the Services.

We went ashore and had our first legal drink for many days. The bar, palm thatched, bulging with bottles, stood on the highest point of Bikini—ten feet above sea level. It was called—and by then one was past caring—"The Up and Atom." It did not prevent several of us getting madly drunk.

As the cannonball sun set on the last pre-atomic evening of the Marshall Islands, Joint Task Force One began to slide out of the lagoon to action-stations beyond the reef, leaving the target fleet empty and alone. One by one the anchored ships began to flutter the red-and-yellow "Y for Yoke" flag, the signal that the ship was cleared. Any forgotten man, abandoned by mischance in that terrible lagoon, was to reach the nearest ship, haul down the Yoke flag and "hoist all available bunting." No one did.

As the night came streaming over the ocean, the *Appalachian* slipped into the procession moving in long line ahead through the reef passage to the open Pacific. It was all carnival with lights springing erratically up and down the line, the hospital ships glowing like showboats, a regatta leaving a graveyard, while the flickering aldis blinker signals kept up the interminable mysterious gossip of ships at sea.

That night we had the final briefing. Dr. Compton told us that if the bomb did not go off at the proper height, and waited until it hit the surface of the water before exploding, we might expect a temporary tidal wave about one hundred feet high, not to speak of diverse other phenomena intensely distracting to the scientific mind. It still continued to cause far less conjecture than the famous radioactive cloud, which had come to hover rather larger than a man's hand around the back of everyone's mind. It was authoritatively stated that the visible cloud would rise to 60,000 feet, but the invisible trail drifting down to the surface was the thing to watch out for—an awkward proposition for those who did not carry geiger counters permanently in their pockets. What danger there might be, they said, would exist from falling radioactive particles which, as was so often pointed out by the Fat Boys of Bikini, you would not know about until you came to pieces in your own hand.

At seven in the morning the first aircraft appeared, a flying-boat wheeling in wide circuits, droning round at three thousand, until abruptly it tired of it and streaked back to the south-east.

The loudspeaker system began a raucous confused chatter, indiscriminate radiophone conversations between ships and planes, filling the air with a backstage buzz of orders and counter-orders. Somewhere about in the roof of the sky already hung the bomb, suspended in the rack of the B-29 Dave's Dream, which had taken off according to plan at Ray Hour. Ray Hour was the moment of the bomber's take off. Even the moments of the day had new and special names. How Hour was the planned moment of the drop. Mike Hour was to be the actual moment of the drop, according to how many dry runs the bombardier needed to get the crimson spot of the *Nevada* trued up in his bombsight.

As the day began to grow one felt the sky filling with aircraft of all kinds, seen and unseen, manned and unmanned, bombers and flying-boats and spotters, pilotless drones from the carrier *Shangri La* and—because by now this operation had achieved in America an importance momentarily even greater than the World Series—a bomberful of Public Relations Officers and broadcasters from radio networks. Then high above, just fleetingly visible as a twinkling speck when the sun caught it, the B-29 began its experimental cast over the target, eighteen miles away square on the starboard beam. Far too lofty and distant to be heard, the bomber flirted for a second like a mote in the sunlight and was lost.

Over the radio, suddenly came the announcement: broadcast transmission began.

"Listen, world—this is Crossroads."

It was dramatic, you could not deny it was intensely dramatic, a *coup de théâtre*. "Listen, world . . ."

Then soon after eight we caught the voice of the bomb-aimer in our loudspeakers. We heard the chant, tinny and remote as an old gramophone in another world: "Skylight here. First simulated bomb release; stand by. Mark: first simulated bomb release. First practice run; stand by."

At fifty-one minutes past eight: "This is a live run. Mark: coming up on thirty-five miles off target, thirty-five miles. Mark: adjust goggles. Stand by."

At eight fifty-eight he said: "Eighteen miles."

In two minutes, for good or ill, the thing would be falling through the empty air, its controlling drogue tight like a drumhead; two bullets face to face, twin charges of plutonium to rush headlong to the uproarious embrace, the critical mass, the meeting of ultimate release.

The loudspeaker said: "Bomb gone. Bomb gone. Bomb gone."

I had on my goggle-mask, so black and deep it was like staring into velvet; behind that opacity all things vanished, sea, and ships and sunlight. At the bomb-aimer's words I began to count. Then I found I was counting too fast; I made an effort to slow down. I felt the sweat dripping down my back and I was glad I had no clothes on. I felt that the time between the beginning and end of the bomb's fall was far too much. I had no consciousness of calculation. I felt that in the nature of things expectancy does not endure so long without anticlimax. When my counting had reached fifty-five the bomb went off.

It is difficult to say what one had foreseen. However keenly you wait for the stage revolver-shot it is always louder than you expect; however long you wait for an atom bomb it is presumably a little less than you feared.

In that first fine edge of a second it might have been a sudden star, low down on the horizon. Then it grew and swelled and became bright, and brighter; it pierced the goggles and struck the eye as a crucible does, and in that moment it was beyond every doubt there ever was an atom bomb, and nothing else.

It was a spheroid, then an uprising wavering thing like a half-filled balloon, then a climbing unsteady dome like a mosque in a dream. It looked as though it were throbbing. I tore off my goggles and the globe had become a column, still rising, a gentle peach-colour against the sky, and from eighteen miles I could see a curtain of water settling like rain back into the lagoon. Somehow I found it not impossible to believe that the thing had produced a hundred million centigrade degrees of heat, ten times that of the surface of the sun, that this was the answer of the little men in pince-nez to ten thousand tons of TNT; yet it was beautiful, in its monstrous way; a writhing lovely mass. Then, just as I remembered the sound of the explosion, it finished its journey and arrived.

It was not a bang, it was a rumble, not overloud, but it thudded into all the corners of the morning like a great door slammed in the deepest hollows of the sea. Beside me a heavy wire stay unexpectedly quivered like a cello-string for a moment, then stopped.

Now, standing up unsteadily from the sea, was the famous Mushroom. In seven minutes fifteen seconds our ship's trigonometry gave it twenty-three thousand feet in height and eleven thousand six hundred feet in diameter. It climbed like a fungus; it looked like a towering mound of firm cream shot with veins and rivers of wandering red; it mounted tirelessly through the clouds as though it were made of dense, solider stuff, as no doubt it was. The only similes that came to mind were banal: a sundae, red ink in a pot of distemper. From behind me I heard a frenetic ticking of typewriters; very soon I found I was fumbling with my own. The reportage had begun. Many of us will never live it down.

Slowly the creamy pillar began to lean awkwardly over. Another spasm somewhere in its base forced a second mushroom bellying upwards until it too tilted and thinned and lost its sculptured excellence. Twenty-five minutes later it too had practically disappeared, and we had all of us stumbled one more step on the path to the twilight.

JAMES CAMERON,
A Point of Departure

1947: Vernon Bartlett

A revolting woman simpered up to me and said: "I hear you are writing a book. Won't you please bring me into it?" To get rid of her I promised I would. This paragraph shows that I keep promises.

VERNON BARTLETT, on board the
S.S. *Fionia* en route to Singapore,
Go East, Old Man

Games at sea

1. 1957: Harold Nicolson

For his seventieth birthday, Harold Nicolson's friends presented him with a handsome cheque which he used to take his wife, Vita Sackville-West, on a sea voyage to Java and back. The writer who (as readers of *A Book of Railway Journeys* will remember) so wittily described the journey to Lausanne of Lord Curzon and his drunken valet Arketall, has in his old age become a little pompous and patronizing. But his curiosity about people and things (which, he said, would always keep a man young) and his general observations are as sharp as ever.

Sunday, March 10th

Already they are playing off the final heats of the deck-tennis, quoits and ping-pong competitions. The Stedalls, who engage with prowess in these pastimes, but who have failed to win in the semi-finals, are evidently under the impression that there has been some dirty business somewhere. Being interested in sports that are played unsportingly, I press them to tell me exactly who cheated whom. They shake their heads sadly, being too gentleman-like to say more. I suggest to them that it is the game that matters and not who wins it. Again they shake their heads with deliberate discretion implanted on their features. "We should not wish," they seem to imply, "to divulge what we have seen or know." This confirms me in my opinion that competitive games, especially when they occur between teams of different nationality, do not create concord or happiness, but leave behind them the suspicions of distrust and the poisons of hatred. "Anyhow," remarks Stedall, in his easy Whites Club voice, "let's say no more about it." So off he goes with his binoculars to gaze at gulls. Mrs. Stedall remains in the saloon stitching away at the appliqué work which I first noticed, before I ever got to know these agreeable people, as we were steaming, almost two months ago, past Finisterre.

———◆———

2. 1962: James Kirkup

The poet James Kirkup is on his way to take up a teaching job in Malaya.

Awful competitive deck-games have been going on ever since we passed Gibraltar. People play them even at the hottest time of the day. I absolutely refuse to take part in any, or to try my luck in the tote on the ship's daily run. Someone in the purser's office, breathing heavily, laboriously enunciates every morning over the public-address system, in a voice thick with adenoidal cockney: "The towt on the ship's dyly run is neow open at the swim-bin pull. The middle number fer t'dy's run is four 'unred an' twenty height. Four 'unred an' twenty height."

People seemed to enjoy the games less and less as the voyage proceeded. There is now often a good deal of crossness and bickering about who should play with whom. The jolly nurse at my table takes part in all the games and beats everyone at deck-tennis; I feel proud of her when she tells me the captain played against her and complimented her on her game. She is a great sport, brings me all the ship's gossip and talks with enthusiasm about her Jaguar in the hold. She invites me to visit her in Hong Kong for a spin round the island: an invitation I was never to take advantage of on my trips to Hong Kong.

There are dances in the evenings, and I who thought my dancing days were over give the nurse an occasional whirl to the very stolid ship's band. One evening there was a fancy-dress party: we all had to go as characters from *Spartacus*, or at least to go looking vaguely Roman. I devised a sort of pleated kirtle and swirling cape from a single bedsheet and constructed a "gold" laurel wreath and bangles from the outer covers of Benson and Hedges cigarette cartons. The smart thing, when dressing as an ancient Roman, is to wear one golden arm-band *above* the elbow: all the men seemed to know this. I made a large brooch and stuck a sucked raspberry-drop in the centre to make a very convincing and barbaric ruby. I covered a pair of rubber Japanese *geta* with golden paper and there I was, as depraved a Roman emperor as one could wish. Always when I put on fancy dress, whatever the period, I wear it to the manner born, which is to me a sure proof of reincarnation.

After the ball was over, I leaned for a long time on the rail, smoking, gradually undoing my bits of cardboard regalia and casting them upon the silvery wreaths of the ship's moonlit wake.

I also took part in a quiz, the other members of my team tight-lipped with disapproval when I got anything wrong, though they never got anything right themselves. We won a second quiz, however, and received scribbling pads and metal propelling pencils as prizes. The scribbling pads had bits of metal inside their plastic covers, and the metal was magnetised so that when you put the propelling pencil on the cover it did not roll off. It was the first time I had seen such a useful and ingenious gift.

JAMES KIRKUP,
Tropic Temper

1965: Ludovic Kennedy

In the course of a visit to the United States Sixth Fleet in the
Mediterranean, as part of research for a book on Americans
abroad, the editor of this anthology was transferred from the
aircraft-carrier *Shangri-La* to the destroyer *Dewey*.

In the morning the *Dewey* came close alongside the *Shangri-La*
and steamed on a parallel course. I was put into a big chair, like
a throne, which was fixed to one of the ship's derricks, and slung
out into space. The sea looked a long way below. I felt rather foolish sitting there in my old raincoat, holding a rope with one hand
and my Panama hat in the other. They lowered me onto the
Dewey's deck, and then the chair went back and my luggage
came over the same way.

A young officer who said his name was Lieutenant Smith took
me to the bridge. It was an enclosed bridge with plenty of glass
windows and central heating, not like the open-air boxes that I
served in during the war. Here I met Captain Tazewell, commodore of the destroyer division, and the ship's captain, Commander Bradley. Captain Tazewell was a neat, small man with
monkey-like features and the build of Eddie Cantor. Commander
Bradley had a lean and handsome look. He introduced me to his
executive officer, Lieutenant-Commander Robinson, and to Lieutenant-Commander Vishenski, the supply officer, who looked like
the Michelin man, round as a rubber ball: he had been in the ship
three years and was going to leave at Rhodes.

We were due to enter the Dardanelles at two-o'clock, so at
11.30 we had an early lunch in the wardroom. The curtains had
been drawn over the portholes, shutting out the light, like in an
American restaurant. I have never understood this thing Americans have against natural light while eating: somebody ought to
make a study of it. About twenty officers sat down, with the captain at the head and on his right. There was a telephone at his
feet, and now and then its bell sounded, and he picked it up and
talked to the officer on the bridge. We had a very good lunch,
steaks which practically covered the plate, a green salad, and
peaches and cream. Captain Tazewell had his in his cabin. The
captain said he spent a lot of time in there learning Italian.

After lunch I went up to the bridge and saw the squadron had formed single line ahead, with the *Shangri-La* leading, *Little Rock* next, ourselves in the middle and two destroyers astern. The captain showed me a signal he had just received from the admiral which said, "Captain, you have one beautiful ship." The entrance to the Dardanelles was about five miles ahead. It was a grey, misty afternoon, but through the drizzle and haze you could see the land coming up on either side. It was green near the water's edge, but higher up it was blotted out by low cloud, like on the west coast of Scotland.

Captain Tazewell sat in a little chair on the left of the bridge and the captain and officer on duty stood in the middle. Now and then the officer on duty said things like "Two-thirds speed, one four two rpm, right ten rudder, steer zero three nine," which the helmsman repeated. On the other side of the bridge Lieutenant-Commander Vishenski had taken up position beside a microphone which fed into the ship's public address system. The *Encyclopaedia Americana* was in front of him, and as we approached the narrows, he began reading the entry marked "Dardanelles." It wasn't terrific prose in the first place, but Vishenski's monotonous, bored delivery killed it dead.

The Dardanelles! The name had been stamped on my mind ever since I could remember. The bloody campaign which the allies had fought there against the Turks might, if it had turned out differently, have changed the course not only of the First World War, but of subsequent European history. It was one of the crucial battlefields of the twentieth century. And the names associated with it were ones to remember: Winston Churchill above all, Asquith, Fisher, Kitchener, Hamilton, de Robeck, Roger Keyes, Dunbar Nasmith, Rupert Brooke, Compton Mackenzie. And the place that was at the centre of it all, that symbolized the whole bloody futile conflict, was Gallipoli. Where along this drab green coastline was it? Where were the beaches where our men had swarmed ashore in such hope, and down which in anger and despair they had retreated, less than a year later?

Aloud, and to no one in particular, I said, "Where's Gallipoli, I wonder?"

No one responded. At length, out of politeness, Captain Tazewell said, "What was that place?" I said it again, I even spelt it, but it was clear they were all hearing it for the first time (it is possible that Vishenski might have mentioned it but everyone had stopped listening to him long ago). I thought, this is astonishing, surely everyone has heard of Gallipoli: then I thought, well is it? have they? What is equivalent to Gallipoli in American history? Say the *Maine* at Havana and the subsequent Spanish-American war. How many British naval officers know about that?

It was the navigating officer who finally found it on the chart. But it was spelt Gelibolu, and when it came into sight a little later, it turned out to be a small dull town of white and yellow houses with red-tiled roofs. I looked at it long and hard, searching for some point of recognition, trying to make a connection between it and the imaginings of my youth. But there was no connection. Gelibolu, Gelibolu, I thought: what have you to do with my Gallipoli? Nothing at all. The false had become real and the real false: it was a surprise and a disappointment.

We went on up the straits, following in the wake of the *Little Rock* and *Shangri-La*, obeying orders from the admiral as to course and speed. Along the green coastline white minarets began to show up, pencil thin. Two Russian merchant-ships passed us going south, and dipped their flags: I knew that would please some of the boys. Then we overtook a Greek steamer called *Hermes*, carrying German tourists. Vishenski, who had finished his running commentary, looked in the *Encyclopaedia* and said: "Hermes is the Greek name for Mercury, that's the messenger of the gods."

LUDOVIC KENNEDY,
Very Lovely People

———◆———

1971: Noel Mostert

There could hardly be a greater contrast between the voyage taken by Eugenio de Salazar in 1573 in the *Nuestra Señora de los Remedios*, a small ship that yet appeared to be crowded, and that of Noel Mostert in 1971 in the P. and O. supertanker *Ardshiel*, a quarter of a mile long and of 215,000 tons, but which often seemed to be empty.

There were moments aboard *Ardshiel* when I felt that I was on one of those very old-fashioned mailboats moving east of Suez a good many decades ago, and never was this more so than at night

when, punctually at seven thirty, Basil Thomson led a small procession of his senior officers down from the evening's sundowner's
party, or "pour-out" as they preferred to call it, to the dining
saloon, all dressed for dinner in "Red Sea rig." An informal dinner
dress for warm climates which dispenses with tie and jacket while
retaining the decorum of proper change for the evening, the en-
semble consists of black dress trousers, silk cummerbund, and
white short-sleeved shirt with gold-braided insignia of rank worn
on the shoulder tabs. We moved into a dining-room where the
Goanese stewards awaited us in stiff white jackets, grouped around
their tables of fresh linen, silverware, and individual printed menus
in silver holders.

Dinner chimes were broadcast throughout the ship at seven,
but these were for the junior officers, who were expected to have
finished by the time the captain's party arrived. Cadet Davis, a
slow eater apparently, occasionally was still munching when we
came in. "Since you're still there, you'd better bring your plate
over here," Thomson would say sharply, with the tone of a man
whose sense of order had been disturbed, and later, when Davis
finally had finished, "You can excuse yourself now!"

The dinner courses came and went silently, arriving upon
salvers and served upon hot chinaware. Not much was ever said,
except by Captain Thomson, who, as masters are wont to do,
exercised the right of monologue.

The food was exceptional, whether breakfast or dinner. A
normal breakfast menu might be stewed apples, cornflakes, oat-
meal, smoked cod in milk, sausage mince cakes, fried potatoes,
cheese or plain omelettes, eggs to order, rolls and toast, tea or
coffee. Lunch always featured a curry: birianis, keftas, Madras,
dry mince and Deil sauce, vindaloos, Sally Mutton; and it was
always served with chutney, popadoms, diced tomato, onion, coco-
nut, and currants. A typical dinner could be mock turtle soup,
grilled sole Tartare, roast veal and stuffing, baked and boiled potatoes, cauliflower, peach Melba, and that essentially English
course, the savoury, such as bloater paste on toast.

After dinner the party moved to the coffee-table in the wardroom. "Who is going to be mum?" someone invariably asked, and
whoever was nearest to the coffee began pouring, while others
handed around the cups, the milk and the sugar. Thomson usually
dominated the conversation, and recounted to the juniors tales of

his past experience, to which they patiently listened. These were stories they'd heard often enough, and would hear many times again before they left the ship. It was not however a lengthy ordeal. After half an hour or so, the master would suddenly announce, "Well, I suppose I'll go up and do my book of words," and vanished. As a rule, he was followed by the chief engineer.

The departure of the two most senior officers brought a distinct lightening of atmosphere to the room; but, however much it lightened, the mood of the wardroom always remained somewhat formal and well-mannered. There was seldom any horseplay or ribaldry. One was again aware of the social lassitude of long confinement: that quality of desultory and inactive converse that is not listlessness but rather that emptiness of real mutual interest that settles upon men who have heard each other out too often. And one was aware not so much of the remoteness of the world at large but of most of the ship itself; it was the feeling of being inside a walled-in community upon one end of an otherwise uninhabited island whose opposite shore few ever bothered to visit and some scarcely knew, and which one actually had to wonder about from time to time.

The wardroom in *Ardshiel* was used a great deal more than it was in other tankers, so they all said; on other ships one apparently could seldom expect more than two or three people to be gathered in it at night; yet it struck me that activity in *Ardshiel*'s wardroom died soon enough. They seemed to prefer gathering in each other's cabins, as if in retreat from the huge and impinging emptiness of the ship; and there, in a fog of smoke and a growing litter of beer cans, the hubbub, ribaldry, affectionate jeering, and repartee absent from the wardroom asserted itself.

When people started to drift from the wardroom one evening I decided to follow the path to the other end of our island and went down and started along the catwalk to the bows. The night was overcast and very black, and the farther one went the stranger and lonelier and more frightening the experience became. The front of a ship's superstructure is always dark, all windows heavily curtained, to avoid spoiling night vision from the bridge, so that one walked from a façade that showed no hint of light; but there was at least the sheltering comfort of its towering proximity. After a while one lacked even that; it was distant and only faintly discernible, and still the steel path ran on into the dark as far as one's straining eyes could see. Ships had always had great appeal for me at night, when their peace and detachment seem greatest. I felt quite different on *Ardshiel*'s main deck, and what I felt was close to the fringe of fear, or even terror if one allowed oneself to be impressionable about it, which would not have been too difficult.

An unpleasant loneliness grew from this apprehension of the ship's gloomy distances. One felt the arid metal acreage spreading invisibly all around, and its impact was one of menace: a mechanical desert of indefinable purpose imposed upon the sea's own emptiness, and with forms and shapes that had no reassuring familiarity; it was filled with wind signs, not those of masts and rigging but of abandoned structures upon a plain, and there was no comfort even from the sea. One did not even feel its presence amidships on that path over the somnolent pipes and obscure fittings; the sea lay somewhere a long way below the remote and unseen edge of the deck on either side, and what saltiness reached one's lips had the taste of steel.

The overpowering impression was of desolation and severance from that vague far-off castle one had left; but when I returned there I found it entirely abandoned as well. Those who had been drinking and talking when I left had gone, presumably into the cabins, and, as aboard the *Mary Celeste*, only the fragments of their recent presence lay about: half-emptied glasses of beer, the open magazines, full ash-trays, and cups of cold untouched coffee. One passed from wardroom to dining saloon, to cinema, games room, hospital, emergency room, up the stairways and along the deserted alleyways, encountering no sound or sign of another human. And when, on sudden compulsion, I took the lift down to the engine room as well, the melancholy surrealism of the experience seemed complete, for the engines are switched to automatic controls at night and over the weekend and left running on their own. The engine room consequently was as fearful as the deck. It was disturbing to follow those narrow fly-overs, suspended sixty feet over the pounding machinery, and to find one's imagination susceptible once more to aloneness in a mechanical world, especially one of such ceaseless and unaccountable activity.

NOEL MOSTERT,
Supership

Part Two

◆

A

MISCELLANY

OF

VOYAGES

NAVAL

OCCASIONS

Loss of H.M.S. *Phoenix*, 1780

Benjamin Archer was first lieutenant of the *Phoenix* when she
was shipwrecked off Cuba in 1780, and has left us this lively
and racy account of it. The captain of the *Phoenix* was Sir
Hyde Parker, later to win doubtful fame at Copenhagen as the
admiral to whose signal for recall Nelson turned a blind eye.

"It blows d————d hard, Archer!" "It does indeed, sir." "I
don't know that I ever remember its blowing so hard before,
but the ship makes a very good weather of it upon this tack, as
she bows the sea; but we must wear her, as the wind has shifted
to the S.E., and we are drawing right upon Cuba; so do you go
forward and have some hands stand by; loose the leeyard-arm of
the foresail, and when she is right before the wind, whip the clue
garnet close up and roll the sail up."

"Sir, there is no canvas can stand against this moment. If we
attempt to loose him, he'll fly into ribands in a moment, and we
may lose three or four of our people; she'll wear by manning the
fore shrouds."

"No, I don't think she will."

"I'll answer for it, sir; I have seen it tried several times on the
coast of America with success."

"Well, try it; if she does not wear, we can only loose the foresail afterwards."

This was a great condescension from such a man as Sir Hyde.
However, by sending about two hundred people into the fore-
rigging, after a hard struggle she wore; found she did not make so
good weather on this tack as the other, for as the sea began to
run across, she had not time to rise from one sea before another
lashed against her. My God! to think that the wind could have
such force.

Sir Hyde now sent me to see what was the matter between decks, as there was a good deal of noise. As soon as I went below, one of the marine officers calls out, "Good God! Mr. Archer, we are sinking; the water is up to the bottom of my cot." "Poh, poh, as long as it is not over your mouth, you are well off; what the devil do you make this noise for?"

While I was standing at the pumps, cheering the people, the carpenter's mate came running to me with a face as long as my arm.—"Oh, sir! the ship has sprung a leak in the gunner's room." "Go, then, and tell the carpenter to come to me, but don't speak a word to anyone else." "Mr Goodinoh, I am told there is a leak in the gunner's room; go and see what is the matter, but don't alarm anybody, and come and make your report privately, to me." A little after this he returned: "Sir, there's nothing there, 'tis only the water washing up between the timbers that this booby has taken for a leak." Shortly afterwards the gunner came to me; "Mr Archer, I should be glad if you would step this way into the magazine for a moment." I thought some d————d thing was the matter, and ran directly: "Well, what's the matter here?" "The ground tier of powder is spoiled: and I want to show you it is not out of carelessness in me in stowing it, for no powder in the world could be better stowed. Now, sir, what am I to do? If you don't speak to Sir Hyde he will be angry with me." I could not but smile to see how easy he took the danger of the ship, and said to him, "Let us shake off this gale of wind first, and talk of the damaged powder afterwards."

At four we had gained upon the ship a little, and I went upon deck, it being my watch. The second lieutenant relieved me at the pumps. Who can attempt to describe the appearance of things upon deck? If I was to write for ever, I could not give you an idea of it—a total darkness all above—the sea on fire—running, as it were, in Alps, or Peaks of Teneriffe; mountains are too common an idea: the wind, roaring louder than thunder (absolutely no flight of imagination); the whole made more terrible, if possible, by a very uncommon kind of blue lightning. The poor ship very much pressed, yet doing what she could; shaking her sides, and groaning at every stroke. Sir Hyde upon deck, lashed to windward! I soon lashed myself alongside of him, and told him the situation of things below; the ship not making more water than might be expected with such weather; that "I was only afraid of a gun breaking loose." "I am not in the least afraid of that: I have commanded her for six years, and have had many a gale of wind in her; so that her iron work is pretty well tried, which always gives way first—hold fast that was an ugly sea; we must lower the lower yards, I believe, Archer: the ship is much pressed." "If we attempt it, sir, we shall lose them, for a man aloft can do nothing; besides, their being down will cease the ship very little; the mainmast is a sprung mast; I wish it was overboard without carrying anything else along with it." Said to Sir Hyde, "This is no time, sir, to think of saving the masts, shall we cut the mainmast away?" "Aye, as fast as you can." I accordingly went into the weather chains with a pole-axe to cut away the lanyards; the boatswain went to leeward, and the carpenters stood by the mast; we were all ready, when a very violent sea broke right on board of us, carried everything upon deck away; filled the ship full of water; the main and mizzen masts went; the ship righted, but was in the last struggle of sinking under us. As soon as we could shake our heads above water, Sir Hyde exclaimed: "We are gone at last, Archer! foundered at sea!" "Yes,

Loss of the *Phoenix* in a hurricane near Cuba

sir, farewell, and the Lord have mercy upon us!" I then turned about to look forward at the ship, and thought she was struggling to get rid of some of the water; but all in vain: she was almost full below. "God Almighty! I thank thee that now I am leaving this world, which I have always considered as only a passage to a better, I die with a full hope of thy mercies, through the merits of Jesus Christ thy Son, our Saviour." I then felt sorry that I could swim, as by that means I might be a quarter of an hour longer dying, than a man who could not, as it is impossible to divest ourselves of a wish to preserve life. At the end of these reflections, I thought I felt the ship thump, and grinding our feet; 'twas so! "Sir, the ship is ashore." "What do you say?" "The ship is ashore, and we may save ourselves yet."

By this time the quarter-deck was full of men that had come up from below, and the "Lord have mercy upon us," flying about from all quarters. The ship made everybody sensible now that she was ashore, for every stroke threatened a total dissolution of her whole frame; found she was stern ashore, and the bow broke the sea a good deal, though it was washing clear at every stroke. Sir Hyde: "Keep to the quarter-deck, my lads, when she goes to pieces, 'tis your best chance."

She was a very strong ship, and did not go to pieces at the first thumping, though her decks tumbled in. I now began to think of getting on shore; so stripped off my coat and shoes for a swim, and looked for a line to carry the end with me. I luckily could not find one, which gave time for reflection. This won't do for me, to be the first man out of the ship, and first lieutenant: we may get to England again, and people may think I paid a great deal of attention to myself, and did not care for anybody else. No, that won't do; instead of being first, I'll see every man, sick and well, out of her before me.

I now thought there was not a probability of the ship's going to pieces, therefore had not a thought of instant death; took a look round with a sort of philosophic eye, to see how the same situation affected my companions, and was not surprised to find the most swaggering, swearing bullies in fine weather, were now the most pitiful wretches on earth, when death appeared before them: several people that could swim went overboard to try for the shore; nine of them were drowned before our eyes. However, two got safe; by which means, with a line, we got a hawser on shore and made it fast to the rocks, upon which many went, and arrived safe. There were some sick and wounded on board, who could not go this way; so we got a spare top-sail yard from the chains, and got one end ashore, and the other into the cabin window, so that most of the sick got ashore this way. As I had determined, so I was the last man out of the ship, which was about ten o'clock.

The gale now began to break. Sir Hyde came to me, and taking me by the hand, was so affected as to be hardly able to speak. "Archer! I am happy beyond expression to see you on shore! but look at our poor *Phoenix!*" I turned about, but could not say a single word, being too full: my mind had been too actively employed before, but everything now rushed upon me at once, so that I could not contain myself; and I indulged for a full quarter of an hour. By twelve it was pretty moderate: got some sails on shore, and made tents; found great quantities of fish, drove up by the sea, in holes amongst the rocks: knocked up a fire, and had a most comfortable dinner. In the afternoon we made a stage from the cabin-windows to the rocks, and got out some provisions and water, lest the ship should go to pieces, and then we must all perish with hunger and thirst, for we were upon a desolate part of the coast, and under a rocky mountain, which could not supply us with a single drop of water.

Slept comfortably this night; and next day, the idea of death vanishing by degrees. Employed in getting more provisions and water on shore, which was not an easy matter, on account of decks, guns, and rubbish, that lay over them, and ten feet of water besides. In the evening I proposed to Sir Hyde, to repair the remains of the only boat left; and that I would venture to Jamaica myself; and if I got safe, would bring vessels to take them all off—a proposal worth thinking of. It was next day agreed to, so got the cutter on shore and set the carpenters to work on her; in two days she was ready, and at four o'clock in the afternoon I embarked, with four volunteers, and a fortnight's provisions; hoisted English colours as we put off from shore, and received three cheers from the lads left behind, which we returned, and set sail with a light heart. Had a very squally night, and a very leaky boat; so had to keep two buckets constantly bailing.

Steered her myself the whole night by the stars, and at eight in the morning arrived in Montego Bay. I instantly sent off an express to the admiral; another to the *Porcupine* man-of-war; and went myself to Martha Bay to get vessels. Got three small vessels, and set out back again to Cuba, where I arrived the fourth day after leaving them. I thought the ship's crew would have devoured me on my landing: they whisked me upon their shoulders presently, and carried me to the tent where Sir Hyde was. I found the *Porcupine* had arrived that day, and the lads had built a boat almost ready for launching, that would hold fifty men, which was intended for another trial, in case I should have foundered. Next day embarked all our people that were left, amounting to two hundred and fifty; for some had died of the wounds they got coming on shore; others by drinking rum; and others had straggled into the country. All our vessels were so full of people, that we could not take away the few clothes that were saved from the wreck; that was a trifle, since our lives and liberties were saved.

BENJAMIN ARCHER

———◆———

Two views of Captain Bligh

1. His own

Just before sun-rising* Mr. Christian, with the master-at-arms, gunner's mate, and Thomas Burkitt, seaman, came into my cabin while I was asleep, and seizing me, tied my hands with a cord behind my back and threatened me with instant death, if I spoke or made the least noise. I, however, called so loud as to alarm everyone; but they had already secured the officers who were not of their party, by placing sentinels at their doors. There were three men at my cabin door, besides the four within; Christian had only a cutlass in his hand, the others had muskets and bayonets. I was hauled out of bed, and forced on deck in my shirt, suffering great pain from the tightness with which they had tied my hands. I demanded the reason of such violence, but received no other answer than threats of instant death if I did not hold my

* On April 27, 1789.

tongue. Mr. Elphinston, the master's mate, was kept in his berth; Mr. Nelson, botanist, Mr. Peckover, gunner, Mr. Ledward, surgeon, and the master were confined to their cabins, and also the clerk, Mr. Samuel, but he soon obtained leave to come on deck. The fore hatchway was guarded by sentinels; the boatswain and carpenter were, however, allowed to come on deck, where they saw me standing abaft the mizzen-mast, with my hands tied behind my back, under a guard, with Christian at their head.

The boatswain was now ordered to hoist the launch out, with a threat, if he did not do it instantly, to take care of himself.

The boat being out, Mr. Hayward and Mr. Hallet, midshipmen, and Mr. Samuel were ordered into it, upon which I demanded the cause of such an order, and endeavoured to persuade someone to a sense of duty; but it was to no effect: "Hold your tongue, sir, or you are dead this instant," was constantly repeated to me.

The master, by this time, had sent to be allowed to come on deck, which was permitted; but he was soon ordered back again to his cabin.

The Mutiny in the *Bounty:* Captain Bligh
and his companions are set adrift.

I continued my endeavours to turn the tide of affairs, when Christian changed the cutlass he had in his hand for a bayonet that was brought to him, and, holding me with a strong grip by the cord that tied my hands, he with many oaths threatened to kill me immediately if I would not be quiet; the villains round me had their pieces cocked and bayonets fixed. Particular people were now called on to go into the boat, and were hurried over the side, whence I concluded that with these people I was to be set adrift.

I therefore made another effort to bring about a change, but with no other effect than to be threatened with having my brains blown out.

The boatswain and seamen who were to go in the boat were allowed to collect twine, canvas, lines, sails, cordage, an eight-and-twenty-gallon cask of water, and the carpenter to take his tool-chest. Mr. Samuel got 150 lb. of bread, with a small quantity of rum and wine. He also got a quadrant and compass into the boat; but was forbidden, on pain of death, to touch either map, ephemeris,* book of astronomical observations, sextant, time-keeper, or any of my surveys or drawings.

The mutineers now hurried those they meant to get rid of into the boat. When most of them were in, Christian directed a dram to be served to each of his own crew. I now unhappily saw that nothing could be done to effect the recovery of the ship: there was no one to assist me, and every endeavour on my part was answered with threats of death.

The officers were called, and forced over the side into the boat, while I was kept apart from everyone, abaft the mizzen-mast; Christian, armed with a bayonet, holding me by the bandage that secured my hands. The guard round me had their pieces cocked, but, on my daring the ungrateful wretches to fire, they uncocked them.

Isaac Martin, one of the guard over me, I saw, had an inclination to assist me, and, as he fed me with shaddock (my lips being quite parched with my endeavours to bring about a change), we explained our wishes to each other by our looks; but this being observed, Martin was instantly removed from me; his inclination then was to leave the ship, for which purpose he got into the boat; but with many threats they obliged him to return.

* Nautical almanac.

The armourer, Joseph Coleman, and the two carpenters, M'Intosh and Norman, were also kept contrary to their inclination; and they begged of me, after I was astern in the boat, to remember that they declared they had no hand in the transaction. Michael Byrne, I am told, likewise wanted to leave the ship.

It is of no moment for me to recount my endeavours to bring back the offenders to a sense of their duty: all I could do was by speaking to them in general; but my endeavours were of no avail, for I was kept securely bound, and no one but the guard suffered to come near me.

To Mr. Samuel I am indebted for securing my journals and commission, with some material ship papers. Without these I had nothing to certify what I had done, and my honour and character might have been suspected, without my possessing a proper document to have defended them. All this he did with great resolution, though guarded and strictly watched. He attempted to save the time-keeper, and a box with all my surveys, drawings, and remarks for fifteen years past, which were numerous; when he was hurried away, with "Damn your eyes, you are well off to get what you have."

It appeared to me that Christian was some time in doubt whether he should keep the carpenter, or his mates; at length he determined on the latter, and the carpenter was ordered into the boat. He was permitted, but not without some opposition, to take his tool-chest.

Much altercation took place among the mutinous crew during the whole business: some swore, "I'll be damned if he does not find his way home, if he gets anything with him" (meaning me); others, when the carpenter's chest was carrying away, "Damn my eyes, he will have a vessel built in a month." While others laughed at the helpless situation of the boat, being very deep, and so little room for those who were in her. As for Christian, he seemed meditating instant destruction on himself and everyone.

I asked for arms, but they laughed at me, and said I was well acquainted with the people where I was going, and therefore did not want them; four cutlasses, however, were thrown into the boat, after we were veered astern.

When the officers and men, with whom I was suffered to have no communication, were put into the boat, they only waited for me, and the master-at-arms informed Christian of it, who then said—"Come, Captain Bligh, your officers and men are now in the boat, and you must go with them; if you attempt to make the least resistance you will instantly be put to death"; and, without any further ceremony, holding me by the cord that tied my hands, with a tribe of armed ruffians about me, I was forced over the side, where they untied my hands. Being in the boat we were veered astern by a rope. A few pieces of pork were then thrown to us, and some clothes, also the cutlasses I have already mentioned; and it was now that the armourer and carpenters called out to me to remember that they had no hand in the transaction. After having undergone a great deal of ridicule, and been kept some time to make sport for these unfeeling wretches, we were at length cast adrift on the open ocean.

*   *   *

Notwithstanding the roughness with which I was treated, the remembrance of past kindnesses produced some signs of remorse in Christian. When they were forcing me out of the ship, I asked him if this treatment was a proper return for the many instances he had received of my friendship; he appeared disturbed at my question, and answered, with much emotion, "That, Captain Bligh, that is the thing;—I am in hell—I am in hell."

As soon as I had time to reflect, I felt an inward satisfaction, which prevented any depression of my spirits; conscious of my integrity, and anxious solicitude for the good of the service in which I was engaged, I found my mind wonderfully supported, and I began to conceive hopes, notwithstanding so heavy a calamity, that I should one day be able to account to my king and country for the misfortune. A few hours before, my situation had been peculiarly flattering. I had a ship in the most perfect order, and well stored with every necessary both for service and health: by early attention to those particulars I had, as much as lay in my power, provided against any accident, in case I could not get through Endeavour Straits, as well as against what might befall me in them; add to this, the plants had been successfully preserved in the most flourishing state: so that, upon the whole, the voyage was two-thirds completed, and the remaining part in a very promising way; every person on board being in perfect health, to establish which was ever amongst the principal objects of my attention.

It will very naturally be asked, what could be the reason for such a revolt? In answer to which, I can only conjecture that the mutineers had assured themselves of a more happy life among the Tahitians than they could possibly have in England; which, joined to some female connections, have most probably been the principal cause of the whole transaction.

*   *   *

The secrecy of this mutiny is beyond all conception. Thirteen of the party who were with me had always lived forward among the people; yet neither they, nor the messmates of Christian, Stewart, Heywood, and Young, had ever observed any circumstances to give them suspicion of what was going on. With such close-planned acts of villainy, and my mind free from any suspicion, it is not wonderful that I have been got the better of. Perhaps, if I had had marines, a sentinel at my cabin-door might have prevented it; for I slept with the door always open, that the officer of the watch might have access to me on all occasions. The possibility of such a conspiracy was ever the farthest from my thoughts. Had their mutiny been occasioned by any grievances, either real or imaginary, I must have discovered symptoms of their discontent, which would have put me on my guard; but the case was far otherwise. Christian, in particular, I was on the most friendly terms with: that very day he was engaged to have dined with me; and the preceding night he excused himself from supping with me, on pretence of being unwell, for which I felt concerned, having no suspicions of his integrity and honour.

Captain Bligh

from E. A. Hughes (ed.),
Bligh of the Bounty

For a long time Bligh's own version of the mutiny was accepted as the definitive account of what had happened. But in 1934 the discovery in Australia of the journal of the boatswain, James Morrison, and its publication by the Golden Cockerel Press, showed Bligh in a rather different light.

2. The boatswain's

In the Afternoon of the 27th Mr. Bligh Came up, and taking
a turn about the Quarter Deck when he missed some of the Cocoa
Nuts which were piled up between the Guns upon which he said
that they were stolen and Could not go without the knowledge
of the Officers, who were all Calld and declared that they had not
seen a Man toutch them, to which Mr. Bligh replied "then you
must have taken them yourselves," and orderd Mr. Elphinstone
to go and fetch evry Cocoa nut in the Ship aft, which He obeyd.
He then questioned evry Officer in turn concerning the Number
they had bought, & Coming to Mr. Christian askd Him, Mr.
Christian answerd "I do not know Sir, but I hope you dont think
me so mean as to be Guilty of Stealing yours." Mr. Bligh replied
"Yes you dam'd Hound I do—You must have stolen them from
me or you could give a better account of them—God dam you,
you Scoundrels, you are all thieves alike, and combine with the
men to rob me—I suppose you'll Steal my Yams next, but I'll
sweat you for it, you rascals, I'll make half of you Jump overboard before you get through Endeavour Streights"—He then
Calld Mr. Samuel and said "Stop these Villains Grog, and Give
them but Half a Pound of Yams tomorrow, and if they steal then,
I'll reduce them to a quarter." The Cocoa Nuts were Carried aft,
& He Went below, the officers then got together and were heard
to murmur much at such treatment, and it was talked among the
Men that the Yams would be next seized, as Lieut. Bligh knew
that they had purchased large quantitys of them and set about
secreting as many as they Could.

The night being Calm we made no way, & in the Morning
of the 28th the Boatswain Came to my hammock and waked me
telling me to my great surprize that the ship was taken by Mr.
Christian. I hurried on deck and found it true—seeing Mr. Bligh
in his shirt with his hands tied behind him and Mr. Christian
standing by him with a drawn Bayonet in his hand and his Eyes
flaming with revenge. Several of the men were under arms, and
the Small Cutter hoisted out, and the large one getting ready. I
applied to the Boatswain to know how I should proceed, but he
was as much at a loss as I, and in a Confused Manner told me
to lend a hand in Clearing the Boat and Getting her out, which

I did, when she was out the Small one was got in—Mr. Christian Calld to Mr. Hayward and Mr. Hallet to get into the Boat and ordered Churchill to See the Master & Clerk into Her. The Lieutenant then began to reason but Mr. Christian replied "Mamoo, Sir, not a word, or deaths your portion." Mr. Hayward & Mr. Hallet begd with tears in their eyes to be sufferd to remain in the ship but Mr. Christian ordered them to be silent. The Boatswain and Carpenter Came aft (the Master & Gunner being Confined below) and beggd for the Launch, which with much hesitation was Granted, and she was ordered out. While I was Clearing her the Master Came up & spoke to Mr. Bligh and afterwards Came to Me, asking me if I had any hand in the Mutiny—I told him I had not, and he then desired me to try what I Could do to raise a party and rescue the Ship, which I promised to do. In consequence of which Jno. Millward who was by me at the time Swore he would stand by me, and went to Musprat, Burket and the Boatswain on that score, but Churchill seeing the Master speaking to me (tho he was Instantly hurried away by Quintrell ordering him down to his Cabbin) Came and demanded what he had said. I told him that He was asking about the Launch but Alexr. Smith who stood on the other side of the Boat told Churchill to look sharp after me saying " 'tis a dam'd lye, Chas, for I saw him and Millward shake hands, when the Master spoke to them, and Calld to the others to stand to their Arms, which put them on their Guard." As I saw none near me that seemd inclined to make a push, and the Officers busy getting the boat in order, I was fain to do so too, and the Boat was got out, when evry one ran to get what He could into her and get in themselves as fast as possible. The officers were hurryd in as fast as possible, and when Mr. Bligh found that He must go, He beggd of Mr. Christian to desist, saying "I'll Pawn my Honor, I'll Give My Bond, Mr. Christian, never to think of this if youll desist"; and urged his wife and family, to which Mr. Christian replyd "No, Captain Bligh, if you had any Honor, things had no[t] come to this; and if you Had any regard for your Wife & family, you should Have thought on them before, and not behaved so much like a villain." Lieutenant Bligh attempted again to speak, but was ordered to be silent; the Boatswain also tryd to pacify Him to which He replied " 'Tis too late, I have been in

Hell for this Fortnight passed and am determined to bear it no
longer, and you know Mr. Cole that I have been used like a Dog
all the Voyage."

Journal of James Morrison,
Boatswain's Mate of the *Bounty*

THE SAILOR'S CONSOLATION

One night came on a hurricane,
    The sea was mountains rolling,
When Barney Buntline slewed his quid
    And said to Billy Bowline:
"A strong nor'-wester's blowing, Bill,
    Hark! don't ye hear it roar now!
Lord help 'em, how I pities them
    Unhappy folks on shore now!

"Fool-hardy chaps as live in towns,
    What danger they are all in,
And now lie quaking in their beds,
    For fear the roof should fall in:

Poor creturs, how they envies us,
    And wishes, I've a notion,
For our good luck, in such a storm
    To be upon the ocean!

"And as for them that's out all day,
    On business, from their houses,
And late at night returning home
    To cheer their babes and spouses;
While you and I, Bill, on the deck
    Are comfortably lying,
My eyes! what tiles and chimney-pots
    About their heads are flying!

"Both you and I have ofttimes heard
   How men are killed and undone,
By overturns from carriages,
   By thieves and fire, in London.
We know what risks these landsmen run,
   From noblemen to tailors,
Then, Bill, let us thank Providence
   That you and I are sailors."

WILLIAM PITT

———◆———

Eccentricities of George III

One of the most delightful of the naval memoirs of the eighteenth and nineteenth centuries are those of Admiral Sir Thomas Byam Martin. In 1791 he served aboard the frigate *Juno*, stationed at Weymouth. Weymouth was the favourite watering-place of George III, and the *Juno* was ordered by the Admiralty to attend on him.

Walking the quarter-deck of the *Juno* one day with Lord Chesterfield, who was taking a passage to Falmouth in the ship to inspect the packets, his lordship being at the time postmaster-general, I ventured to say I supposed the King felt a good deal annoyed at the revolutionary movements in France. Lord Chesterfield replied: "Yes, very much. It was only the day before we left Weymouth that his Majesty had said, putting down the newspaper: 'I am much grieved to see such an unruly temper throughout the French nation, and the bad feeling it has produced in this country, as we see so strongly expressed at public meetings. All this must lead to great mischief, Lord Chesterfield, and I am very anxious for the royal family of France; they are placed in awful circumstances, and no one can foresee how it may all end. It may not come to pass in my time, I do not expect it will, but you may be assured, Lord Chesterfield, there is a feeling gaining ground which is likely to occasion a great change in this country, and may cost my children much trouble. It will require on their part more than common fortitude and prudence. God grant it may go well with them!' "

The postmaster-general, in the pride of office, proposed to the King to have one of the Falmouth packets ordered round, and accordingly the *Chesterfield* soon joined our squadron. The person who commanded this vessel, Captain Jones, was not in the least conversant with naval manœuvres; it was therefore a material object for safety's sake, in a space so limited for evolutions as Weymouth and Portland roads, to keep the *Chesterfield* as much separated from us as due delicacy towards her godpapa would permit. It happened, however, that the packet (a very nice-looking ship) was placed by her captain one day, when there was a fresh breeze, in a position quite unwarranted by only three days' experience in naval tactics. The consequence was that the *Shark* sloop of war, commanded by that excellent and greatly beloved man the Honourable Arthur Legge, was forced into such a situation that she could not escape running on board the *Juno* where the royal family covered the quarter-deck, or on board the *Chesterfield*. It may be supposed Legge did not hesitate which should receive the shock, and to avoid the *Juno* bore up athwart the *Chesterfield*'s course, having ineffectually made all sorts of signs and signals for her to get out of the way. The collision of the two ships in so fresh a breeze was no joke. In an instant away went the figure-head (a well carved representation of his lordship in his robes of Parliament), the bowsprit, fore top-mast and main top-gallant mast, with such an awful crash that one might have thought both ships knocked to pieces, but happily no lives were lost, and the *Shark* escaped without any material damage.

The good old King, who knew what delight we had in doing whatever might tend to his amusement, took this to be a part of the designed exhibitions of the day, and immediately called out in a rapturous tone: "Very fine, very fine, how beautiful, very fine indeed!" (addressing the Princess Royal), "I never saw anything finer." It was quite impossible to stand all this, and off we went, a parcel of us, to have our laugh out where it could be indulged without offence to the royal ears.

*   *   *

Whenever the royal family came on board, and the ship under sail, the people were kept at their different stations, and the lower deck quite clear. One day the King and Queen came out of the cabin together and were inclined to pay a visit to the lower deck. When I discovered the intended frolic, I found his Majesty with infinite awkwardness trying how it was best to go down the ladder; first his foot was planted on the upper step, as if to descend in the usual way of going down stairs, presently he turned to try the other way to make a stern board of it; but not quite satisfied that he was right, I found on my approach that he and the Queen were holding a council of war, and being called in to assist in the deliberations, the latter mode of proceeding was adopted.

My accidental appearance was very fortunate; I do believe if left to themselves they would have encountered a very bumping, disagreeable passage from one deck to the other, for if the heel slips in going down, the hinder part of the human body is sure to strike each step in the descent. I endeavoured to explain this hazard in the most delicate terms I could employ, and with suffi-

Admiral of the Fleet
Sir Thomas Byam Martin

cient clearness to make her Majesty at once take the lead with her face towards the ladder. This is a caution which I always give to ladies, however contrary to court etiquette such mode of presentation may be.

Having reached the lower deck my duty was to think of the safety of another part of the royal person, and that a very tender one, too, considering the King's then recent malady—I mean the head. The height of a frigate of the *Juno* class, the old 32, is about 5 feet 4 inches between decks, so that there was a constant danger of his Majesty throwing his head suddenly up and receiving a severe blow; it kept me quite in a nervous fidget the whole time. We were the only three persons at the time on the lower deck, and I was desired to explain everything as they walked round. His Majesty, getting tired of stooping so long, was not sorry to sit himself down in the midshipmen's berth, and then commenced innumerable questions as to my professional service, &c., &c. Finding I had served with Prince William (Duke of Clarence) in every ship he had ever commanded, the conversation became very interesting, and occasioned them to tarry so long in this unfrequented part of the ship that a sort of hue and cry made us aware that some uneasiness prevailed on account of their Majesties' long absence from the quarter-deck. This was still more increased when one of the anxious attendants, Colonel Price, reconnoitred the cabin and found the royal couple missing. The alarm soon reached those above, and set one of the lords off, accompanied by one of the officers of the ship, in search of the absentees. We were found very snug in the midshipmen's berth; the Queen in the enjoyment of a half-broken chair, while his Majesty was politely content to take his seat on a poor mid.'s chest. For myself I can't say much for enjoyment; I stood before them almost exhausted, answering the thousand questions put to me, and they ceased not even when the intruders discovered our retreat. The King long recollected his visit to the lower deck, and had always a question ready for me relating to the conversation on that occasion.

ADMIRAL SIR THOMAS BYAM MARTIN,
Memoirs

Song for All Seas, All Ships

1

Today a rude brief recitative,
Of ships sailing the seas, each with its special flag or ship-
   signal,
Of unnamed heroes in the ships—of waves spreading and
   spreading far as the eye can reach,
Of dashing spray, and the winds piping and blowing,
And out of these a chant, for the sailors of all nations,
Fitful, like a surge.

Of sea-captains young or old, and the mates, and of all
   intrepid sailors,
Of the few, very choice, taciturn, whom fate can never sur-
   prise nor death dismay,
Picked sparingly, without noise, by thee old ocean, chosen
   by thee,
Thou sea that pickest and cullest the race in time, and
   unitest nations,
Suckled by thee, old husky nurse, embodying thee,
Indomitable, untamed as thee.

(Ever the heroes on water or on land, by ones or twos
   appearing,
Ever the stock preserved, and never lost, though rare—
   enough for seed preserved.)

2

Flaunt out O sea your separate flags of nations!
Flaunt out visible as ever the various ship-signals!
But do you reserve especially for yourself and for the soul
   of man one flag above all the rest,
A spiritual woven signal for all nations, emblem of man
   elate above death,
Token of all brave captains and all intrepid sailors and
   mates,
And all that went down doing their duty,
Reminiscent of them, twined from all intrepid captains
   young or old,
A pennant universal, subtly waving all time, o'er all brave
   sailors,
All seas, all ships.

WALT WHITMAN

Admiral Collingwood dreams of home

Lord Nelson's friend and second-in-command at Trafalgar, Admiral Collingwood, was at sea for most of the fifty years he spent in the Navy. Between 1793 and his death on board his flagship in 1810, he spent only a year in England, and for one period of twenty-two months never went ashore. In these letters to his wife and a friend he conveys something of the loneliness and isolation of those whose task it was to retain Britain's mastery of the seas.

To his wife:

Ocean, *June 16, 1806*

This day, my love, is the anniversary of our marriage, and I wish you many happy returns of it. If ever we have peace, I hope to spend my latter days amid my family, which is the only sort of happiness I can enjoy. After this life of labour, to retire to peace and quietness is all I look for in the world. Should we decide to change the place of our dwelling, our route would of course be to the southward of Morpeth: but then I should be forever regretting those beautiful views, which are nowhere to be exceeded; and even the rattling of that old wagon that used to pass our door at 6 o'clock in a Winter's morning had its charms. The fact is, whenever I think how I am to be happy again, my thoughts carry me back to Morpeth, where, out of the fuss and parade of the world, surrounded by those I loved most dearly and who loved me, I enjoyed as much happiness as my nature is capable of. Many things that I see in the world give me a distaste to the finery of it. The great knaves are not like those poor unfortunates, who, driven perhaps to distress from accidents which they could not prevent, or at least not educated in principles of honour and honesty, are hanged for some little thievery; while a knave of education and high breeding, who brandishes his honour in the eyes of the world, would rob a state to its ruin. For the first, I feel pity and compassion; for the latter, abhorrence and contempt: they are tenfold vicious.

Have you read—but what I am more interested about, is your sister with you, and is she well and happy? Tell her—God bless her!—I wish I were with you, that we might have a good laugh.

God bless me! I have scarcely laughed these three years. I am here, with a very reduced force, having been obliged to make detachments to all quarters. This leaves me weak, while the Spaniards and French within are daily gaining strength. They have patched and pierced until they have now a very considerable fleet. Whether they will venture out I do not know: if they come, I have no doubt we shall do an excellent deed, and then I will bring them to England myself.

Admiral Lord Collingwood

How do the dear girls go on? I would have them taught geometry, which is of all sciences in the world the most entertaining: it expands the mind more to the knowledge of all things in nature, and better teaches to distinguish between truths and such things as have the appearance of being truths, yet are not, than any other. Their education and the proper cultivation of the sense which God has given them, are the objects on which my happiness most depends. To inspire them with a love of every thing that is honourable and virtuous, though in rags, and with contempt for vanity in embroidery, is the way to make them the darlings of my heart. They should not only read, but it requires a careful selection of books; nor should they ever have access to two at the same time: but when a subject is begun, it should be finished before anything else is undertaken. How would it enlarge their minds, if they could acquire a sufficient knowledge of mathematics and astronomy to give them an idea of the beauty and wonders of the creation! I am persuaded that the generality of people, and particularly fine ladies, only adore God because they are told it is proper and the fashion to go to Church; but I would have my girls gain such knowledge of the works of creation, that they may have a fixed idea of the nature of that Being who could be the author of such a world. Whenever they have that, nothing on this side of the moon will give them much uneasiness of mind. I do not mean that they should be Stoics, or want the common feelings for the sufferings that flesh is heir to; but they would then have a source of consolation for the worst that could happen.

Tell me how do the trees which I planted thrive? Is there shade under the three oaks for a comfortable summer seat? Do the poplars grow at the walk, and does the wall of terrace stand firm? My bankers tell me that all my money in their hands is exhausted by fees on the peerage, and that I am in their debt, which is a new epoch in my life, for it is the first time I was ever in debt since I was a Midshipman. Here I get nothing; but then my expenses are nothing, and I do not want it, particularly now that I have got my knives, forks, teapot, and the things you were so kind as to send me.

To his lifelong friend J. E. Blackett, Esq.:

Ocean, *January 1st, 1807*

. . . I have lived now so long in a ship, always engaged in serious employments, that I shall be unfit for any thing but the quiet society of my family: it is to them that I look for happiness, if ever I am relieved from this anxious and boisterous life, and in them I hope for every thing. Tell the children that Bounce is very well and very fat, yet he seems not to be content, and sighs so piteously these long evenings, that I am obliged to sing him to sleep, and have sent them the song.

> Sigh no more, Bouncey, sigh no more,
> Dogs were deceivers never;
> Though ne'er you put one foot on shore,
> True to your master ever.
> Then sigh not so, but let us go
> Where dinner's daily ready,
> Converting all the sounds of woe
> To heigh phiddy diddy!

To his wife:

Ocean, *off Cadiz, July 28th, 1808*

I am sorry to find my picture was not an agreeable surprise. I did not say any thing to you about it, because I would always guard you as much as I could against disappointment; but you see, with all my care, I sometimes fail. The painter was reckoned the most eminent in Sicily; but you expected to find me a smooth-skinned, clear-complexioned gentleman, such as I was when I left home, dressed in the newest taste, and like the fine people who live gay lives ashore. Alas! it is far otherwise with me. The painter was thought to have flattered me much: that lump under my chin was but loose skin, from which the flesh has shrunk away; the redness of my face was not, I assure you, the effect of wine, but of burning suns and boisterous winds; and my eyes, which were once dark and bright, are now faded and dim. The painter represented me as I am; not as I once was. It is time and toil that have worked the change, and not his want of skill. That the countenance is stern, will not be wondered at, when it is considered how many sad and anxious hours and how many heartaches I have. I shall be very glad when the war is over. . . .

ADMIRAL LORD COLLINGWOOD

HOME-THOUGHTS FROM THE SEA

Nobly, nobly Cape Saint Vincent to the North-west died
    away;
Sunset ran, one glorious blood-red, reeking into Cadiz Bay;
Bluish 'mid the burning water, full in face Trafalgar lay;
In the dimmest North-east distance dawn'd Gibraltar
    grand and gray;
"Here and here did England help me: how can I help
    England?"—say,
Whoso turns as I, this evening, turn to God to praise and
    pray,
While Jove's planet rises yonder, silent over Africa.

ROBERT BROWNING

1815: Journey's end

1. Napoleon boards the *Bellerophon*

General Bertrand came first up the ship's side, and said to me,
"The Emperor is in the boat." He then ascended, and, when he
came on the quarter-deck, pulled off his hat and, addressing me
in a firm tone of voice, said, "I am come to throw myself on the
protection of your Prince and laws." When I showed him into
the cabin, he looked round and said, "Une belle chambre. This is
a handsome cabin." I answered, "Such as it is, Sir, it is at your
service while you remain on board the ship I command." He then
looked at a portrait that was hanging up, and said, "Who is that
young lady?" "My wife," I replied. "Ah! She is both young and
pretty." He then asked if I had any children, and put a number
of questions respecting my country, and the service I had seen.
He next requested I would send for the officers, and introduce
them to him: which was done according to their rank. He asked
several questions of each, as to the place of his birth, the situation
he held in the ship, the length of time he had served, and the
actions he had been in. He then expressed a desire to go round
the ship; but as the men had not done cleaning, I told him it was

customary to clean the lower decks immediately after their breakfast, that they were then so employed, and if he would defer
visiting the ship until they had finished, he would see her to more
advantage.

CAPTAIN FREDERICK MAITLAND,
*A Narrative of the Proceedings
on Board* (1826)

The barge approached, and ranged alongside. The first lieutenant
came up the side, and to Maitland's eager and blunt question,
"Have you got him?" he answered in the affirmative. After the
lieutenant came Savary, followed by Marshal Bertrand, who
bowed and fell back a space on the gangway, to await the ascent
of their master. And now came the little great man himself,

Napoleon on board the *Bellerophon*

wrapped up in his grey greatcoat buttoned up to the chin, three-cocked hat and Hussar boots, without any sword; I suppose as emblematical of his changed condition. Maitland received him with every mark of respect due to a crowned head, which was afterwards insidiously thrown out against Maitland. So far from that, the captain, on Napoleon's addressing him, only removed his hat, as to a general officer, and remained covered while the Emperor spoke to him. His expressions were brief, I believe only reiterating what he had stated the day previous in his letter to the Prince Regent, "that he placed himself under the protection of the British nation, and under that of the British commander as the representative of his sovereign." The captain again removed his hat, and turned to conduct the Emperor to the cabin. As he passed through the officers assembled on the quarter-deck, he repeatedly bowed slightly to us, and smiled. What an ineffable beauty there was in that smile; his teeth were finely set, and as white as ivory, and his mouth had a charm about it that I have never seen in any other human countenance. I marked his fine robust figure as he followed Captain Maitland into the cabin, and, boy as I was, I said to myself, "Now have I a tale for futurity!"

MIDSHIPMAN GEORGE HUME,
*Reminiscences of the Emperor
Napoleon*

We were received by the ex-Emperor with all his former dignity; and the party consisting of Napoleon, Bertrand, Sir Henry Hotham, Captain Maitland, Mr. Irving, and myself, were kept standing the whole time.

Napoleon's person I was very desirous of seeing, but on doing so, I was disappointed. His figure is bad, he is short with a large head, his hands and legs small, and his body so corpulent as to project very considerably, his coat made very plain, as you see it in most prints, and from being very short in the back it gives his figure a more ridiculous appearance than it has naturally. His profile is good and is exactly what his busts and portraits represent him, but his full face is bad. His eyes are a light blue, heavy and totally contrary to what I had expected, his teeth are bad, but the expression of his countenance is versatile, and expressive beyond measure of the quick and varying passions of the mind. His face at one moment bears the stamp of good humour and again immediately changes to a dark, penetrating scowl denoting the character of the thought that excites it. He speaks quick, and runs from one subject to another, with great rapidity. His knowledge is extensive and very various, and he surprised me much by his remembrance of men of every character in England. He spoke much of America and asked many questions concerning Spanish and British America, and also of the United States.

He plays the Emperor in everything, and has taken possession of Maitland's after-cabin. As a specimen, he sent this morning to Captain Maitland to request the pleasure of his company to breakfast at Maitland's own table. In consequence of this assumption Napoleon walked into the dinner cabin as into his own palace, and Marshal Bertrand was left to usher in the strangers and staff. Dinner was served in the French style by Napoleon's domestics. Without any ceremony, he commenced eating, no notice was taken of any individual, and we had all only to eat and drink as fast as the servants plied our plates and glasses with food and wine. Directly after dinner we had coffee and then adjourned to the after-cabin; very little conversation took place; afterwards we were principally amused by seeing a very compact bed of Napoleon's set up, and his bed made by 3 or 4 of his valets.

Soon after this we went to the Quarter Deck, by Napoleon's desire, with the ladies, and remained under ½ past 7, when Sir Henry Hotham, Mr. Irving and I returned on board. At dinner Napoleon said little, but ate heartily; as little was said afterwards, and on going on deck he amused himself much in talking with the subordinate officers and midshipmen by turns, and in walking the deck with Bertrand. At an early hour he retired to bed apparently much fatigued.

CAPTAIN HUMPHREY SENHOUSE

Commodore Perry throws a party at Lew Chew

In 1852 Commodore Matthew Perry of the United States Navy, flying his broad pennant in the *Susquehanna*, made his famous visit to Japan—whose ports had hitherto been closed to foreign ships—to open up the country to trade. Before arriving in Japan proper Perry took his squadron to visit the island of Okinawa, then called Lew Chew, which lies between Formosa (or Taiwan) and the Japanese mainland. During a visit ashore there was a misunderstanding regarding the Regent, and after visiting the Bonin Islands Perry returned to Lew Chew to find the old Regent dismissed and a new one appointed in his place. At this time the wardrooms of United States naval ships were still wet.

The Commodore, who was quite satisfied with the conciliatory measures that had been pursued during his absence, now renewed his invitation to the regent and treasurer to dine on board the *Susquehanna*, on Tuesday, the 28th of June, offering to send boats for them. This invitation was accepted; and the Commodore had reason to doubt the whole story of the old Regent's degradation, from the fact that the new Regent, *Shang Hung Hiun*, a member of the family of his predecessor, and a much younger man, did not hesitate to accept an invitation to the dinner, but went even further in his courtesies and attentions than the old Regent had ever done. As far as he could ascertain the facts, the Commodore believed that the old man had voluntarily resigned in favor of the young one.

On the appointed day of the feast, three of the ship's boats were sent off to the creek at Tumai to bring on board the invited guests. On their arrival, and after the usual presentation of crimson cards, they came on board in robes of the finest and cleanest grass-cloth, and with *hatchee matchees* of showy color on their heads. Captain Buchanan received them at the gangway, and conducted them through the various parts of the ship. The day was oppressively warm, and the visitors found it so sultry between decks, and especially in the engine room, that they were glad once more to stand upon the upper deck. The marines were under arms, and the band played to give honor to their reception. When dinner was announced they were ushered into the Commodore's cabin, and immediately sat down to the table. The entertainment was, of course, entirely in accordance with European and American customs. The Commodore took the centre of the table, with the Regent on his right hand and the chief treasurer on his left, while the mayor of Napha and one of the other treasurers were seated near the ends of the table, where they were taken in charge by the commanders of the different vessels of the squadron. Mr. Williams and Dr. Bettelheim were present as guests and interpreters; while at a smaller table were Messrs. O. H. Perry, Portman, Taylor, and Heine. None of the Regent's suite were allowed to sit at table with him, but remained in attendance. His interpreter, Ichirazichi, stood behind him.

The new Regent was a small man, apparently about forty-five years old, of more swarthy complexion than any of his suite, and with a slight cast in his left eye. He was remarkably grave and taciturn, seemed to be perpetually awake to the novelty of his position, having at times a restless and uneasy expression of countenance, and never spoke except when he was particularly addressed. It was very evident that he was less at his ease than any person present. This, perhaps, arose from his newly acquired rank, to which he had not yet become accustomed, and possibly some embarrasment may have been caused by the apprehension that he should be wanting in some of the proprieties of etiquette at an American dinner table. Perhaps, too, he was not without his fears that, surrounded as he knew himself to be by spies, his visit might bring in its train some unpleasant political consequences. His dress consisted of a dark purple or violet-colored robe and a cap of crimson. The treasurers, both old men with wrinkled faces and scanty grey beards, wore similar caps, while their robes were yellow. The mayor was attired in a robe of pearl-white grass-cloth, and had on his head a crimson cap. The hair of all was put up with massive gold pins, and their girdles were of rich Chinese silk. These various dresses were presumed to be official, and in their diversity of color indicative of difference of rank. The inferior attendants who stood behind these dignitaries were dressed in blue and yellow with scarlet caps.

Knives and forks were placed, in our usual fashion, for each guest. The first seemed to be very much in the way of the Lew Chewans; with the last they did better, and showed some dexterity in making them answer the purpose of chop sticks. This, however, was a matter of but little moment, as, be the implements used what they may, hungry men will contrive in some mode to convey food to their mouths, and the Lew Chewans, like sensible men, manifested no intention of avoiding awkwardness at such a heavy price as the loss of a good dinner; and the dinner was very good. Turtle soup, goose, kid curry, and various delicacies formed part of the feast which was spread with bountiful profusion. To the soup the mayor and treasurer did ample justice, and in their appreciation of its excellence were not unworthy rivals of a London Alderman. The cabin was sultry, and as the feast proceeded the guests grew warmer (for they were very much in earnest) until finally they asked permission to remove their caps, and this having been done, the attendant of each, standing, vigorously fanned the uncovered head of his master. Punch followed the soup and furnished them with a new gustatory enjoyment. They had given the Commodore some of their *saki*, and he was now resolved to give them a taste of the *saki* made in all other parts of the world. So there were French and German wines, Scotch and American whiskey, madeira and sherry, and the gin of Holland, winding up with the sweet, smooth, strong maraschino, which decidedly, in their estimation, bore away the palm. They smacked their lips and shut their eyes at each sip of the delicacy, and, in short, showed but a very sorry appreciation of the virtue of temperance. And while they were thus almost equalling Christendom in genteel dissipation, Mr. Heine, at the small table, was making a sketch of the group, and Mr. Portman was taking a portrait of the Regent.

After feeding heartily on the substantials, they asked leave to smoke their pipes; it was of course accorded, and the chief treasurer, after a few whiffs, presented his, with the embroidered tobacco pouch attached, to the Commodore. The mayor and other treasurers followed his example by handing theirs to Captains Buchanan and Adams. There seemed to be no end to the capacity of stomach in some of these officials. Preserved oysters and other articles of food sealed up in America, excited an admiration as boundless as their appetites. Part of the dessert consisted of melons and bananas brought from the Bonin Islands. These took them completely captive and they begged that they might carry some home to their wives. They were, of course, told to do so, and forthwith the loose folds of each one's robe above his girdle was converted into a pocket and loaded with what it would hold.

When things had reached this stage, there was but too much reason to fear that "the tide of wine and wassail was fast gaining on the dry land of sober judgment." All reserve was now fully thawed out. The quiet repose of a calm contentment sat enthroned on the shining face of the jolly old mayor of Napha. The wrinkled visages of the two withered old treasurers flushed and expanded into rubicund fullness. The Regent alone preserved his silent, anxious demeanor, and all he drank was neutralized in its effects by his excessive dignity. He appeared cordial and friendly but once, and that was when the Commodore offered him an assortment of American garden seed and vegetables. These he promised to plant and carefully cultivate. The Commodore had previously landed, as a present, cattle and buffaloes; these he also promised should be carefully looked to and their offspring preserved.

The band had been playing on the deck while the guests were feasting, and when the weightier part of the festival was over the Commodore ordered down some of the more expert performers, to

The midshipmen's berth, c. 1830

play solos on the flageolet, hautboy, clarionet, and cornet-a-piston. The Regent listened attentively, but the mayor and treasurers were too busy in stowing away the epular fragments to be moved by any "concord of sweet sounds." Coffee was offered them, under the name of "American tea." They did not relish it, and resorted once more to their pipes. The attendants had not been forgotten. They had enjoyed an abundance of meat and drink in the steward's pantry, and relished it quite as much as their masters. But all earthly enjoyment must have an end, and the feast at last was over. The guests were put on shore at Tumai, leaving the ship under a salute of three guns; and so ended the dinner given to the Regent on board the *Susquehanna*.

FRANCIS L. HAWKS,
*Narrative of the Expedition of an American
Squadron to the China Seas and Japan*

Opening the door to Japan

The following year Commodore Perry took his squadron into Edo (now Tokyo) Bay.

To the astonishment of the Japanese lining the shore of Edo Bay on the morning of July 8, 1853, four black-hulled warships hove into sight. Amazement turned into panic when they saw smoke pouring from the funnels of two side-wheelers, each with a sloop in tow and their guns run out for action. The thunder of a thirteen-gun salute was Commodore Perry's way of announcing his arrival to a "weak and semi-barbarous people" as he anchored defiantly within sight of the sprawling city of Edo at the head of what would later become Tokyo Bay. President Fillmore had instructed Perry to secure "friendship, commerce, a supply of coal and provisions and protection for our shipwrecked people." Shrewdly assessing the Japanese character, the Commodore, dressed resplendently in his dress uniform, refused to treat with underlings, and made the unheard-of demand of an audience with the Mikado. He threatened to blow the Shōgun's boats from the water when they ordered him to Nagasaki.

Perry was a believer in "manifest destiny"; he saw his mission as "God's purpose," and thought it was his responsibility to "bring a singular and isolated people into the family of nations." His daughter was married into the Belmont banking family, which had invested heavily in the Far East trade, so he was well aware of the commercial importance of opening trade with Japan before "our great maritime rival England" could do so. His show of bravado impressed the Shōgun. After Shinto priests' prayers for a "Kamikaze" had failed to raise the "Divine Wind" to scatter the foreign vessels, as the great storm of 1281 had saved Japan from a Mongol invasion, the Shōgun agreed to a ceremonial acceptance of the casket containing a letter from the President to the Mikado. Perry then sailed away, promising to come back with a stronger fleet. The Japanese were left to reflect on their first lesson in gunboat diplomacy.

JOHN COSTELLO,
The Pacific War

Rescue of the Sillibaboos

The same year one of Perry's storeships made an unusual rescue in the South China Sea.

On the morning of the 5th of August, 1853, in about latitude 18° 46′ N., longitude 124° E., the store-ship *Southampton*, Lieutenant Commanding Boyle, was steering S.W. by W., the wind blowing from the northward and westward a fresh top-gallant breeze, with considerable swell, when a boat was discovered to windward. The ship was hove to, and presently succeeded in getting on board the boat and its contents. When hoisted in and measured, the craft was found to be twelve feet long, four wide, and seventeen inches deep. On board of the boat, when the ship thus picked her up, were six males, four of whom were adults and two were boys, the one about ten and the other fourteen years of age. They were all of healthy appearance, of medium stature, of a dark color, the hair cut close, not tattooed, and did not appear to be much exhausted. Captain Boyle supposed, from their appearance, that they might have been adrift some two or three days. They had in the boat about two or three dozen ears of Indian corn (maize), a few sweet potatoes, some prepared betel nuts, a cask, two gongs, a fishing net, an axe, a small piece of grass cloth as a sail, and a colored piece of cloth supposed to be a flag. Of water they had none; but, from the frequent showers encountered by the ship, Captain Boyle concluded they had not suffered much from the want of it.

To what nation or people these poor creatures belonged no one could tell, as nobody on board could understand their language. It was observed, however, that the word most frequently on their lips was *Sil-li-ba-boo*. The nearest land to the ship was Cape Engano, the N.E. point of Luconia, distant about one hundred miles. The Babuan and Bashee group were about one hundred and eighty miles directly to windward; and the first conjecture was that possibly they might belong to these. Their dress consisted of wide-legged trowsers extending a little below the knee, with a dark-colored gown enveloping the entire person, and secured around the neck by a drawing string; their heads they would sometimes bind around with a cotton handkerchief, after a fashion not unlike that used by the blacks of the southern States. Though seemingly not much exhausted when they were taken on board the ship, yet they evidently experienced great difficulty in walking, from their long confinement in a cramped position. Sleep, with suitable diet, however, soon restored them to their usual condition.

When the ship came near and passed through the group of islands just named, the commander watched closely to observe if they showed any mark of recognition. Their attention was called to them by signs, and they seemed to understand the pantomimic inquiry, for they invariably shook their heads as if to imply that their home was not there, and pointing towards the eastward, said "*Sil-li-ba-boo*." Soon after the ship arrived at Cum-sing-moon, in China, and here great pains were taken to discover, if possible, where these poor adventurers belonged. There were many ships lying there, and the Commodore directed that diligent search should be made among them all, in the hope that, perchance, some one might be found who could communicate with them. They were visited by many from the various vessels, and, from their timidity, they fell at first under the suspicion that they were anxious to remain unknown; but Captain Boyle became quite convinced that their shyness, and repugnance to leave the ship, proceeded from fear alone. They were taken on board each of the trading ships at Cum-sing-moon, and out of the numerous tongues spoken on board not one was found like that spoken by these men. At length they uttered some words when on the deck of the English ship *Bombay*, which Captain Jamieson, the commander, thought he recognized as belonging to the language of the natives of the Bentinck Isles. On perceiving that their words were attracting notice, they made their usual salaam, and uttering *Sil-li-ba-boo*, afterwards held their peace. There is an island called by that name, and mentioned by Horsburg as being in latitude 4° N., longitude 127° E., but this is so remote from the spot where they were picked up, some twelve or fifteen hundred miles, that Captain Boyle could not suppose it possible they had drifted such a

The Sillibaboos

distance. The wind had, indeed, for several days been strong from the southward and eastward, just before the boat was seen, though at the time they were picked up it was from the northward and westward. Notwithstanding this, however, it seemed most improbable that in their frail craft they could have floated so many miles. Captain Jamieson and his crew interested themselves much for these poor creatures, and persevered in their efforts to communicate with them by means of the slight vocabulary they had acquired in their voyagings; and though such communication was very imperfect, of course, yet it was plain some words were understood, and the unfortunate men were evidently pleased, and sought opportunities of mingling with those who could comprehend any portion, however small, of their language. With these imperfect means of knowledge, the best account Captain Jamieson could gather from them was, that they did come from Sil-li-ba-boo, distant as it was; that they left the land in their boat with some articles of food for a vessel in the offing, met a fresh breeze which carried them out to sea, and, by its continuance, prevented their return to land, and that they had been in the boat fifteen days when the *Southampton* picked them up. By direction of the Commodore, two of the surgeons of the squadron made a minute examination of these Sil-li-ba-boos, and reported in substance as follows:

"The Sil-li-ba-boos are of medium height and well set, with moderate muscular development, and, though possessed of no great strength, are active in movement. Destitute of the fatty tissue beneath the skin which generally gives roundness and fullness to the forms of northern races, the Sil-li-ba-boos have, from this deficiency, a sharp and angular contour that deprives them of all claim to physical beauty. Their features have the irregular expression of the negro, though their color resembles that of the mulatto. Their heads are small and round, with a large disproportionate development of the posterior part of the skull; their faces are oval, their foreheads moderately high, their eyes dark, but not very brilliant or intelligent, and their chins broad and massive. Their noses are long and flat, their lips thick and prominent, and their large mouths display strong well-formed teeth, which, however, are generally blackish, from the use of the betel nut. The skin is smooth, with a small supply of black coarse hair in those parts where it is usually found, except on the head; there it grows profusely and straight, but is worn short. Their limbs are lithe, and their hands and feet small. Their language is soft and agreeable to the ear, but, although it is supposed to be a derivation from the Malayan, it is not intelligible to those on board familiar with the ordinary dialect of the Malays. They are, however, believed to be of Malay origin, much modified by the effects of climate and accidental causes. The intelligence of the Sil-li-ba-boos is so far blunted as to place them within the category of the savage races, to which, in habits and social characteristics, they are closely allied."

One purpose of the visit of the *Macedonian* to Manilla was to hand over the Sil-li-ba-boos to the governor general of the Philippines, that they might be protected and sent home. The governor, with many expressions of gratitude for the kindness that had been shown toward these involuntary wanderers, received them; and we may indulge the hope that, long ere this, they have reached their native island, there to tell to their wondering countrymen the story of their providential preservation and marvellous adventures.

FRANCIS L. HAWKS,
Narrative of the Expedition of an American
Squadron to the China Seas and Japan

———◆———

An unwanted rescue

The Northern States in the American Civil War fought those of the south on the issue of slavery. At Charleston, West Virginia, in the summer of 1861, the officers of the Northern supply-ship *Rhode Island* had an opportunity of putting their beliefs into practice.

While at this place the Union officers experienced one of those serio-comic difficulties that were so common during the war. The officers of the *Rhode Island* had the kindest of dispositions, and held human slavery to be the most abominable of institutions. They entered upon their first active service in this war with a resolute determination to do all in their power to release the negro from his "horrible bondage." The first opportunity occurred off Charleston. Two negroes, about nineteen years of age, were innocently paddling along the shore in a canoe enjoying themselves thoroughly, and apparently unconscious of their danger in being rescued from their "horrible bondage." When they were discovered, a boat from the *Rhode Island* promptly pulled off with a marine guard, and after a vigorous effort it overtook the canoe and brought the negroes aboard.

So far everything had progressed as satisfactorily as the most ardent humanitarian could desire. But soon the question arose, "What shall we do with the negroes?" Dirty, and almost destitute of clothing, they were most persistent in obtruding themselves in just those parts of the ship where they were least wanted. In the first gush of kindliness for waifs rescued from "horrible bondage," the Union officers did not like to order their visitors around like the rest of the crew; and the result was that Sambo and Jupiter soon became intolerable nuisances, especially for the officers; for the negroes seemed to think no part of the ship too good for them, and that the persons of the officers were not too sacred to be handled. They took a fancy especially to the gold lace on the uniforms, and insisted on passing their horny hands over it. The nuisance became so great that after a consultation it was decided to send the "released slaves" aboard the *Roanoke*. But Flag-Officer Pendergrast had been on the station longer than the officers of the *Rhode Island*, and undoubtedly had had experience with the escaped slaves aboard his ship, so he promptly sent them back to the *Rhode Island* with instructions to land them under a flag of truce, or to keep them on board until they fell in with Flag-Officer Stringham, to whom they might be given up.

But here another difficulty arose. It was doubtful if the *Rhode Island* would fall in with the old commodore, short of several months, and the idea began to prevail among the *Rhode Island*'s officers that perhaps even Stringham might have so far satiated his desire to release the poor negro from his "horrible bondage," as to refuse to take them aboard of his ship and again send them back to the *Rhode Island*, with further indefinite instructions. The prospect of having the negroes aboard the ship several months, during the hottest part of the year, in a tropical climate, was too much for the intensely anti-slavery officers of the *Rhode Island*, and finally it was decided to land them under a flag of truce, and leave them—to their "horrible bondage." On no other occasion do we find the *Rhode Island*'s officers taking aboard fugitive negroes; still less sending armed boats out to capture them.

EDGAR STANTON MACLAY,
Reminiscences of the Old Navy

1914: The Fleet recalled

We dropped out under a soft air, which soon died away. We spent the whole mortal day drifting down to the Mewstone, and then, in that exasperating calm, the turn of the tide took us up again towards the breakwater. It was not till the fall of day that a breeze arose; I cannot remember from what quarter, but I think it was off the land—that is, from the north-east—but, at any rate, it served us; we could go eastward without having to beat, and we made out down the Sound. It was still light when we passed the Mewstone again. Through the last of evening and through all the darkness we ran along the coast to Devon for the Start.

I knew that the times were perilous, but I knew no more than any other man, in that odd week's lull before the storm, exactly how perilous they were. It was nearly a month, I think, since I had heard the priest read out, from those altar steps of Salisbury, prayers for the Archduke who had been murdered at Sarajevo.

When I had set out from Plymouth there was nothing but rumour, nothing certain. The Fleet had dispersed already some days past from the great review at Spithead, and was, as we were told, in the Atlantic at manœuvres. A night, a day, and now another night had passed; I had heard no news.

Nothing was further from my mind than war and armament as the sun rose on that glorious July morning, right out of a clean horizon, towards which the wind blew fresh and cool. It was a light but steady wind of morning that filled my sails as I sat at the tiller with a blanket about me, and laying her head to the north.

We had just rounded the Start at dawn. My companion went below to sleep. I watched, over the quarter, the Start Light flashing pale and white in the broadening day, and at last extinguished. Then the sun rose, as I have said. Immediately after its rising a sort of light haze filled the air to eastward. It was denser than it seemed to be, for it did not obscure the low disc of the sun, nor redden it, but, as you will read in a moment, it performed a mystery. The little ship slipped on, up past the Skerries Bank, and I could see far off the headland which bounds Dart Bay. There was no sail in sight. I was alone upon the sea; and the breeze neither freshening nor lowering, but giving a hearty line of course (along which we slipped, perhaps, five knots or six) made the water speak merrily upon the bows and along the run of our low sides. In this loneliness and content, as I sailed northward, I chanced to look after an hour's steering or so, eastward again towards the open sea—and then it was that there passed me the vision I shall remember for ever, or for so long as the longest life may last.

Like ghosts, like things themselves made of mist, there passed between me and the newly risen sun, a procession of great forms, all in line, hastening eastward. It was the Fleet recalled.

"Like ghosts . . . there passed between me and the newly-risen sun,
a procession of great forms, all in line, hastening eastward."
The mobilisation of the British Grand Fleet, 1914

The slight haze along that distant water had thickened, perhaps, imperceptibly; or perhaps the great speed of the men-of-war buried them too quickly in the distance. But, from whatever cause, this marvel was of short duration. It was seen for a moment, and in a moment it was gone.

Then I knew that war would come, and my mind was changed.

HILAIRE BELLOC,
The Cruise of the Nona

————◆————

MINESWEEPERS
1914

Dawn off the Foreland—the young flood making
  Jumbled and short and steep—
Black in the hollows and bright where it's breaking—
  Awkward water to sweep.
  "Mines reported in the fairway,
  Warn all traffic and detain.
  Sent up *Unity, Claribel, Assyrian, Stormcock*, and
    Golden Gain."

Noon off the Foreland—the first ebb making
  Lumpy and strong in the bight.
Boom after boom and the golf-hut shaking
  And the jackdaws wild with fright!
  "Mines located in the fairway,
  Boats now working up the chain,
  Sweepers—*Unity, Claribel, Assyrian, Stormcock*, and
    Golden Gain."

Dusk off the Foreland—the last light going
  And the traffic crowding through,
And five damned trawlers with their syreens blowing
  Heading the whole review!
  "Sweep completed in the fairway.
  No more mines remain.
  Sent back *Unity, Claribel, Assyrian, Stormcock*, and
    Golden Gain."

RUDYARD KIPLING

1918: Journey's end

2. The High Seas Fleet

In the early morning of 21st November, 1918, the light cruiser *Cardiff*, flying the flag of Rear-Admiral Alexander-Sinclair, stole quietly out of the Firth of Forth, on perhaps the most stirring mission a British warship has ever had to perform. She was to meet the German battle fleet, and lead it to a pre-arranged rendezvous with the British Commander-in-Chief. Shortly afterwards Beatty left harbour with the whole Grand Fleet, consisting of no less than thirteen squadrons, in two huge columns. The German ships were sighted about 8 A.M. Their fleet consisted of nine modern battleships, five battle cruisers, seven modern light cruisers, and forty-nine destroyers, all in single line ahead, with the *Cardiff* in the van. Forty miles west of May Island, the *Cardiff* led the German Fleet between the two British columns, approaching on an opposite course. As soon as they were in position, Beatty turned the Grand Fleet 180°, which placed him abeam of the German Flagship. This manœuvre, which was beautifully executed, brought the two fleets into three columns, with the Germans in the centre, all steering for the Forth. Describing the scene, Admiral Rodman, U.S.N., said the *Cardiff* reminded him of "the old farm in Kentucky, where many times he had seen a little child leading by the nose a herd of fearsome bullocks." In the early afternoon the German Fleet anchored off Aberlady Bay, while the Grand Fleet proceeded to its anchorage above the Forth Bridge. In the British Fleet the feeling was more of sober triumph than of jubilation. Everyone had good cause to remember the tough fighting qualities of the German warships, now mere impotent hulks with demoralised crews. As of old, the great traditions of the British fighting seamen had prevailed, not only in battle, but in the dull routine of keeping open the sea communications throughout a long, weary war. Adversity never dismayed them. Victory they took as a matter of course.

The officers and men of the Grand Fleet all knew how much they owed to Beatty's inspiration and leadership. While the ships, big and little, passed the Fleet Flagship, one by one, they gave vent to their pent-up feelings by cheering their Commander-in-

1917.   *George R.I.*

Admiral of the Fleet Sir David Beatty,
Commander-in-Chief of the British Grand Fleet,
with King George V, 1917

Chief as few men have ever been cheered before. But Beatty felt
that it was not to himself that thanks should be given, so in words
reminiscent of Nelson's signal after the battle of the Nile, he made
a general signal to the British Fleet: "It is my intention to hold
a service of thanksgiving at 6 P.M. today, for the victory which
Almighty God has vouchsafed to His Majesty's arms, and every
ship is recommended to do the same."

When the last ships had gone by, and the *Queen Elizabeth*
had secured to her buoy, Chatfield asked Beatty to address the
ship's company assembled on the quarter-deck. Beatty, knowing
that the men's thoughts were his own, expressed them in a very
few words. Then, as if wishing to escape from it all, he made for
the ladderway leading to his cabin. To the delight of the ship's
company he suddenly stopped, and with the familiar flash of the
eye and a smile on his lips, said: "Didn't I tell you they would
have to come out?"

The dramatic finale to this historic day had yet to be enacted.
At eleven o'clock Beatty had signalled to Admiral von Reuter:
"The German flag will be hauled down at sunset today, Thurs-
day, and will not be hoisted again without permission. 1104."

H.M.S. *Cardiff* leads the German High Seas Fleet
to surrender in the Firth of Forth, 1918.

Whether Beatty had the right to make such a signal has been questioned, but he was not concerned with legal niceties or the continental school of thought at such a moment. He would organise the surrender in his own way, and being still at war, he felt that it would be intolerable to have enemy ships flying their national flag in a British harbour. So, at dusk, as the sky reddened over the Scottish hills, and the buglers of the British Fleet sounded the call of "Sunset," the ensigns of the Imperial German Navy fluttered slowly down for the last time. And darkness closed like a curtain on the final act of this mighty drama of the sea.

REAR-ADMIRAL W. S. CHALMERS,
Life and Letters of David Beatty

H.M.S. *HERO*

Pale grey, her guns hooded, decks clear of all impediment,
Easily, between the swart tugs, she glides in the pale
    October sunshine:
It is Saturday afternoon, and the men are at football,
The wharves and the cobbled streets are silent by the slow
    river.

Smoothly, rounding the long bend, she glides to her place
    in history,
Past the grimed windows cracked and broken,
Past Swan Hunter's, Hawthorn Leslie's, Armstrong's,
Down to the North Sea, and trials, and her first commission.

Here is grace; and a job well done; built only for one end.
Women watch from the narrow doorways and give no sign,
Children stop playing by the wall and stare in silence
At gulls wheeling above the Tyne, or the ship passing.

MICHAEL ROBERTS

1945: Journey's end

3. The U-boats

The beaten foe emerged.

All over the broad Atlantic, wherever they had been working or lying hid, the U-boats surfaced, confessing the war's end. A few of them, prompted by determination or struck by guilt, scuttled or destroyed themselves, or ran for shelter, not knowing that there was none; but mostly they did what they had been told to do, mostly they hoisted their black surrender flags, and said where they were, and waited for orders.

They rose, dripping and silent, in the Irish Sea, and at the mouth of the Clyde, and off the Lizard in the English Channel, and at the top of the Minches where the tides raced: they rose near Iceland, where *Compass Rose* was sunk, and off the northwest tip of Ireland, and close to the Faroes, and on the Gibraltar run where the sunk ships lay so thick, and near St. John's and Halifax, and in the deep of the Atlantic, with three thousand fathoms of water beneath their keel.

They surfaced in secret places, betraying themselves and their frustrated plans: they rose within sight of land, they rose far away in mortal waters where, on the map of the battle, the crosses that were sunken ships were etched so many and so close that the ink ran together. They surfaced above their handiwork, in hatred or in fear: sometimes snarling their continued rage, sometimes accepting thankfully a truce they had never offered to other ships, other sailors.

They rose, and lay wherever they were on the battlefield, waiting for the victors to claim their victory. . . .

So their battle ended, and so, all over the Atlantic, the fighting died—a strangely tame finish, after five-and-a-half years of bitter struggle. There was no eleventh-hour, death-or-glory assault on shipping, no individual attempt at piracy after the surrender date: the vicious war petered out in bubbles, blown tanks, a sulky yielding, and the laconic order: "Follow me." But no anti-climax, no quiet end, could obscure the triumph and the pride inherent in this victory, with its huge cost—30,000 seamen killed, 3,000 ships sent to the bottom in this one ocean—and its huge toll of 780 U-boats sunk, to even the balance.

May 1945. The U-boat U.1009 surrenders
to the British frigate *Byron*.

It would live in history, because of its length and its unremit-
ting ferocity: it would live in men's minds for what it did to themselves and to their friends, and to the ships they often loved. Above
all, it would live in naval tradition, and become legend, because of
its crucial service to an island at war, its price in sailors' lives, and
its golden prize—the uncut lifeline to the sustaining outer world.

NICHOLAS MONSARRAT,
The Cruel Sea

4. Japan

General MacArthur established temporary headquarters in the
Yokohama customhouse and various Japanese agencies located
themselves nearby. Here the final arrangements were made for the
formal signing of the instrument of surrender, now set for 0900
September 2. It was intended that it be done in a frame of impres-

sive dignity, accompanied by an appropriate display of Allied air and sea power. General MacArthur, having obtained the prior occupation of Japan proper, gracefully yielded to Admiral Nimitz the choice of place. Battleship *Missouri* (Captain S. S. Murray), which was named for President Truman's native state and sponsored by his daughter Margaret, and which had been Admiral Halsey's flagship during the last weeks of the war, became the scene of the ceremony. She anchored in Tokyo Bay, about four and a half miles NE ½ E from Commodore Perry's second anchorage. On a bulkhead overlooking the surrender ceremony was displayed the 31-starred flag that Perry carried into Tokyo Bay in 1853. In contrast to the tiny fleet that had opened Japan 92 years earlier, there were now anchored in Tokyo Bay 258 warships of all types from battleship to the smallest beaching craft, representing the Allied nations which had been at war with Japan. Most of the aircraft carriers remained outside the bay in order to launch planes at the appropriate moment of this "V-J Day."

Sunday, 2 September, dawned with scattered clouds that dissipated during the morning. *Missouri* was especially rigged for the occasion. On the admiral's veranda deck on the starboard side was set up an ordinary mess table covered with a green baize cloth. There the surrender documents, in English and Japanese, were laid out ready for signature. At Morning Colors the flag that had flown over the Capitol in Washington on 7 December 1941 was raised on the battleship's flagstaff. It had also been displayed at Casablanca, Rome, and Berlin, and would rise again over the American Embassy in Tokyo when General MacArthur moved in, a few days later.

Visitors began to arrive on board shortly after seven. Destroyer *Buchanan* closed the starboard side at 0803 to deliver high-ranking officers and Allied representatives. When Fleet Admiral Nimitz came on board at 0805, his five-starred flag was broken at the main, Admiral Halsey in the meantime having shifted his four-starred flag to *Iowa*. General of the Army Douglas MacArthur came up *Missouri*'s starboard gangway from destroyer *Nicholas* at 0843, to be received by Admirals Nimitz and Halsey and a full set of sideboys. His personal flag was promptly broken alongside that of Admiral Nimitz. The General and the two Admirals went directly to flag cabin.

At 0856 the Japanese delegation, lifted from Yokohama in destroyer *Lansdowne*, mounted the starboard gangway. They were headed by the Foreign Minister, Mamoru Shigemitsu, who, having lost a leg to an assassin's bomb many years before, negotiated the ladder with difficulty. He was followed by General Yoshijiro Umezu, chief of the Army general staff, to sign on behalf of Imperial General Headquarters. It was reported that the General, who had consistently opposed surrender, turned white with rage when he learned that he was being considered for this part and threatened to commit hara-kiri; but after personal intervention by the Emperor he consented to carry it out. The rest of the party consisted of three representatives each from the Foreign Office, the Army and the Navy. The civilians were in formal morning dress with top hats, in contrast to the ill-fitting uniforms of the military members and to the khaki uniforms with open-necked shirts worn by the United States Navy and Army officers. Sideboys were stationed and the Japanese delegation were piped on board. As they arrived on deck, their faces expressing no emotion, complete silence fell over the assembled multitude.

Immediately abaft the table on which the documents lay stood representatives of the Allied Nations to sign the surrender for their respective governments, and observers from their armed services. On their right and under *Missouri*'s No. 2 turret were a score of flag and general officers of the United States who had taken a leading part in the war against Japan. Cameramen were everywhere and bluejackets manned every vantage point from which to view the proceedings.

The atmosphere was frigid. The Japanese, performing an act unprecedented in their country's history, preserved their dignity. Toshikazu Kase, a member of the Foreign Office who noted the significance of the miniature rising-sun flags painted on the wing of *Missouri*'s bridge, felt that the delegation was "subjected to the torture of the pillory. A million eyes seemed to beat on us with the million shafts of a rattling storm of arrows barbed with fire." As they stood immobile, facing the table, in position indicated by an aide, the ship's chaplain spoke an invocation over the loud-speaker system, and was followed by "The Star-Spangled Banner" played from a disc. A Russian photographer tried to secure a position close to the table and was firmly removed to his proper place.

After three or four minutes had elapsed, General MacArthur appeared with Admirals Nimitz and Halsey. The General took his place before the microphones to open the ceremony. At his side were Lieutenant General Jonathan M. Wainwright USA, who had surrendered the Philippines in 1942, and Lieutenant General Sir Arthur E. Percival, who had surrendered Singapore the same year. Both had been flown from prison camps in Manchuria. General MacArthur made a short speech stating the purpose of the occasion, concluding with a ringing expression of hope for the future:—

It is my earnest hope—indeed the hope of all mankind—that from this solemn occasion a better world shall emerge out of the blood and carnage of the past, a world founded upon faith and understanding, a world dedicated to the dignity of man and the fulfillment of his most cherished wish for freedom, tolerance and justice.

Mr. Kase, at least, was profoundly moved by the General's speech. It transformed the battleship's quarterdeck, he recorded, "into an altar of peace."

The General now pointed to a chair at the other side of the table, and motioned to the Japanese delegates to come forward and sign. Mr. Shigemitsu fumbled with his hat, gloves and cane and seemed puzzled as to which paper he was supposed to sign. It was a tense moment; some of the onlookers suspected the Foreign Minister of stalling, but what really bothered him was pain from his ill-fitting artificial leg. MacArthur's voice punctuated the dead silence with a crisp order to his chief of staff, "Sutherland, show him where to sign." Sutherland did, and Shigemitsu signed the instrument of surrender at 0904, thus officially ending the war, which had lasted exactly 1364 days, 5 hours and 44 minutes. He was immediately followed as signatory by General Umezu.

General of the Army Douglas MacArthur then signed the acceptance of the surrender for all Allied powers. Next, Fleet Admiral Nimitz, with Admiral Halsey and Rear Admiral Forrest Sherman as supporters, signed for the United States. Then, in order, came General Hsu Yung-chang for China, Admiral Sir Bruce Fraser RN for the United Kingdom, Lieutenant General Derevyanko for the Soviet Union, General Sir Thomas Blamey for Australia, Colonel Moore-Gosgrove for Canada, General Jacques LeClerc for France, Admiral Helfrich for the Netherlands, and Air Vice Marshal Isitt for New Zealand.

After all had signed, General MacArthur spoke a final word:—

"Let us pray that peace be now restored to the world and that God will preserve it always. These proceedings are now closed."

In this firm and stern setting, Japan acknowledged her defeat in a war forced upon her by an ambitious and reckless military clique. The ceremony was conducted in an atmosphere of cold formality; no pageantry, no roll of drums, no handing over of swords or colors, not even a handshake; nothing to recall historic surrenders such as those of Saratoga, Yorktown and Appomattox. Nevertheless, the atmosphere was charged with emotion. Vice Admiral John S. McCain, who had only four more days to live, thought that the mask behind which the Japanese delegation hid their feelings concealed a spirit of non-compliance or revenge; he could not have been more wrong. Admiral Halsey's feeling was one of undisguised elation. "If ever a day demanded champagne, this was it," he recorded; but when, after the ceremony, the Allied representatives flocked into flag cabin he had nothing to offer but coffee and doughnuts. General MacArthur and Admiral Nimitz entertained a feeling of compassion toward the fallen foe; Nimitz revoked an order from Halsey to the C.O. of destroyer *Lansdowne* not to offer coffee, cigarettes or other courtesies to the Japanese delegation. The Japanese delegates received customary honors as they approached the gangway in order to symbolize the fact that they were no longer enemies.

As the formalities came to a close at 0925, the sun broke through, and a flight of 450 carrier aircraft, together with several hundred of the Army Air Force, swept over *Missouri* and her sister ships.

One famous flag officer of the Pacific Fleet, Vice Admiral Theodore S. Wilkinson, was too busy to attend the surrender, since as Commander III Amphibious Force he was responsible for landing the 1st Cavalry Division while the ceremony was going on. Owing to this circumstance we have a good description of what happened in Tokyo Bay outside the *Missouri* in a letter from the Admiral to his wife, written that evening on board his flagship *Mount Olympus*.

We stood in after an all-night approach through several islands, in a rainy night, in a long column of thirty-odd transports. We reached the lower entrance . . . just after dawn and filed slowly up the harbor, to avoid fouling four destroyers reported to be bringing out visitors (including the Japs) to the surrender party. As we approached last night I got a general message from Bill Halsey that all flag officers not engaged in operations were invited to the ceremony at 9, to be aboard by 8:15. I couldn't leave my flock, but I lowered a fast boat and sent Dick Byrd on ahead at 6. Our column, however, passed during the ceremony, and should have made an impressive 10-mile long backdrop. . . .

We anchored our large squadron off Yokohama and sent our boats scurrying in, filled with men. By shortly after noon all our "assault" troops were landed, though fortunately without the usual accompaniment of an assault, and the reserve troops went ashore, followed by the usual tedious and lengthy unloading of supplies, which we hope to complete in two days.

In the afternoon I went down the harbor to see Bill Halsey and the old Third Fleet crowd; they were most cordial. He promptly took me over to a very impressive sunset ceremony Admiral Fraser was having in the *Duke of York*. Massed bands of all the British ships played splendid martial music and a hymn. The flags of all the signatory Allies were flying from the signal yards, and all were slowly lowered in unison during the sunset hymn.

The hymn was John Ellerton's "The Day Thou Gavest, Lord, Is Ended."

> The day thou gavest, Lord, is ended,
>   The darkness falls at thy behest;
> To thee our morning hymns ascended,
>   Thy praise shall sanctify our rest.
>
> So be it, Lord; thy throne shall never,
>   Like earth's proud empires, pass away:
> Thy kingdom stands, and grows for ever,
>   Till all thy creatures own thy sway.

Nothing could have been more appropriate to the occasion than this Sunday evening hymn to the "Author of peace and lover of concord." The familiar words and music, which floated over the now calm waters of the Bay to American bluejackets, touched the mystic chords of memory and sentiment, reminding all hands of the faith that had sustained them through travail and sacrifice. It brought sailors back to base and made them feel that their Navy had achieved something more than a military victory.

They were right. If victory over Japan meant anything beyond a change in the balance of power, it meant that eternal values and

immutable principles, which had come down to us from ancient
Hellas, had been reaffirmed and reestablished. Often these principles are broken, often these values are lost to sight when people
are struggling for survival; but to them man must return, and
does return, in order to enjoy his Creator's greatest gifts—life,
liberty and the pursuit of happiness.

SAMUEL ELIOT MORRISON,
*A History of United States
Naval Operations in World War II*

———◆———

The new navy

In 1959, the nuclear-powered submarine U.S.S. *Skate* made
history by surfacing at the North Pole. Here her commander,
James Calvert, describes the last leg of a perilous journey.

After supper we submerged and once more headed for the Pole,
now less than 250 miles away. A night of travel under the ice
covered the distance and on the morning of the seventeenth we
were nearing our destination.

When we reached the Pole we would start a slow crisscrossing
search of the immediate vicinity. If nothing showed up at first, we
would be patient and keep searching. The ice cover was constantly
shifting, and the new ice coming over might be better. Assuming
the ice was moving at 2½ miles a day (an average speed), in
twenty-four hours 5000 yards of ice would drift over the North
Pole. In that stretch we might be able to find what we wanted.

The test would not be without military value. After we returned from the Arctic in the fall of 1958, many senior officers
wanted to know what our chances were of surfacing at a *given*
geographic location in the Arctic—not a place like Drift Station
Alfa, which shifted with the ice, but an assigned latitude and
longitude. Well, we would see.

At the breakfast table the talk was, as usual, of ice. We began
discussing the clumsiness of our name for these areas of thin ice

which were so vital to us. Actually they were newly frozen leads but that seemed an awkward way to put it. What we needed was a new name. Many were suggested but none seemed to convey the idea. Then Dr. Lyon, who had heard me discussing what they looked like through the periscope, said, "Why don't you just call them skylights?"

And that's what they resembled. They were like a stretch of blue-green translucent glass in an otherwise black ceiling. The places where the ice was thin enough to let in the light to the dark sea below were the places we were looking for to reach the light and air above. *Skylights* they would be.

But we found no skylights as we approached the Pole. We cruised slowly, adjusting our course carefully according to the instructions of Bill Layman. Zane Sandusky and Bob Wadell methodically plotted the readings from their green tubes on reams of orange graph paper. Slowly but surely, the submarine was delicately conned into the spot where every direction is south. The *Skate* had returned to the Pole.

I made a brief announcement to the crew, reminding them of something most of them already knew—that almost exactly fifty years ago (it had been April 6, 1909) Robert Peary had first reached the Pole. How different his circumstances from ours! Accompanied by four Eskimos and his steward, Matt Henson, Peary had had no scientific marvels to guide him to his goal. He measured distance traveled with a crude wheel attached to one of the sledges. His determination of position was by observation of the sun—and this depended partially on a timepiece that had gone for weeks without an accurate check. But Peary had known what he was about. After he had reached the Pole, according to his best navigation, he spent thirty hours marching and countermarching around the general area to make certain he had achieved his goal. He had spent twenty years of his life in its quest and had no desire to miss it by a few miles through miscalculation. When he was certain he had located the Pole as well as his limited equipment would allow, he planted his flags and took his pictures. And then, in a few hours, the drifting ice of the Arctic had carried his flags away from the Pole. The shifting signs of fame!

Our task still lay ahead of us. Thanks to the marvels of inertial navigation, we had reached the Pole with little difficulty. Reaching the surface would be a different matter—that would be up to us.

There was not a sign of a skylight. With the ship stopped 200 feet under the sea directly at the North Pole, I raised the periscope in the hope of seeing something. But the sea was black—absolutely and completely. Not the faintest glimmer shone through the ice above; we were sealed in.

We began our crisscross search in the immediate area, proceeding at very slow speed and using the periscope as well as the ice detector and the television. No luck.

Here at the Pole the sun would still be below the horizon; if the overcast were as heavy as the day before, there wouldn't be much light anyway. Well, I thought, we'd just have to wait and see. Several hours went by with no results.

And then we saw it. At first it was just a faint glimmer of emerald green, visible only through the periscope. It looked too small for the ship, but it was worth investigating. Carefully we maneuvered the *Skate* under it and looked at our ice detector. The trace showed thin ice.

This was a different game from that of last summer, when we made long leisurely loops under lakes, taking care to get ourselves safely in the middle of a relatively large piece of open water. Here, trying to surface at a pre-chosen spot in winter, we had to be satisfied with a patch of thin ice scarcely large enough to hold us. No need to maneuver the ship beneath it to plot its shape—it was so small we could see the whole area at a glance through the periscope, outlined sharply by the black floes around it. At the same time, we would simply not have had the courage or skill to try such a dangerous and delicate task without the confidence that had come of last summer's experience.

We drifted up to 100 feet. The skylight was dog-legged in shape and treacherously small; we had never attempted anything like this. However, I knew that if we could once break through the ice above us the *Skate* would be held as tightly as in a vise. There would be no danger of damage from drifting into the sides of the small opening.

"Stand by to hit the ice," I said. "Bring her up."

We had barely started up again when Al Kelln, standing at the ice detector, called out nervously, "Heavy ice overhead—better than twelve feet!"

I could see what had happened. The ice was moving, and the skylight was simply drifting away from the submarine.

"Flood her down, Guy!" I said. Reluctantly the three-thousand-ton ship reversed her course and began to sink slowly back into the black depths. Patiently we realigned the ship under the small opening, twisting first one way and then the other with the propellers.

The second try was no better than the first; again we drifted out from under the tiny skylight.

"We'd better try an offset," said Bill. He quickly calculated how far to the side we should position ourselves in order to come up from 100 feet and find ourselves in the right position. Painstakingly the *Skate* was maneuvered into position.

This time, as we started upward, Kelln told us that we had heavy ice overhead. Not a very comfortable feeling, with the top of the sail only 50 feet or so below the ice, but we could only count on the drift to carry us into position.

As we rose, I was forced to lower the periscope. Now we were blind except for the television camera, which showed only the fuzzy edge of the heavy ice.

Now the top of the sail was only 25 feet under the heavy ice. "Heavy ice, still heavy ice," Kelln reported, the strain apparent in his voice. How much longer can we wait?

"Flood her down—emergency!" I snapped. We could wait no longer. The wave of air pressure slapped into my ears as Shaffer opened the vent of the negative tank and sent tons of water cascading into the ship to bring her down. Quickly we fell away from the ominous ice cliffs.

"Blow negative to the mark," Shaffer ordered, trying to regain control of the now swiftly falling *Skate*. The roar of high-pressure air filled the room.

"Blow secured; negative at the mark," reported Chief Dornberg at his side.

"Shut the flood, vent negative, pump from auxiliaries to sea," said Guy, watching his gauges through narrowed eyes.

Slowly our downward momentum slackened and finally, far deeper than we had intended to go, we were once more motionless.

Beads of perspiration were standing out on my brow and I could sense the feeling of strain that ran through the ship. With grim determination, we started all over again.

"There are heavy pressure ridges on either side of this opening except at the dog-leg corner," reported Al Kelln. "I've had a chance to catch them on the ice detector."

Once more Bill Layman calculated the offset required, this time allowing for a little less drift.

I attempted to set the ship near the corner of the dog-leg to avoid the ridges Al had mentioned. The whir of the trimming pump announced our slow ascent.

"Heavy ice, still heavy ice," intoned Kelln like the voice of doom. Time for the periscope to go down.

"Thin ice! There she is! Looks good!" exclaimed Al.

The television screen showed us very close. We braced ourselves. With a sickening lurch we hit and broke through.

"Don't let her drop out, Guy," I warned. Again I had the feeling of having a tenuous foothold at the top of an impossible peak.

Shaffer put a puff of air into the ballast tanks; we seemed to be maintaining our position. I raised the periscope on the chance of seeing something; I was most reluctant to surface blind when I knew heavy pressure ridges were close by.

The periscope went up, but revealed nothing but a field of blank white. Frozen.

I glanced at the diving instruments; we were holding our position well. If we could break through, we would make history.

"Stand by to surface at the Pole," I announced over the speaker system.

Swiftly preparations were made, and Shaffer turned to me with a smile, "Ready to surface," he said, "at the Pole!"

Slowly we blew the tanks and the *Skate* moved reluctantly upward. It was apparent we were under heavier ice here than any we had experienced before. After what seemed an eternity of delay, the upper hatch was far enough above the ice to be opened. Our tenuous foothold was becoming more firm.

"Open the hatch!" I shouted, and raced up the ladder. The ice we had broken was so heavy that it had not fallen into the bridge but had split and fallen outside. I leaped to the bridge and was struck by the first heavy wind I had ever experienced in the Arctic. It howled and swirled across the open bridge, carrying stinging snow particles which cut like flying sand. Heavy gray clouds hung in the sky; the impression was of a dark and stormy twilight about to fade into night.

We had broken through almost exactly at the bend of the dog-leg. The lead was narrow and heavily hummocked on either side, wandering into the blowing snow like a meandering creek for the quarter of a mile or so I could see. These hummocks were the tallest we had yet seen in the Arctic—we later estimated their height at 18 feet.

Although we were closer to one side of the narrow lead than I would have liked, we seemed to have a clear path in which to surface the rest of the way. Only our sail protruded from the ice, but the ship was held tightly—there was no chance of drifting.

The phones were rigged and the tanks blown with high-pressure air. With loud cracks that sounded like gunshots, the deck began to break through. This lead had frozen with many large chunks of heavier ice floating in it. They were now caught in the matrix of the thinner ice like almonds in chocolate.

Finally the *Skate* lay on the surface—the first ship in history to sit at the very top of the world. In every direction—ahead, astern, to port, to starboard—was south. The planet turned ponderously beneath us. When the sun rose on March 19, just two days away, it would swing around the horizon for twenty-four hours in a perpetual sunrise.

The *Skate* had arrived at her goal. Last summer's attainment of the Pole had brought little satisfaction because we had been forced to remain submerged where, for all the difference it made to us, we could have been anywhere else in the oceans of the world. Only our instruments had told us we were there.

But this—with its blowing snow and lowering sky—this was the North Pole. The lodestone of the Arctic, which had lured brave men to their deaths for over a century and which had even been denied to the indomitable Nansen, had fallen to the modern submarine.

JAMES CALVERT,
Surface at the Pole

SMALL

BOATS

Sailing in small boats across the Atlantic or around the world, either alone or with one or two companions, is now commonplace; and it is surprising to recall that it is only fifteen years since the late Sir Francis Chichester first blazed the way in *Gypsy Moth IV*, to the wonder and admiration of the world.

There would seem to be a book in almost every small boat sailor who ventures beyond the Azores, if for no other reason than that advance royalties are often needed to pay for the voyage. But that royalties should be so readily advanced is itself evidence for the continuing popularity of such books. Among literally scores of accounts of modern small boat voyages, I have selected three: Robert Manry's on board *Tinkerbelle*, because of the vivid descriptions of his hallucinations; Ann Davison on *Reliance*, because her story is both terrible and profoundly moving; and Dougal Robertson's adventures in a dinghy, because not only are he and his family lucky to be alive, but he has some kind things to say about the perennially bewildering Japanese.

Yet however much one admires these modern small-boat sailors, there is one who towers above them all. This is the American Captain Joshua Slocum, who more than eighty years ago at the age of fifty-one, long before it became fashionable or such niceties as the self-steering gear were invented, took his little sloop *Spray* out of Boston, Massachusetts, sailed her round the world, and then wrote a classic about it, *Sailing Alone Around the World*. As Arthur Ransome said of him, he was "confident, serene, modest and blessed with the most infectious of all gifts, an immense power of enjoyment. He makes no fuss about anything but relishes each moment as it comes and shares his gusto with the reader."

1. *Spray*

I had resolved on a voyage around the world, and as the wind on the morning of April 24, 1895, was fair, at noon I weighed anchor, set sail, and filled away from Boston, where the *Spray* had been moored snugly all winter. The twelve-o'clock whistles were blowing just as the sloop shot ahead under full sail. A short board was made up the harbour on the port tack, then coming about she stood seaward, with her boom well off to port, and swung past the ferries with lively heels. A photographer on the outer pier at East Boston got a picture of her as she swept by, her flag at the peak throwing its folds clear. A thrilling pulse beat high in me. My step was light on deck in the crisp air. I felt that there could be no turning back, and that I was engaging in an adventure the meaning of which I thoroughly understood. I had taken little advice from anyone, for I had a right to my own opinions in matters pertaining to the sea. That the best of sailors might do worse than even I alone was borne in upon me not a league from Boston docks, where a great steamship, fully manned, officered, and piloted, lay stranded and broken. This was the *Venetian*. She was broken completely in two over a ledge. So in the first hour of my lone voyage I had proof that the *Spray* could at least do better than this full-handed steamship, for I was already farther on my voyage than she. "Take warning, *Spray*, and have a care," I uttered aloud to my bark, passing fairylike silently down the bay.

The wind freshened, and the *Spray* rounded Deer Island light at the rate of seven knots.

Passing it, she squared away direct for Gloucester to procure there some fishermen's stores. Waves dancing joyously across Massachusetts Bay met her coming out of the harbour to dash them into myriads of sparkling gems that hung about her at every surge. The day was perfect, the sunlight clear and strong. Every particle of water thrown into the air became a gem, and the *Spray*, bounding ahead, snatched necklace after necklace from the sea, and as often threw them away. We have all seen miniature rainbows about a ship's prow, but the *Spray* flung out a bow of her own that day, such as I had never seen before. Her good angel had embarked on the voyage; I so read it in the sea.

Bold Nahant was soon abeam, then Marblehead was put astern. Other vessels were outward bound, but none of them passed the *Spray* flying along on her course. I heard the clanking of the dismal bell on Norman's Woe as we went by; and the reef where the schooner *Hesperus* struck I passed close aboard. The "bones" of a wreck tossed up lay bleaching on the shore abreast. The wind still freshening, I settled the throat of the mainsail to ease the sloop's helm, but I could hardly hold her before it with the whole mainsail set. A schooner ahead of me lowered all sail and ran into port under bare poles, the wind being fair. As the *Spray* brushed by the stranger, I saw that some of his sails were gone, and much broken canvas hung in his rigging, from the effects of a squall.

I made for the cove, a lovely branch of Gloucester's fine harbour, again to look the *Spray* over and again to weigh the voyage, and my feelings, and all that. The bay was feather-white as my little vessel tore in, smothered in foam. It was my first experience of coming into port alone, with a craft of any size, and in among shipping. Old fishermen ran down to the wharf for which the *Spray* was heading, apparently intent upon braining herself there. I hardly know how a calamity was averted, but with my heart in my mouth, almost, I let go the wheel, stepped quickly forward, and downed the jib. The sloop naturally rounded in the wind, and just ranging ahead, laid her cheek against a mooring-pile at the windward corner of the wharf, so quietly, after all, that she would not have broken an egg. Very leisurely I passed a rope around the post, and she was moored.

*   *   *

The weather was mild on the day of my departure from Gloucester. On the point ahead, as the *Spray* stood out of the cove, was a lively picture, for the front of a tall factory was a flutter of handkerchiefs and caps. Pretty faces peered out of the windows from the top to the bottom of the building, all smiling *bon voyage*. Some hailed me to know where away and why alone. Why? When I made as if to stand in, a hundred pairs of arms reached out, and said come, but the shore was dangerous! The sloop worked out of the bay against a light southwest wind, and about noon squared

away off Eastern Point, receiving at the same time a hearty salute
—the last of many kindnesses to her at Gloucester. The wind
freshened off the point and, skipping along smoothly, the *Spray*
was soon off Thatcher's Island lights. Thence shaping her course
east, by compass, to go north of Cashes Ledge and the Amen
Rocks, I sat and considered the matter all over again, and asked
myself once more whether it were best to sail beyond the ledge
and rocks at all. I had only said that I would sail around the world
in the *Spray*, "dangers of the sea excepted," but I must have said
it very much in earnest. The "charter-party" with myself seemed
to bind me, and so I sailed on. Toward night I hauled the sloop
to the wind, and baiting a hook, sounded for bottom-fish, in thirty
fathoms of water, on the edge of Cashes Ledge. With fair success
I hauled till dark, landing on deck three cod and two haddocks,
one hake, and, best of all, a small halibut, all plump and spry.
This, I thought, would be the place to take in a good stock of provisions above what I already had; so I put out a sea-anchor that
would hold her head to windward. The current being southwest,
against the wind, I felt quite sure I would find the *Spray* still on
the bank or near it in the morning. Then "stradding" the cable
and putting my great lantern in the rigging I lay down, for the
first time at sea alone, not to sleep, but to doze and to dream.

I had read somewhere of a fishing-schooner hooking her anchor into a whale, and being towed a long way and at great speed.
This was exactly what happened to the *Spray*—in my dream! I
could not shake it off entirely when I awoke and found that it was
the wind blowing and the heavy sea now running that had disturbed my short rest. A scud was flying across the moon. A storm
was brewing; indeed, it was already stormy. I reefed the sails,
then hauled in my sea-anchor, and setting what canvas the sloop
could carry, headed her away for Monhegan light, which she
made before daylight on the morning of the 8th. The wind being
free, I ran on into Round Pond harbour, which is a little port east
from Pemaquid. Here I rested a day while the wind rattled among
the pine-trees on shore. But the following day was fine enough,
and I put to sea, first writing to my log from Cape Ann, not omit-
ting a full account of my adventure with the whale.

*   *   *

I now stowed all my goods securely, for the boisterous Atlantic was before me, and I sent the top mast down, knowing that the *Spray* would be the wholesomer with it on deck. Then I gave the lanyards a pull and hitched them afresh, and saw that the gammon was secure, also that the boat was lashed, for even in summer one may meet with bad weather in the crossing.

In fact, many weeks of bad weather had prevailed. On July 1, however, after a rude gale, the wind came out nor'west and clear, propitious for a good run. On the following day, the head sea having gone down, I sailed from Yarmouth, and let go my last hold on America. The log of my first day on the Atlantic in the *Spray* reads briefly: "9.30 A.M. sailed from Yarmouth. 4.30 P.M. passed Cape Sable; distance, three cables from the land. The sloop making eight knots. Fresh breeze N.W." Before the sun went down I was taking my supper of strawberries and tea in smooth water under the lee of the east-coast land, along which the *Spray* was now leisurely skirting.

At noon on July 3 Ironbound Island was abeam. The *Spray* was again at her best. A large schooner came out of Liverpool, Nova Scotia, this morning, steering eastward. The *Spray* put her hull down astern in five hours. At 6.45 P.M. I was in close under Chebucto Head light, near Halifax harbour. I set my flag and squared away, taking my departure from George's Island before dark to sail east of Sable Island. There are many beacon lights along the coast. Sambro, the Rock of Lamentations, carries a noble light, which, however, the liner *Atlantic*, on the night of her terrible disaster, did not see. I watched light after light sink astern as I sailed into the unbounded sea, till Sambro, the last of them all, was below the horizon. The *Spray* was then alone, and sailing on, she held her course. July 4, at 6 A.M. I put in double reefs, and at 8.30 A.M. turned out all reefs. At 9.40 P.M. I raised the sheen only of the light on the west end of Sable Island, which may also be called the Island of Tragedies. The fog, which till this moment had held off, now lowered over the sea like a pall. I was in a world of fog, shut off from the universe. I did not see any more of the light. By the lead, which I cast often, I found that a little after midnight I was passing the east point of the island, and should soon be clear of dangers of land and shoals. The wind was holding free, though it was from the foggy point, south south-west. It is said that within a few years Sable Island has been reduced from forty miles in length to twenty, and that of three lighthouses built on it since 1880, two have been washed away and the third will soon be engulfed.

On the evening of July 5 the *Spray*, after having steered all day over a lumpy sea, took it into her head to go without the helmsman's aid. I had been steering southeast by south, but the wind hauling forward a bit, she dropped into a smooth lane, heading southeast, and making about eight knots her very best work. I crowded on sail to cross the track of the liners without loss of time, and to reach as soon as possible the friendly Gulf Stream. The fog lifting before night, I was afforded a look at the sun just as it was touching the sea. I watched it go down and out of sight. Then I turned my face eastward, and there, apparently at the very end of the bowsprit, was the smiling full moon rising out of the sea. Neptune himself coming over the bows could not have startled me more. "Good evening, sir," I cried; "I'm glad to see you." Many a long talk since then I have had with the man in the moon; he had my confidence on the voyage.

About midnight the fog shut down again denser than ever before. One could almost "stand on it." It continued so for a number of days, the wind increasing to a gale. The waves rose high, but I had a good ship. Still, in the dismal fog I felt myself drifting into loneliness, an insect on a straw in the midst of the elements. I lashed the helm, and my vessel held her course, and while she sailed I slept.

During these days a feeling of awe crept over me. My memory worked with startling power. The ominous, the insignificant, the great, the small, the wonderful, the commonplace—all appeared before my mental vision in magical succession. Pages of my history were recalled which had been so long forgotten that they seemed to belong to a previous existence. I heard all the voices of the past laughing, crying, telling what I had heard them tell in many corners of the earth.

The loneliness of my state wore off when the gale was high and I found much work to do. When fine weather returned, then came the sense of solitude, which I could not shake off. I used my voice often, at first giving some order about the affairs of a ship, for I had been told that from disuse I should lose my speech. At the meridian altitude of the sun I called aloud, "Eight bells," after the custom on a ship at sea. Again from my cabin I cried to an imaginary man at the helm, "How does she head there?" and again, "Is she on her course?" But getting no reply, I was reminded the more palpably of my condition. My voice sounded hollow on the empty air, and I dropped the practice. However, it was not long before the thought came to me that when I was a lad I used to sing; why not try that now, where it would disturb no one? My musical talent had never bred envy in others, but out on the Atlantic, to realize what it meant, you should have heard me sing. You should have seen the porpoises leap when I pitched my voice for the waves and the sea and all that was in it. Old turtles, with large eyes, poked their heads up out of the sea as I sang "Johnny Boker," and "We'll Pay Darby Doyl for his Boots," and the like. But the porpoises were, on the whole, vastly more appreciative than the turtles; they jumped a deal higher. One day when I was humming a favourite chant, I think it was "Babylon's a-Fallin," a porpoise jumped higher than the bowsprit. Had the *Spray* been going a little faster she would have scooped him in. The sea-birds sailed around rather shy.

July 10, eight days at sea, the *Spray* was twelve hundred miles east of Cape Sable. One hundred and fifty miles a day for so small a vessel must be considered good sailing. It was the greatest run the *Spray* ever made before or since in so few days. On the evening of July 14, in better humour than ever before, all hands cried, "Sail ho!" The sail was a barkantine, three points on the weather bow, hull down. Then came the night. My ship was sailing along now without attention to the helm. The wind was south; she was heading east. Her sails were trimmed like the sail of the nautilus. They drew steadily all night. I went frequently on deck, but found all well. A merry breeze kept on from the south. Early in the morning of the 15th the *Spray* was close aboard the stranger, which proved to be *La Vaguisa* of Vigo, twenty-three days from Philadelphia, bound for Vigo. A lookout from his masthead had spied the *Spray* the evening before. The captain, when I came near enough, threw a line to me and sent a bottle of wine across slung by the neck, and very good wine it was. He also sent his card, which bore the name of Juan Gantes. I think he was a good man, as Spaniards go. But when I asked him to report me "all well" (the *Spray* passing him in a lively manner), he hauled his shoulders much above his head; and when his mate, who knew of my expedition, told him that I was alone, he crossed himself and made for his cabin. I did not see him again. By sundown he was as far astern as he had been ahead the evening before.

There was now less and less monotony. On July 16 the wind was northwest and clear, the sea smooth, and a large bark, hull down, came in sight on the lee bow, and at 2.30 P.M. I spoke to the stranger. She was the bark *Java* of Glasgow, from Peru for Queenstown for orders. Her old captain was bearish, but I met a bear once in Alaska that looked pleasanter. At least, the bear seemed pleased to meet me, but this grizzly old man! Well, I suppose my hail disturbed his siesta, and my little sloop passing his great ship had somewhat the effect on him that a red rag has upon a bull. I had the advantage over heavy ships, by long odds, in the light winds of this and the two previous days. The wind was light; his ship was heavy and foul, making poor headway, while the *Spray*, with a great mainsail bellying even to light winds, was just skipping along as nimbly as one could wish. "How long has it been calm about here?" roared the captain of the *Java*, as I came within hail of him. "Dunno, cap'n," I shouted back as loud as I could bawl. "I haven't been here long." At this the mate on the forecastle wore a broad grin. "I left Cape Sable fourteen days ago," I added. (I was now well across toward the Azores.) "Mate," he roared to his chief officer—"mate, come here and listen to the Yankee's yarn. Haul down the flag, mate, haul down the flag!" In the best of humour, after all, the *Java* surrendered to the *Spray*.

The acute pain of solitude experienced at first never returned. I had penetrated a mystery, and, by the way, I had sailed through a fog. I had met Neptune in his wrath, but he found that I had not treated him with contempt, and so he suffered me to go on and explore.

During the next three years Slocum circumnavigated the world from east to west. In the Magellan Straits near Cape Horn he was attacked by natives, and discouraged them by putting tintacks on the deck each night. He spent several days on the island of Juan Fernandez, which lies to the west of Chile. Here Admiral George Anson had called in after his crews had be-

come decimated by scurvy, and Alexander Selkirk had lived
alone for several years, becoming the inspiration for Defoe's
Robinson Crusoe. In Samoa, Slocum called on the lately wid-
owed Mrs. Robert Louis Stevenson, whose husband's books had
helped him to pass many empty hours. In South Africa he was
received by President Kruger who told him, astonishingly, that
he had not gone *round* the world but *on* it, as everyone knew
the world was flat.

By the early summer of 1898 he was once more in sight of
home.

The experiences of the voyage of the *Spray*, reaching over three
years, had been to me like reading a book, and one that was more
and more interesting as I turned the pages, till I had come now to
the last page of all, and the one more interesting than any of the
rest.

When daylight came I saw that the sea had changed colour
from dark green to light. I threw the lead and got soundings in
thirteen fathoms. I made the land soon after, some miles east of
Fire Island, and sailing thence before a pleasant breeze along the
coast, made for Newport. The weather after the furious gale was
remarkably fine. The *Spray* rounded Montauk Point early in the
afternoon; Point Judith was abeam at dark; she fetched in at
Beavertail next. Sailing on, she had one more danger to pass—
Newport harbour was mined. The *Spray* hugged the rocks along
where neither friend nor foe could come if drawing much water,
and where she would not disturb the guard-ship in the channel.
It was close work, but it was safe enough so long as she hugged
the rocks close, and not the mines. Flitting by a low point abreast
of the guard-ship, the dear old *Dexter*, which I knew well, some
one on board of her sang out, "There goes a craft!" I threw up a
light at once and heard the hail, "*Spray*, ahoy!" It was the voice of
a friend, and I knew that a friend would not fire on the *Spray*. I
eased off the main-sheet now, and the *Spray* swung off for the
beacon-lights of the inner harbour. At last she reached port in
safety, and there at 1 A.M. on June 27, 1898, cast anchor, after
the cruise of more than forty-six thousand miles round the world,
during an absence of three years and two months, with two days
over for coming up.

Was the crew well? Was I not? I had profited in many ways
by the voyage. I had even gained flesh, and actually weighed a

pound more than when I sailed from Boston. As for ageing, why, the dial of my life was turned back till my friends all said, "Slocum is young again." And so I was, at least ten years younger than the day I felled the first tree for the construction of the *Spray*.

My ship was also in better condition than when she sailed from Boston on her long voyage. She was still as sound as a nut, and as tight as the best ship afloat. She did not leak a drop—not one drop! The pump, which had been little used before reaching Australia, had not been rigged since that at all.

The first name on the *Spray*'s visitors' book in the home port was written by the one who always said, "The *Spray* will come back." The *Spray* was not quite satisfied till I sailed her around to her birthplace, Fairhaven, Massachusetts, farther along. I had myself a desire to return to the place of the very beginning whence I had, as I have said, renewed my age. So on July 3, with a fair wind, she waltzed beautifully round the coast and up the Acushnet River to Fairhaven, where I secured her to the cedar spile driven in the bank to hold her when she was launched. I could bring her no nearer home.

If the *Spray* discovered no continents on her voyage, it may be that there were no more continents to be discovered. She did not seek new worlds, or sail to pow-wow about the dangers of the seas. The sea has been much maligned. To find one's way to lands already discovered is a good thing, and the *Spray* made the discovery that even the worst sea is not so terrible to a well-appointed ship. No king, no country, no treasury at all, was taxed for the voyage of the *Spray*, and she accomplished all that she undertook to do.

To succeed, however, in anything at all, one should go understandingly about his work and be prepared for every emergency. I see, as I look back over my own small achievement, a kit of not too elaborate carpenters' tools, a tin clock, and some carpet-tacks, not a great many, to facilitate the enterprise as already mentioned in the story. But above all to be taken into account were some years of schooling, where I studied with diligence Neptune's laws, and these laws I tried to obey when I sailed overseas; it was worth the while.

And now, without having wearied my friends, I hope, with detailed scientific accounts, theories, or deductions, I will only say that I have endeavoured to tell just the story of the adventure itself. This, in my own poor way, having been done, I now moor ship, weather-bitt cables, and leave the sloop *Spray*, for the present, safe in port.

CAPTAIN JOSHUA SLOCUM,
Sailing Alone Around the World

———◆———

2. *Tinkerbelle*

Of all the books about solo voyaging, the best written, the funniest, the most touching, is to my mind *Tinkerbelle* by Robert Manry. Manry, a sub-editor on the Cleveland *Plain Dealer*, had, like many others before and since, a lifelong ambition to sail the Atlantic in his own boat. He finally achieved it in the summer of 1965 in a boat he kept in his garage *and which was only 13½ feet long*. He left Falmouth, Massachusetts, on 1 June 1965 and arrived to a great welcome in Falmouth, England, on 17 August. During the voyage he suffered a number of hallucinations due to lack of sleep, and was knocked overboard six times.

By this time I had gone without sleep for more than forty-eight hours, except for the nap I'd had in the cockpit the second day out, and although I'd been taking stay-awake pills to keep myself alert, my body's desperate need for rest (ashore it had been used to a full eight hours' sleep every night) was becoming acute, unmistakable. Or rather, it should have been unmistakable. Actually, I didn't recognize the symptoms immediately because the pills I was taking contained a chemical mood elevator that made me feel great even though I was on the borderline of exhaustion. The symptoms were so unexpectedly fantastic, so far removed from any previous experience, that I didn't realize their import until many days later, after I'd encountered them once or twice more. Lack of sleep may not have been the sole cause; the pills themselves could have been partly to blame. But, whatever the cause, I floated off in the early afternoon into a realm of wild fantasy, a strange world of mixed illusion and reality such as I had never known before. I lived through an hours-long hallucination.

It provided an interesting subject for contemplation, after it was all over, but while it was occurring it was most vexatious, decidedly unpleasant. It made me waste a whole afternoon sailing hither and yon about the ocean. And the incident was so unusual, so completely different from any earlier happening in my life, that I have great difficulty in describing it satisfactorily, especially for anyone who has not had a similar experience. I suppose, in a sense, I went off the deep end, out of my mind, into a Never Land, where real things and dream things existed side by side without distinction; where reality and imagination merged, leaving no hint of which was which. I have attributed what took place to lack of sleep and stay-awake pills, but anxiety and, even more likely, loneliness, as my mother had feared, may have contributed to it, too. Like a person in a hypnotic trance, I simply began seeing and hearing things that weren't really there.

I became aware, gradually, that I was not alone; someone, a man, was on *Tinkerbelle* with me. This man had no face that I can recall; nor can I remember what he wore, although his clothing seemed to be appropriate for sailing. He was a quiet man with very little to say, and he was friendly. At first I reciprocated with equal friendliness, but later on his presence became inexpressibly annoying, intolerable.

It developed that he was on *Tinkerbelle* as a seagoing hitch-hiker and I was taking him to his home, which was on a small island somewhere in our vicinity. (Of course, there really was no island in that part of the Atlantic.) But we had a terrible time finding the place. We sailed this way, and that way, and around, and back, and north, and south, and east, and west, trying to catch sight of a scrap of treeless land with a couple of houses on it.

Sometime during the afternoon I recalled the storm *Tinkerbelle* and I had been through the night before and, fearful that we might be hit by a southeast wind that would batter us toward a lee shore, I decided I should try out the storm sails I'd made of heavy canvas to see if they would enable us to beat away from such a hazard. However, my phantom companion thought I should take him to his home before I spent any time experimenting with the storm sails, and we got into a slight hassle about it. My arguments prevailed, though, for at sea the skipper's word is law. I tried out the storm sails.

I replaced the white genoa with a minute jib and the red main with a small trysail. The heavy-weather suit of canvas seemed to fit the boat all right, but beyond that the tryout was a flop; there simply wasn't enough wind to move the boat with such small sails. The only adequate tryout would be in a storm.

So I reset the original sails and we continued our island hunt, to the great satisfaction of the hitch-hiker. In fact, preposterous as it seems, my airy chum took over the tiller and I became the passenger. Such is the remarkable stuff of hallucinations. On we sailed. We never seemed to talk out loud; that is, we seldom actually moved our lips, but we did converse in a miraculous, soundless way. I kept pressing my shipmate for descriptions of the island and for clues to the course to be sailed to reach it, all the while straining my eyes to spot a bit of sand or rock.

My companion then admitted that the island would be hard to find because it rose only a few feet above the level of the sea and was mostly rocky, the rocks being a blue that blended almost perfectly with the colour of the sea—camouflage *par excellence*. Several times I thought I'd spotted the island and cried out to the phantom to steer in that direction, but when we drew close it became evident that what I'd seen was merely rock-like wave forms. It was discouraging and irritating. This bloke I had on board was wasting my time on a wild-goose chase. I grew more

Tinkerbelle, seventy-seven days out

and more peevish, more and more impatiently eager to find his blasted rock pile and put him on it so that I could continue on my way. I had started out as a good Samaritan, but now I was entirely disenchanted with that role.

I guess he sensed my rising exasperation because he kept saying, "It won't be much longer. Just be patient, we'll soon be there."

By early evening I was in a frenzy. I'm reluctant to own up to it because of what it may indicate about my character, but I was ready to run amok and toss my unwanted guest into the sea. Then I could resume my own hunt, for England. But at that very moment, in the nick of time, he yelled, "There it is! There it is!" And, sure enough, there it was. I saw it too.

It was a solid patch no bigger than a city block, and if it was composed of anything besides sea-blue rocks I couldn't see what it was. No sand was visible anywhere, and no vegetation of any sort. There was nothing but rock, rock, rock. Even the two small houses at the centre of the island were made of the same type of rock, which made it hard to distinguish between them and their surroundings. About the only way you could tell they were houses was by the windows and doors.

Some people came out of one of them and waved to us and we waved back. The hitch-hiker (I never learned his name, unfortunately) wanted to sail right up to the shore, but I was determined not to risk *Tinkerbelle*'s life on such foolishness. Why, she'd be battered into splinters! So, to be on the safe side, I took over the steering again.

We sailed around the island looking for a place to land, but there was no suitable place. Good Lord! Now what? Was I going to have to put up with this guy even longer? I'd had about all the delays I could take. I was on the point of telling him to swim for it or else when, through the magic that exists only in fantasies, he was suddenly ashore with his family, grinning and waving me on my way. I waved back happily, delighted to be rid of him at last, and without wasting another minute I resumed my original course of 50°. The daylight was waning fast and I wanted to get as far away from that island as I could before turning in for some badly needed sleep.

*   *   *

I was tired. So far I'd gone more than twenty-three hours without sleep and goodness only knew how much longer I'd have to go. The skin of my face felt stretched taut. It burned from the protracted buffeting of wind and spray. I was shocked to discover my eyelids were beginning to droop and my head to nod. I even had some trouble focusing my eyes.

This is no good, I said to myself. I've got to snap out of it.

Quickly, I opened the cabin hatch, leaned inside, rummaged in my medical kit until I found a stay-awake pill, downed it with a swallow or two of fresh water and closed the hatch again. I moved fast, for I didn't relish the prospect of maybe having *Tinkerbelle* flipped over while the hatch was open.

The pill took effect swiftly. In a minute or two I was bright-eyed and bushy-tailed, the need for sleep seemingly vanished. That was better, much better.

I thought how wonderful it would be to crawl into the cabin and at least get out of the reach of the wind, but I didn't have the courage or the faith in *Tinkerbelle* to do it. I feared she might be capsized, trapping me inside her, and I imagined that that wouldn't be much fun. So I remained outside in the pitching, bounding, rolling, yawing, dipping, swaying, reeling, swivelling, gyrating cockpit, exposed to the merciless clawing of what by then was either a full gale or the next thing to it.

Hanging on to avoid being tossed overboard by my little craft's furious bucking, I offered up prayers to God, and Neptune, and Poseidon, and all the sprites who might be induced to lend a hand in my hour of need. And then, just to be sure I hadn't overlooked a bet, I prayed "To whom it may concern."

I hunched down behind the cabin to escape the worst of the wind and flying spindrift, but every ten minutes or so I popped up to take a quick look around the horizon to see if there were any ships about. It would have been a splendid time, while we were riding to the sea anchor, helpless, unable to manœuvre, for a big freighter to come along and run us down. We made a dandy target with that hundred and fifty feet of line stretched out from the bow. A picture flitted into my mind of *Tinkerbelle* and me being chopped into little pieces by the slashing cleaver-like propellers of an Atlantic juggernaut.

From the tops of the waves I could see four or five miles,

maybe farther. A reddish glow in the east foretold the imminent
appearance of the sun. How I yearned for its heat! It would make
life worth living again. Banks of orange-looking clouds hugged
the northwest quadrant of the horizon, making it seem as if there
must be land there, although of course there wasn't. The sky had
already turned from black to grey to white and now was turning
from white to pale blue. Except for the northwest sector, close to
the sea, it was almost clear. Only a few small billowy clouds
dotted its vastness.

With the arm I didn't need for holding on, I beat my chest
and rubbed my legs in a frantic effort to generate warmth. I
wriggled my toes and, as well as I could under the circumstances,
made my legs pedal an imaginary bicycle. The exercise and the
friction helped. It produced a mild internal glow that dulled the
icy sting of the wind. It also gave me something to do, which, for
the moment at least, relieved the mounting apprehension aroused
by the incessant crashing of breaking waves and raving of the
wind.

In another twenty minutes or so, at about 4.30 A.M., the sun
bobbed up and so did my spirits. The red-gold rays burnished the
varnished mahogany of *Tinkerbelle*'s cabin and sent waves of
radiant relief deep into my chilled hide. The sight of my own
shadow made life appear ever so much brighter and, somehow,
this deep blue ocean of the day didn't seem nearly as threatening
as the inky black one of the night had seemed.

What happened soon afterwards happened so fast and, believe
it or not, so unexpectedly, that I still don't have a clear picture
of it in my mind. I remember I was revelling in the growing
warmth of the sun and in the improved prospects for the day
when a wall of hissing, foaming water fell on *Tinkerbell* from
abeam, inundating her, knocking her down flat and battering me
into the ocean with a backward somersault. One moment I was
sitting upright in the cockpit, relatively high and dry, and the
next I was upside down in the water, headed in the direction of
Davy Jones's locker.

I flailed my arms and legs, fighting to gain the surface. I
wasn't exactly frightened; it had all taken place too fast for that.
But the horrible thought of sharks passed through my mind and
I was gripped by the awesome feeling of being suspended over an

abyss as I recalled that not long before I had figured out from the chart that the sea was about three miles deep at that spot. No use trying to touch bottom and push myself up to the surface.

I struggled harder as pressure began to build up in my lungs and behind my eyeballs. I hoped I could get my head above water in time to avoid taking that first fatal underwater breath that would fill my lungs and, no doubt, finish me off.

My lungs were at the bursting point when, at last, my head broke out of the water and I gasped for air. I expected to find *Tinkerbelle* floating bottom up, her mast submerged and pointed straight at the ocean floor, but she had righted herself and was riding the waves again like a gull. We were no more than eight or ten feet apart.

I reached down, caught hold of the lifeline around my waist and hauled myself back to my loyal friend. Then, gripping the grab rail on her cabin top, I tried to pull myself on board. I couldn't do it; the weight of my wet clothes made the task too great for my limited strength. Nevertheless, I tried again. Still no go, so I rested a moment.

There must be an easier way, I thought, as the boat and I rose and fell to the waves in unison. Of course, I could have taken off my clothes, put them on board, and then climbed aboard after them, but I hoped there was a quicker way. And then it came to me: hold the grab rail with one hand while floating close to the surface, get a leg hooked over the rub rail and on to the deck, and then pull up. I was given extra impetus by the mental image of a vicious, snaggle-toothed shark possibly lurking nearby and preparing to take pounds of flesh out of my quivering body, so, on the next try, I made it.

Puffing heavily, I flopped into the cockpit and lay there clutching the handhold above the compass as my breathing slowly returned to normal. The situation, to state the case mildly, could have been a lot worse. I had been given a bad scare and was soaked through, but nothing really calamitous had happened. *Tinkerbelle* was still right side up and clear of water, and neither she nor I had suffered so much as a scratch. And, best of all, I now had evidence of exactly how stable she was. That one piece of empirically gained knowledge transformed the whole harrowing experience into a blessing in disguise. There would be no more torturous nights in the cockpit; from now on I would sleep in comfort in the cabin, even in the foulest weather, with the assurance that my boat would remain upright. No longer did I need to fear being trapped there by a capsize. This discovery made the remainder of the voyage immensely more enjoyable than it would otherwise have been.

ROBERT MANRY,
Tinkerbelle

---

from ROUNDING THE HORN

Then came the cry of "Call all hands on deck!"
The Dauber knew its meaning; it was come:
Cape Horn, that tramples beauty into wreck,
And crumples steel and smites the strong man dumb.
Down clattered flying kites and staysails: some
Sang out in quick, high calls: the fair-leads skirled,
And from the south-west came the end of the world. . . .

"Lay out!" the Bosun yelled. The Dauber laid
Out on the yard, gripping the yard, and feeling
Sick at the mighty space of air displayed
Below his feet, where mewing birds were wheeling.
A giddy fear was on him; he was reeling.
He bit his lip half through, clutching the jack.
A cold sweat glued the shirt upon his back.

The yard was shaking, for a brace was loose.
He felt that he would fall; he clutched, he bent,
Clammy with natural terror to the shoes
While idiotic promptings came and went.
Snow fluttered on a wind-flaw and was spent;
He saw the water darken. Someone yelled,
"Frap it; don't stay to furl! Hold on!" He held.

Darkness came down—half darkness—in a whirl;
The sky went out, the waters disappeared.
He felt a shocking pressure of blowing hurl
The ship upon her side. The darkness speared
At her with wind; she staggered, she careered,

Then down she lay. The Dauber felt her go;
He saw his yard tilt downwards. Then the snow

Whirled all about—dense, multitudinous, cold—
Mixed with the wind's one devilish thrust and shriek,
Which whiffled out men's tears, deafened, took hold,
Flattening the flying drift against the cheek.
The yards buckled and bent, man could not speak.
The ship lay on her broadside; the wind's sound
Had devilish malice at having got her downed.

* * *

How long the gale had blown he could not tell,
Only the world had changed, his life had died.
A moment now was everlasting hell.
Nature an onslaught from the weather side,
A withering rush of death, a frost that cried,
Shrieked, till he withered at the heart; a hail
Plastered his oilskins with an icy mail . . .

"Up!" yelled the Bosun; "up and clear the wreck!"
The Dauber followed where he led: below
He caught one giddy glimpsing of the deck
Filled with white water, as though heaped with snow.
He saw the streamers of the rigging blow
Straight out like pennons from the splintered mast,
Then, all sense dimmed, all was an icy blast

Roaring from nether hell and filled with ice,
Roaring and crashing on the jerking stage,
An utter bridle given to utter vice,
Limitless power mad with endless rage
Withering the soul; a minute seemed an age.
He clutched and hacked at ropes, at rags of sail,
Thinking that comfort was a fairy-tale

Told long ago—long, long ago—long since
Heard of in other lives—imagined, dreamed—
There where the basest beggar was a prince
To him in torment where the tempest screamed,
Comfort and warmth and ease no longer seemed
Things that a man could know: soul, body, brain,
Knew nothing but the wind, the cold, the pain.

JOHN MASEFIELD

3. *Reliance*

Before the war Ann Davison was a qualified air pilot and her future husband, Frank, the owner and manager of an aerodrome in the north of England. They married in 1939. Frank had always had a secret ambition to buy a boat and sail round the world, and in 1947 they purchased an old seventy-foot fishing trawler, the *Reliance*, lying at Fleetwood, Lancashire. Fitting her out proved more expensive than they had bargained for, and before she was completed their creditors had foreclosed on them.

This was not enough to deter Frank, and on a summer evening in 1948 he and Ann cast off the mooring ropes and took *Reliance* to sea. They had hoped to sail direct to Cuba and a new life, but they soon found themselves in a succession of appalling gales which drove them through the Irish Sea and into the English Channel. The engine packed up more than once, there was a fire in the galley, they lost the main anchor, and Frank, like Robert Manry, suffered from hallucinations due to exhaustion and lack of sleep. Here Ann recounts the grim end to their story.

Inevitably the wind eased off: we bucketed slowly away from the shore, out of green into grey water, up towards Portland Bill. If only we could clear one of the horns of this damned Bay and get into mid-Channel again. If only this infernal wind would blow from another direction . . .

It was in melancholy mood I waited in the saloon for a weather report from the radio. The sky had been still full of wind at dawn, and I hoped to hear that the sky was a liar. The radio bleated a song popular in my early flying days, "There's a Small Hotel," evoking a host of memories—was life really so gay, so carefree?—all sounding both appropriate and incongruous. It had changed to "Put Your Shoes On, Lucy," when Frank came in and we giggled at it foolishly.

We listened to a gale warning and Frank said, "We'd better fix the engine in that case." He seemed quite brisk and cheerful. I picked a book at random from the top of the pile at my feet. *Ulysses*. Flicked the pages—". . . made weak by time and fate, but strong in will to strive, to seek, to find, and not to yield."

Not to yield. I followed Frank into the engine-room.

It was an easier task to free the piston this time, knowing exactly what the trouble was and how to tackle it. We felt when we left it ready for starting that it was a good job done, and that we were catching up on the work bit by bit. But we hadn't got round to the mainsail yet. It was still pretty wild though not yet the gale of the warning and we were too jelly-boned to cope with a halyard up the pendulum-swinging mast. Tomorrow, we promised ourselves, if it is fit.

By night we were coming up to the Bill, having pinched and scraped all the sea-room possible. The sou'westerly wind had hardened considerably. *Reliance* under jib and mizzen was tugging away to clear the Bill, upon which the light flashed brightly. Frank took a last look round; satisfied that all was well, he turned in. It was tacitly understood that rest for him was all-important.

For a while I stayed in the wheelhouse watching the Portland light and our steady progress. We were going to have ample margin. The movement of the ship underfoot had become second nature and I did not notice it. Nor hear the shrilling of the wind. But I felt the cold and lashed the wheel and nipped below for a cup of coffee.

As one is oblivious of the noise of a well-known engine and is instantly aware of a change in the beat, so I recognised when *Reliance* changed direction. Immediately I was on deck to see what she was up to.

For no known reason she had swung off course and was belting downwind for the Bill.

Knowing her reluctance to go through the wind and the amount of sea-room she required gybing, and desperately anxious not to lose all we had gained, I called Frank.

As she was coming slowly round, Charles, way up at the top of the mast, played his ace—the rope grommet parted and the jib blew over the side.

Reliance drifted stern first.

"Engine," cried Frank. On the way down I slipped into the galley and turned off the stove. It was bound to be an all-night session. It always was. And I knew the situation was going to be tough by the waves of drowsiness that swept over me. A sure sign.

As the torches roared I looked out of the hatch. Bright were the lights behind Chesil Bank. Bright were the lights on the

Portland radio masts. Brilliantly swept the beam of the light-house.

The tide was making six knots, or more. Taking us with it . . .

"We haven't much time," I said to Frank, who nodded as if I had said it was raining.

The engine started on one cylinder. I went to the wheelhouse and Frank wedged the fuel injector on the for'ard cylinder. There was no time to play around. We had covered an amazing distance whilst the heads were heating and were very near to the high cliffs of Portland Bill. But half-power was not enough. With the throttle wide *Reliance* was going astern. Stern first she passed under the light, its white beam slicing the night sky overhead.

Frank took over and put her into reverse in the hope she would steer better.

I looked out of the door aft. Black waves were breaking high and white on outlying pinnacles of rock. Right in our path.

"Don't think we'll make it."

I felt faintly surprised and automatically unhooked the life-jackets. Each time she lifted we listened—waiting . . .

Ahead or reverse it made no difference. *Reliance*, fast in the grip of wind and tide, passed under the end of the Bill, missing the rocks by a matter of inches. The swift immutable current swept round the point and up the eastern side of the Bill. *Reliance* went with it, stern first round the point, then broadside, bow on to the cliffs, closing nearer and nearer in every long-drawn minute.

We dropped the mizzen, and Frank went to try and clear the atomiser on number one.

"Bring her round," he said, "if you can."

With unusual docility she turned, was coming round, was nearly round, then a sharp bark, and the engine stopped. She swung back to face the cliffs. And plunged towards them, in-exorably.

I thought: I know this. I've been through it all before.

As Frank bounded up through the hatch, cursing, I switched on the deck-lights and together we ran up the deck. The anchor was already shackled to wire and chain, but as we tore at the lashings, he looked up at the towering cliffs above us and straight-ened.

"No use. No time," he said. "We'll have to look to ourselves . . ."

Quickly he got the paraffin and as I handed him a bundle of garments for a flare, he hesitated—"Won't you want these again?"—and laughed shortly and soaked them in paraffin.

The flare cast an orange glow over the deck and by its weird light we unlashed the float and moved it over to the lee side, ready for launching.

We were putting on lifejackets, Frank grumbling he couldn't work in one, when she struck. Lightly at first then harder and harder. We were in front of the wheelhouse. He shouted, "Hold tight!" and we grabbed the mainsheet. Jolting and bumping on the bottom, louder and louder she crashed. Each crash the knell for our hopes and beliefs. Sounding the end of all for which we had laboured and endured.

And I could believe none of it.

I heard Frank saying, "What a shame, what a shame," as the ship rent beneath our feet.

Then the tall cliff face was upon us with a tremendous splintering crash. The bowsprit snapped like kindling. The flare was out. The night was dark. We clung to the mainsheets in a pool of light thrown by the lamps in front of the wheelhouse. She began to roll. From side to side, rails under, with incredible speed, as if she would roll right over. A colossal jolt; the shock travelling from stem to stern. The mainmast sagged, came over, seemed to hang suspended. The boom dropped and we leapt from under. Before our horrified eyes the bows of the vessel buried into the very face of the cliff.

And above the roaring sea came the terrible noise of a dying ship.

Frank yelled: "Float!" and we heaved it over the side. It swung in the water, level with the deck, in the depths below, streaming away under the counter.

"Jacket OK?" he shouted. "Over you go!"

I swung over the side, facing it, and, as the ship rolled, felt out with my feet for the float, missed it, and was left hanging by my arms. He leant over and gripped my wrists. But the ship, rolling prodigiously, flung me off. I shouted: "Let go!" and dropped into the sea.

In the float I got a leg in the ropeworks. Each time the ship came over, the mizzen-boom on the counter rail drove within a hair's breadth of my chest. I was trapped, helpless and infuriated. Frank, not seeing this, shouted, "Right?" and without waiting for a reply climbed on to the bulwarks and leapt overboard.

I happened to look up, got an imprint of him silhouetted on the rail high above—the ship having rolled the other way—then he jumped clear into the sea, swam to the float, clambered aboard and handed me a paddle as, panting and angry, I wrenched free. Muttering about the dangerousness of the ropeworks in the float (incomprehensible to Frank), I dug in a paddle and sculled away to the end of the line out of reach of the boom. Frank said, "Got your knife?" and cut the painter.

It struck me as an unnecessarily dramatic gesture, just as making a flare from a bundle of real clothes had appeared to him. It was impossible to believe in our predicament.

As far as we could judge—it was too dark to see more than the faint outline of the cliff-tops and the white smudge of waves dashing against the face—*Reliance* was aground at the foot of a bluff round which the coast fell back a bit. There was no landing for us there, the cliffs were sheer, and the high-flung spray of the bellowing breakers warned us to keep off. We struck out along the coast in the direction of Weymouth, taking care to keep clear of the boiling turmoil at the foot of the cliffs.

Our queer little craft was a lozenge-shaped ring of cork, or some other unsubmersible substance, canvas-bound and painted red and yellow. The ring was woven about with an intricate system of life-lines, and in the centre of the ring, suspended by a rope network was a wooden box. It was in this network I had got entangled. The box was double-sided, with two compartments either side with sliding lids, for the containing of provisions (a point we had not taken advantage of, unfortunately). It was immaterial which way up it floated, for both sides were the right side.

We sat on the ring and paddled, with our feet on the box and water up to our knees. Sometimes the water swept across our laps. The float swooped gamely to the top of a wave and dived down into the trough. Frank said she was a good little craft—but wet. We were very cold.

We were both wearing woollen sweaters and jackets but our clothes were soaked through, of course. Frank had cast off his shoes and his feet gleamed very white in the black water. I was still wearing the light rubber-soled sneakers that had hardly left my feet since we sailed from Fleetwood. In my pockets was the "shipwreck" equipment carried since the night off Land's End, torch, four one-pound notes, watch, knife and lucky photograph. The watch was still going in spite of its immersion. We left the ship shortly after 2 A.M. and it did not stop until twenty-three minutes past eight. Then it stopped irrevocably.

As we paddled along the coast, careering up and over and down the swift waves, we saw terrific activity burst out on the cliff-tops. A rocket shot up with a bang, leaving a white trail against the night sky. Torch, bicycle and car lights appeared and ran about in a purposeful manner. An organisation was going into operation. We visualised telephonings, shouts, orders; a lifeboat launched, coast-guards in action . . . because of a ship in distress . . . *our* ship, we realised, unable to rid ourselves of astonishment and incredulity. Simultaneously we looked back. A yellow pin-point of light still burned at the foot of the bluff.

"What a shame," burst out Frank, thinking of his beloved ship, "what an utter, bloody shame."

Right back to the beginning again . . . with four pounds and a pocket-knife . . . No *Reliance*, no future, no hope. I made some boy-scout remark about everything going to be all right. But apart from the overriding surprise I was beyond feeling anything but a thankfulness that Frank and I were together and a yearning to lie down and sleep for about a week.

He said, "Aren't we getting too far out?"

It was hard to say.

"No. Yes. We are a bit."

There was a point a mile or so ahead along the coast, and we thought if we could get round that we might find a lee and a landing, and paddled towards it for all we were worth. Yet we seemed to draw no nearer.

A steamer making for Weymouth passed on our starboard hand, not too far away. We shouted, competing ineffectively with the roaring sea, and shone the torch, but the battery was almost spent, and it gave only a feeble glow. At the same time we spotted the lights of a lifeboat coming round the point we were trying to make for.

By now we realised that the fierce current that had wrecked *Reliance* was turning and carrying us out to sea. Inexorably, we were going back, some distance out, and parallel to the way we had come. But the ship's lights were consoling and the knowledge there was a lifeboat looking for us, comforting. We had complete faith in being picked up.

We could see the masthead light of the lifeboat rising and falling. From the tops of waves we could see the navigation lights. Then it moved close inshore, and passed us.

We yelled at the top of our voices and waved the torch. The torch went out irrevocably, and our shouts were drowned in the tumult of wind and water.

Our puny efforts with the paddles were no match for the sea. Drawn relentlessly away we watched the lifeboat work up the coast to *Reliance*, then down and back again, shining a searchlight on the cliffs.

Frank said peevishly, "What the hell do they think we are? Goats?" And I said, "It will be dawn soon, and then they'll see us."

We passed *Reliance* . . . the end of Portland Bill.

When daylight came they did not see us. Nor by then could we see them. Only from wave-crests could we see land at all. The seas were tremendous, and very steep. From the top we looked down into impenetrable depths, from the troughs we gazed, awestruck at huge walls of water. The cold was intense.

Wilder and wilder came the seas. Wilder and whiter. Instead of the float riding over the crests, the crests rode over the float. We paddled one-handed, holding on to the life-lines.

"I do not see"—I found it extraordinarily difficult to move my frozen lips—"how anyone could pick us up in this . . . even if we were seen. . . ."

Frank did not reply, but looked round and round at the awful sea as if he did not believe what he saw.

The current took us into the very centre of Portland Race. The sea was white with insensate rage. Towering pinnacles of water rushed hither and yon, dashing into one another to burst with a shrapnel of foam—or to merge and grow enormous.

From the level of the sea itself it was as the wrath of God, terrifying to behold.

Seated on the bottomless coracle, filled with wonder and awe, we worked away with the paddles to meet the seas. Bravely the little craft tugged up the precipitous slopes and plunged into the depths. I was thinking I would rather be in her than in a dinghy, when suddenly I was in the sea, underneath the float, looking up through the centre where the water was bright green.

There was time to wonder—is this drowning?—and—how green the water is from this side—then I surfaced, found I was gripping a life-line.

The float was swinging uneasily at the bottom of a trough. There was no sign of Frank. Terror-stricken, I shrieked for him at the very top of my voice.

He came up about ten yards away. Swam strongly to the float, still holding his paddle, whereon I realised I had lost mine.

We heaved aboard, and lay athwart the ring, gasping, clinging to the life-lines.

"What did that?" I panted.

"Don't know. This is *not* funny."

Then we saw my paddle, swung upright and set off in pursuit, chasing it up hill and down stormy dale, but it remained forever out of reach.

Suddenly we were in the water again. Under the float. Green water above. This time we were slower getting aboard. Took longer to recover. We looked at one another in great fear.

"What do we *do?* How do we fight this?"

The upset was so sudden, happened so quickly, we had no notion as to the cause of it. And that was the frightening part.

Dizzily the float tore up and down, swinging and swaying. Tensely we watched the advance of each white-headed mountain. Frank had lost his paddle in the last upset and we could not even make a pretence of fighting.

Then we were flung into the sea again. And this time saw how it happened. Saw with slow-motion clarity how the float was sucked up under a great overhanging crest, and thrown over backwards in the boiling tumult as the wave broke.

This time it was very hard to get back on to the float.

Frank threw an arm about my shoulders: "All right?"

"Yes."

"Good-oh."

We got right inside the float, crouching on the wooden box with water up to our armpits.

There must be some way of stopping it turning over, I thought.

He shouted: *"Look out!"*

Instinctively I leant forward, head down on the ring to meet what was coming. And we did not turn over. But took the full force of the wave as it exploded upon us.

I found myself shouting: "That's it. That's it. Lean forward. Head down. That foxes 'em."

Shivering violently with cold I remembered something once read about the mechanics of shivering and put up a great show of exaggerated shudders, partly to offset the numbing cold, and partly as a manifestation of triumph. Frank smiled wanly.

But the conquest was short-lived. The seas grew worse. Boiled in a white lather all about us. Breaking in endless succession . . . We hardly recovered from the onslaught of one before gasping under the next. The weight of water and shock of cold were stunning. Each time a wave broke over us it was with the effect of an icy plunge, although we were actually crouching in water all the time.

Hours dragged out in immeasurable misery as the sea struck with a sledge-hammer to kill a pair of gnats.

No longer buoyed by the slightest hope of rescue we sank into an apathy of endurance, huddled together, heads on the ring, hands grasping life-lines with the prehensile, immovable grip of the newborn. Or the dying. Passively fighting for the lives which were a little less living after every blow.

In a comparative lull, from a wave-top, I glimpsed land, Portland Bill, thin and attenuated in the distance. Pointed to it. Frank slowly stood up and called in a whisper for help.

It was such a pitiful travesty of his usual stentorian bellow I was inexpressibly shocked, and with a surge of protective energy reached up to pull him down, dreading a recurrence of the horror of the other night. Then I saw it was not that . . . and looked wildly round for help. But there was none.

He did not speak. He put out a hand, pressed mine, reassuringly, smiled at me.

And gradually, the smile fixed and meaningless and terrible, faded into unconsciousness, into a slow delirium when, blank-eyed, he tried to climb out of the float. I held on to him and feebly tried to rub his hands, my own unfeeling.

A monster wave rose above the rest. Fury piled on fury. Curling foaming crest. Sweeping down on us. Inescapable. I threw an arm round Frank, leant forward.

The little float drove into the wall of water and was lost within it.

When it broke free Frank was dead.

I stared at the edge of the ring. At the ropes intertwined about it. At the froth and bubbles on the water.

Nothing mattered now. No point in trying any more. The fight was over. I laid my head on my arms and closed my eyes, engulfed in a blessed darkness.

ANN DAVISON,
Last Voyage

Ann Davison was washed up on some rocks and succeeded in scrambling ashore. The experience, instead of crushing her, acted as a spur to further challenges, including a solo voyage across the Atlantic in her sloop *Felicity*. She wrote several books about her adventures, including *My Ship Is So Small*.

———◆———

4. *Lucette*

Dougal Robertson and his family were crossing the Pacific in their boat *Lucette* when she was wrecked by a killer whale. They took to their dinghy, *Ednamair*, and at the start of this extract, have been adrift for thirty-seven days.

Noon position 8°21′ North and 85 miles west of Espinosa, twelve miles nearer land, was not a great boost to our morale but I pointed out that throughout all the time we had been adrift we had either been becalmed or the wind had been favourable. There hadn't been a day yet when I had had to record an adverse run. The calming seas also indicated that we might soon be able to row although the heavy cross swell would have to diminish a little too before that would be possible.

Lyn bathed the twins that afternoon and after their daily exercises and a half-hour apiece on the centre thwart to move around a bit, they retreated under the canopy again as a heavy shower threatened. The dorado, caught in the morning, now hung in wet strips from the forestay while the drying turtle meat festooned the stays and cross lines which had been rigged to carry the extra load of meat from two turtles. We worked a little on the thole pins, binding canvas on them to save wear on the rope, then, realising that we were neglecting the most important job of making a flotation piece, took the unused piece of sleeve and started to bind one end with fishing line. The clouds grew thicker as the afternoon advanced; it was going to be a wet night again and perhaps we would be able to fill the water sleeve. Seven gallons of water seemed like wealth beyond measure in our altered sense of values.

I chopped up some dried turtle meat for tea, and Lyn put it with a little wet fish to soak in meat juice. She spread the dry sheets for the twins under the canopy, then prepared their little supper as we started to talk of Dougal's Kitchen and if it should have a wine licence. As we pondered the delights of Gaelic coffee, my eye, looking past the sail, caught sight of something that wasn't sea. I stopped talking and stared; the others all looked at me. "A ship," I said. "There's a ship and it's coming towards us!" I could hardly believe it but it seemed solid enough. "Keep still now!" In the sudden surge of excitement, everyone wanted to see. "Trim her! We mustn't capsize now!" All sank back to their places.

I felt my voice tremble as I told them that I was going to stand on the thwart and hold a flare above the sail. They trimmed the dinghy as I stood on the thwart. "Right, hand me a flare, and remember what happened with the last ship we saw!" They suddenly fell silent in memory of that terrible despondency when our signals had been unnoticed. "Oh God!" prayed Lyn, "please let them see us." I could see the ship quite clearly now, a Japanese tunny fisher. Her grey and white paint stood out clearly against the dark cross swell. "Like a great white bird," Lyn said to the twins, and she would pass within about a mile of us at her nearest approach. I relayed the information as they listened excitedly, the tension of not knowing, of imminent rescue, building like a tangible, touchable, unbearable unreality around me. My eye caught the outlines of two large sharks, a hundred yards to starboard. "Watch the trim," I warned. "We have two man-eating sharks waiting if we capsize!" Then, "I'm going to light the flare now, have the torch ready in case it doesn't work."

I ripped the caps off, pulled out the striker and struck the primer. The flare smoked then sparked into life, the red glare illuminating *Ednamair* and the sea around us in the twilight. I could feel my index finger roasting under the heat of the flare and waved it to and fro to escape the searing heat radiating outwards in the calm air, then unable to bear the heat any longer, I dropped my arm, nearly scorching Lyn's face, and threw the flare high in the air. It curved in a brilliant arc and dropped into the sea. "Hand me another, I think she's altered course!" My voice was hoarse with pain and excitement and I felt sick with apprehension that it might only be the ship cork-screwing in the swell, for she had made no signal that she had seen us. The second flare didn't work. I cursed it in frustrated anguish as the priming substance chipped off instead of lighting. "The torch!" I shouted, but it wasn't needed, she had seen us, and was coming towards us.

I flopped down on the thwart. "Our ordeal is over," I said quietly. Lyn and the twins were crying with happiness; Douglas, with tears of joy in his eyes, hugged his mother. Robin laughed and cried at the same time, slapped me on the back and shouted "Wonderful! We've done it. Oh! Wonderful!" I put my arms about Lyn, feeling the tears stinging my own eyes: "We'll get these boys to land after all." As we shared our happiness and watched the fishing boat close with us, death could have taken me quite easily just then, for I knew that I would never experience another such pinnacle of contentment.

The high flared bows of *Tokamaru I* towered over us as she closed in, pitching and rolling in the uneasy swell. We emptied turtle oil on the sea to try to smooth it as the dinghy rocked violently in the cross chop of waves deflected from the steel wall of the ship's side; then, as they drew near enough, the Japanese seamen lining the bulwarks threw heaving lines, snaking through the air to land in the water beside us. The rise and fall of the dinghy was too great to make the line fast so I held it as we were pulled alongside the bulwark door. Willing hands reached down and we were hauled bodily through the bulwark door, Neil first, then Sandy. "Come on Douglas, you next," I said, as Douglas hesitated, waiting for his mother to go first, but to do so would have resulted in too much weight on one side and the sharks were still waiting. *Ednamair* bumped heavily as the swell flung her against the side of the ship; with aching arms I wound the line round my wrist and, "Right Lyn, on you go," Lyn's legs kicked as she was hoisted aboard. "Come on Robin, lad." I looked at the empty *Ednamair* with sudden desolation in my heart, we must have her too! I threw the polythene bag containing the dried turtle and my log book, and one or two of the little trinkets from the sewing basket, on to the deck of the fishing vessel, then passed the line round the mast and brought the end with me as I was lifted to the deck.

Lyn, Douglas, Robin and the twins lay in a line along the deck and I wondered what was wrong with them, until I tried to walk and my legs wouldn't work. I clutched at the bulwark for support, then, to my dismay, saw the Japanese sailor cast off the *Ednamair*—they were going to leave her. I gestured wildly, for no one spoke our language, that we must have the boat as well but they shook their heads and held their noses. (I couldn't smell the fish and turtle drying on the rigging but to them it must have been overpowering!) I leaned out trying to catch the rigging and something in my appeal must have reached them, for at a word of command from the bridge, they brought boat hooks and lifted *Ednamair*'s stern up to the deck. I grasped at the handles to help them but they motioned me away, then they cut all the lashings to the mast, canopy, oars and sea anchor, tipped *Ednamair* upside down and emptied everything into the sea; with a heave *Ednamair* was brought on deck. The sucker fish which we had thrown over from the turtles were still clinging to the fiberglass bottom and were knocked off as the hosepipe and brushes got to work in the capable hands of the Japanese seamen. We smiled and said "Thank you." They smiled back and nodded, unable to communicate their understanding.

My blistered fingers smarted painfully from the burn of the flare as I staggered to the companionway leading to the bridge. Pulling myself up with my arms I greeted the Captain of the *Tokamaru* at the top and thanked him warmly in sign language for the efficiency of his crew in spotting us. We could only gesture for I had no Japanese and he no English, but gestures were adequate. I produced my log book and we went into the chartroom to check positions and to give details of who we were and where we had come from, for as far as I knew we had not yet been reported missing!

My estimated latitude at 8°20′ North was good, only five miles wrong, but my estimated longitude, though a hundred miles wrong, was better, for we were a hundred miles nearer land than I had estimated and would have reached it five days sooner than I had said! We were rescued in position 8°15′ North, 90°55′ West. My estimate of 8°20′ North, 92°45′ West, without sextant, chart or compass, wasn't a bad guess after thirty-seven days adrift in the cross currents and trade drifts which complicate that particular part of the Pacific Ocean. We had travelled over seven hundred and fifty miles by raft and dinghy and had about two hundred and ninety to go. We would have reached the American Coastal shipping lanes in ten more days and the coast in fifteen. Laboriously, I drew in on the chart the position of our sinking, and pointed out on the calendar the date we had been sunk. I drew a small picture of *Lucette* and the killer whales, then wrote a list of our names and nationality so that our worried relatives would know we were safe. The Captain nodded his understanding and, shaking hands once more, he wrinkled his nose and, pointing at my tattered underclothing, said "Showa! Showa!" I could well imagine the powerful odours emanating from my blood and grease-soaked rags though I could smell nothing. (I remembered how during my days in the Mercantile Marine, we had picked up some survivors in the Karimata Straits near Indonesia after they had been adrift for ten days, and they had smelled with a pretty powerful odour then.) The only part of our bodies that seemed to be in no need of cleaning was our teeth! They were unfurred and felt smooth and polished to the feel of our tongues.

I staggered back to the foredeck where the family and Robin were seated with their backs against the hatch coaming, in their

hands tins of cool orange juice, and a look of blissful content on
their faces. I picked up the tin that was left for me, smiled my
thanks to the Japanese who grinned broadly back at me, then
lifting my arm said "Cheers." I shall remember the taste of that
beautiful liquid to the end of my days. I looked at the twins, the
juice seemed to be reflected in their bright eyes and their smiling
lips, and suddenly my legs gave way and I flopped on the deck,
holding my can of juice from spilling. We all laughed at my
awkwardness and I crawled beside Lyn, sat down with the can
to my lips and sucked like a child at the breast; mother's milk
must taste like this to a hungry child, and I thought how lucky I
was; an hour ago I had been ready to accept death and here I
was, being re-born!

The Japanese crew carried the twins to the large four-feet
deep, hot sea-water bath, Robin and Douglas tottering along
behind on uncertain legs. There in the fresh water shower (we
had to readjust our ideas to the notion that fresh water could be
used for other things besides drinking!) they soaped and lathered
and wallowed in luxury, scrubbing at the brown scurf which our
skins had developed, but this took many days to disappear. Then
Lyn and I luxuriated in the warmth of the deep tub. The ecstasy
of not having to protect boil-covered parts of our anatomies from
solid contacts had to be experienced to be believed, and the simple
joy of soap lathering in fresh water is surely one of the greatest
luxuries of civilised mankind.

New clothes had been laid out for us from the ship's stores
and the kind concern shown us by these smiling warm-hearted
seamen was almost too much for our shattered emotions. How
cosy to have garments that were soft and dry. With the tingling
sensation of cleanliness came awareness of the rags we had taken
off. Poor worn done things, they had kept the sun off and had held
the moisture next to our skins to keep us cool; they had even, on
occasion, helped to keep us warm when the night winds blew
on our rain-soaked bodies; now destined for the broad reaches of
the Pacific, I felt thankful that my bones were not inside them.

On our return to the foredeck, there on the hatch stood a huge
tray of bread and butter and a strange brown sweet liquid called
coffee. Our eyes gleamed as our teeth bit into these strange luxuries and in a very short space of time the tray was empty, the

coffee pot was empty and our stomachs were so full that we couldn't squeeze in another drop. It felt rather like having swallowed a football. We tried to settle down to sleep on the tarpaulins and flags spread out on the deck inside the fo'c'stle for us, but the unaccustomed warmth became a stifling heat; the vibration of the engines, the whole attitude of relaxation and freedom to move around was so strange that sleep would not come, exhausted as we were. I lay thinking strange thoughts of the life in the sea, like a merman suddenly abstracted from an environment which has become his own and returned to a forgotten way of life amongst strangers. I felt lonely for the sea and for the uncomplicated issues there at stake, until I realised that my thoughts had for so long been centred on devising ways to reach land that this unexpected interruption of our plans, the destruction of our painfully acquired stores of food and water, the sudden abrogation of the survival laws, the tyranny of which still dominated our minds, was all rather overwhelming and we would need a few days to readjust to civilised channels of thought.

At about midnight, we could stand it no longer and staggered out on deck to seek the cool night air, the starlit skies, and the swell of the ocean. Robin, lucky man, was asleep. The junior watchkeeper, Hidemi Saito, a personable young Japanese who could speak one or two words in English, and had a phrase book with the usual inappropriate situations, came up the foredeck and after enquiring the cause of our unease, brought us our second meal, a noodle congé with small pieces of beef. The flavour was enchanting! He then plied us with sleeping pills which didn't make the slightest difference to our mental turmoil. Robin appeared just in time to finish off the remainder of the congé and we brought our pieces of bedding out on deck and rested under the stars.

In the days that followed we indulged in the luxury of eating and drinking wonderful food, the meals growing in quantity and sophistication. The familiar figure of the cook, Sakae Sasaki, became the symbol around which our whole existence revolved as he bore tray after tray up the foredeck to us. Spinach soup, prawns, fruit juices, fried chicken, roast pork, tinned fruit, fermented rice water, coffee and, a special treat, lemon-flavoured tea; and always in the background of our diet, like the foundation stones of a building, bread and butter. The assault upon our stomachs seemed unending and even when they were full, we still felt hungry—a most frustrating sensation! Our bones and bodies ached in contact with the unyielding deck, luxuriated in the deep, hot sea-water bath, groaned under the burden of indigestion, relaxed in the cool of the tropical night, and each day we gently exercised our swollen ankles and weakly legs, learning to walk again.

The Japanese crew took the twins to their hearts and showered them with kindness. They had already made gifts of clothing to us all, soap and toilet requisites, towels, notebooks and pens. They delighted in watching the twins draw, write and play together.

It took four days for *Tokamaru* to reach Balboa, by which time we had to some extent learned to use our legs again; in four days Captain Kiyato Suzuki and his wonderful crew brought the milk of human kindness to our tortured spirits and peace to our savage minds. They also removed the bitter canker of revenge from my character for when I had been a young man, my ship had been bombed and sunk by the Japanese war machine, and the memory of the screams of the trapped firemen in the stokehold and the flesh hanging in strips from the bodies of my friends had lived with me in bitterness through the years, through my later visits to Japan, and even through the rescue of my family and myself. These kindly fishermen were a new generation of men whose character bore no resemblance to the ogres in my memory, for they not only bore friendship to us, but also to each other. Their humanity regained my respect for their nation.

If for no other reason than this one, the voyage of *Lucette* had been worth my while, but as we watched Douglas and the twins talking and drawing pictures with their new-found Japanese friends, Lyn and I felt that they too had become citizens of the world, learning to communicate without the help of language, knowing that men and women of other nations and races had hopes, fears and ambitions which were not so different from our own.

DOUGAL ROBERTSON,
Survive the Savage Sea

WHEN

THE

GOING

WAS

ROUGH

Scurvy (1740)

This horrible disease, caused by lack of fresh fruit, vegetables, or milk, was a perpetual hazard for all early ocean-going travellers. When Admiral George Anson set out on his famous voyage round the world in 1740, he had with him six ships and 1,872 men. A little over a year later, scurvy and ship-wreck had reduced these to one ship and 201 men. Here Richard Walter, Anson's chaplain, describes the onset of the disease soon after rounding Cape Horn.

Soon after our passing Streights Le Maire, the scurvy began to make its appearance amongst us, and our long continuance at sea, the fatigue we underwent, and the various disappointments we met with, had occasioned its spreading to such a degree that at the latter end of April there were but few on board who were not in some degree afflicted with it, and in that month no less than forty-three died of it on board the *Centurion*. But though we thought that the distemper had then risen to an extraordinary height, and were willing to hope that as we advanced to the north-ward its malignity would abate, yet we found, on the contrary, that in the month of May we lost near double that number; and as we did not get to land till the middle of June, the mortality went on increasing, and the disease extended itself so prodigiously that, after the loss of above two hundred men, we could not at last muster more than six fore-mast men in a watch capable of duty.

This disease, so frequently attending long voyages, and so particularly destructive to us, is surely the most singular and unaccountable of any that affects the human body. Its symptoms are inconstant and innumerable, and its progress and effects extremely irregular; for scarcely any two persons have complaints exactly resembling each other, and where there hath been found some conformity in the symptoms, the order of their appearance has been totally different. However, though it frequently puts on the form of many other diseases, and is therefore not to be described by any exclusive and infallible criterions, yet there are some symptoms which are more general than the rest, and occurring the oftenest, deserve a more particular enumeration. These common appearances are large discoloured spots dispersed over the whole surface of the body, swelled legs, putrid gums, and above all, an extraordinary lassitude of the whole body, especially after any exercise, however inconsiderable; and this lassitude at last degenerates into a proneness to swoon, and even die, on the least exertion of strength, or even on the least motion.

This disease is likewise usually attended with a strange dejection of the spirits, and with shiverings, tremblings, and a disposition to be seized with the most dreadful terrors on the slightest accident. Indeed it was most remarkable, in all our reiterated experience of this malady, that whatever discouraged our people, or at any time damped their hopes, never failed to add new vigour to the distemper; for it usually killed those who were in the last stages of it, and confined those to their hammocks who were before capable of some kind of duty; so that it seemed as if alacrity of mind, and sanguine thoughts, were no contemptible preservatives from its fatal malignity.

But it is not easy to compleat the long roll of the various concomitants of this disease; for it often produced putrid fevers, pleurisies, the jaundice, and violent rheumatic pains, and sometimes it occasioned an obstinate costiveness, which was generally attended with a difficulty of breathing, and this was esteemed the most deadly of all the scorbutick symptoms; at other times the whole body, but more especially the legs, were subject to ulcers of the worst kind, attended with rotten bones, and such a luxuriancy of fungous flesh as yielded to no remedy. But a most extraordinary circumstance, and what would be scarcely credible upon any single evidence, is, that the scars of wounds which had been for many years healed were forced open again by this virulent distemper. Of this there was a remarkable instance in one of the invalids on board the *Centurion*, who had been wounded above fifty years before at the battle of the Boyne, for though he was cured soon after, and had continued well for a great number of years past, yet on his being attacked by the scurvy, his wounds, in the progress of his disease, broke out afresh, and appeared as if they had never been healed: nay, what is still more astonishing, the callus of a broken bone, which had been compleatly formed for a long time, was found to be hereby dissolved, and the fracture seemed as if it had never been consolidated. Indeed, the effects of this disease were in almost every instance wonderful; for many of our people, though confined to their hammocks, appeared to have no inconsiderable share of health, for they eat and drank heartily, were cheerful, and talked with much seeming vigour, and with a loud strong tone of voice; and yet, on their being the least moved, though it was from only one part of the ship to the other, and that too in their hammocks, they have immediately expired; and others, who have confided in their seeming strength, and have resolved to get out of their hammocks, have died before they could well reach the deck; nor was it an uncommon thing for those who were able to walk the deck, and to do some kind of duty, to drop down dead in an instant, on any endeavours to act with their utmost effort, many of our people having perished in this manner during the course of this voyage.

RICHARD WALTER, M.A.,
A Voyage Round the World

Despite these privations, Anson pushed on, captured the Spanish treasure ship off the Philippines, and returned to England in 1744 with three million pounds worth of specie.

———◆———

Dog soup 1. (1773)

In pursuing his course to the north, Captain Cook became well assured that the discovery of Juan Fernandez, if any such was ever made, could be nothing more than a small island. At this time, the captain was attacked by a bilious colic, the violence of which confined him to his bed. The management of the ship upon this occasion, was left to Mr. Cooper, the first officer, who conducted her entirely to his commander's satisfaction. It was several days before the most dangerous symptoms of Captain Cook's disorder were removed; during which time, Mr. Patten, the surgeon, in attending upon him, manifested not only the skilfulness of a physician, but the tenderness of a nurse. When the captain began to recover, a favourite dog, belonging to Mr. Forster, fell a sacrifice to his tender stomach. There was no other fresh meat whatever on board, and he could eat not only of the broth which was made of it, but of the flesh itself, when there was nothing else that he was capable of tasting. Thus did he derive nourishment and strength from food which to most people in Europe, would have been in the highest degree disgusting, and productive of sickness. The necessity of the case overcame every feeling of dislike.

ANDREW KIPPIS,
Life and Voyages of Captain James Cook

———◆———

Dog soup 2. (1891)

During our stay, our wardroom steward, an Italian from the borders of the Adriatic, became a shining star on shore. He was a large, clumsy man, forty years of age, with a full round face, at times as red as the rising moon. Blessed as he was at all times with a fair amount of assurance, when his face was red he thought he knew everything. Having a large mess to provide for, and a full purse, he became an authority with the native population. Being told that a man was ill from an engorgement of the liver, he went to see him, and said his case was not serious; he could cure him by treating him as persons similarly afflicted were treated in his country. All that he required was a black dog. Great difficulty was experienced in securing the animal, the whole country being searched in vain, but the fortuitous arrival of a coasting-brig brought the much-longed-for black dog. The captain of the vessel did not like to part with him, but when informed that the doctor thought a black dog was the only remedy that would save a sick man's life his instinct of humanity prompted him to hand over the animal at once. It was killed and his skin wrapped closely around the body of the sick man over the region of the liver; a dog soup was made, also a dog stew, and dog steaks were prepared, and the patient fed on this savory diet to repletion. The self-constituted doctor said that after eating freely of this food the patient would vomit up the diseased liver, and a new one would form. The man vomited freely, but some obstruction prevented the liver from being thrown up, and the patient died notwithstanding the physician's skill. While undergoing this treatment, the man was surrounded by hopeful friends, who were sadly disappointed at the result. This occurrence was narrated at our dinner-table, much to the chagrin of the steward who had assumed the *rôle* of doctor. His practice on shore did not increase; he gained a title, but no other patients presented themselves.

The Old Navy and the New,
REAR-ADMIRAL DANIEL AMMEN, U.S.N.

The slave trade

1. The *Zong* case

The ship *Zong*, or *Zung*, Luke Collingwood master, sailed from the island of St. Thomas, on the coast of Africa, the 6th September, 1781, with four hundred and forty slaves (or four hundred and forty-two) and seventeen Whites on board, for Jamaica; and on the 27th November following she fell in with that island; but, instead of proceeding to some port, the master, either through ignorance or a sinister intention, ran the ship to leeward, alleging that he mistook Jamaica for Hispaniola.

Sickness and mortality had by this time taken place, which is almost constantly the case on board slave-ships, through the avarice of those most detestable traders, which induces them to crowd, or rather to pack, too many slaves together in the holds of their ships; so that on board the *Zong*, between the time of her leaving the cost of Africa and the 29th of November 1781, sixty slaves and upwards, and seven White people, died; and a great number of the remaining slaves, on the day last mentioned, were sick of some disorder or disorders, and likely to die, or not to live long.

These circumstances of sickness and mortality are necessary to be remarked, and also the consequences of them—*viz.* that the dead and dying slaves would have been a dead loss to the owners, and, in some proportion, a loss also to the persons employed by the owners, unless some pretence or expedient had been found to throw the loss upon the insurers, as in the case of Jetsam or Jetson —*i.e.* a plea of necessity to cast overboard some part of a cargo to save the rest. These circumstances, I say, are necessary to be remarked, because they point out the most probable inducement to this enormous wickedness.

The sickness and mortality on board the *Zong*, previous to the 29th November 1781 (the time when they began to throw the poor Negroes overboard alive), was not occasioned by the want of water; for it was proved that they did not discover till that very day, the 29th November (or the preceding day) that the stock of fresh water was reduced to two hundred gallons: yet the same day, or in the evening of it, "before any soul had been put to short allowance," and before there was any present or real want of water, "the master of the ship called together a few of the officers, and told them to the following effect:—that, if the slaves died a natural death, it would be the loss of the owners of the ship; but if they were thrown alive into the sea, it would be the loss of the underwriters": and, to palliate the inhuman proposal, he the said Collingwood pretended, that "it would not be so cruel to throw the poor sick wretches (meaning such slaves) into the sea, as to suffer them to linger out a few days under the disorders with which they were afflicted, or expressed himself to the like effect." To which proposal the mate (whose name is Colonel James Kelsal) objected, it seems, at the first, and said "there was no present want of water to justify such a measure": But "the said Luke Collingwood prevailed upon the crew, or the rest of them, to listen to his said proposal; and the same evening, and two or three or some few following days, the said Luke Collingwood picked, or caused to be picked out, from the cargo of the same ship, one hundred and thirty-three slaves, all or most of whom were sick or weak, and not likely to live; and ordered the crew by turns to throw them into the sea; which most inhuman order was cruelly complied with." I am informed, by a memorandum from the deposition of Kelsal the chief mate (one of the murderers), that fifty-four persons were actually thrown overboard alive on the 29th of November; and that forty-two more were also thrown overboard on the 1st December. And on this very day, 1st December, 1781, before the stock of water was consumed, there fell a plentiful rain, which, by the confession of one of their own advocates, "continued a day or two, and enabled them to collect six casks of water, which was full allowance for eleven days, or for twenty-three days at half-allowance"; whereas the ship actually arrived at Jamaica in twenty-one days afterwards—*viz.* on the 22nd December, 1781. They seem also to have had an opportunity of sending their boat for water no less than thirteen days sooner, *viz.* on the 9th December, when they "made the west end of Jamaica, distant two or three leagues only," as I am informed by a person who was on board: and yet, notwithstanding this proof of a possibility that they might perhaps obtain further supplies by rain, or that they might be able to hold out with their new-increased stock of water till they might chance to meet with some ship, or be able to send to some island for a further supply, they nevertheless cast twenty-six more human persons alive into the sea, even after the rain, whose hands were also fettered or

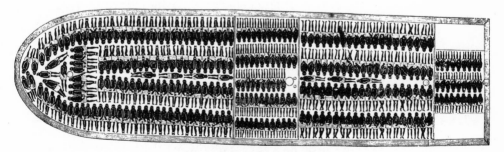

Plan of accommodation
in slave ship, 1844

bound; and which was done, it seems, in the sight of many other unhappy sufferers that were brought up upon deck for the same detestable purpose, whereby ten of these miserable human creatures were driven to the lamentable necessity of jumping overboard, to avoid the fettering or binding of their hands, and were likewise drowned.

Granville Sharp to the Prime
Minister and Lords of the Admiralty,
18th July 1783

ed. ELIZABETH DONNAN,
A Summation of the Zong *Case*

THE SLAVE CHASE

Set every stitch of canvas to woo the fresh'ning wind;
Our bowsprit points to Cuba, the coast lies far behind.
Filled to the hatches full, my boys, across the seas we go;
There's twice five hundred niggers in the stifling hold
    below.
"A sail! What say you, boys? Well—let him give us chase
A British man-o-war you say—well, let him try the race;
There's not a swifter vessel ever floated on the waves
Than our tidy little schooner well ballasted with slaves."

Now stronger yet and stronger still came down the fiery
    breeze,
And ever fast and faster sped the strange ship on the seas,
Flinging each rude and bursting surge in glittering haloes
    black,
And bearing high to heaven aloft the English Union Jack!
"Now curses on that ensign," the slaving captain said:
"There's little luck for slavers when the English bunting's
    spread,

But pack on sail and trim the ship; before we'll captured be
We'll have the niggers up, my boys, and heave them in the
  sea."

Hoarse was the slaving captain's voice, and deep the oath
  he swore:
"Haul down the flag: that's shot enough, we don't want
  any more."
Alongside dashed the cruiser's boat to board and seize the
  prize.
Hark to that rattling British cheer that's ringing to the
  skies!
"Up, up with negroes speedily; up, up, and give them
  breath;
Clear out the hold from stem to stern: that noisome den is
  death;
And run aloft St. George's Cross, all wanton let it wave,
The token proud that under it there never treads a slave."

ANON

---

2. Evidence relating to the slave trade

Lunae, 8° die Martii, 1790

MR. ALEXANDER FALCONBRIDGE was called in, and examined.

What is your present situation?
A surgeon.

How many voyages have you been to the Coast of Africa. . . ?
I have been four voyages to the Coast of Africa. . . .

Do you examine the Slaves previous to purchasing them?
They are always examined by some officers on board; it is generally understood to be the surgeon's business.

Do they appear dejected when brought on board?
All that I have seen in my voyages did appear so.

Did this dejection continue, or did it soon wear off?
With some it continued the whole voyage, and with others till death put a period to their misery.

Have you known instances of Slaves refusing sustenance?
I have known several instances.

With what design. . . ?
With a design to starve themselves, I am persuaded.

Are compulsive means used to induce the Slaves to take their food?
In every ship that I have been, it has been the case.

Have you ever known them refuse to take their medicines when sick?
I have known many instances of it.

With what intention do you imagine?
With the same intention that they refused their food—that they would wish to die. I had a woman on board the *Alexander*, who was dejected from the moment she came on board; she was taken ill of a dysentery, and would neither take food or medicines: I often tried to make her swallow wine, but never could. I desired the interpreter to ask her what she wanted, or what I should get for her; she replied, she wanted nothing but to die—and she did die. . . .

What was the mode used in stowing the Slaves in their night apartments . . . ?
They had not so much room as a man has in his coffin, neither in length or breadth, and it was impossible for them to turn or shift with any degree of ease. I have had occasion very often to go from one side of their rooms to the other; before I attempted it I have always taken off my shoes, and notwithstanding I have trod with as much care as I possibly could to prevent pinching them, it

has unavoidably happened that I did so; I have often had my feet bit and scratched by them, the marks of which I have now. . . .

Have you ever observed that the confinement in this situation has been injurious to the health of the Slaves?

So much so, that I have known them go down apparently in good health at night, and found dead in the morning. In my last voyage I remember a very stout man going down in the evening, to all appearance in good health, and he was found dead in the morning; I had the curiosity to open him, Mr. Fraser [the master] permitting that, provided it was done with decency: after all the Slaves were off the deck I opened the thorax and abdomen, and found the respective contents in a healthy state; I therefore conclude he must have been suffocated, or died for want of fresh air.

Were you ever yourself below when the Slaves were there; and describe the effects you perceived from it.

It is the surgeon's business to go below every morning the first thing; and I was never amongst them above ten minutes, but my shirt was as wet as if it had been dipt in water. In the *Alexander*, in coming out of the River Bonny, the ship got on ground on the Bar, she hung on her rudder, and detained us there six or seven days in consequence; during that time there was a great swell, and a good deal of heavy rain; the air-ports were obliged to be shut, and part of the gratings on the weather side of her covered; almost all the men Slaves were taken ill with the flux [dysentery], I went down repeatedly amongst them; the last time that I went down it was so extremely hot that I took off my shirt, upwards of twenty of them had fainted, or were fainting. I got several of them hauled upon deck, and two or three of them died, and most of the rest before I arrived in the West Indies. I think I had been down about fifteen minutes, and it made me so very ill, that I could not get up without assistance. I was taken ill of a dysentery myself, and was unable to do my duty the whole passage afterwards. . . .

Have you known the Slaves to suffer from the want of better accommodation?

They suffer exceedingly, especially those who are much emaciated, so much so, that I have seen the prominent part of their
bones about the shoulder-blade and knees frequently bare—if I
have put any kind of plaister or bandage on them, they generally
remove them, and apply them to other purposes.

What are the most prevalent disorders on board a Negro ship?
I believe fevers and dysenteries.

Are the consequences ever extremely noxious and nauseous of
great numbers being ill at once of this latter disorder?
It was the case in the *Alexander*, as I have said before when I
was taken ill—I cannot conceive any situation so dreadful and disgusting, the deck was covered with blood and mucus, and approached nearer to the resemblance of a slaughter-house than anything I can compare it to, the stench and foul air were likewise
intolerable. . . .

Do those who are sick under these circumstances often recover?

I never myself could recover one who had a bad dysentery, nor
do I believe the whole college of physicians, if they were there,
could be of the least service, for I humbly conceive a disease cannot be cured while the cause remains.

What do you apprehend to be the main cause?
I think the principal causes are a diseased mind, sudden tran-
sitions from heat to cold, breathing a putrid atmosphere, wallowing in their own excrement, and being shackled together.

On what grounds do you ascribe the sickness of the [male]
Slaves in any degree to the circumstances of their being shackled?
From their dying in above twice the number of the women,
who are not shackled . . .

Have you known any other inconveniences resulting from their
being thus shackled?

The inconvenience is great. In each apartment are placed three or four tubs, more or less; the Slaves that are at the greatest distance from these tubs find it very difficult to get over the other Slaves to them; and sometimes when one wants to go his companion will not agree to go with him; and while they are disputing, if one of them happens to be a little relaxed, he exonerates over his neighbours, which is the cause of great disturbance.

Have you ever known an instance of a Slave dying whilst still shackled to another?

In the *Alexander* I have known two or three instances of a dead and living Slave being found in the morning shackled together. . . .

Slaves bound for the West Indies forced
to dance to keep them fit

Have you known any instances of Slaves destroying themselves?

In my first voyage to Bonny, in the *Alexander*, I went on board brought on board, who was continually crying, and was emaciated very much in the course of three or four days; she refused her food: it was thought proper, for the recovery of her health, to send her on shore to the town of Bonny; I was informed that she soon got chearful again; but hearing by accident she was to be sent on board the ship, she hung herself. . . .

Did you ever know instances of insanity among the Slaves on board ship?

In my first voyage to Bonny, in the *Alexander*, I went on board the *Amelia*, then lying in the river, and which was about to sail; I saw a woman chained on deck, and I asked the chief mate what was the matter with her; he said she was mad.

Do you recollect any other instance?

I recollect, on my second voyage in the *Amelia*, we had a woman on board, whom we were forced to chain at certain times; at other times she appeared perfectly well; and, in one of those intervals, she was sold at Port Maria, in Jamaica.

To what cause do you describe the insanity in these instances?

To their being torn from their nearest connections, and carried away from their country.

How are the male Slaves secured when on deck?

While lying on the coast, as they come up in the morning a person examines their irons, and a large chain is reeved through a ring on the shackles of each, and through the ring-bolts on deck, and locked.

Do the male Slaves ever dance under these circumstances?

After every meal they are made to jump in their irons but I cannot call it dancing. . . .

Is compulsion ever used, to make the Slaves take the exercise of dancing?

I have often been desired myself, in all the ships which I have been in, to flog such as would not jump or dance voluntarily. . . .

Have you ever known the Slaves sing when on board the ship?
I have.

Did you ever hear what was the subject of their songs?
I have desired the interpreter at Bonny to ask what they were singing about; and he has always told me, they were lamenting the loss of their country and friends. . . .

*   *   *

Lunae, 10° die Maii 1790
ISAAC PARKER, ship-keeper on board the *Melampus* frigate in ordinary, called in; and examined.

Were you ever in Africa?
Yes.

How often, when, and in what ship?
Three times; once in the *Black Joke*, in the year 1764, captain Joseph Pollard, from Liverpool, to the river Gambia: we slaved at Culloreen.

How were the Slaves treated in that voyage?
The Slaves were treated very well, except one child that was used ill.

Did Captain Pollard command the ship during the whole of your voyage?
No; he died off the island of St. Jago, and Captain Marshall, who was the chief mate, succeeded to the command. . . .

Was the child to which you refer ill-treated by Captain Pollard or Captain Marshall?
By Captain Marshall.

What were the circumstances of this child's ill treatment?
The child took sulk, and would not eat.

What followed?
The captain took the child up in his hand, and flogged it with the cat.

Did he say anything when he did so?
Yes; he said, "Damn you, I will make you eat, or I will kill you."

Could the Slaves who were on board see the captain while he was flogging the child?
Yes; they could.

How could they see him, and how did they behave on the occasion?
They saw it through the barricado, looking through the crevices; they made a great murmuring, and did not seem to like it.

Do you remember anything more about this child?
Yes; the child had swelled feet; the captain desired the cook to put on some water to heat to see if he could abate the swelling, and it was done. He then ordered the child's feet to be put into the water, and the cook putting his finger into the water, said, "Sir, it is too hot." The captain said, "Damn it, never mind it, put the feet in," and so doing the skin and nails came off, and he got some sweet oil and cloths and wrapped round the feet in order to take the fire out of them; and I myself bathed the feet with oil, and wrapped the cloths around; and laying the child on the quarter deck in the afternoon at mess time, I gave the child some victuals, but it would not eat; the captain took the child up again, and flogged it, and said, "Damn you, I will make you eat," and so he continued in that way for four or five days at mess time, when the child would not eat, and flogged it, and he tied a log of mango, eighteen or twenty inches long, and about twelve or thirteen pound weight, to the child by a string round its neck. The last time he took the child up and flogged it, and let it drop out of his hands, "Damn you (says he) I will make you eat, or I will be the death

of you"; and in three quarters of an hour after that the child died. He would not suffer any of the people that were on the quarter deck to heave the child overboard, but he called the mother of the child to heave it overboard. She was not willing to do so, and I think he flogged her; but I am sure that he beat her in some way for refusing to throw the child overboard; at last he made her take the child up, and she took it in her hand, and went to the ship's side, holding her head on one side, because she would not see the child go out of her hand, and she dropped the child overboard. She seemed to be very sorry, and cried for several hours. . . .

> Minutes of Evidence relating to
> the Slave Trade, delivered before
> a Select Committee of the House of
> Commons, 1790
>
> *ed.* CHARLOTTE AND DENIS PLIMMER,
> *Slavery*

———◆———

THE YARN OF THE *NANCY BELL*

'Twas on the shores that round our coast
  From Deal to Ramsgate span,
That I found alone on a piece of stone
  An elderly naval man.

His hair was weedy, his beard was long,
  And weedy and long was he,
And I heard this wight on the shore recite,
  In a singular minor key:

"Oh, I am a cook and a captain bold,
  And the mate of the *Nancy* brig,
And a bo'sun tight, and a midshipmite,
  And the crew of the captain's gig."

And he shook his fists and he tore his hair,
    Till I really felt afraid,
For I couldn't help thinking the man had been drinking,
    And so I simply said:

"Oh, elderly man, it's little I know
    Of the duties of men of the sea,
But I'll eat my hand if I understand
    How you can possibly be

"At once a cook, and a captain bold,
    And the mate of the *Nancy* brig,
And a bo'sun tight, and a midshipmite,
    And the crew of the captain's gig."

Then he gave a hitch to his trousers, which
    Is a trick all seamen larn,
And having got rid of a thumping quid,
    He spun this painful yarn:

" 'Twas in the good ship *Nancy Bell*
    That we sailed to the Indian sea,
And there on a reef we come to grief,
    Which has often occurred to me.

"And pretty nigh all o' the crew was drowned
    (There was seventy-seven o' soul),
And only ten of the *Nancy*'s men
    Said 'Here!' to the muster-roll.

"There was me and the cook and the captain bold,
    And the mate of the *Nancy* brig,
And the bo'sun tight, and a midshipmite,
    And the crew of the captain's gig.

"For a month we'd neither wittles nor drink,
    Till a-hungry we did feel,
So we drawed a lot, and accordin' shot
    The captain for our meal.

"The next lot fell to the *Nancy*'s mate,
   And a delicate dish he made;
Then our appetite with the midshipmite
   We seven survivors stayed.

"And then we murdered the bo'sun tight,
   And he much resembled pig;
Then we wittled free, did the cook and me
   On the crew of the captain's gig.

"Then only the cook and me was left,
   And the delicate question, 'Which
Of us two goes to the kettle?' arose
   And we argued it out as sich.

"For I loved that cook as a brother, I did,
   And the cook he worshipped me;
But we'd both be blowed if we'd either be stowed
   In the other chap's hold, you see.

" 'I'll be eat if you dines off me,' says Tom,
   'Yes, that,' says I, 'you'll be,'—
'I'm boiled if I die, my friend,' quoth I,
   And 'Exactly so,' quoth he.

"Says he, 'Dear James, to murder me
   Were a foolish thing to do,
For don't you see that you can't cook *me*,
   While I can—and will—cook *you!*'

"So he boils the water, and takes the salt
   And the pepper in portions true
(Which he never forgot), and some chopped shalot,
   And some sage and parsley too.

" 'Come here,' says he, with a proper pride,
   Which his smiling features tell,
' 'Twill soothing be if I let you see,
   How extremely nice you'll smell.'

"And he stirred it round and round and round,
    And he sniffed at the foaming froth;
When I ups with his heels, and smothers his squeals
    In the scum of the boiling broth.

"And I eat that cook in a week or less,
    And—as I eating be
The last of his chops, why, I almost drops,
    For a wessel in sight I see!

                    *   *   *

"And I never grin, and I never smile,
    And I never larf nor play,
But I sit and croak, and a single joke
    I have—which is to say:

"Oh, I am a cook and a captain bold,
    And the mate of the *Nancy* brig,
And a bo'sun tight, *and* a midshipmite,
    And the crew of the captain's gig!"

W. S. GILBERT,
The Bab Ballads

———◆———

Piracy (1822)

In the early part of June, 1822, I sailed from Philadelphia in the schooner *Mary*, on a voyage to New Orleans. My principal object in going by sea was the restoration of my health, which had been for many months declining. Having some friends in New Orleans, whose commercial enterprises were conducted on an extensive scale, I was charged with the care of several sums of money in gold and silver, amounting altogether to nearly $18,000. This I communicated to the captain, and we concluded to secure it in the best manner our circumstances would permit. A plank was taken off the ribs of the schooner in my own cabin, the money was deposited in the vacancy, the plank nailed down in its original place, and the seams filled and tarred over. Being thus relieved from any apprehension that the money would be found upon us in case of an attack from pirates, my mind was somewhat easier. What other articles of value I could conveniently carry about with me, I did so.

I had also brought a quantity of bank notes to the amount of $15,000. Part of these I caused to be carefully sewed in the left lapel of my coat, supposing that in case of my being lost at sea, my coat, should my body be found, would still contain the most valuable of my effects. The balance was carefully quilted into my black silk cravat. Our crew consisted of the captain and four men, with a supply of livestock for the voyage, and a Newfoundland dog, valuable for his fidelity and sagacity. He had once saved his master from a watery grave when he had been stunned and knocked overboard by a sudden shifting of the boom. I was the only passenger. Our voyage at first was prosperous, and time went rapidly. I felt my strength increase the longer I was at sea, and

Pirates lying in wait

when we arrived off the southern coast of Florida, my feelings were like those of another man.

It was towards the evening of the fourteenth day, two hours before sunset, that we espied a sail astern of us. As twilight came it neared us with astonishing rapidity. Night closed, and all around was impenetrable darkness. Now and then a gentle wave would break against our bow and sparkle for a moment, and at a distance behind us we could see an uneven glow of light occasioned by the foaming of the strange vessel. The breeze that filled our canvas was gentle, though it was fresh.

We coursed our way steadily through the night, though once or twice the roaring of the waves increased so suddenly as to make us believe we had passed a breaker.

At the time it was unaccountable to me, but I now believe it to be occasioned by the schooner behind us, coming rather near in the darkness of the night. At midnight I went on deck. Nothing but an occasional sparkle was to be seen, and the ocean was undisturbed. Still it was a fearful and appalling darkness, and in spite of my endeavours I could not compose myself. At the windlass, on the forecastle, three of the sailors, like myself unable to sleep, had collected for conversation. On joining them, I found our fears were mutual. They all kept their eyes steadily fixed upon the unknown vessel, as if anticipating some dreadful event. They informed me that they had put their arms in order and were determined to stand or die.

At this moment a flash of light, perhaps a burning musket priming, proceeded from the vessel in pursuit, and we saw distinctly that her deck was covered with men. My heart almost failed me. I had never been in battle, and knew not what it was. Day at length dawned, and setting all her canvas, our pursuer gained alarmingly upon us. It was evident that she had followed us the whole night, being unwilling to attack us in the dark. In a few minutes she fired a gun and came alongside. She was a pirate. Her boat was lowered, and about a dozen hideous-looking objects jumped in, with a commander at their head. The boat pushed off and was fast nearing us, as we arranged ourselves for giving her a broadside. Our whole stock of arms consisted of six muskets and an old swivel used as a signal gun, belonging to the *Mary*, and a pair of pistols of my own, which I carried in my belt. The pirate-boat's crew were armed with muskets, pistols, swords, cutlasses, and knives; and when she came within her own length of us we fired five of our muskets and the swivel into her.

Her fire was scarcely half given when she filled and went down, with all her crew. At this success we were inclined to rejoice, but looking over the pirate schooner we observed her deck swarming with more horrid-looking wretches. A second boat's crew pushed off, with their muskets pointed directly at us the whole time. When they came within the same distance as the other, we fired, but with little, if any effect. The pirates immediately returned the fire, and with horrid cries jumped aboard us. Two of our brave crew lay dead upon the deck, and the rest of us expected nothing better. French, Spanish, and English were spoken indiscriminately and all at once. The most horrid imprecations were uttered against us, and threats that fancy cannot imagine.

A wretch whose black, shaggy whiskers covered nearly his whole face, whose eyes were only seen at intervals from beneath his bushy eyebrows, and whose whole appearance was more that of a hellhound than of a human being, approached me with a drawn cutlass in his hand. I drew one of my pistols and snapped it in his face, but it flashed in the pan, and before I could draw the other, the pirate, with a brutality that would have disgraced a cannibal, struck me over the face with his cutlass and knocked me down. I was too much wounded to resist, and the blood ran in torrents from my forehead. In this situation the wretch seized me by the scalp, and thrusting his cutlass in my cravat cut it through completely. I felt the cold iron glide along my throat, and even now the very thought makes me shudder.

The worst idea I had ever formed of human cruelty seemed now realized, and I could see death staring me in the face. Without stopping to examine the cravat, he put it in his pocket, and in a voice of thunder exclaimed, "*levez-vous*"; I accordingly rose to my feet, and he pinioned my hands behind my back, led me to the vessel's bulwark, and asked another of the gang, in French, whether he should throw me overboard. At the recollection of that scene I am still staggered. I endeavoured to call the prospects of eternity before me, but could think of nothing except the cold and quiverless apathy of the tomb. His infamous companion replied, "*Il est trop bien habillé pour l'envoyer au diable*," and led me to the foremast, where he tied me with my face to the stern of the vessel. The cords were drawn so tight around my arms and legs that my agony was excruciating. In this situation he left me.

On looking round, I found them all employed in plundering and ransacking everything we had. Over my left shoulder one of our sailors was strung up to the yardarm, apparently in the last agonies of death; while before me our gallant captain was on his knees and begging for his life. The wretches were endeavouring to extort from him the secret of our money; but for a while he was firm and dauntless. Provoked at his obstinacy, they extended his arms and cut them off at the elbows. At this human nature gave way, and the injured man confessed the spot where we had concealed our specie. In a few moments it was aboard their own vessel. To revenge themselves on our unhappy captain, when they had satisfied themselves that nothing else was hidden, they spread a bed of oakum on the deck, and after soaking it through with turpentine, tied the captain on it, filled his mouth with the same combustibles, and set the whole on fire. The cries of the unfortunate man were heart-rending, and his agonies must have been unutterable, but they were soon over. All this I was compelled to witness. Heartsick with the sight, I once shut my eyes, but a musket discharged close to my ear was a warning sufficient to keep them open.

On casting my eyes towards the schooner's stern, I discovered that our boatswain had been nailed to the deck through his feet, and the body spiked through to the tiller. He was writhing in the last agonies of crucifixion. Our fifth comrade was out of sight during all this tragedy; in a few minutes, however, he was brought upon the deck blindfolded. He was then conducted to the muzzle of the swivel and commanded to kneel. The swivel was then fired off, and his head was dreadfully wounded by the discharge. In a moment after it was agonizing to behold his torments and convulsions—language is too feeble to describe them; I have seen men hung upon the gibbet, but their death is like sinking in slumber when compared with his.

Excited with the scene of human butchery, one of those wretches fired his pistol at the captain's dog; the ball struck his shoulder and disabled him; he finished him by shooting him again, and at last by cutting out his tongue! At this last hell-engineered act my blood boiled with indignation at such savage brutality on a helpless inoffensive dog! But I was unable to give utterance or action to my feelings.

Seeing that the crew had been every one despatched I began to think more of myself. My old enemy, who seemed to forget me, once more approached me, but shockingly besmeared with blood and brains. He had stood by the side of the unfortunate sailor who suffered before the swivel, and supported him with the point of his bayonet. He drew a stiletto from his side, placed its point upon my heart, and gave it a heavy thrust. I felt its point touch my skin; but the quilting of my bank bills prevented its further entrance. This savage monster then ran it up my breast, as if intending to divide my lungs, and in doing so the bank notes fell upon the deck. He snatched them up greedily and exclaimed, "*Ah! laissez-moi voir ce qui reste!*" My clothes in a few moments were ripped to pieces, at the peril of my life. He frequently came so near as to tear my skin and deluge me with blood; but by the mercy of Providence, I escaped from every danger.

At this moment a heavy flaw struck the schooner, and I heard one of the pirates say, "*Voilá un vaisseau!*" They all retreated precipitately, and gaining their own vessel, were soon out of sight.

Helpless as I now was, I had the satisfaction of knowing that the pirates had been frightened by the appearance of a strange sail, but it was impossible for me to see it. Still tied to the fore-mast, I knew not what was my prospect of release. An hour or two had elapsed after they left me, and it was now noon. The sun played violently upon my head, and I felt a languor and debility that indicated approaching fever. My head gradually sank upon my breast, when I was shocked by hearing the water pouring into the cabin windows. The wretches had scuttled the schooner, and left me pinioned to go down with her. I commended my spirit to my Maker, and gave myself up for lost. I felt myself gradually dying away, and the last thing I remembered was the foaming noise of the waves. This was occasioned by a ship passing by me. I was taken in and restored to health, but am now a poor, ruined, helpless man.

ANON

THE SMUGGLER

O my true love's a smuggler and sails upon the sea,
And I would I were a seaman to go along with he;
To go along with he for the satins and the wine,
And run the tubs at Slapton when the stars do shine.

O Hollands is a good drink when the nights are cold,
And brandy is a good drink for them as grows old.
There is lights in the cliff-top when the boats are home-
    bound,
And we run the tubs at Slapton when the word goes round.

The King he is a proud man in his grand red coat,
But I do love a smuggler in a little fishing-boat;
For he runs the Mallins lace and he spends his money free,
And I would I were a seaman to go along with he.

ANON

———◆———

Emigrants

Not all of the voyages made by emigrants from the Old World
to the New during the nineteenth century were as pleasant as
that described by Robert Louis Stevenson in *The Amateur
Emigrant* (see pp. 72–76). Here are two accounts of less
agreeable journeys. The first is by Herman Melville. This
description of an epidemic that attacked passengers in an emigrant ship comes from his book *Redburn* which, although
strictly fiction, is based on a journey he made in 1839 in the
emigrant ship *St. Lawrence*, plying between Liverpool and
New York.

1. Typhoid

During the frequent hard blows we experienced, the hatchways
on the steerage were, at intervals, hermetically closed; sealing

down in their noisome den, those scores of human beings. It was something to be marveled at, that the shocking fate, which, but a short time ago, overtook the poor passengers in a Liverpool steamer in the Channel, during similar stormy weather, and under similar treatment, did not overtake some of the emigrants of the *Highlander*.

Nevertheless, it was, beyond question, this noisome confinement in so close, unventilated, and crowded a den; joined to the deprivation of sufficient food, from which many were suffering; which, helped by their personal uncleanliness, brought on a malignant fever.

The first report was, that two persons were affected. No sooner was it known, than the mate promptly repaired to the medicine-chest in the cabin: and with the remedies deemed suitable, descended into the steerage. But the medicines proved to no avail; the invalids rapidly grew worse; and two more of the emigrants became infected.

Upon this, the captain himself went to see them; and returning, sought out a certain alleged physician among the cabin-passengers; begging him to wait upon the sufferers; hinting that, thereby, he might prevent the disease from extending into the cabin itself. But this person denied being a physician; and from fear of contagion—though he did not confess that to be the motive —refused even to enter the steerage.

The cases increased: the utmost alarm spread through the ship: and scenes ensued, over which, for the most part, a veil must be drawn; for such is the fastidiousness of some readers, that, many times, they must lose the most striking incidents in a narrative like mine.

Many of the panic-stricken emigrants would fain now have domiciled on deck; but being so scantily clothed, the wretched weather—wet, cold, and tempestuous—drove the best part of them again below. Yet any other human beings, perhaps, would rather have faced the most outrageous storm than continue to breathe the pestilent air of the steerage. But some of these poor people must have been so used to the most abasing calamities, that the atmosphere of a lazar-house almost seemed their natural air.

The first four cases happened to be in adjoining bunks; and the emigrants who slept in the farther part of the steerage, threw up a barricade in front of those bunks; so as to cut off communication. But this was no sooner reported to the captain, than he ordered it to be thrown down; since it could be of no possible benefit; but would only make still worse, what was already direful enough.

It was not till after a good deal of mingled threatening and coaxing, that the mate succeeded in getting the sailors below, to accomplish the captain's order.

The sight that greeted us, upon entering, was wretched indeed. It was like entering a crowded jail. From the rows of rude bunks, hundreds of meagre, begrimed faces were turned upon us; while seated upon the chests, were scores of unshaven men, smoking tea-leaves, and creating a suffocating vapor. But this vapor was better than the native air of the place, which from almost unbelievable causes, was foetid in the extreme. In every corner, the females were huddled together, weeping and lamenting; children were asking bread from their mothers, who had none to give; and old men, seated upon the floor, were leaning back against the heads of the water-casks, with closed eyes and fetching their breath with a gasp.

At one end of the place was seen the barricade, hiding the invalids; while—notwithstanding the crowd—in front of it was a clear area, which the fear of contagion had left open.

"That bulkhead must come down," cried the mate, in a voice that rose above the din. "Take hold of it, boys."

But hardly had we touched the chests composing it, when a crowd of pale-faced, infuriated men rushed up; and with terrific howls, swore they would slay us, if we did not desist.

"Haul it down!" roared the mate.

But the sailors fell back, murmuring something about merchant seamen having no pensions in case of being maimed, and they had not shipped to fight fifty to one. Further efforts were made by the mate, who at last had recourse to entreaty; but it would not do; and we were obliged to depart, without achieving our object.

About four o'clock that morning, the first four died. They were all men; and the scenes which ensued were frantic in the extreme. Certainly, the bottomless profound of the sea, over which we were sailing, concealed nothing more frightful.

Orders were at once passed to bury the dead. But this was unnecessary. By their own countrymen, they were torn from the clasp of their wives, rolled in their own bedding, with ballast-stones, and with hurried rites, were dropped into the ocean.

At this time, ten more men had caught the disease; with a degree of devotion worthy all praise, the mate attended them with his medicines; but the captain did not again go down to them.

It was all-important now that the steerage should be purified; and had it not been for the rains and squalls, which would have made it madness to turn such a number of women and children upon the wet and unsheltered decks, the steerage passengers would have been ordered above, and their den have been given a thorough cleansing. But, for the present, this was out of the question. The sailors peremptorily refused to go among the defilements to remove them; and so besotted were the greater part of the emi-

Dinnertime on board emigrant ship
en route to Australia, 1849

grants themselves, that though the necessity of the case was forcibly painted to them, they would not lift a hand to assist in what seemed their own salvation.

The panic in the cabin was now very great; and for fear of contagion to themselves, the cabin passengers would fain have made a prisoner of the captain, to prevent him from going forward beyond the mainmast. Their clamors at last induced him to tell the two mates, that for the present they must sleep and take their meals elsewhere than in their old quarters, which communicated with the cabin.

On land, a pestilence is fearful enough; but there, many can flee from an infected city; whereas, in a ship, you are locked and bolted in the very hospital itself. Nor is there any possibility of escape from it; and in so small and crowded a place, no precaution can effectually guard against contagion.

Horrible as the sights of the steerage now were, the cabin, perhaps, presented a scene equally despairing. Many, who had seldom prayed before, now implored the merciful heavens, night and day, for fair winds and fine weather. Trunks were opened for Bibles; and at last, even prayer-meetings were held over the very table across which the loud jest had been so often heard.

Strange, though almost universal, that the seemingly nearer prospect of that death which any body at any time may die, should produce these spasmodic devotions, when an everlasting Asiatic Cholera is forever thinning our ranks; and die by death we all must at last.

On the second day, seven died, one of whom was the little tailor: on the third, four; on the fourth, six, of whom one was the Greenland sailor, and another, a woman in the cabin, whose death, however, was afterward supposed to have been purely induced by her fears. These last deaths brought the panic to its height; and sailors, officers, cabin-passengers, and emigrants—all looked upon each other like lepers. All but the only true leper among us—the mariner Jackson, who seemed elated with the thought, that for *him*—already in the deadly clutches of another disease—no danger was to be apprehended from a fever which only swept off the comparatively healthy. Thus, in the midst of the despair of the healthful, this incurable invalid was not cast down; not, at least, by the same considerations that appalled the rest.

And still, beneath a gray, gloomy sky, the doomed craft beat on; now on this tack, now on that; battling against hostile blasts, and drenched in rain and spray; scarcely making an inch of progress toward her port.

On the sixth morning, the weather merged into a gale, to which we stripped our ship to a storm-stay-sail. In ten hours' time, the waves ran in mountains; and the *Highlander* rose and fell like some vast buoy on the water. Shrieks and lamentations were driven to leeward, and drowned in the roar of the wind among the cordage; while we gave to the gale the blackened bodies of five more of the dead.

But as the dying departed, the places of two of them were filled in the rolls of humanity, by the birth of two infants, whom the plague, panic, and gale had hurried into the world before their time. The first cry of one of these infants, was almost simultaneous with the splash of its father's body in the sea. Thus we come and we go. But, surrounded by death, both mothers and babes survived.

At midnight, the wind went down; leaving a long, rolling sea; and, for the first time in a week, a clear, starry sky.

In the first morning-watch, I sat with Harry on the windlass, watching the billows; which, seen in the night, seemed real hills, upon which fortresses might have been built; and real valleys in which villages, and groves, and gardens, might have nestled. It was like a landscape in Switzerland; for down into those dark, purple glens, often tumbled the white foam of the wave-crests, like avalanches; while the seething and boiling that ensued, seemed the swallowing up of human beings.

By afternoon of the next day this heavy sea subsided; and we bore down on the waves, with all our canvas set; stun'-sails alow and aloft; and our best steersman at the helm; the captain himself at his elbow—bowling along, with a fair, cheering breeze over the taffrail.

The decks were cleared, and swabbed bone-dry; and then, all the emigrants who were not invalids, poured themselves out on deck, snuffing the delightful air, spreading their damp bedding in the sun, and regaling themselves with the generous charity of the captain, who of late had seen fit to increase their allowance of food. A detachment of them now joined a band of the crew, who proceeding into the steerage, with buckets and brooms, gave it a thorough cleansing, sending on deck, I know not how many bucketsful of defilements. It was more like cleaning out a stable, than a retreat for men and women. This day we buried three; the next day one, and then the pestilence left us, with seven convalescent; who, placed near the opening of the hatchway, soon rallied under the skilful treatment, and even tender care of the mate.

HERMAN MELVILLE,
Redburn

2. Prostitution

It may be worth pausing here to enquire into the system adopted to bring about the destruction of those young women, which is exactly alike in all the cases I have witnessed. During the first two or three days passengers are perfectly terrified by the atrocities and frightful bodily injuries which they see inflicted around them. They themselves getting a few drives and knocks and plenty of curses, they soon perceive that they are now embarked on a long and dreary passage, helpless and unarmed, perfectly at the mercy of miscreants, whose acts have so frequently of late been brought before the public by the press, that I need not more particularly describe them. When night sets in each passenger retires to rest with a foreboding mind; when all is quiet and supposed asleep a sudden shriek or shrieks are heard from a female! Some gather round her, whilst others hurry for the medical officer. He arrives, and finds a girl generally very young, say about sixteen or seventeen, lying on the floor of the between decks, with pale and terrified countenance gazing wildly around from face to face;—he interrogates those around as to the cause; they shake their heads, but are dumb; he asks the girl herself; she turns her eyes quickly around; they rest for one moment on some object, and are as quickly averted; she shudders, makes an effort to sit, and says she is better; she turns to look again, and sees an officer of the ship, who has most officiously attended, lantern in hand, standing a little aside. The mystery is now perfectly intelligible, at least to any medical man who has been twice across the Atlantic with passengers. In all cases enquiries are useless, because terror has taken possession of the unfortunate passengers. The next night there may be repetition of the same scene and with the same girl; I have not known it occur oftener than twice; but watch that girl; ask her, during the day following, the cause of her alarm. She was frightened, she says; but at what? No art can extract from her an answer, but before one week has elapsed, that girl has become the worst prostitute in the ship; she is perpetually about galley and forecastle in the midst of the sailors. She has been visited at night, and not being found a ready victim, was upon the alarm, threatened with the knife, or being thrown overboard if she told. The threat had its effect on her, and on her companions around her also. This scene of atrocious villainy occurred in the last ship I sailed in. The girl was not more than between fifteen and sixteen; and although I daily conversed with her for four days during my visits between decks, nothing could induce her to give me the slightest information; but a male passenger who slept in a bunk adjoining hers said "She is all right now; we shall have no more screaming; it's all right, Doctor." There was no mistaking his manner and mode of giving this information; and the poor girl's conduct was sufficiently confirmatory of it, for she became one of the most unblushing prostitutes on board.

Recollections of a ship's surgeon,
Mona's Herald of Anglesey, September 1857

Sea monsters

The whale having been secured alongside, all hands were sent below, as they were worn out with the day's work. The third mate being ill, I had been invested with the questionable honour of standing his watch, on account of my sea experience and growing favour with the chief. Very bitterly did I resent the privilege at the time, I remember, being so tired and sleepy that I knew not how to keep awake. I did not imagine that anything would happen to make me prize that night's experience for the rest of my life, or I should have taken matters with a far better grace.

At about eleven P.M. I was leaning over the lee rail, gazing steadily at the bright surface of the sea, where the intense radiance of the tropical moon made a broad path like a pavement of burnished silver. Eyes that saw not, mind only confusedly conscious of my surroundings, were mine; but suddenly I started to my feet with an exclamation, and stared with all my might at the strangest sight I ever saw. There was a violent commotion in the sea right where the moon's rays were concentrated, so great that, remembering our position, I was at first inclined to alarm all hands; for I had often heard of volcanic islands suddenly lifting their heads from the depths below, or disappearing in a moment, and, with Sumatra's chain of active volcanoes so near, I felt doubtful indeed of what was now happening. Getting the night-glasses out of the cabin scuttle, where they were always hung in readiness, I focussed them on the troubled spot, perfectly satisfied by a short examination that neither volcano nor earthquake had anything to do with what was going on; yet so vast were the forces engaged that I might well have been excused for my first supposition. A very large sperm whale was locked in deadly conflict with a cuttle-fish, or squid, almost as large as himself, whose interminable tentacles seemed to enlace the whole of his great body. The head of the whale especially seemed a perfect net-work of writhing arms—naturally, I suppose, for it appeared as if the whale had the tail part of the mollusc in his jaws, and, in a business-like, methodical way, was sawing through it. By the side of the black columnar head of the whale appeared the head of the great squid, as awful an object as one could well imagine even in a fevered dream. Judging as carefully as possible, I estimated it to be at least as large as one of our pipes, which contained three hundred and fifty gallons; but it may have been, and probably was, a good deal larger. The eyes were very remarkable from their size and blackness, which, contrasted with the livid whiteness of the head, made their appearance all the more striking. They were, at least, a foot in diameter, and, seen under such conditions, looked decidedly eerie and hobgoblin-like. All around the combatants were numerous sharks, like jackals round a lion, ready to share the feast, and apparently assisting in the destruction of the huge cephalopod. So the titanic struggle went on, in perfect silence as far as we were concerned, because, even had there been any noise, our distance from the scene of conflict would not have permitted us to hear it.

Fight between giant squid and whale

Thinking that such a sight ought not to be missed by the captain, I overcame my dread of him sufficiently to call him, and tell him of what was taking place. He met my remarks with such a furious burst of anger at my daring to disturb him for such a cause, that I fled precipitately on deck again, having the remainder of the vision to myself, for none of the others cared sufficiently for such things to lose five minutes' sleep in witnessing them. The conflict ceased, the sea resumed its placid calm, and nothing remained to tell of the fight but a strong odour of fish, as of a bank of seaweed left by the tide in the blazing sun. Eight bells struck, and I went below to a troubled sleep, wherein all the awful monsters that an over-excited brain could conjure up pursued me through the gloomy caves of ocean, or mocked my pigmy efforts to escape.

The occasions upon which these gigantic cuttle-fish appear at the sea surface must, I think, be very rare. From their construction, they appear fitted only to grope among the rocks at the bottom of the ocean. Their mode of progression is backward, by the forcible ejection of a jet of water from an orifice in the neck, beside the rectum or cloaca. Consequently their normal position is head-downward, and with tentacles spread out like the ribs of an umbrella—eight of them at least; the two long ones, like the antennae of an insect, rove unceasingly around, seeking prey.

The imagination can hardly picture a more terrible object than one of these huge monsters brooding in the ocean depths, the gloom of his surroundings increased by the inky fluid (sepia) which he secretes in copious quantities, every cup-shaped disc, of the hundreds with which the restless tentacles are furnished, ready at the slightest touch to grip whatever is near, not only by suction, but by the great claws set all round within its circle. And in the centre of this net-work of living traps is the chasm-like mouth, with its enormous parrot-beak, ready to rend piecemeal whatever is held by the tentaculæ. The very thought of it makes one's flesh crawl. Well did Michelet term them "the insatiable nightmares of the sea."

F. T. Bullen,
The Cruise of the Cachalot

VOYAGING

IN

STYLE

The *Great Eastern*

The first, and in some ways most astonishing, of the ocean liners was the *Great Eastern*, brainchild of the legendary Isambard Kingdom Brunel. Launched at the Isle of Dogs, Kent, on January 31, 1858, 693 feet long, 22,500 tons deadweight, and with passenger accommodation for 3,000 people, she was five times larger than any ship yet built. She had six masts (named Monday, Tuesday, Wednesday, etc.), five funnels, 6,500 square yards of sail, 58-foot paddle wheels, a 24-foot screw (the biggest ever built before or since) and a coal-carrying capacity of 15,000 tons.

The day before she was to leave for her ocean adventures, a faltering, white-faced man painfully climbed aboard to inspect the ship. His associates were heavy in heart when they looked at I. K. Brunel. He was fifty-three years old, and had changed in months from the tough, tanned little engineer who bossed great manipulations of earth, iron, and minds, to a quaking ancient. He posed for Nottage of the London Stereoscope Company against the gigantic mainmast. When he took off his high beaver, no memoranda fell out and they saw that his thick brown hair was gone. The twin lenses took the image. Brunel staggered away and fell with a stroke. He was carried tenderly through the great ship to a cargo port at the waterline, placed in "the flying hearse," and slowly driven home to his house in Duke Street, St. James's.

The *Great Eastern* did not sail the next day. Bales of bedding, stacks of furniture and barrels of crockery were still coming aboard in an ant-like procession. Men tried to hang chandeliers while riveters were still banging away at the bulkheads. The ship waited for more bargeloads of china, sofas, rugs, guns, anchors and cables, received in a vast din of hammers and forges' flares. The ship left a day late under tow to Purfleet with the artificers still aboard. The pilot trumpeted, "Let slip the moorings!" Six huge chains dropped through the hawseholes with a shower of sparks and a roar heard for miles. The tugs, *Victoria, Napoleon, Victor, Punch,* and *True Briton,* drew her away in a din of orders and counter-orders, which could scarcely be heard down on the tugs. The bridge telegraph, which was to transmit helm orders from the bridge to the afterdeck wheelhouse, was not yet installed. Captain Comstock, an American master who was studying the great ship, stood at the aft wheelhouse, trying to relay to the six helmsmen the distant trumpeted orders of the bridge. When the paddle-wheels finally turned, the population of the river lost their seven-years' disillusionment. "Boats of every kind were launched," said *The Times,* and "thousands upon thousands crowded to the water's edge with an outburst of enthusiasm and delight. Even the wan inmates of the Seamen's Hospital crowded the ports to give one shout or a wave to the vessel, as she slid grandly past."

The *Great Eastern* navigated the tricky point at Blackwall and released carrier pigeons to spread the news in the City. The shore features of Woolwich could hardly be distinguished for humans. Men in ship's shrouds bounced "three times three" cheers against the banks as she came to anchor for the night in the river at Purfleet. Purfleet and Gravesend came out in boats to watch her. Little steamers ran round and round with brass bands playing "Rule, Britannia!" and "See the Conquering Hero Comes." The Marquis of Stafford arrived panting from Scotland to get aboard for her next morning's progress to the Nore.

"The long-nursed pet of the shipbuilders" left for the Channel with a piper playing "King of the Cannibal Islands" for the eighty men who walked her anchor capstans. They had the muscular aid of the Lords Stafford, Mountcharles, Alfred Paget and Vane Tempest. Fifteen merchant and navy captains beat time for the men who went down the iron sides "like kittens on a tree" to adjust the anchors. She sailed in a mass caterwaul from the banks, "which triumphant as may be her reception in the States is never likely to be surpassed," said the proud *Times*. The tugs cast off, and in ten minutes, "she set at rest for ever all doubt as to her being the fastest [steam] vessel beyond compare in the world."

The *Great Eastern* ran up twelve knots by the time the breakfast bugle blew. She skirted the treacherous Goodwin Sands on a typical windy September day in the Channel, into waves rolling high from Biscay, but "their foaming surge seemed but sportive elements of joy, over which the new mistress of the ocean held her undisputed sway." Rain and spray scudded through a burst of sunlight in a marine panorama of the *Great Eastern*, and pitching steamers, yachts and brigs come out under the leaden Channel sky to see her pass. The guests did not linger for after-dinner wine and toasts, but hurried on deck to enjoy the sensation un-

The *Great Eastern*

known since Channel voyages began. The great ship moved on that unruly strait with a slight sway of chandeliers.

Off Hastings, "there was throughout the whole vessel a sound of most awful import." The forward funnel blew out of the ship, followed by the sibilants of escaping steam. The mirrors in the grand saloon, which the passengers had just left, "were shattered into ten thousand fragments." Captain Comstock ran out on the paddle-wheel guardwalk to look at the explosion hole in the side. The *Great Eastern* "deviated a few yards, then her paddles wafted her lightly along." The American saw that the hull was intact, despite the most "terrific explosion a vessel has ever survived." The scene was hidden in clouds of steam. Glass, ornamentation and bits of wood fell like hail. Captain Harrison ran from the bridge and yelled for six men to follow him. He went hand under hand down a line into the shattered saloon and searched it for survivors. There had been no one in the room when the explosion came, except Captain Harrison's little daughter. He found her behind a bulkhead which had preserved her from the blast. Harrison passed the child up through the broken lights and continued to search. He almost fell through the hole in the saloon deck. He saw below a red glare of open furnace doors, fed by the downdraught from the craters above. The furnaces were spewing flame and ashes. Captain Harrison yelled for the donkey pumps to pour sea water into the boiler-room fires.

The cry "Man overboard!" was raised. People threw out lifebelts and wooden debris of the explosion. There was a man receding in the sea, a fireman who had escaped being boiled alive by diving down a coal-chute. He was drawn into the paddle-wheel and left broken in the wake. Crewmen went into the forward stokehole and brought out fifteen men. "None who had ever seen blown-up men before could fail to know at a glance some had only two or three hours to live," said an eyewitness. "Three walked up to the deck with an indescribable expression in their faces resembling intense astonishment and a certain faltering gait like one that walks in his sleep. One man walked along and seemed unconscious that the flesh of his thighs was burnt to deep holes. He said quietly, 'I am all right, there are others worse than me, so look after them.'" He was the second of the five explosion victims to die. The oak stairways into the grand saloon were broadcast in splinters. Not a book on the shelves near the exploded funnel had been disturbed.

That evening the *Great Eastern* put into Portland Bill. The captains declared no other ship could have survived such an explosion. The cause was steam building up in the funnel casing. The escape cock on the standpipe had been closed by some unknown person; so John Scott Russell testified at the inquest on the dead fireman. Three of the passengers blamed Russell, who

Brunel. Photograph taken by Robert Howlett for
The Illustrated Times, November 1857. In the
background are the anchor cables of the *Great Eastern*.

had been standing on deck, issuing general orders to the engine-room. The inquest brought in a verdict of accidental death, but stated that "sufficient caution was not used by the engineers." Brunel, paralysed in his bed, was not told of the explosion and his partner's humiliation for four days. The news killed the Little Giant.

By May 1860, after further adventures that included being driven ashore in a gale, the *Great Eastern* was ready for her maiden voyage to the United States.

In New York "public expectation was on tiptoe" as the *Great Eastern* lay in Southampton water in May of 1860, taking on passengers for the maiden voyage. It was a portentous summer in New York. Bell, Breckenridge, Douglas, and Lincoln had just been nominated for the Presidency. Captain John Brown was restless in his grave. The city had reached a million population; Central Park and the Croton Reservoir at Fifth Avenue and Forty-second Street were new. The first Japanese to visit the United States were on their way. What the *New York Herald* called "the governing classes"—the street boys and sporting element—were clamouring for news by steamer of the first world's heavy-weight fight involving a native pugilist, John C. Heenan, "The Benicia Boy," who was fighting Tom Sayers in London. Meteors were being plentifully reported from rural parts and, although the 1858 Atlantic cable was dead, New Yorkers were reading late "interestings" by another briefly lived medium, the Pony Express. Not only was the British monster coming, but the Chicago Zouaves, nonpareil of drill teams; and later the Prince of Wales and Prince Napoleon. The *élite* shunned Newport and other resorts to stay in the baking city for the summer of spectacles.

Michael Murphy, a vaunted Sandy Hook pilot, who was known as Commodore Murphy, was quietly sent to Britain in the fast steamer *Teutonia*, to pilot the great ship into New York harbour. Eight cities were still vying to become the North American port of the *Great Eastern*: Montreal, Quebec, Portland (Maine), Boston, Philadelphia, Baltimore, Norfolk, and New York. When the word came back that a New York pilot had been seen on the bridge during the big ship's last trial, seven rival cities echoed

with lamentations and charges of double-dealing, particularly
Portland, which had built the £25,000 Victoria Pier especially to
handle her.

*   *   *

The great ship actually left Southampton on June 16, thereby
confounding the company secretary who was in New York preparing for a sailing a week later. When "the monster struck out
for the New World," said Holley, it was "the final embarkation,
the real trial trip, the first ocean voyage of a ship that has been
the parent of more talk, speculation and wonder, and world-wide
interest, than any craft since Noah's Ark." A solitary tug saw
them off, in a grey, squally morning. The *Times* man looked
down at the melancholy faces on the tug and was reminded of a
chromo of his youth, "The Last Mourner," which depicted a
drunkard's dog following his corpse to a pauper burial. Just east
of The Needles, they passed a troopship that had been blown
ashore the night before—"a decidedly cheerless sight," Holley
said.

> There were 418 crew but only 35 paying passengers, one of
> whom "was carrying an English fighting-cock and three hens
> in wicker cages to a chicken fighter in California."

The passengers were lost in the ship. They wandered through her
like children discovering marvels. They stared at the four huge
paddle-cylinders swinging on their trunnions. As in a dream they
watched leviathan walking smoothly and puffing billows of smoke
from her Quaker-grey funnels. The ship burned mixed Welsh and
Lancashire bituminous, a slaggy coal that blistered the funnel
casings which passed up through the saloons. The passengers had
to abandon the main dining-saloon because of the heat.

In mid-passage the *Great Eastern* encountered a half-gale. She
passed the emigrant ship, *Martha's Vineyard*, which rolled like a
yacht. The wind grew. At its peak velocity an eighteen-degree
roll was recorded on the oscillograph the journalists had brought
along. Such an inclination in nineteenth-century seafaring was almost unnoticeable. To one of the Royal Navy captains aboard it

was welcome evidence that she was seaworthy. "Thank God, she rolls!" he declared. Only three persons reported seasick to Dr. Watson, the ship's chief surgeon (she carried three doctors). They were firemen overcome in the stifling boiler-rooms.

Most of the days were fair. Gamecock Wilkes had crossed the North Atlantic five times but he had never seen so much sail. Several times a day little ships closed in over the hills of the sea to look at her: the *Great Eastern* stood so much higher than any ship afloat that she could be spied from far away. Holley liked to take "a lonely and contemplative walk, these fine summer evenings, around our acre of door-yard." The spell-bound passengers discovered an irresistible resort, the guardwalk outside the paddle-boxes, at the extremes of the 120-foot width. "The guardwalks will wellnigh hold all of us," said Holley. "Standing fifteen feet outside the vessel and watching her giant bulk gliding through the sea, which she scarcely seems to ripple, is a sight so decidedly indescribable that I would advise you not to be content until you witness it." They stayed on the guardwalks for hours, staring along her sheer or sticking their noses through the vents of the paddle-box to watch the gigantic red wheel rolling over the waves.

At night there were musicales in the grand saloon. The ship carried a six-piece band, led by Professor MacFarlane, a mighty artist on the cornet-à-pistons. He rendered solos, accompanied on the rosewood grand piano, and crew and passengers alike made vocal offerings. Captain Vine Hall joined the entertainment with concertos on the flute. Occasionally the harmonic evenings were marred by the music of the deck hands, blaring down through the open skylights. The crew had its own cornetist, who played a deafening rendition of "Wait Till the Wagon Comes" on a dented instrument, to inspire the hauling of sail. The boatswain, who was seven feet tall, led the heaving deck hands in "Adieu, My Johnny Boker," to which they roared innumerable responses, many unfit for the ladies' hearing.

They were Olympian days for those who sailed on the maiden voyage of the first ocean mammoth. No account of it—and there were inspired literary workers and diarists aboard—fails to mention divine sunsets, and storm effects, and the seraphic moods that came upon them as the *Great Eastern* strode homerically across the brine. She left a long triple wake, "like two bridlepaths and a turnpike," and on the sixth night in the Gulf Stream, they stayed half the night at the taffrail, bewitched with the wakes receding phosphorescently into the dark. Holley said the ship ploughed "a pathway as wide as the passage of the Israelites in the Red Sea."

They did not dine on salt junk. The cattle pens on deck supplied fresh-killed mutton and fowl. At dinner the trumpet sounded "The Roast Beef of Old England," and at supper, "Polly, Put the Kettle On." Champagne bubbled like the ship's wake. "Enough wine to float her" was wagered on each day's mileage.

"Early risers got up appetite by walking nearly downtown and back," said the *New York Times* correspondent. One of the Englishmen brought along nine-pins and set up an alley "on a vacant lot somewhere." This unknown fellow probably invented deck games. Daniel Gooch called him "Skittles" and referred to Mary Ann Herbert as "Miss Skittles." In the balmy airs of the Gulf Stream the urge came upon them to have a quarter-mile

Sunday service in the *Campania*

foot race round the teak deck. Betting accounts were opened for
an international match between a long-legged British officer, Captain Drummond, and Commodore Murphy, the short, thickset
Sandy Hook pilot. Captain Drummond finished while Commodore
Murphy was still rounding a bow capstan. "Several vineyards
changed hands," said the *Times* man. They discovered the gym-
nastic possibilities of the rigging, and in the late afternoons the
ladies were treated to the sight of the men hanging or stunting
in the jungle of shrouds.

The crew was unusually well behaved. The log listed only
two minor imbroglios among the black gang and the case of a
fireman who was seized and put in irons for attempting to stab a
mate. The joy of the trip had caught the engine crew: they were
heard singing hilariously in the dark pits. In the number two and
three cargo holds, the ship's carpenters worked all the way across
building sightseers' stairs, installing ticket booths and a turnstile,
a contraption that had not yet been seen in America.

> On June 28 the *Great Eastern*'s maiden voyage across the
> Atlantic was almost over, and by 10 A.M. "the big ship was
> surrounded by hundreds of little ones, full of enraptured New
> Yorkers."

At 2 P.M. Commodore Murphy telegraphed to the engine-room,
"Head slow with her paddles," and the monster made for the
questionable sand bar. She crossed it without a bump, although
watchers at the stern saw mud clouds boiling to the surface.
Murphy ordered the screw engaged and the *Great Eastern* drew
away from the escorts which swam below like waterfowl. Gamecock Wilkes said, "The boy who saw the Bay of New York yesterday witnessed a spectacle that he will not be likely to forget, if he
should outlive Methuselah." As she passed Fort Hamilton the
garrison fired a twenty-one-gun salute, which the great ship answered with a majority from her four big brass Dahlgren guns.
Harbour pieces joined in the ovation to her march. In the upper
bay she passed the frigate U.S.S. *Niagara*, next largest vessel in
the world. The *Niagara* dipped her ensign but did not fire a salute.
Augustus Schell, collector of the port, came 'longside while she
was under way. His boat was nearly drawn under the paddle-

wheel, but he grabbed for a lower cargo port and was handed safely aboard. When the *Great Eastern* passed Castle Garden at the toe of Manhattan, thousands threw heads back and roared, then broke ranks and run up West Street after her.

JAMES DUGAN,
The Great Iron Ship

——————◆——————

from THE YEAR OF METEORS

Nor forget I to sing of the wonder, the ship as she swam
    up my bay,
Well-shaped and stately the *Great Eastern* swam up my
    bay, she was 600* feet long,
Her moving swiftly surrounded by myriads of small craft I
    forget not to sing.

WALT WHITMAN

——————◆——————

The *Great Eastern* is abandoned . . .

Being entirely uneconomic, the *Great Eastern* was sold from company to company, and in 1867 was chartered by a French syndicate to bring American visitors from New York to the Paris World Exhibition.

She attracted only 191 passengers, but one of them was Jules Verne who, if the great ship had not existed, might well have invented her, and in any case wrote a book about the voyage, called *A Floating City*. Because there was no superstructure she

---

* Actually 692 feet.

had a vaster expanse of open deck than ever seen again on such a ship. American children ran about throwing ball and bowling hoops. To go and look over the stern was known as walking in the country. In the saloons, Verne listened to the tones of an organ and three pianos. The *Great Eastern* still relied partly on sails, but on Sunday the captain would not allow them to be hoisted, though the weather was fine, saying it would be improper on the Sabbath. Verne wondered why, in that case, the machinery was still allowed to continue. "Sir," replied the captain, a fierce Puritan, "that which comes directly from God must be respected; the wind is in His hand, but the steam is in the power of man." On the Sabbath the captain assumed the position of pastor. No pianos, cards, chess, or billiards were played. At a holy concert in the grand saloon, passengers sat on the side sofas or glided about from time to time, catching hold of one another silently but almost without talking. Once the Sabbath had passed the captain himself organized a race between sailors, three times round the deck, and there was betting on the result. Verne sat in a deck chair. When the French charterers got her into Brest they abandoned her without even paying off the crew.

... And a new generation appears

The *Great Eastern* was reduced to laying cables across the Atlantic, and in 1888 she was broken up. But by now a new generation of steamers was entering Atlantic service.

By the time of *Umbria* and *Etruria* the Atlantic crossing was still an adventure but could no longer be called by any stretch of the imagination a calculated risk of one's life. By the 1880s the advice given in 1878 by an American woman, Kate Ledoux, in a guide called *Ocean Notes for Ladies*, had an archaic sound. She advised lady saloon passengers to dress sensibly but well, because she had always felt that a body washed ashore in good clothes would receive more respect and kinder care than if dressed in clothes only fit for the rag bag.

White Star, like so many other companies in these early days, had their shipwrecks. In 1873 their *Atlantic* found herself, at the end of a crossing, with less than enough coal to make New York, tried to make for Halifax instead, and there stranded and broke up in sight of land with the loss of 546 lives. Patrick Leahy, an Irishman, said: "Then I saw the first and awful sight . . . a large mass of something drifted past the ship on the top of the waves, and then it was lost to view in the trough of the sea. As it passed by a moan—it must have been a shriek but the tempest dulled the sound—seemed to surge up from the mass, which extended over fifty yards of water: it was the women. The sea swept them out of the steerage, and with their children, to the number of 200 or 300, they drifted thus to eternity."

It was ships of the *Oceanic* and *Atlantic* class that were first described as having all the comforts of Swiss hotels. Their smok-

Dressing for dinner

ing-rooms—rooms and not just the deck awnings Cunard offered at the time—were described as narcotic paradises. And it was over cabins in a slightly later White Star liner, the *Britannic*, that two American railroad millionaires came into dispute. Both William Henry Vanderbilt and John Pierpont Morgan wanted the same state-rooms. Vanderbilt thought he settled the matter by booking the same cabin for five years in advance, only he died soon after doing so. Morgan, having won there, also made sure of getting what he wanted elsewhere by reserving several cabins on several dates on several ships, also for years ahead. He survived, but there arrived a time when he had no need of advance bookings since he came, in the course of his later business career, to own half the Atlantic shipping lines.

To advertise the *Umbria* and *Etruria*, a booklet appeared entitled *An Aristocrat of the Atlantic*, by Maev, a lady of fashion, and a close inspection reveals that it was published by Cunard. The text would soon have revealed that anyway. "The Cunard," it said, "has something. It has a name. Half the pleasure of doing a thing really well consists in letting the other people—the people who are not doing the thing at all but would like to if they could—know that one is enjoying the very best that can be had." If one said one was crossing by Cunard, the sleepiest inhabitant of a duck-ridden village would know what that meant. Maev then reported a conversation between a young American girl and her mother, who were returning from Europe. "Say, Momma, don't you think the sofa-covers and curtains in the music room are just like the brocaded Court trains we saw in London? I tell you, I'd like a Watteau train of that myself: it's a real elegant colour, that sea-green Genoese velour. Do you think that the purser would know where they got it and how much it was?"

The only jarring note on board, said Maev, not apparently thinking the wretched girl and her green velour at all jarring, was that provided by passengers. Rough tweed ulsters, plain inexpensive tailor-mades, and heavy boots such as people would wear at sea, were all shown up by the coquettish elegancies of the vessel, just as a lady's boudoir might intensify the roughness of a shaggy-coated retriever. She gave other advice on dress. The skirts chosen for deck wear should be very heavy, as sea breezes were no respecters of persons, and draperies behaved embarrassingly at gusty corners. It was a good plan to sew dress weights at intervals round the hem or three or four inches up. Little coins in packets of three apiece could be used instead. Coloured under-skirts, if such were worn, were preferable to white. Maev said ten meals a day would be provided, and regretted that even the necessity of "paying with one's person" did not prevent some people, who had paid their money in advance, from eating right through their

Women passengers embarking at Le Havre, 1905

ticket, so to speak. Here is a summary of the ten meals a day
Cunard offered to first-class passengers in the 1890s:

Before breakfast: grapes, melons, etc.
Breakfast: "Almost anything on earth"
11 am: Pint cup of bouillon
Noon: Sandwiches carried about the decks
1 pm: Lunch
3 pm: Trays of ices
4 pm: Tea
5 pm: Toffee or sweets carried round on trays
7 pm: Dinner
9 pm: Supper

In the matter of food, Maev advised ladies to "moderate their
transport, you know." In other matters, she remarked that lady
passengers, especially those travelling alone, should not sit out on
deck in the dark. She quoted Mark Twain as saying that Cunard
were such hard-headed, practical, unromantic people, that they
would not take Noah himself as first mate until they had worked
him up all the lower grades.

And of all the grades the firemen were the lowest.

They were Liverpool Irish, who often arrived on board more or
less drunk. At sea, they worked two four-hour spells in each
twenty-four, lifting five tons of coal each a day. The trimmers
brought coal from the bunkers and wheeled it to piles handy for
the firemen to shovel into the furnaces. They worked in twenty-
one-minute spells. There were seven minutes to feed coal into
furnaces whose heat scorched the firemen, then seven minutes for
cutting and clearing clinkers with long slicers, and then another
seven for raking over. A man who was behind in any seven minutes could not escape being seen by his fellows to be weaker, and
so the weak drove themselves to keep up with the strong. After
the three periods of seven minutes there was a short pause, and
then a gong announced the beginning of another twenty-one minutes. This was the fireman's work for four hours on end, scorched
by furnaces and choked by coal dust and by gases from white-hot

clinkers and ashes. When they had finished their watches they often took the air with chests open to the cold Atlantic wind. They worked, and ate, and then slept exhausted. They could not obtain drink aboard, so when they did get ashore they made up for this by getting and staying drunk. As firemen, only the Hungarians were as good as the Liverpool Irish.

TERRY COLEMAN,
The Liners

———◆———

LEAVE HER, JOHNNY

I thought I heard the captain say,
Leave her, Johnny, leave her;
You may go ashore and touch your pay,
It's time for us to leave her.

You may make her fast, and pack your gear,
Leave her, Johnny, leave her;
And leave her moored to the West Street Pier,
It's time for us to leave her.

The winds were foul, the work was hard,
Leave her, Johnny, leave her;
From Liverpool Docks to Brooklyn Yard,
It's time for us to leave her.

She would neither steer, nor stay, nor wear,
Leave her, Johnny, leave her;
She shipped it green and she made us swear,
It's time for us to leave her.

She would neither wear, nor steer, nor stay,
Leave her, Johnny, leave her;
Her running rigging carried away,
It's time for us to leave her.

The winds were foul, the trip was long,
   Leave her, Johnny, leave her;
Before we go we'll sing a song,
   It's time for us to leave her.

We'll sing, Oh, may we never be,
   Leave her, Johnny, leave her;
On a hungry ship the like of she,
   It's time for us to leave her.

ANON

The only way to go

To the rich, the liners were extensions of their lives ashore, floating luxury hotels.

They crossed the Atlantic aboard the magnificent vessels of North German Lloyd, Hamburg American, Cunard, White Star, French Line, Red Star, and for a time, Inman, at a time when twenty pieces of hold luggage were an absolute basic minimum for social survival and when even a gentleman required a wardrobe or innovation trunk in the corridor outside his stateroom to hold the four changes of clothes he was expected to make daily on an eight- or nine-day passage. They went with valets and maids, hatboxes and shoe trunks, jewel cases and, in some fastidious instances, their own personal bed linen. Invalids brought their own doctors and nurses, dog lovers traveled with mastiffs and St. Bernards. Occasional magnificoes or eccentrics brought their own barbers, and food faddists carried their special rations of sanitized lettuce leaves or graham nut bread. The transatlantic entourage of a well-placed man and woman might well number half a dozen persons, while there was no limit at all to the number of secretaries and couriers that could be kept usefully at hand.

Clarence Barron never traveled with fewer than three male secretaries. The Lloyd Hilton Smiths of Houston, upholstered with Humble Oil money aboard the French Line *Liberté* as recently as the 1950s, took their own automobiles with them for a tour of France, one for Mr. and Mrs. Smith, one for the children and their own entourage of nurses and governesses. People frequently made the westward passage on board the *Mauretania* or *Olympic* with vastly more luggage and motorcars than they had started out with. Many of the elite and doomed who took passage on the first and last voyage of the *Titanic* went well dressed for eternity with twenty trunks full of Paris frocks and evening dresses.

LUCIUS BEEBE,
The Big Spenders

The *Titanic*

From Thursday noon to Friday noon the *Titanic* ran 386 nautical miles. Friday to Saturday 519 miles, and Saturday to Sunday 546 miles. She was making 22 knots. Everyone agreed she was the most comfortable ship they had travelled in. There was, though, a vibration, which was most noticeable as one lay in the bath. The throb of the engines came straight up from the floor through the metal sides of the tub so that one could not put one's head back with any comfort. Throughout her voyage, the *Titanic* slightly listed to port, but it was nothing. As the second-class passengers sat at table in the dining-room they could, if they watched the skyline through the portholes, see both skyline and sea on the port side but only sky to starboard. The purser thought this was probably because more coal had been used from the starboard bunkers.

When some passengers went on deck on Sunday morning they found the temperature had dropped so rapidly that they did not care to stay outside, although there was no wind, or only that artificial wind created by the passage of the ship. Both the French liner *Touraine* and the German *Amerika* had wirelessed the

Titanic reporting ice, and the *Titanic* had replied thanking them. Sunday dinner was served, and then coffee. Thomas Andrews, the shipbuilder, strolled down to the kitchens to thank the baker for making some special bread for him. The passengers went to bed with the presumption, perhaps already mentally half-realized, as [Lawrence] Beesley put it, that they would be ashore in New York in forty-eight hours time. At the evening service, after coffee, Rev. Mr. Carter had caused the hymn "For Those in Peril on the Sea" to be sung, but he had brought the service to a close with a few words on the great confidence all on board felt in the *Titanic*'s great steadiness and size. At 11.40, in Lat. 41° 46′ N. Long. 50° 14′ W. Frederick Fleet, the look-out in the crow's-nest, saw or sensed an iceberg ahead. The *Titanic* veered to port, so that it was her starboard plates which were glanced open. The engines were stopped. There was a perfectly still atmosphere. It was a brilliantly starlit night but with no moon, so that there was little light that was of any use. She was a ship that had come quietly to rest without any indication of disaster. No ice was visible: the iceberg had been glimpsed by the look-out and then gone. There was no hole in the ship's side through which water could be seen to be pouring, nothing out of place, no sound of alarm, no panic, and no movement of anyone except at a walking pace.

Within ten minutes the water had risen fourteen feet inside the ship. Mail bags were floating about in the mail room. The passengers had no idea of danger. Beesley, who was in bed, noticed no more than what he took to be the slightest extra heave of the engines. What most people noticed first was the sudden lack of engine vibration. This had been with them so constantly for the four days of the voyage that they had ceased to be conscious of it, but when it stopped they noticed the supervening silence and stillness. The only passengers who saw an iceberg were a few still playing cards in the smoking room. They idly discussed how high it might have been, settled on an estimate of eighty feet, and went back to their cards. One pointed to a glass of whisky at his side and, turning to an onlooker, suggested he should just run along on deck to see if any ice had come on board. If so, he would like some more in his whisky. They laughed. In fact, as the crew discovered, the decks were strewn with ice, but even then, so unaware were they of danger, that Edward Buley, an able seaman, picked up a handful of it, took it down to his bunk, and turned in again. There was no panic because there was no awareness. The *Titanic* was assumed to be unsinkable. The shipbuilders had said so. Practically everyone believed she was as unsinkable as a railway station. A Rothschild, asked to put on his life-jacket, said he did not think there was any occasion for it, and walked leisurely away. Stewards rode bicycles round and round in the gym. She was in fact sinking very fast, and by midnight was a quarter sunk already. There was something unusual about the stairs, a curious sense of something out of balance, a sense of not being able to put one's foot down in the right place. The stairs were tilting forward and tended to throw your feet out of place. There was no visible slope, just something strange perceived by the sense of balance. The *Titanic* was settling by the head.

* * *

The *Titanic*. Main hall, promenade deck

There is going to be no coherent account of what happened in the last hour of the *Titanic*, because nothing coherent happened. The *Titanic* was a sixth of a mile long and had eleven decks. What happened in one place did not happen in another. What happened on the starboard side did not happen on the port. On the port side, women and children only were allowed into the boats which were even sent away half-empty when there were not women enough at that moment to fill them, although there were men. On the starboard side, men were allowed to enter the boats when there were not at any given moment enough women to fill them. There was even a difference of opinion as to what constituted a woman. Second Officer Lightoller took any women, except stewardesses. Fifth Officer Lowe accepted any women, "whether first class, second class, third class, or sixty-seventh class . . . regardless of class or nationality or pedigree. Stewardesses just the same." Lowe, however, said he fended off a lot of Italian men. Latin people, all along the ship's rails, "more or less like wild beasts, ready to spring." But the severe Lightoller saw none of this, and said that the men whom he refused to allow into his boats "could not have stood quieter if they had been in church." Major Arthur Peuchen, who held his commission in the Canadian militia and got away into a boat because he was a yachtsman and could help to handle it, saw a hundred stokers with their bags crowd a whole deck in front of the boats until an officer he did not recognize, a very powerful man, drove them right off the deck like a lot of sheep. Others said not a soul emerged from the engine room. Certainly no single engineer survived. Lowe said they were never seen.

Everyone agrees that the band played until the last. There were eight of them, and none survived. They had played throughout dinner and then gone to their berths. About twenty to one, when the ship was foundering, the cellist ran down the deserted starboard deck, his cello trailing behind him with the spike dragging along the floor. Soon after that the band began to play ragtime. They were still playing ragtime when the last boat was launched.

Colonel Astor, having placed his young bride in one of the boats, lit a cigarette and looked over the rails. Benjamin Guggenheim changed into evening dress, saying that if he had to die he would die like a gentleman. Thomas Andrews leaned against a mantelpiece in the smoking room. A steward asked him, "Aren't you going to try for it, sir?" He did not reply. John Collins, aged seventeen, an assistant cook making his first sea voyage, saw the stewards with their white jackets steering some passengers along, making a joke of it. One steward was helping a woman with two children. The steward was carrying one child and the woman the other. Collins took the child the woman was carrying. "Then," he said, "the sailors and the firemen that were forward seen the ship's bow in the water and seen that she was intending to sink her bow, and they shouted out for all they were worth we were to go aft, and we were just turning round and making for the stern when the wave washed us off the deck, washed us clear of it, and the child was washed out of my arms: and the wreckage, and the people that was around me, they kept me down for at least two or three minutes under the water." The sea was calm as a board, but when the bow went under the water it created a wave that washed the decks clear, and there were hundreds on it.

The *Titanic* goes down,
from *The Illustrated London News*, 27 April 1912

These are the detailed figures for survivors given in the report of the British Board of Trade Inquiry:

	Number on board	Number saved	Percentage saved
First-class passengers			
Men	173	58	34
Women	144	139	97
Children	5	5	100
Second-class passengers			
Men	160	13	8
Women	93	78	84
Children	24	24	100
Third-class passengers			
Men	454	55	12
Women	179	98	55
Children	76	23	30
Total passengers	1308	493	38
Crew	898	210	23
Total	2206	703	32

Taking each class of passenger as a whole, of the first class 63 per cent were saved, of the second class 42 per cent, and of the third class 23 per cent.

TERRY COLEMAN,
The Liners

Dr. Crippen's attempted escape . . .

A couple of years before the sinking of the *Titanic*, two fugitives from English justice had endeavoured to make their getaway to America by ocean steamer. They were the American-born doctor, Hawley Harvey Crippen, and his mistress, Ethel le Neve. On January 31, 1910, Crippen had murdered his wife Cora, also an American, at their house in London, cut up her body, and buried it beneath the floorboards in the cellar. After repeated questioning by Chief Inspector Dew, Crippen took fright and bolted with le Neve to Antwerp where, in the names of John and Master Robinson, they joined the Quebec-bound steamer *Montrose*. Before sailing, the master, Captain Kendall, had received the police description of the missing pair and was immediately suspicious of the Robinsons. After observing them for two days, he sent a wireless message to his owners.

The man on board the *Montrose*, supposed to be Crippen, answers all the descriptions given in the police report, as does also his companion, Miss Le Neve.

I discovered them two hours after leaving Antwerp, but did not telegraph to my owners until I had found out good clues. I conversed with both, and at the same time took keen observations of all points, and felt quite confident as to their identity.

They booked their passage in Brussels as Mr. John Robinson and Master Robinson, and came on board at Antwerp in brown suits, soft grey hats, and white canvas shoes. They had no baggage except a small handbag bought on the Continent. My suspicion was aroused by seeing them on the deck beside a boat. Le Neve squeezed Crippen's hand immoderately. It seemed to me unnatural for two males, so I suspected them at once.

I was well posted as to the crime, so got on the scent at once. I said nothing to the officers till the following morning, when I took my chief officer into my confidence. He then detected the same suspicious circumstances as myself. I warned him that it must be kept absolutely quiet, as it was too good a thing to lose, so we made a lot of them, and kept them smiling.

During lunch I examined both their hats. Crippen's was stamped "Jackson, Boulevard le Nord." Le Neve's hat bore no name, but it was packed round the rim with paper to make it fit. Le Neve has the manner and appearance of a very refined, modest girl. She does not speak much, but always wears a pleasant smile. She seems thoroughly under his thumb, and he will not leave her for a moment. Her suit is anything but a good fit. Her trousers are very tight about the hips, and are split a bit down the back and secured with large safety pins.

You will notice I did not arrest them. The course I am pursuing is the best, as they have no suspicion, and, with so many passengers, it prevents any excitement. They have been under strict observation all the voyage, as if they smelt a rat, he might do something rash. I have not noticed a revolver in his hip pocket. He continually shaves his upper lip, and his beard is growing nicely. I often see him stroking it and seeming pleased, looking more like a farmer every day. The mark on the nose caused through wearing spectacles has not worn off since coming on board.

Ethel le Neve disguised as a boy, 1910

He sits about on the deck reading, or pretending to read, and both seem to be thoroughly enjoying all their meals. They have not been seasick, and I have discussed various parts of the world with him. He knows Toronto, Detroit, and California well and says he is going to take his boy to California for his health (meaning Miss Le Neve). Has in conversation used several medical terms. Crippen says that when the ship arrives he will go to Detroit by boat, if possible, as he prefers it. The books he has been most interested in have been—

> *Pickwick Papers*
> *Nebo the Nailer* (S. B. Gould)
> *Metropolis*
> *A Name to Conjure With*

And he is now busy reading *The Four Just Men*, which is all about a murder in London and £1000 reward.

*   *   *

When my suspicions were aroused as to Crippen's identity I quietly collected all the English papers on the ship which mentioned anything of the murder, and I warned the chief officer to collect any he might see. This being done, I considered the road was clear. I told Crippen a story to make him laugh heartily, to see if he would open his mouth wide enough for me to ascertain if he had false teeth. This ruse was successful.

All the "boy's" manners at table when I was watching him were most lady-like, handling knife and fork, and taking fruit off dishes with two fingers. Crippen kept cracking nuts for her, and giving her half his salad, and was always paying her the most marked attention.

During the evening of July 25, which they spent in the saloon, enjoying songs and music, he was quite interested, and spoke to me next morning, saying how one song, "We All Walked into the Shop," had been drumming in his head all night, and how his boy had enjoyed it, and had laughed heartily when they retired to their room. In the course of one conversation he spoke about American drinks, and said that Selfridge's was the only decent place in London to get them at.

On two or three occasions when walking on the deck I called after him by his assumed name, Mr. Robinson, and he took no notice. I repeated it, and it was only owing to the presence of mind of Miss Le Neve that he turned round. He apologised for not hearing me, saying that the cold weather had made him deaf.

One night he did not appear at the concert in the saloon, and he made an apology to me next morning, saying he wanted to come but the young fellow did not feel well and would not let him come, and he did not like to be left alone. During the day he would often look at the track chart which shows the ship's position, and count the number of days remaining to the end of the passage.

He would often sit on deck and look up aloft at the wireless aerial, and listen to the cracking electric spark messages being sent by the Marconi operator. He said, "What a wonderful invention it is!" He said one day that, according to our present rate of steaming, he ought to be in Detroit on Tuesday, August 2.

At times both would sit and appear to be in deep thought. Though Le Neve does not show signs of distress, and is, perhaps, ignorant of the crime committed, she appears to be a girl with a very weak will. She has to follow him everywhere. If he looks at her she gives him an endearing smile, as though she were under his hypnotic influence.

Crippen was very restless on sighting Belle Isle, and asked where we stopped for the pilot, how he came off, how far from the pilot station to Quebec, and said he would be glad when we arrived, as he was anxious to get to Detroit.

I had them both in my room talking over various things connected with the United States, mostly about San Francisco. Crippen says he does not suppose he would know it now, as he had not been there since he was eighteen years of age, but how he loved California, and said he thought of settling down on a nice fruit farm there. Throughout the whole conversation Le Neve never spoke, but gave the usual laugh of response to anything funny, and looked as though she would like to give vent to her feelings.

(signed) KENDALL, Commander

Daily Mail, London
July 31, 1910

. . . And subsequent trial

The wireless message having been passed on to Chief Inspector Dew, he took a train to Liverpool in time to catch a fast steamer leaving there on July 23—the day after Captain Kendall had sent the message. Dew had with him a warrant executed at Bow Street for Crippen's arrest. When the *Montrose* reached Father Point at the entrance to the St. Lawrence, Dew was already waiting. What happened then he described to the jury at Crippen's subsequent trial.

On 31st July I went on board the steamship *Montrose* at Father Point: she was on the voyage from Antwerp to Quebec. Near the captain's cabin on the deck I saw the prisoner Crippen. He was clean shaven then. He was brought into the captain's cabin. I said, "Good morning, Dr. Crippen; I am Chief Inspector Dew." He said, "Good morning, Mr. Dew." I said, "You will be arrested for the murder and mutilation of your wife, Cora Crippen, in London, on or about the 2nd of February last." Chief Inspector M'Carthy, of the Canadian Provincial Police, cautioned him, and he made no reply. Mr. M'Carthy and Inspector Dennis then searched him in my presence. Exhibits 7, 8, 9, 10, and 11, which are the same articles of jewellery as he had shown me as being the ones which his wife had left behind her, were found on the lower part of his under-vest: the two rings were sewn in and the two brooches were pinned in. Exhibit 12 was fastened to his under-vest with a pin. There were also two cards found upon him. I then left him and went to No. 5 cabin, where I found Miss Le Neve. In the same cabin I found some of Crippen's clothes. At that time Miss Le Neve was dressed as a boy, with her hair cut short. After speaking to her I returned to the captain's cabin, where Crippen was, and then he was taken from that to another cabin. As we were doing that he said, "I am not sorry: the anxiety has been too much." I then read the warrant in detail to him, but he did not make any reply. Mr. M'Carthy then put handcuffs on him, and I said, "We must put these on, because on a card found on you you have written that you intend jumping overboard." He replied, "I won't. I am more than satisfied, because the anxiety has been too awful." Exhibit 2 is one of the cards found upon him. It is a printed card, "E. Robinson & Co., Detroit, Mich. Presented by Mr. John Robinson," and on the back is written, "I cannot stand the horror I go through every night any longer, as I see nothing bright ahead." Exhibit 3 is the other card, a piece of similar card, and on it is written, "Shall we wait until to-night about 10 or 11 o'clock? If not, what time?" In my opinion the handwriting on those cards is Dr. Crippen's. In his portmanteau I found several other similar printed cards.

By the LORD CHIEF JUSTICE—The cabin that Miss Le Neve was in was a two-berth cabin, which could be converted into a four-berth cabin. The cards to which I have spoken were found almost immediately after my first speaking to Dr. Crippen on the steamer. He was searched immediately.

Examination continued—Referring to the signature upon the manifest which is now shown to me, "Robinson" is written backwards, but it seems to me to be Dr. Crippen's handwriting. While Dr. Crippen was being further searched he said, "How is Miss Le Neve?" I said, "Agitated, but I am doing all I can for her." He said, "It is only fair to say that she knows nothing about it: I never told her anything." On 20th August I left with the prisoner and Miss Le Neve in my custody for England on board the steamer *Majestic*. On 21st August I again read to the prisoner the warrants charging him with the wilful murder of his wife, and in reply he said "Right." On 24th August, during the voyage, I was taking Crippen for deck exercise, and on that occasion he said, "I want to ask you a favour, but I will leave it till Friday." I said, "Tell me what it is now and I can answer as well now as on Friday." He said, "When you took me off the ship I did not see Miss Le Neve, and I don't know how things may go; they may go all right or they may go all wrong with me, and I may never see her again: and I want to ask you if you will let me see her; but I won't speak to her. She has been my only comfort for the last three years." On 29th August, having arrived in England, he was formally charged at Bow Street Police Court. He did not make any reply.

Trial of Hawley Harvey Crippen
Notable British Trials
ed. FILSON YOUNG

Crippen was hanged at Pentonville Prison, London, on November 23, 1910.

The V.I.P.s

World War I saw the sinking by U-boat of the liner *Lusitania*, a factor contributing to America's entry into the war. Afterwards the rich began their journeyings again.

Going Cunard as a friend of the company or an important personage with letters from Sir Ashley Sparks, the line's American manager, in the early twenties entailed almost as much inconvenience as it did prestige. The institution of cocktails served every night while at sea by the captain as is the practice today did not exist and the ultimate in social recognition was to be asked to sit at the captain's table, which had about it overtones of royalty. Captain's tables differed in their conduct at the whim of the master of the vessel. Cunard didn't select its captains on a basis of gregariousness or Chesterfieldian courtliness, although most senior sea dogs were fairly well indoctrinated by the time they reached this exalted rank in the social and financial status of the line's clientele.

It was possible to sail with a strict disciplinarian like Sir Arthur Rostron, who had been in command of the *Carpathia* at the time of the *Titanic* rescue, whose table was a tall tower of the maritime proprieties but small geniality, or a voyager of importance could be invited to sit with Sir James Charles, commodore of the Cunard Line and a legend of seagoing joviality and bonhomie.

Sir James's pennant flew from the masthead of the *Aquitania* and represented the ultimate cachet of nautical rank and dignity combined with voluptuary table practices which were a preview of Maxim's and the Café de Paris in an age when Americans were refugees from prohibition with an illimitable thirst for champagne washed down with Niagaras of gin, vodka, arrack, tequila, cognac, slivovitz, and bourbon, whatever was handy in the most substantial quantities.

Guests at Sir James's table lived by protocol. It was an age when the dinner jacket was not in universal acceptance among Englishmen as evening attire, and one's steward, on instructions from the bridge, laid out smoking or tails as the commodore might have decreed and left a note naming the dinner hour. You didn't dine at your convenience but the commodore's and on evenings of the Captain's Dinner full evening dress was required with decorations, which put Americans, unless they were of military background, at a disadvantage in the matter of crosses, ribbons, and miniatures.

Sir James's tastes at table were vaguely those of Emil Jannings playing Henry VIII. Stewards wheeled in carcasses of whole roasted oxen one night and the next evening small herds of grilled antelope surrounded a hilltop of Strasbourg *foie gras* surmounted with peacock fans. Electrically illuminated *pièces montées* representing the battle of Waterloo and other patriotic moments made an appearance while the ship's orchestra played Elgar. Chefs in two-foot-high hats emerged to make thrusts in tierce at turrets of Black Angus beef that towered above the arched eyebrows of the diners, and soufflés the size of the chef's hats blossomed to-

Poster for Royal Mail Line, 1924

ward the end, like the final set pieces of a Paine's fireworks display on the Fourth of July. Throughout these flanking movements and skirmishes champagne circulated in jeroboams, Mumm's 1916, Irroy, and Perrier-Jouet, ditto.

Sir James Charles, a grandee of the sea lanes so portly and full of honors that his mess jackets required structural bracing in their internal economy to support the weight of his decorations, died in line of duty, at sea, almost literally leading an assault on a citadel of pastry moated with diamondback turtle stew *au Madeira*. When they took him ashore at Southampton it was necessary to open both wings of the *Aquitania*'s half-ports to accommodate his going. It was the exit of a nobleman and a warrior.

*   *   *

Transatlantic commuters aboard the *Berengaria*, the *Paris*, or *Rotterdam* in the 1920s became familiar with a personable and very stout French gentleman who traveled the sea lanes on his business occasions named Count La Riboissier. An affable and chatty member of the international set, the Count carried considerable sums of money about his person at all times and in all national currencies. He had, he disclosed to smoke-room acquaintances, about him whenever he was away from home the equivalent of $1000 each in pounds, francs, guilders, zloty, milreis, taler, yen, pesos, marks, pengö, drachmas, and the like, perhaps a total of $10,000 in all the currencies of the then traveled world. Invariably friends would ask why he exposed himself thus to possible robbery when traveler's checks were so much handier?

"It is this way," said Count La Riboissier. "I am, as you see, a fat man, nearly twenty stone on the hoof, and one day I am in a public café in Rio de Janeiro when a young lady acquaintance stops to give me good day. Chivalry is not dead. I leap to my feet and I break a leg in so doing. I have no appreciable money on me, so they throw me in the public pest house. You have never been in a charity hospital in Rio de Janeiro? A good thing. It is deplorable. So now wherever I am, I carry ample money of that country to be able to break a leg in ten languages. I am then a first-class street accident."

LUCIUS BEEBE,
The Big Spenders

ON DECK

Midnight in the mid-Atlantic. On deck.
Wrapped up in themselves as in thick veiling
And mute as mannequins in a dress shop,
Some few passengers keep track
Of the old star-map on the ceiling.
Tiny and far, a single ship

Lit like a two-tiered wedding cake
Carries its candles slowly off.
Now there is nothing much to look at.
Still nobody will move or speak—
The bingo players, the players at love
On a square no bigger than a carpet

Are hustled over the crests and troughs,
Each stalled in his particular minute
And castled in it like a king.
Small drops spot their coats, their gloves:
They fly too fast to feel the wet.
Anything can happen where they are going.

The untidy lady revivalist
For whom the good Lord provides (He gave
Her a pocketbook, a pearl hatpin
And seven winter coats last August)
Prays under her breath that she may save
The art students in West Berlin.

The astrologer at her elbow (a Leo)
Picked his trip-date by the stars.
He is gratified by the absence of icecakes.
He'll be rich in a year (and he should know)
Selling the Welsh and English mothers
Nativities at two-and-six.

And the white-haired jeweller from Denmark is carving
A perfectly faceted wife to wait
On him hand and foot, quiet as a diamond.
Moony balloons tied by a string
To their owners' wrists, the light dreams float
To be let loose at news of land.

Sylvia Plath

The *Normandie* approaches New York,
having won the blue riband of the Atlantic
on her maiden voyage.

The *Normandie*

The *Normandie*'s maiden voyage from Le Havre was on 29 May
1935. The *corps de ballet* of the Paris Opera arrived on board,
and so did Madame Lebrun, wife of the living President of the
French Republic; she was to make the crossing in the Trouville
suite, of four bedrooms, living-room, dining-room, and kitchen.
It was not quite ready: as in many of the other first-class cabins,
the hot running water was not yet running and water had to be
brought in pitchers, but though the plumbing might have failed,

On board the *Atlantique*, 1931

1. Main hall and shops
2. The bathing pool
3. The first class
   dining-saloon
4. Oval saloon
5. First class lounge

La piscine. (Hennequin et Lardat, archit.)

2.

1.

3.

4.

5.

the panache had not, and Madame President's suite was guarded by a sailor with a pike. The other of the two great suites, Deauville, was occupied by the Maharajah of Karpurthala, who, however, offered an unjustified slight to the *Normandie*'s 200 chefs by bringing his own cook with him. Colette was on board, writing for a Paris newspaper, but even her sharp observations collapsed into lofty prose and she wrote about the great liner struggling for the record, and the ocean obeying the ship in silence, and so on. There never was any struggle. The sceptics had said she might break in two, but no liner, however large, had ever done so badly as that even on her maiden voyage, and the *Normandie* did easily what she had been built to do, and took the blue riband at the first attempt. She sailed from Bishop's Rock to the Ambrose light in four days, three hours, fourteen minutes. She had not been officially trying for the record. No liner of breeding ever openly did. But as soon as she happened to break it, little commemorative medals with blue ribbons were spontaneously produced and there were just enough to go round, one to each passenger.

Her dash and gaiety are perhaps best captured by Ludwig Bemelmans, who travelled aboard her and wrote a short story about it. In her decor, he said, she leaned towards excess. There was something of the *femme fatale* about her. Everybody was satisfied, particularly with the Lalique ashtrays. The great hall— silver, gold, glass, and high windows—was as large as a theatre. On the sun deck, children rode the merry-go-round that was built inside the first funnel, which was there for no purpose except decoration and proportion. On the outside of that funnel was a small plaque, like the charm on a bracelet, elegant and right. On it was inscribed: *Normandie, Chantiers Penhoet, Saint Nazaire*, and the date she was built. A young widow aboard travelled with an icebox full of flowers which helped her bear up through the voyage. She appeared with fresh blooms at every meal. Each lift had not only one operator, but also a second man whose purpose it was to squeeze himself into the car, pushing the first one against the wall. The second man then asked the passenger his destination, and passed this information to the first. The second man also opened the door and then rushed ahead to guide the passenger to whatever room he had asked for. When Bemelmans went to buy railway tickets at the ship's travel bureau he

On board the *Normandie*, 1935.
The first class swimming pool

told the man there he wanted to go to Zuerrs in the Tyrol, and started to add that Zuerrs was on the top of the Arlberg between . . . But he got no further. The man at the bureau stopped him and explained, "It is I, Monsieur, who will tell you where Zuerrs is found." Bemelmans thought that the tips on that crossing amounted to more than the whole price of the voyage.

TERRY COLEMAN,
The Liners

The *Ile de France*

The *Normandie* had a gracious older relation, the *Ile de France*.

Every unattached man aboard the ship had approached the tall,
coolly beautiful blonde who held herself aloof and alone throughout the westbound crossing; everyone was icily rebuffed. Everyone knew, from the Passenger List and from scuttlebutt, that the
lady had a bed-ridden husband; yet there was something indefin-
ably approachable about her in spite of the consistency with which
she discouraged invitations to dinner, to deck sports, to cocktails
—or the more blatant tip to a deck steward to place another chair
next to hers. *Something* about her suggested, delicately but un-
mistakably, that she was only flirtatiously waiting for the man
who would catch her fancy.

The elderly and eminently respectable gentleman who suddenly and unexpectedly received an unmistakable smile of invitation on the last night of the voyage was, therefore, thunderstruck.
He had certainly never considered entering the lists himself, having a wife and several children aboard and possessing no lupine
proclivities as a rule anyway, but he had been entertained by the
long succession of optimistic—and unsuccessful—suitors for her
attention. In fact, it had been his wife who had first drawn his
attention to the glamorous blonde, and they had both watched her
with shared amusement throughout the crossing.

But on this last evening his wife had retired early to finish
packing, and the old gentleman was left alone to sip a cognac in
the Salon de Conversation. He never did quite understand how the
lady came to join him, although he supposed he must have exceeded himself in gallantry somehow, but he was not unaware of
the amazed and envious glances of the unattached men in the room
as he waltzed creakily with her and ordered champagne and
waltzed again, and found himself a far more brilliant conversa-
tionalist than he had supposed, to judge from the starry-eyed attention of his beautiful audience.

He never could explain exactly how he had got inside the lady's
cabin, either, once he had delivered her courteously to her door;
certainly he had not had any such intention. Not for years. But
there he indisputably was when the "bed-ridden" husband burst

in from the adjoining cabin, ranting about his outraged honour and declaring that his wrath could only be assuaged by the receipt of a considerable sum of money—which had better be forthcoming at once if the old gentleman didn't want *his* wife to hear about this scandalous affair.

But the old gentleman had been married too long, and too happily, to have any fear at all of such a threat. He remarked rather wistfully that he would be only too pleased if his wife could still believe him capable, after all these years, of captivating such a charming young woman; as it was, he feared that the story would only reduce her to tears of helpless laughter. And he thereupon bade the scheming couple a most courteous good night, and went directly to the Purser and related the whole story. And the Purser, Roger Raulin, notified the would-be blackmailers that *he* was reporting the incident to the F.B.I., the New York Police Department, and to his own head office and the head offices of all the other major steamship companies, and that it would be inadvisable for them to try anything of the kind again.

DONALD K. STANFORD,
Ile de France

Business as before

In 1946 the *Queen Elizabeth* brought back the copy of Magna Carta which had gone to the New York World's Fair of 1939 and then, for safety, had stayed in America for the war. The captain was presented with a metal box lined with copper and sealed with lead, and invited to sign a receipt for "One Tin Box Containing the Magna Carta." This he altered to "One Tin Box Alleged to Contain the Magna Carta," and then signed. Of the two Queens, the *Elizabeth* was released first from war service, and was fitted out for the first time as an ocean liner, her entire previous career having been that of a troopship. The master's cabin was lined with Waterloo elm, from piles driven under old Waterloo bridge in 1811 and recently recovered when the new bridge was built.

During the eighteen months after the war the *Queen Mary* carried 12,886 G.I. brides to America, who were naturally welcomed by bands aboard New York tugboats playing "Here Comes the Bride," but then she too was handed back to Cunard and refitted with the 10,000 bits of furniture that had been stripped from her and stored in New York, Sydney, and the New Forest. One hundred and twenty female French polishers were brought in to restore the woodwork in which American soldiers had carved their initials. Very soon the two Queens were running the weekly Southampton–New York service they had been designed for. The new *Mauretania* was also running to New York, and the old *Aquitania* to Canada, and Cunard were thriving. Aboard the *Queen Mary*, Henry Ford II and Greta Garbo dined, incommunicado and separately, in the Verandah Grill. On the *Queen Elizabeth*, Crown Prince Akihito of Japan won the ship's table-tennis tournament. On the *Mauretania* Miss Lana Turner, on honeymoon, required for breakfast minced raw beef beaten up with egg-yolks, and champagne to wash it down. The Queen of England, returning from New York on the *Queen Mary* after visiting the United States, watched the nightly film shows on three evenings of the crossing, asking to be called just before the main feature began because she did not like cartoons. In the first-class dining-room, passengers were as pampered as ever they had been, and earnestly invited not to limit their choice to the enormous menu, but to ask for anything else that took their fancy. An American oil magnate asked for rattlesnake steaks for four. His order was gravely taken, and his party was served eels in a silver salver born by two stewards shaking rattles. There were sixteen kinds of breakfast cereal every morning, and each liner, on each crossing, carried fifty pounds of mint leaves to make mint juleps. A very few extravagances were moderated. It was noticed that the best people now required smaller suites. Before the war it had been nothing for Count Rossi of Martini Rossi to book a suite of twenty cabins. After the war, the largest suite demanded was only of twelve rooms, by Sir William Rootes, the car manufacturer. Even King Peter of Yugoslavia, no longer having a kingdom, made do with the simplest of royal suites consisting only of three rooms, bathroom, and pantry. But otherwise the tone was maintained. The Marquis and Marquise de la Falaise exacted the same suite with the identical furnishings every crossing, and there was a bed-room steward whose greatest pride it was to store such details in his memory. Mrs. Fern Bedaux, at whose château the Windsors had been married, liked quarts of lilac scent to be sprayed round her suite before she came aboard. The Duchess of Windsor herself always sent advance details of the colour schemes she required to be executed throughout her suite, usually electric greens or blues. Stewards were still stewards, working all hours, travelling light with only two shirts to their name, receiving up to £50 a passage in tips and themselves tipping the pantrymen to ensure their particular passengers got the quickest service, the pantrymen in their turn tipping the chefs. Cunard stewardesses, whether married or unmarried, were according to long custom addressed by other members of the crew as Mrs. though by the passengers of course by their surname alone, with no prefix.

TERRY COLEMAN,
The Liners

Decline and fall

In the early 1960s the old Queens were often criticized. Magazines ran articles with headlines like "Cunard-on-Sea," comparing the deserted Queens to deserted English holiday resorts in rainy summers. In 1962 John Rosselli, an English journalist and historian, crossed the Atlantic both ways in the Queens, one way on each, with his wife and two children. He travelled tourist, and wrote an article entitled "The Notion of Steerage." He suspected that the fall of 7 per cent in the numbers of passengers carried by these ships in the previous year had come about partly because some of the missing 7 per cent had heard what it was like from previous passengers and had decided to try the jets instead. The tourist-class decorations reminded him of the Winter Gardens at Hoylake, near Blackpool. The crew seemed helpful in an Ealing Films way, courteous at all times but noticeably at their best in an emergency. The surest way to get magnificent service was to be seasick from the moment you went on board. But he and his family were not seasick, and found the Queens rather a trial. The ships tended to superimpose on the seedy grandeur of the Odeon the trade-union demarcation lines of the sixties. He wanted to bath his children but found the bathroom doors locked. He called the stewardess who called for the Lady Bath Attendant, who, in turn, when she discovered that he wished to bath the children himself, and was a man, said in that case the Male Bath Attendant was required. After another wait, they all had to go to the deck below, where the Male Bath Attendant had his bathroom. Later, in the restaurant, the wine waiter had never heard of a carafe, though the menu said there was one for nine shillings, and the bottle of wine they ordered instead did not arrive until after the meal. The tiny deckspace for tourists on both Queens suggested that the notion of steerage died hard. On the *Queen Mary* there was no covered deck space where you could sit and look at the sea. It was wind and view, or no wind and no view. The *Queen Elizabeth* did have a small lounge on the top deck, a bit dingy, but with a view. Rosselli suggested fewer waiters and simpler meals. Passengers should be allowed to open their own bathroom doors and fetch their own drinks from the bar without having to wait for a steward to serve them. And generally Cunard could do a lot to make its ships pleasanter and cheaper.

About the same time, passengers in first class were claiming that the service there was not what it used to be, saying that some of the stewards did not even speak English and sounded like the Real Madrid football team. "Do you gents want something to drink?" though uttered in a perfectly friendly manner, was not quite the way for a wine waiter to address first-class passengers. It could also have been said that some of the passengers were not what they used to be either. In 1963, only forty-two took their own manservants or maidservants with them at the special rates traditionally offered by the company.

TERRY COLEMAN,
The Liners

OPEN

BOATS

The sea is a great test of character, and nowhere has man's will to survive been more bravely demonstrated than in involuntary journeys in small boats across big oceans, at the mercy of wind and sea, without adequate food, water, warmth or shelter.

The four stories here are shining examples of the struggle for survival. What happened on three of the journeys we can read for ourselves; the fourth we can only imagine.

Elephant Island to South Georgia

In 1916, after his ship the *Endurance* had been crushed by the Antarctic ice and abandoned, Sir Ernest Shackleton and a few companions set out from Elephant Island in a seven-metre boat, the *James Caird*, to sail to South Georgia, eight hundred miles away, to seek help for those who had to be left behind. That voyage is one of the most remarkable in the history of the sea, a classic not only of courage and endurance but of brilliant navigation. Sir Ernest's own account of the sixteen-day journey is strictly factual, yet somehow he enables the reader to share it with him, to experience the cold and wet, the perpetual depressing grayness of sea and sky, the utter monotony of each day and night, broken only by miserable regulated little meals. It says much for Shackleton's leadership that the journey was successful and that those left behind on Elephant Island were eventually rescued.

By midday the *James Caird* was ready for the voyage. Vincent and the carpenter had secured some dry clothes by exchange with members of the shore party (I heard afterwards that it was a full fortnight before the soaked garments were finally dried), and the boat's crew was standing by waiting for the order to cast off. A moderate westerly breeze was blowing. I went ashore in the

Stancomb Wills and had a last word with Wild, who was remaining in full command, with directions as to his course of action in the event of our failure to bring relief, but I practically left the whole situation and scope of action and decision to his own judgment, secure in the knowledge that he would act wisely. I told him that I trusted the party to him and said good-bye to the men. Then we pushed off for the last time, and within a few minutes I was aboard the *James Caird*. The crew of the *Stancomb Wills* shook hands with us as the boats bumped together and offered us the last good wishes. Then, setting our jib, we cut the painter and moved away to the north-east. The men who were staying behind made a pathetic little group on the beach, with the grim heights of the island behind them and the sea seething at their feet, but they waved to us and gave three hearty cheers. There was hope in their hearts and they trusted us to bring the help that they needed.

I had all sails set, and the *James Caird* quickly dipped the beach and its line of dark figures. The westerly wind took us rapidly to the line of pack, and as we entered it I stood up with my arm around the mast, directing the steering, so as to avoid the great lumps of ice that were flung about in the heave of the sea. The pack thickened and we were forced to turn almost due east, running before the wind towards a gap I had seen in the morning from the high ground. I could not see the gap now, but we had come out on its bearing and I was prepared to find that it had been influenced by the easterly drift. At four o'clock in the afternoon we found the channel, much narrower than it had seemed in the morning but still navigable. Dropping sail, we rowed through without touching the ice anywhere, and by 5.30 P.M. we were clear of the pack with open water before us. We passed one more piece of ice in the darkness an hour later, but the pack lay behind, and with a fair wind swelling the sails we steered our little craft through the night, our hopes centred on our distant goal. The swell was very heavy now, and when the time came for our first evening meal we found great difficulty in keeping the Primus lamp alight and preventing the hoosh splashing out of the pot. Three men were needed to attend to the cooking, one man holding the lamp and two men guarding the aluminium cooking-pot, which had to be lifted clear of the Primus whenever the movement of

the boat threatened to cause a disaster. Then the lamp had to be
protected from water, for sprays were coming over the bows and
our flimsy decking was by no means water-tight. All these operations were conducted in the confined space under the decking,
where the men lay or knelt and adjusted themselves as best they
could to the angles of our cases and ballast. It was uncomfortable,
but we found consolation in the reflection that without the decking we could not have used the cooker at all.

The tale of the next sixteen days is one of supreme strife amid
heaving waters. The sub-Antarctic Ocean lived up to its evil
winter reputation. I decided to run north for at least two days
while the wind held and so get into warmer weather before turning to the east and laying a course for South Georgia. We took
two-hourly spells at the tiller. The men who were not on watch
crawled into the sodden sleeping-bags and tried to forget their
troubles for a period; but there was no comfort in the boat. The
bags and cases seemed to be alive in the unfailing knack of pre-
senting their most uncomfortable angles to our rest-seeking
bodies. A man might imagine for a moment that he had found a
position of ease, but always discovered quickly that some unyielding point was impinging on muscle or bone. The first night aboard
the boat was one of acute discomfort for us all, and we were
heartily glad when the dawn came and we could set about the
preparation of a hot breakfast.

This record of the voyage to South Georgia is based upon
scanty notes made day by day. The notes dealt usually with the
bare facts of distances, positions, and weather, but our memories
retained the incidents of the passing days in a period never to be
forgotten. By running north for the first two days I hoped to get
warmer weather and also to avoid lines of pack that might be
extending beyond the main body. We needed all the advantage
that we could obtain from the higher latitude for sailing on the
great circle, but we had to be cautious regarding possible ice-
streams. Cramped in our narrow quarters and continually wet by
the spray, we suffered severely from cold throughout the journey.
We fought the seas and the winds and at the same time had a
daily struggle to keep ourselves alive. At times we were in dire
peril. Generally we were upheld by the knowledge that we were
making progress towards the land where we would be, but there

were days and nights when we lay hove to, drifting across the storm-whitened seas and watching, with eyes interested rather than apprehensive, the uprearing masses of water, flung to and fro by Nature in the pride of her strength. Deep seemed the valleys when we lay between the reeling seas. High were the hills when we perched momentarily on the tops of giant combers. Nearly always there were gales. So small was our boat and so great were the seas that often our sail flapped idly in the calm between the crests of two waves. Then we would climb the next slope and catch the full fury of the gale where the wool-like whiteness of the breaking water surged around us. We had our moments of laughter—rare, it is true, but hearty enough. Even when cracked lips and swollen mouths checked the outward and visible signs of amusement we could see a joke of the primitive kind. Man's sense of humour is always most easily stirred by the petty misfortunes of his neighbours, and I shall never forget Worsley's efforts on one occasion to place the hot aluminium stand on top of the Primus stove after it had fallen off in an extra heavy roll. With his frost-bitten fingers he picked it up, dropped it, picked it up again, and toyed with it gingerly as though it were some fragile article of lady's wear. We laughed, or rather gurgled with laughter.

The wind came up strong and worked into a gale from the north-west on the third day out. We stood away to the east. The increasing seas discovered the weaknesses of our decking. The continuous blows shifted the box-lids and sledge-runners so that the canvas sagged down and accumulated water. Then icy trickles, distinct from the driving sprays, poured fore and aft into the boat. The nails that the carpenter had extracted from cases at Elephant Island and used to fasten down the battens were too short to make firm the decking. We did what we could to secure it, but our means were very limited, and the water continued to enter the boat at a dozen points. Much bailing was necessary, and nothing that we could do prevented our gear from becoming sodden. The searching runnels from the canvas were really more unpleasant than the sudden definite douches of the sprays. Lying under the thwarts during watches below, we tried vainly to avoid them. There were no dry places in the boat, and at last we simply covered our heads with our Burberrys and endured the all-pervading

water. The bailing was work for the watch. Real rest we had
none. The perpetual motion of the boat made repose impossible;
we were cold, sore, and anxious. We moved on hands and knees
in the semi-darkness of the day under the decking. The darkness
was complete by 6 P.M., and not until 7 A.M. of the following day
could we see one another under the thwarts. We had a few scraps
of candle, and they were preserved carefully in order that we
might have light at meal-times. There was one fairly dry spot in
the boat, under the solid original decking at the bows, and we
managed to protect some of our biscuit from the salt water; but I
do not think any of us got the taste of salt out of our mouths during the voyage.

The difficulty of movement in the boat would have had its
humorous side if it had not involved us in so many aches and
pains. We had to crawl under the thwarts in order to move along
the boat, and our knees suffered considerably. When a watch

The *James Caird* nearing South Georgia

turned out it was necessary for me to direct each man by name when and where to move, since if all hands had crawled about at the same time the result would have been dire confusion and many bruises. Then there was the trim of the boat to be considered. The order of the watch was four hours on and four hours off, three men to the watch. One man had the tiller-ropes, the second man attended to the sail, and the third bailed for all he was worth. Sometimes when the water in the boat had been reduced to reasonable proportions, our pump could be used. This pump, which Hurley had made from the Flinders bar case of our ship's standard compass, was quite effective, though its capacity was not large. The man who was attending the sail could pump into the big outer cooker, which was lifted and emptied overboard when filled. We had a device by which the water could go direct from the pump into the sea through a hole in the gunwale, but this hole had to be blocked at an early stage of the voyage, since we found that it admitted water when the boat rolled.

While a new watch was shivering in the wind and spray, the men who had been relieved groped hurriedly among the soaked sleeping-bags and tried to steal a little of the warmth created by the last occupants; but it was not always possible for us to find even this comfort when we went off watch. The boulders that we had taken aboard for ballast had to be shifted continually in order to trim the boat and give access to the pump, which became choked with hairs from the moulting sleeping-bags and finneskoe. The four reindeer-skin sleeping-bags shed their hair freely owing to the continuous wetting, and soon became quite bald in appearance. The moving of the boulders was weary and painful work. We came to know every one of the stones by sight and touch, and I have vivid memories of their angular peculiarities even to-day. They might have been of considerable interest as geological specimens to a scientific man under happier conditions. As ballast they were useful. As weights to be moved about in cramped quarters they were simply appalling. They spared no portion of our poor bodies. Another of our troubles, worth mention here, was the chafing of our legs by our wet clothes, which had not been changed now for seven months. The insides of our thighs were rubbed raw, and the one tube of Hazeline cream in our medicine-chest did not go far in alleviating our pain, which was increased by the bite of the salt water. We thought at the time that we never slept. The fact was that we would doze off uncomfortably, to be aroused quickly by some new ache or another call to effort. My own share of the general unpleasantness was accentuated by a finely developed bout of sciatica. I had become possessor of this originally on the floe several months earlier.

Our meals were regular in spite of the gales. Attention to this point was essential, since the conditions of the voyage made increasing calls upon our vitality. Breakfast, at 8 A.M., consisted of a pannikin of hot hoosh made from Bovril sledging ration, two biscuits, and some lumps of sugar. Lunch came at 1 P.M., and comprised Bovril sledging ration, eaten raw, and a pannikin of hot milk for each man. Tea, at 5 P.M., had the same menu. Then during the night we had a hot drink, generally of milk. The meals were the bright beacons in those cold and stormy days. The glow of warmth and comfort produced by the food and drink made optimists of us all. We had two tins of Virol, which we were keeping for an emergency; but, finding ourselves in need of an oil-lamp to eke out our supply of candles, we emptied one of the tins in the manner that most appealed to us, and fitted it with a wick made by shredding a bit of canvas. When this lamp was filled with oil it gave a certain amount of light, though it was easily blown out, and was of great assistance to us at night. We were fairly well off as regarded fuel, since we had 6½ gallons of petroleum.

A severe south-westerly gale on the fourth day out forced us to heave to. I would have liked to have run before the wind, but the sea was very high and the *James Caird* was in danger of broaching to and swamping. The delay was vexatious, since up to that time we had been making sixty or seventy miles a day; good going with our limited sail area. We hove to under double-reefed mainsail and our little jigger, and waited for the gale to blow itself out. During that afternoon we saw bits of wreckage, the remains probably of some unfortunate vessel that had failed to weather the strong gales south of Cape Horn. The weather conditions did not improve, and on the fifth day out the gale was so fierce that we were compelled to take in the double-reefed mainsail and hoist our small jib instead. We put out a sea-anchor to keep the *James Caird*'s head up to the sea. This anchor consisted of a triangular canvas bag fastened to the end of the painter and allowed to stream out from the bows. The boat was high enough to catch the wind, and, as she drifted to leeward, the drag of the anchor kept her head to windward. Thus our boat took most of the seas more or less end on. Even then the crests of the waves often would curl right over us and we shipped a great deal of water, which necessitated unceasing bailing and pumping. Looking out abeam, we would see a hollow like a tunnel formed as the crest of a big wave toppled over on to the swelling body of water. A thousand times it appeared as though the *James Caird* must be engulfed; but the boat lived. The south-westerly gale had its birthplace above the Antarctic Continent, and its freezing breath lowered the temperature far towards zero. The sprays froze upon the boat and gave bows, sides, and decking a heavy coat of mail. This accumulation of ice reduced the buoyancy of the boat, and to that extent was an added peril; but it possessed a notable advantage from one point of view. The water ceased to drop and trickle from the canvas, and the spray came in solely at the well in the after part of the boat. We could not allow the load of ice to grow beyond a certain point, and in turns we crawled about the decking forward, chipping and picking at it with the available tools.

When daylight came on the morning of the sixth day out we saw and felt that the *James Caird* had lost her resiliency. She was not rising to the oncoming seas. The weight of the ice that had formed in her and upon her during the night was having its effect, and she was becoming more like a log than a boat. The situation called for immediate action. We first broke away the spare oars, which were encased in ice and frozen to the sides of the boat, and threw them overboard. We retained two oars for use when we got inshore. Two of the fur sleeping-bags went over the side; they were thoroughly wet, weighing probably 40 lb. each, and they had frozen stiff during the night. Three men constituted the watch below, and when a man went down it was better to turn into the wet bag just vacated by another man than to thaw out a frozen bag with the heat of his unfortunate body. We now had four bags, three in use and one for emergency use in case a member of the party should break down permanently. The reduction of weight relieved the boat to some extent, and vigorous chipping and scraping did more. We had to be very careful not to put axe or knife through the frozen canvas of the decking as we crawled over it, but gradually we got rid of a lot of ice. The *James Caird* lifted to the endless waves as though she lived again.

About 11 A.M. the boat suddenly fell off into the trough of the sea. The painter had parted and the sea-anchor had gone. This was serious. The *James Caird* went away to leeward, and we had no chance at all of recovering the anchor and our valuable rope, which had been our only means of keeping the boat's head up to the seas without the risk of hoisting sail in a gale. Now we had to set the sail and trust to its holding. While the *James Caird* rolled heavily in the trough, we beat the frozen canvas until the bulk of the ice had cracked off it and then hoisted it. The frozen gear worked protestingly, but after a struggle our little craft came up to the wind again, and we breathed more freely. Skin frost-bites were troubling us, and we had developed large blisters on our fingers and hands. I shall always carry the scar of one of these frost-bites on my left hand, which became badly inflamed after the skin had burst and the cold had bitten deeply.

We held the boat up to the gale during that day, enduring as best we could discomforts that amounted to pain. The boat tossed interminably on the big waves under grey, threatening skies. Our thoughts did not embrace much more than the necessities of the hour. Every surge of the sea was an enemy to be watched and circumvented. We ate our scanty meals, treated our frost-bites, and hoped for the improved conditions that the morrow might bring. Night fell early, and in the lagging hours of darkness we were cheered by a change for the better in the weather. The wind dropped, the snow-squalls became less frequent, and the sea moderated. When the morning of the seventh day dawned there was not much wind. We shook the reef out of the sail and laid our course once more for South Georgia. The sun came out bright and clear, and presently Worsley got a snap for longitude. We hoped that the sky would remain clear until noon, so that we could get the latitude. We had been six days out without an observation, and our dead reckoning naturally was uncertain. The boat must have presented a strange appearance that morning. All hands basked in the sun. We hung our sleeping-bags to the mast and spread our socks and other gear all over the deck. Some of the ice had melted off the *James Caird* in the early morning after the gale began to slacken, and dry patches were appearing in the decking. Porpoises came blowing round the boat, and Cape pigeons wheeled and swooped within a few feet of us. These little black-and-white birds have an air of friendliness that is not possessed by the great circling albatross. They had looked grey against the swaying sea during the storm as they darted about over our heads and uttered their plaintive cries. The albatrosses, of the black or sooty variety, had watched with hard, bright eyes, and seemed to have a quite impersonal interest in our struggle to keep afloat amid the battering seas. In addition to the Cape pigeons an occasional stormy petrel flashed overhead. Then there was a small bird, unknown to me, that appeared always to be in a fussy, bustling state, quite out of keeping with the surroundings. It irritated me. It had practically no tail, and it flitted about vaguely as though in search of the lost member. I used to find myself wishing it would find its tail and have done with the silly fluttering.

We revelled in the warmth of the sun that day. Life was not so bad, after all. We felt we were well on our way. Our gear was drying, and we could have a hot meal in comparative comfort. The swell was still heavy, but it was not breaking and the boat rode easily. At noon Worsley balanced himself on the gunwale and clung with one hand to the stay of the mainmast while he got a snap of the sun. The result was more than encouraging. We had done over 380 miles and were getting on for half-way to South Georgia. It looked as though we were going to get through.

The wind freshened to a good stiff breeze during the afternoon, and the *James Caird* made satisfactory progress. I had not realized until the sunlight came how small our boat really was. There was some influence in the light and warmth, some hint of happier days, that made us revive memories of other voyages, when we had stout decks beneath our feet, unlimited food at our command, and pleasant cabins for our ease. Now we clung to a battered little boat, "alone, alone, all, all alone, alone on a wide, wide sea." So low in the water were we that each succeeding swell cut off our view of the sky-line. We were a tiny speck in the vast vista of the sea—the ocean that is open to all and merciful to none, that threatens even when it seems to yield, and that is pitiless always to weakness. For a moment the consciousness of the forces arrayed against us would be almost overwhelming.

Then hope and confidence would rise again as our boat rose to a wave and tossed aside the crest in a sparkling shower like the play of prismatic colours at the foot of a waterfall. My double-barrelled gun and some cartridges had been stowed aboard the boat as an emergency precaution against a shortage of food, but we were not disposed to destroy our little neighbours, the Cape pigeons, even for the sake of fresh meat. We might have shot an albatross, but the wandering king of the ocean aroused in us something of the feeling that inspired, too late, the Ancient Mariner. So the gun remained among the stores and sleeping-bags in the narrow quarters beneath our leaking deck, and the birds followed us unmolested.

The eighth, ninth, and tenth days of the voyage had few features worthy of special note. The wind blew hard during those days, and the strain of navigating the boat was unceasing, but always we made some advance towards our goal. No bergs showed on our horizon, and we knew that we were clear of the ice-fields. Each day brought its little round of troubles, but also compensation in the form of food and growing hope. We felt that we were going to succeed. The odds against us had been great, but we were winning through. We still suffered severely from the cold, for, though the temperature was rising, our vitality was declining owing to shortage of food, exposure, and the necessity of maintaining our cramped positions day and night. I found that it was now absolutely necessary to prepare hot milk for all hands during the night, in order to sustain life till dawn. This meant lighting the Primus lamp in the darkness and involved an increased drain on our small store of matches. It was the rule that one match must serve when the Primus was being lit. We had no lamp for the compass and during the early days of the voyage we would strike a match when the steersman wanted to see the course at night; but later the necessity for strict economy impressed itself upon us, and the practice of striking matches at night was stopped. We had one water-tight tin of matches. I had stowed away in a pocket, in readiness for a sunny day, a lens from one of the telescopes, but this was of no use during the voyage. The sun seldom shone upon us. The glass of the compass got broken one night, and we contrived to mend it with adhesive tape from the medicine-chest. One of the memories that comes to me from those days is of Crean singing at the tiller. He always sang while he was steering, and nobody ever discovered what the song was. It was devoid of tune and as monotonous as the chanting of a Buddhist monk at his prayers; yet somehow it was cheerful. In moments of inspiration Crean would attempt "The Wearing of the Green."

On the tenth night Worsley could not straighten his body after his spell at the tiller. He was thoroughly cramped, and we had to drag him beneath the decking and massage him before he could unbend himself and get into a sleeping-bag. A hard north-westerly gale came up on the eleventh day (May 5) and shifted to the south-west in the late afternoon. The sky was overcast and occasional snow-squalls added to the discomfort produced by a tremendous cross-sea—the worst, I thought, that we had experienced. At midnight I was at the tiller and suddenly noticed a line of clear sky between the south and south-west. I called to the other men that the sky was clearing, and then a moment later I realized that what I had seen was not a rift in the clouds but the white crest of an enormous wave. During twenty-six years' experience of the ocean in all its moods I had not encountered a wave so gigantic. It was a mighty upheaval of the ocean, a thing quite apart from the big white-capped seas that had been our tireless enemies for many days. I shouted, "For God's sake, hold on! It's got us!" Then came a moment of suspense that seemed drawn out into hours. White surged the foam of the breaking sea around us. We felt our boat lifted and flung forward like a cork in breaking surf. We were in a seething chaos of tortured water; but somehow the boat lived through it, half-full of water, sagging to the dead weight and shuddering under the blow. We bailed with the energy of men fighting for life, flinging the water over the sides with every receptacle that came to our hands, and after ten minutes of uncertainty we felt the boat renew her life beneath us. She floated again and ceased to lurch drunkenly as though dazed by the attack of the sea. Earnestly we hoped that never again would we encounter such a wave.

The conditions in the boat, uncomfortable before, had been made worse by the deluge of water. All our gear was thoroughly wet again. Our cooking-stove had been floating about in the bottom of the boat, and portions of our last hoosh seemed to have permeated everything. Not until 3 A.M., when we were all chilled

almost to the limit of endurance, did we manage to get the stove
alight and make ourselves hot drinks. The carpenter was suffering particularly, but he showed grit and spirit. Vincent had for
the past week ceased to be an active member of the crew, and I
could not easily account for his collapse. Physically he was one of
the strongest men in the boat. He was a young man, he had served
on North Sea trawlers, and he should have been able to bear hardships better than McCarthy, who, not so strong, was always
happy.

The weather was better on the following day (May 6), and
we got a glimpse of the sun. Worsley's observation showed that
we were not more than a hundred miles from the north-west corner of South Georgia. Two more days with a favourable wind
and we would sight the promised land. I hoped that there would
be no delay, for our supply of water was running very low. The
hot drink at night was essential, but I decided that the daily allowance of water must be cut down to half a pint per man. The
lumps of ice we had taken aboard had gone long ago. We were
dependent upon the water we had brought from Elephant Island,
and our thirst was increased by the fact that we were now using
the brackish water in the breaker that had been slightly stove in
in the surf when the boat was being loaded. Some sea-water had
entered at that time.

Thirst took possession of us. I dared not permit the allowance
of water to be increased since an unfavourable wind might drive
us away from the island and lengthen our voyage by many days.
Lack of water is always the most severe privation that men can
be condemned to endure, and we found, as during our earlier boat
voyage, that the salt water in our clothing and the salt spray that
lashed our faces made our thirst grow quickly to a burning pain.
I had to be very firm in refusing to allow any one to anticipate the
morrow's allowance, which I was sometimes begged to do. We
did the necessary work dully and hoped for the land. I had altered
the course to the east so as to make sure of our striking the island,
which would have been impossible to regain if we had run past
the northern end. The course was laid on our scrap of chart for
a point some thirty miles down the coast. That day and the following day passed for us in a sort of nightmare. Our mouths were
dry and our tongues were swollen. The wind was still strong and

the heavy sea forced us to navigate carefully, but any thought of our peril from the waves was buried beneath the consciousness of our raging thirst. The bright moments were those when we each received our one mug of hot milk during the long, bitter watches of the night. Things were bad for us in those days, but the end was coming. The morning of May 8 broke thick and stormy, with squalls from the north-west. We searched the waters ahead for a sign of land, and though we could see nothing more than had met our eyes for many days, we were cheered by a sense that the goal was near at hand. About ten o'clock that morning we passed a little bit of kelp, a glad signal of the proximity of land. An hour later we saw two shags sitting on a big mass of kelp, and knew then that we must be within ten or fifteen miles of the shore. These birds are as sure an indication of the proximity of land as a lighthouse is, for they never venture far to sea. We gazed ahead with increasing eagerness, and at 12.30 P.M., through a rift in the clouds, McCarthy caught a glimpse of the black cliffs of South Georgia, just fourteen days after our departure from Elephant Island. It was a glad moment. Thirst-ridden, chilled, and weak as we were, happiness irradiated us. The job was nearly done.

ERNEST SHACKLETON,
South

And Then There Were Two

Angus Macdonald was a member of the crew of the Ellerman liner *City of Cairo*, which, on November 6, 1942, five days out from Capetown, was torpedoed by a German U-boat. Three passengers and eighteen crew were killed or went down with the ship. The remainder took to the boats.

I was a quartermaster and had charge of No. 4 lifeboat. After seeing everything in order there and the boat lowered, I went over to the starboard side of the ship to where my mate, quartermaster Bob Ironside, was having difficulty in lowering his boat. I climbed inside the boat to clear a rope fouling the lowering gear, and was standing in the boat pushing it clear of the ship's side as it was being lowered, when a second torpedo exploded right underneath and blew the boat to bits. I remember a great flash, and then felt myself flying through space, then going down and down. When I came to I was floating in the water, and could see all sorts of wreckage around me in the dark. I could not get the light on my life-jacket to work, so I swam towards the largest bit of wreckage I could see in the darkness. This turned out to be No. 1 lifeboat and it was nearly submerged, it having been damaged by the second explosion. There were a few people clinging to the gunwale, which was down to water-level, and other people were sitting inside the flooded boat.

I climbed on board, and had a good look round to see if the boat was badly damaged. Some of the gear had floated away, and what was left was in a tangled mess. There were a few lascars, several women and children, and two European male passengers in the boat, and I explained to them that if some of them would go overboard and hang on to the gunwale or the wreckage near us for a few minutes we could bail out the boat and make it seaworthy. The women who were there acted immediately. They climbed outboard and, supported by the life-jackets every one was wearing, held on to an empty tank that was floating near by. I felt very proud of these women and children. One woman (whose name, if I remember rightly, was Lady Tibbs) had three children, and the four of them were the first to swim to the tank. One young woman was left in the boat with two babies in her arms.

We men then started to bail out the water. It was a long and arduous task, as just when we had the gunwale a few inches clear, the light swell running would roll in and swamp the boat again. Eventually we managed to bail out the boat, and then we started to pick up survivors who were floating on rafts or just swimming. As we worked we could see the *City of Cairo* still afloat, but well down in the water, until we heard someone say, "There she goes." We watched her go down, stern first, her bow away up in the air, and then she went down and disappeared. There was no show of emotion, and we were all quiet. I expect the others, like myself, were wondering what would happen to us.

We picked up more survivors as the night wore on, and by the first light of dawn the boat was full. There were still people on the rafts we could see with the daylight, and in the distance were other lifeboats. We rowed about, picking up more people, among them Mr. Sydney Britt, the chief officer, and quartermaster Bob Ironside, who was in No. 3 boat with me when the second torpedo struck. Bob's back had been injured, and one of his hands had been cut rather badly. We picked up others, then rowed to the other boats to see what decision had been made about our future. Mr. Britt had, naturally, taken over command of our boat, and now he had a conference with Captain Rogerson, who was in another boat. They decided we would make for the nearest land, the island of St. Helena, lying five hundred miles due north. We transferred people from boat to boat so that families could be together. Mr. Britt suggested that, as our boat was in a bad way, with many leaks and a damaged rudder, and at least half its water-supply lost, all the children should shift to a dry boat and a few adults take their places in our boat.

When everything was settled we set sail and started on our long voyage. Our boat was now overcrowded with fifty-four persons on board—twenty-three Europeans, including three women, and thirty-one lascars. There was not enough room for everyone to sit down, so we had to take turns having a rest. The two worst injured had to lie down flat, so we made a place in the bows for Miss Taggart, a ship's stewardess, and cleared a space aft for my mate, quartermaster Bob Ironside. We did not know exactly what was wrong with Bob's back. We had a doctor in the boat, Dr. Taskar, but he was in a dazed condition and not able to attend to the injured, so we bandaged them up as best we could with the first-aid materials on hand. The youngest person among us, Mrs. Diana Jarman, one of the ship's passengers, and only about twenty years of age, was a great help with the first-aid. She could never do enough, either in attending to the sick and injured, boat work, or even actually handling the craft. She showed up some of the men in the boat, who seemed to lose heart from the beginning.

Once we were properly under way Mr. Britt spoke to us all. He explained all the difficulties that lay ahead, and asked every one to pull their weight in everything to do with managing the boat, such as rowing during calm periods and keeping a look-out at night. He also explained that as we had lost nearly half our drinking water we must start right away on short rations. We could get two tablespoonfuls a day per person, one in the morning and one in the evening. He told us there were no passengers in a lifeboat, and every one would have to take turns bailing as the boat was leaking very badly.

Before noon on that first day we saw our first sharks. They were enormous, and as they glided backward and forward under the boat it seemed they would hit and capsize us. They just skimmed the boat each time they passed, and they were never to leave us all the time we were in the boat.

The first night was quiet and the weather was fine, but we didn't get much rest. A good proportion of us had to remain standing for long periods, and now and then someone would fall over in their sleep. I was in the fore-part of the boat attending to the sails and the running gear, helped by Robert Watts from Reading, whom we called "Tiny" because he was a big man. He didn't know much about seamanship, as he was an aeronautical

Survivors from a torpedoed ship (Richard Eurich)

engineer, but he said to me that first day, "If you want anything done at any time just explain the job to me and I'll do it." His help was very welcome as we did not have many of the crew available for the jobs that needed to be done. From the very beginning the lascars refused to help in any way, and just lay in the bottom of the boat, sometimes in over a foot of water.

On the second day the wind increased, and we made good speed. Sometimes the boats were close together and at other times almost out of sight of each other. Our boat seemed to sail faster than the others, so Mr. Britt had the idea that we might go ahead on our own. If we could sail faster than the others, and as we were leaking so badly, we should go ahead and when we got to St. Helena we could send help to the others. Mr. Britt had a talk with Captain Rogerson when our boats were close, and the captain said that if the mate thought that was the best plan to go ahead. So we carried on on our own.

During the hours of darkness the wind rose stronger, and, as we could see the running gear was not in the best of condition, we hove to. As it got still worse, we had to put out a sea anchor and take turns at the steering-oar to hold the boat into the seas. We had a bad night, and two or three times seas broke over the heavily laden boat and soaked us all to the skin. It was during this night that we noticed Dr. Taskar was failing mentally. Every now and then he shouted, "Boy, bring me my coffee," or, "Boy, another beer." He had a rip in his trousers, and in the crowded boat during the night he cut a large piece out of the trousers of the ship's storekeeper, Frank Stobbart. I noticed the doctor with the knife and a piece of cloth in his hand. He was trying to fit the cloth over his own trousers. I pacified him and took his knife, a small silver knife with a whisky advertisement on the side. I had the same knife all through the years I was a prisoner in Germany, and only lost it after the war while serving in another Ellerman liner.

At noon on the third day the wind abated, and we set sails again and went on. We had lost sight of the other boats now and were on our own. We all expected to see a rescue ship or plane at any time, but nothing turned up. On the evening of the fourth day the doctor got worse, and rambled in his speech. He kept asking for water, and once Mr. Britt gave him an extra ration, although there was not much to spare. During the night the doctor slumped over beside me, and I knew he was dead. That was the first death in the boat. We cast the body overboard at dawn while Mr. Britt read a short prayer. We all felt gloomy after this first burial, and wondered who would be next.

Later in the day I crawled over to have a yarn with my mate Bob, and he said, "Do you think we have a chance, Angus?" I said, "Everything will be all right, Bob. We are bound to be picked up." Bob hadn't long been married, and he was anxious about his wife and little baby in Aberdeen. He couldn't sit up, and I was afraid his back was broken or badly damaged.

Day and night the lascars kept praying to Allah, and repeating "Pani, sahib, pani, sahib," and they would never understand that the water was precious and had to be rationed out. On the sixth morning we found three of them dead in the bottom of the boat. The old engine-room serang read a prayer for them, and Tiny and I pushed them overboard, as the lascars never would help to bury their dead. The only two natives who helped us at any time were the old serang, a proper gentleman, and a fireman from Zanzibar, and they couldn't do enough to help.

We were getting flat calms for long periods, and we lowered the sails and used the oars. We didn't make much headway, but the work helped to keep our minds and bodies occupied. I know that doing these necessary tasks helped to keep me physically fit and able to stand up to the ordeal that lay ahead. There were a few Europeans who never gave a helping hand, and I noticed that they were the first to fail mentally. They died in the first two weeks.

I was worried about Miss Taggart's sores, as they had now festered and we had nothing to dress them with except salt water. With her lying in the same position all the time her back was a mass of sores. Tiny knew more about first-aid than the rest of us, and with the aid of old life-jackets he padded her up a bit. But on the seventh night she died and slipped down from her position in the bows. As she fell she got tangled up with another passenger, a Mr. Ball from Calcutta, and when we got things straightened out they were both dead. A few more lascars died during the same night, and we had to bury them all at daybreak. The sharks were there in shoals that morning, and the water was churned up as they glided backward and forward near the bodies. Things were now getting worse on board, and a good few of the people sat all day with their heads on their chests doing and saying nothing. I talked to one young engineer, and told him to pull himself together as he was young and healthy and to take a lesson from Diana, who was always cheerful and bright. She had told us, "Please don't call me Mrs. Jarman; just call me Diana." The young engineer did pull himself back to normal but within two days he dropped back and gave up hope and died. As we buried the bodies the boat gradually became lighter and the worst leaks rose above the water-line, so there was not so much water to bail out, although we had still to bail day and night.

Our own ship's stewardess, Annie Crouch, died on the tenth day. She had been failing mentally and physically for a time, and persisted in sitting in the bottom of the boat. We shifted her to drier places, but she always slid back. Her feet and legs had swollen enormously. Her death left only one woman among us, Diana. She was still active and full of life, and she spent most of her time at the tiller. Mr. Britt was beginning to show signs of mental strain, and often mumbled to himself. If I asked him a question he would answer in a dazed sort of way. I worried about him a lot, for he was always a gentleman, and every one thought the world of him. On the twelfth day he was unable to sit up or talk, so we laid him down alongside Bob Ironside, who was also failing fast. Bob called me over one day, and asked me if I thought there was still a chance. I said certainly there was, and urged him not to give up hope as he would soon be home. He said, "I can't hang on much longer, Angus. When I die, will you take off my ring and send it home if you ever get back?" There were only a few able-bodied men left among the Europeans now, and Tiny Watts, my right-hand man, died on the fourteenth morning. He hadn't complained at any time, and I was surprised when I found him dead. We buried seven bodies that morning; five lascars, Tiny, and Frank Stobbart. It took a long time to get them overboard, and I had to lie down and rest during the operation.

On the fifteenth morning at dawn both Mr. Britt and Bob were dead, also three other Europeans, and a few lascars. A few more lascars died during the day. One of the firemen said that if

he couldn't get extra water he would jump overboard, and later
in the day he jumped over the stern. He had forgotten to take
off his life-jacket, and as we were now too weak to turn the boat
round to save him, the sharks got him before he could drown.
The remaining survivors voted that I should take over command.
On looking through Mr. Britt's papers I could see the estimated
distances for each day up to about the tenth day, but after that
there were only scrawls and scribbles. When I checked up on the
water I found we had enough only for a few days, so I suggested
cutting down the issue to one tablespoonful a day. There were
plenty of biscuits and malted-milk tablets, but without water to
moisten the mouth the biscuits only went into a powder and fell
out of the corner of the mouth again. Those people with false
teeth had still more trouble as the malted milk tablets went into
a doughy mess and stuck to their teeth.

The boat was now much drier, and there was not so much
bailing to do as we rode higher in the water and most of the leaks
were above the surface. The movement, however, was not so
steady as when we were heavier laden, but about the middle of
the seventeenth night the boat appeared to become very steady
again. I heard Diana cry out, "We're full of water," and I jumped
up and found the boat half-full of water. I could see the plug-hole
glittering like a blue-light, and I started looking for the plug. I
put a spare one in place, and a few of us bailed out the water.
There were two people lying near the plug-hole, and they seemed
to take no interest in what was happening. About an hour later I
discovered the plug gone again and water entering the boat. I put
the plug back, and this time I lay down with an eye on watch.
Sure enough, in less than half an hour I saw a hand over the plug
pulling it out. I grasped the hand and found it belonged to a
young European. He was not in his right mind, although he knew
what he was doing. When I asked him why he tried to sink the
boat he said, "I'm going to die, so we might as well go together."
I shifted him to the fore part of the boat, and we others took turns
in keeping an eye on him, but he managed to destroy all the contents of the first-aid box and throw them over the side. He died
the next day, with seven or eight lascars, and a banker from Edin-
burgh, a Mr. Crichton. Mr. Crichton had a patent waistcoat fitted
with small pockets, and the valuables we found there we put with

rings and other things in Diana's handbag. Among Mr. Crichton's possessions were the three wise monkeys in jade and a silver brandy flask that was empty.

At the end of the third week there were only eight of us left alive in the boat: the old engine-room serang, the fireman from Zanzibar, myself, Diana, Jack Edmead, the steward, Joe Green from Wigan, Jack Oakie from Birmingham, and a friend of his, Jack Little. Two of them had been engineers working on the new Howrah bridge at Calcutta.

There was still no rain, we had not had a single shower since we started our boat voyage, and the water was nearly finished. Only a few drops were left on the bottom of the tank. About the middle of the fourth week I was lying down dozing in the middle of the night when the boat started to rattle and shake. I jumped up, thinking we had grounded on an island. Then I discovered a large fish had jumped into the boat and was thrashing about wildly. I grabbed an axe that was lying handy, and hit the fish a few hard cracks. The axe bounded off it like rubber, and it was a while before I made any impression, but when it did quieten down I tied a piece of rope round the tail and hung the fish on the mast. It took me all my time to lift the fish, as it was about three feet long and quite heavy. I lay down again, and at daybreak examined the fish closer. It was a dog-fish. During the struggle with it I had gashed a finger against its teeth, and as we now had no bandages or medicine all I could do was wash the cut in sea water before I proceeded to cut up the fish. I had heard and read about people drinking blood, and I thought that I could get some blood from the carcase for drinking. I had a tough job cutting up the fish with my knife, and only managed to get a few tea-spoonsful of dirty, reddish-black blood. I cut the liver and heart out, and sliced some of the flesh off. By this time all hands were awake, although every one was feeling weak. I gave the first spoonful of blood to Diana to taste, but she spat it out and said it was horrible. I tried every one with a taste, but nobody could swallow the vile stuff. I tried it myself, but couldn't get it down. It seemed to swell the tongue. We tried eating the fish, but that was also a failure. I chewed and chewed at my piece, but couldn't swallow any and eventually spat it into the sea.

The day following my encounter with the big dog-fish my

hand and arm swelled up, and Diana said I had blood-poisoning. The following day it was much worse, and throbbed painfully. I asked Diana if she could do anything for it, as we had no medical supplies left. She advised me to let the hand drag in the water, and that seemed to draw out more poison. At intervals Diana squeezed the arm from the shoulder downward, and gradually got rid of the swelling, although the sore didn't heal for months, and the scar remains to this day.

There was no water left now, and Jack Oakie, Jack Little, and the Zanzibar fireman all died during the one night. It took the remainder of us nearly a whole day to lift them from the bottom of the boat and roll them overboard. The serang was now unconscious and Joe Green was rambling in his speech. There were a few clouds drifting over us, but no sign of rain, and I had lost count of the days. I had written up Mr. Britt's log-book to the end of the fourth week, but after that day and night seemed to be all the same. Diana had the sickness that nearly every one in turn had suffered: a sore throat and a thick yellow phlegm oozing from the mouth. I think it was due to us lying in the dampness all the time and never getting properly dry. The sails were now down and spread across the boat as I was too feeble to do anything in the way of running the boat. Against all advice, I often threw small quantities of sea water down my throat, and it didn't seem to make me any worse, although I never overdid it.

One night Joe Green would not lie in the bottom of the boat in comfort, but lay on the after end in an uncomfortable position. When I tried to get him to lie down with us he said, "I won't last out the night, and if I lie down there you will never be able to lift me up and get me over the side." The next morning he was dead. So was the serang. Two grand old men, though of different races. There were only three of us left now. Jack Edmead was pretty bad by now, and Diana still had the sore throat. But we managed to get the bodies over the side. The serang by this time was very thin and wasted, and if he had been any heavier we would not have managed to get him over.

By this time we were only drifting about on the ocean. I had put the jib up a couple of times, but discovered we drifted in circles, so I took it down again. One day I had a very clear dream as I lay there in the bottom of the boat. I dreamed that the three of us were walking up the pierhead at Liverpool, and the dream was so clear that I really believed it would happen. I told Diana and Jack about the dream, and said I was sure we would be picked up. There wasn't a drop of water in the boat now, and the three of us just lay there dreaming of water in all sorts of ways. Sometimes it was about a stream that ran past our house when I was a child, another time I would be holding a hose and spraying water all round, but it was always about water. Jack was getting worse, and was laid out in the stern, while Diana was forward where it was drier. Sick as she was, she always used to smile and say, "We still have a chance if we could only get some rain."

Then one night rain came. I was lying down half asleep when I felt the rain falling on my face. I jumped up shouting, "Rain, rain," but Jack wasn't able to get up and help me. Diana was in pretty bad condition, but she managed to crawl along and help me spread the main sail to catch the water. It was a short sharp shower and didn't last long, but we collected a few pints in the sail and odd corners of the boat. We didn't waste a drop, and after pouring it carefully into the tank we sucked the raindrops from the woodwork and everywhere possible. Diana had trouble swallowing anything as her throat was swollen and raw, but I mixed some pemmican with water, and we had a few spoonfuls each. The water was very bitter as the sail had been soaked in salt water for weeks, but it tasted good to us. We all felt better after our drink, and I sat down in the well of the boat that day and poured can after can of sea water over myself, and gave Diana a bit of a wash. She was in good spirits now, although she could only speak in whispers. She told me about her home in the South of England: I think she said it was Windsor, on the Thames. She was very fond of horses and tennis and other sports, and she said, "You must come and visit us when we get home," which showed that like myself she had a firm conviction that we would get picked up.

The three days after the rain were uneventful. Diana was a bit better, but Jack was in a bad way, and lying down in the stern end. On the third day I had another shower-bath sitting down in the boat, as it had livened me up a lot the last time. Afterwards I set the jib and tried to handle the main sail, but couldn't make it, so I spread the sail and used it as a bed. I had the best sleep in weeks. In the early hours of the morning Diana shook me, and said excitedly, "Can you hear a plane?" I listened, and heard what sounded like a plane in the distance, so I dashed aft and grabbed one of the red flares and tried to light it. It didn't go off, so I struck one of the lifeboat matches. It ignited at once, and I held it up as high as I could, and immediately a voice shouted, "All right, put that light out." It was still dark, but on looking in the direction of the voice we could see the dim outline of a ship, and hear the sound of her diesel engines. The same voice shouted, "Can you come alongside?" God knows how we managed, but manage it we did. Even Jack found enough strength to give a hand, and with Diana at the tiller he and I rowed the boat alongside the ship. A line was thrown to us, and I made it fast. A pilot ladder was dropped, and two men came down to help us on board. They tied a rope round Diana, and with the help of others on the ship hauled her on board. I climbed up unaided, and the men helped Jack. The first thing I asked for was a drink, and we sat on a hatch waiting to see what would happen. We thought we were on a Swedish ship at first, but I saw a Dutch flag painted across the hatch. Then I heard a couple of men talking, and I knew then we were on a German ship, as I had a slight knowledge of the language. I told the other two, and Diana said, "It doesn't matter what nationality it is as long as it is a ship."

A man came to us soon and asked us to go with him and meet the captain. Two of the crew helped Diana and Jack, and we were taken amidships to the doctor's room, where a couch had been prepared for Diana. The captain arrived, and asked us about our trip in the boat and inquired how long we had been in it. I told him our ship had been torpedoed on the 6th of November, and that I had lost count of the days. He said this was the 12th of December, and that we were on board the German ship *Rhakotis*, and we should be well looked after. I remembered the bag of valuables in the boat, and told the captain where Diana's bag was. The bag was found and passed up, and given into the captain's charge. It was probably lost when the ship was sunk three weeks later. The lifeboat was stripped and sunk before the ship got under way again.

We were given cups of coffee, but were told that the doctor's orders were for us not to drink much at a time, and only eat or drink what he ordered. Diana was lying on the doctor's couch, and when the three of us were left alone for a while she bounced up and down on the springs and said, "This is better than lying in that wet boat." Later Jack and I were given a hot bath by a medical attendant, and my hand was bandaged, as it was still festering. We were taken aft to a cabin, and Diana was left in the doctor's room. The crew had orders not to bother us and to leave us on our own, as we had to rest as much as possible. When I looked at myself in the mirror I didn't recognize myself with a red beard and haggard appearance. There didn't seem to be any flesh left on my body, only a bag of bones. Jack looked even worse with his black beard and hollow cheeks.

We had been given some tablets and injected, and were now told to go to bed. Before I did so I asked one of the crew to fetch me a bottle of water. Although this was against the doctor's orders the man did so, and I hid the bottle under my pillow. Then I asked another man to bring me a bottle of water, and in this way I collected a few bottles and I drank the lot. Jack was already asleep when I turned in after drinking the water, and I turned in on the bunk above him. We slept for hours and when I awoke I found I had soaked the bedding. Later I discovered I had soaked Jack's bed too. He was still asleep. I wakened him and apologized, but he only laughed. The steward brought us coffee at 7 A.M. and when I told him about my bladder weakness he didn't seem annoyed, but took the bedclothes away to be changed. It was over a year before I was able to hold any liquid for more than an hour or so.

We were well looked after and well fed on the German ship, and from the first day I walked round the decks as I liked. Jack was confined to bed for a few days. We were not allowed to visit Diana, but the captain came aft and gave us any news concerning her. She couldn't swallow any food, and was being fed by injections. When we had been five days on the ship the doctor and the captain came along to our cabin, and I could see they were worried. The captain did the talking, and said that as the English girl still hadn't been able to eat, and couldn't go on living on injections, the doctor wanted to operate on her throat and clear the inflammation. But first of all he wanted our permission. I had never liked the doctor and had discovered he was disliked by nearly everyone on board, but still, he was the doctor, and should know more about what was good for Diana than I could. So I told the captain that if the doctor thought it was necessary to operate he had my permission as I wanted to see Diana well again. Jack said almost the same, and the captain asked if we would like to see her. We jumped at the chance, and went with the doctor. She seemed quite happy, and looked well, except for being thin. Her hair had been washed and set, and she said she was being well looked after. We never mentioned the operation to her, but noticed she could still talk only in whispers.

That evening at seven o'clock the captain came to us, and I could see that something was wrong. He said, "I have bad news for you. The English girl has died. Will you follow me, please?" We went along, neither of us able to say a word. We were taken to the doctor's room where she lay with a bandage round her throat. You would never know she was dead, she looked so peaceful. The doctor spoke, and said in broken English that the operation was a success, but the girl's heart was not strong enough to stand the anaesthetic. I couldn't speak, and turned away broken-hearted. Jack and I went aft again, and I turned into my bunk and lay crying like a baby nearly all night. It was the first time I had broken down and cried, and I think Jack was the same. The funeral was the next day, and when the time came we went along to the foredeck where the ship's crew were all lined up wearing uniform and the body was in a coffin covered by the Union Jack. The captain made a speech in German, and then spoke in English for our benefit. There were tears in the eyes of many of the Germans, as they had all taken an interest in the English girl. The ship was stopped, and after the captain had said a prayer the coffin slid slowly down a slipway into the sea. It had been weighted, and sank slowly. The crew stood to attention bareheaded until the coffin disappeared. It was an impressive scene, and a gallant end to a brave and noble girl. We had been through so much together, and I knew I would never forget her.

QUARTERMASTER ANGUS MACDONALD

So, of fifty-four passengers originally in the lifeboat, only two survived. At 4 A.M. on New Year's Day, 1942, the *Rhakotis*— a blockade runner bound for St. Nazaire—was attacked and sunk by the British cruiser *Scylla* after crew and prisoners had been given time to abandon ship. Macdonald's boat was found by a U-boat, which took its occupants to a French port, from where Macdonald was escorted to a prisoner-of-war camp in Germany. Jack Edmead's boat reached Spain. He was repatriated to England where he joined another ship, which was later torpedoed and sunk with the loss of all hands.

———◆———

The ordeal of Poon Lim

The most astonishing of all stories of survival at sea—and one that has earned a place in the *Guinness Book of Records*—is that of the Chinese steward Poon Lim.

Second Steward Poon Lim, of Hongkong, of the British Merchant Navy, was serving aboard the S.S. *Ben Lomond* when it was torpedoed in the Atlantic Ocean 750 miles off the Azores at 11.45 A.M. on 23 November, 1942. He spent 133 days alone on a raft until he was picked up by a Brazilian fishing vessel off Salinas, Brazil, on 5 April, 1943, and was able at last to walk ashore.

For this feat Poon Lim was awarded the British Empire Medal in July, 1943. It was a tribute to his courage, will-power and ability to fight for survival with assistance from no other human being.

Poon Lim was twenty-five years old when he underwent his ordeal. As a youth he had been keen on basketball and football and had spent much of his childhood fishing "which was to stand me in very good stead later on."

Most of his shipmates perished when the ship was torpedoed. Poon Lim managed to reach a raft that was floating on the water after his ship had sunk. There was nobody else on that raft.

"It was about six feet square and of standard design, with containers fore and aft," said Poon Lim in telling his story afterwards. "One contained water and in the other were provisions including chocolate, barley sugar, biscuits, fish paste and a bottle of lime juice. There was also Verey light apparatus, some 'yellow smoke' for signalling.

"My first meal was of barley sugar. My shoes and trousers had been washed away while I was in the water and my vest and pants were covered in oil. So I took them off, washed them in the sea and hung them out to dry, and, as night came on, I fell asleep.

"I awoke cold and shivering, naked in the rain. My pants had been washed away and my vest was soaking. However, the sun came out later and I got warm and dry again. I took careful stock of my provisions and decided to eat six biscuits a day, or two per meal."

Poon Lim's first problem was how to fish. The only rope aboard the raft was too thick so he had to unravel it and spin a line for himself. He made a hook out of the fastener of the yellow smoke container. For bait he made a paste out of biscuit powder, but found this washed off too quickly. Eventually he found some barnacles on the side of the raft and with their meat he baited his hook.

Poon Lim's provisions for 133 days

"My first catch was a brownish-coloured fish with hard scales. 'Little fish, you have saved my life!' I said as I cut it up. My second catch was much better—a small shark of about ten pounds.

"This I also cut up for bait, but the fish would not take its meat. I noticed, however, that the blood and part of the entrails of the shark attracted a school of whiting. I tried tying pieces of the entrails on to the line without using the hook. In this way I scooped several of the small fish on to the deck and felt very pleased with myself. In my home village the housewives dry their clothes on a *loo-tai*, a kind of platform on top of the house. I rigged my lines on the four posts of the raft in imitation of a *loo-tai* and dried my fish in this way."

After seven days Poon Lim sighted a steamer and he fired all the Verey lights and used up the yellow smoke, but, close as the ship appeared to be, she steamed on without altering course. This was Poon Lim's darkest moment of all.

"However, I cheered myself by singing songs from Chinese operas and my success with fishing made me feel better. To replenish my supplies of water there was plenty of rain at times, but there were also drought periods that caused me concern until I learned to condense water from the humid atmosphere by dangling my water can in the sea.

"On the hundredth day, as near as I can guess, I struck a bad patch. The fish would not take for some reason and I had eaten all my provisions, dried fish and bait included. For five days I was without food.

"On the fifth day some small birds settled on the raft. They were black with white spots on their foreheads. I waited till nightfall and then when they were asleep, I seized one and tied it up. Altogether I caught thirteen of these birds, but one got away. They tasted like the fish.

"I used parts of the birds for bait and caught more fish. I spent all my time improving my fishing lines and trying new ways of fishing. I found that by swishing my bait through the water and dibbling it up and down, I could catch more fish. This discovery probably saved my life.

"I was so hungry that I ate some of the fish raw."

As Poon Lim approached the Brazilian coast he noticed that the water was changing colour and that there were some fish like salmon which suggested he was near a river mouth, in fact, he was at the approaches to the Amazon.

Even then Poon Lim had some more bad luck. He spotted a fishing vessel, but failed to attract its attention; he saw other ships which only disappeared over the horizon. Then an aeroplane flew over him and dropped a flare. A few days later a Brazilian fishing craft rescued him.

Although he was able to walk ashore, Poon Lim went to hospital for 45 days. "I was a bit thin when I landed, but I never had a headache the whole time I was on the raft and I had slept soundly every night. I do not attribute my survival to any philosophy peculiar to China unless it is that we Chinese are very practical. I concentrated all my thoughts and efforts on getting food and water."

Later Poon Lim was able to tell the full story of his 133-day ordeal to King George VI.

DONALD McCORMICK,
Master Book of Escapes

———◆———

Journey without end

Lost Ken's boat is found

The last sad chapter of Kenneth Kerr's ill-fated attempt to row the Atlantic was written yesterday.

His empty boat, Bass Conqueror, was spotted by a Norwegian vessel 70 miles off Denmark.

All hope for Kenneth, a Royal Navy submariner, was given up last October.

With all hope of fresh water and food supplies gone the search for the submariner was called off.

It was the second time the 13ft boat had completed the Atlantic crossing from Newfoundland.

Kenneth Kerr in the boat in which
he planned to row across the Atlantic

Back in 1979 when Kenneth, 28, a petty officer from Port
Seton, East Lothian, capsized while 1,00 miles out, the boat
drifted ashore on the Irish coast.

A spokesman for the Department of Trade said there was no
sign of life on the Bass Conqueror, but the boat was still afloat.

FRANK URQUHART,
Daily Express
London, 19 January 1981

FICTION

The *Victory* passes

The wild, herbless, weather-worn promontory was quite a solitude, and, saving the one old lighthouse about fifty yards up the
slope, scarce a mark was visible to show that humanity had ever
been near the spot. Anne found herself a seat on a stone, and
swept with her eyes the tremulous expanse of water around her
that seemed to utter a ceaseless unintelligible incantation. Out of
the three hundred and sixty degrees of her complete horizon two
hundred and fifty were covered by waves, the *coup d'œil* including the area of troubled waters known as the Race, where two
seas met to effect the destruction of such vessels as could not be
mastered by one. She counted the craft within her view: there
were five; no, there were only four; no, there were seven, some of
the specks having resolved themselves into two. They were all
small coasters, and kept well within sight of land.

Anne sank into a reverie. Then she heard a slight noise on her
left hand, and turning beheld an old sailor, who had approached
with a glass. He was levelling it over the sea in a direction to the
south-east, and somewhat removed from that in which her own
eyes had been wandering. Anne moved a few steps thitherward,
so as to unclose to her view a deeper sweep on that side, and by
this discovered a ship of far larger size than any which had yet
dotted the main before her. Its sails were for the most part new
and clean, and in comparison with its rapid progress before the
wind the small brigs and sketches seemed standing still. Upon
this striking object the old man's glass was bent.

"What do you see, sailor?" she asked.

"Almost nothing," he answered. "My sight is so gone off lately
that things, one and all, be but a November mist to me. And yet
I fain would see to-day. I am looking for the *Victory*."

"Why?" she said quickly.

"I have a son aboard her. He's one of three from these parts.
There's the captain, there's my son Ned, and there's young Love-
day of Overcombe—he that lately joined."

"Shall I look for you?" said Anne after a pause.

"Certainly, mis'ess, if so be you please."

Anne took the glass, and he supported it by his arm. "It is a large ship," she said, "with three masts, three rows of guns along the side, and all her sails set."

"I guessed as much."

"There is a little flag in front—over her bowsprit."

"The jack."

"And there's a large one flying at her stern."

"The ensign."

"And a white one on her fore-topmast."

"That's the admiral's flag, the flag of my Lord Nelson. What is her figure-head, my dear?"

"A coat-of-arms, supported on this side by a sailor."

Her companion nodded with satisfaction. "On the other side of that figure-head is a marine."

"She is twisting round in a curious way, and her sails sink in like old cheeks, and she shivers like a leaf upon a tree."

"She is in stays, for the larboard tack. I can see what she's been doing. She's been re'ching close in to avoid the flood tide, as the wind is to the sou'-west, and she's bound down; but as soon as the ebb made, d'ye see, they made sail to the west'ard. Captain Hardy may be depended upon for that; he knows every current about here, being a native."

"And now I can see the other side; it is a soldier where a sailor was before. You are *sure* it is the *Victory?*"

"I am sure."

After this a frigate came into view—the *Euryalus*—sailing in the same direction. Anne sat down, and her eyes never left the ships. "Tell me more about the *Victory*," she said.

"She is the best sailer in the service, and she carries a hundred guns. The heaviest be on the lower deck, the next size on the middle deck, the next on the main and upper decks. My son Ned's place is on the lower deck, because he's short, and they put the short men below."

Bob, though not tall, was not likely to be specially selected for shortness. She pictured him on the upper deck, in his snow-white trousers and jacket of navy blue, looking perhaps towards the very point of land where she then was.

The great silent ship, with her population of bluejackets, marines, officers, captain, and the admiral who was not to return alive, passed like a phantom the meridian of the Bill. Sometimes her aspect was that of a large white bat, sometimes that of a grey one. In the course of time the watching girl saw that the ship had passed her nearest point; the breadth of her sails diminished by foreshortening, till she assumed the form of an egg on end. After this something seemed to twinkle, and Anne, who had previously withdrawn from the old sailor, went back to him, and looked again through the glass. The twinkling was the light falling upon the cabin windows of the ship's stern. She explained it to the old man.

"Then we see now what the enemy have seen but once. That was in seventy-nine, when she sighted the French and Spanish fleet off Scilly, and she retreated because she feared a landing. Well, 'tis a brave ship, and she carries brave men!"

Anne's tender bosom heaved, but she said nothing, and again became absorbed in contemplation.

The *Victory* was fast dropping away. She was on the horizon, and soon appeared hull down. That seemed to be like the beginning of a greater end than her present vanishing. Anne Garland could not stay by the sailor any longer, and went about a stone's-throw off, where she was hidden by the inequality of the cliff from his view. The vessel was now exactly end on, and stood out in the direction of the Start, her width having contracted to the proportion of a feather. She sat down again, and mechanically took out some biscuits that she had brought, foreseeing that her waiting might be long. But she could not eat one of them; eating seemed to jar with the mental tenseness of the moment; and her undeviating gaze continued to follow the lessened ship with the fidelity of a balanced needle to a magnetic stone, all else in her being motionless.

The courses of the *Victory* were absorbed into the main, then her topsails went, and then her top-gallants. She was now no more than a dead fly's wing on a sheet of spider's web; and even this fragment diminished. Anne could hardly bear to see the end, and yet she resolved not to flinch. The admiral's flag sank behind the watery line, and in a minute the very truck of the last topmast stole away. The *Victory* was gone.

THOMAS HARDY,
The Trumpet Major

————◆————

THE OLD SHIPS

I have seen old ships sail like swans asleep
Beyond the village which men still call Tyre,
With leaden age o'ercargoed, dipping deep
For Famagusta and the hidden sun
That rings black Cyprus with a lake of fire;
And all those ships were certainly so old
Who knows how oft with squat and noisy gun,
Questing brown slaves or Syrian oranges,
The pirate Genoese
Hell-raked them till they rolled
Blood, water, fruit, and corpses up the hold.
But now through friendly seas they softly run,
Painted the mid-sea blue or shore-sea green,
Still patterned with the vine and grapes in gold.

But I have seen,
Pointing her shapely shadows from the dawn
And image tumbled on a rose-swept bay,
A drowsy ship of some yet older day;
And, wonder's breath indrawn,
Thought I—who knows—who knows—but in that same
(Fished up beyond Ææa, patched up new
—Stern painted brighter blue—)
That talkative, bald-headed seaman came
(Twelve patient comrades sweating at the oar)
From Troy's doom-crimson shore,
And with great lies about his wooden horse
Set the crew laughing, and forgot his course.
It was so old a ship—who knows—who knows?
—And yet so beautiful, I watched in vain
To see the mast burst open with a rose,
And the whole deck put on its leaves again.

JAMES ELROY FLECKER

————◆————

Captain Ahab declares himself

The hours wore on;—Ahab now shut up within his cabin; anon, pacing the deck, with the same intense bigotry of purpose in his aspect.

It drew near the close of day. Suddenly he came to a halt by the bulwarks, and inserting his bone leg into the auger hole there, and with one hand grasping a shroud, he ordered Starbuck to send everybody aft.

"Sir!" said the mate, astonished at an order seldom or never given on ship-board except in some extraordinary case.

"Send everybody aft," repeated Ahab. "Mast-heads, there! come down!"

When the entire ship's company were assembled, and with curious and not wholly unapprehensive faces, were eyeing him, for he looked not unlike the weather horizon when a storm is coming up, Ahab, after rapidly glancing over the bulwarks, and then darting his eyes among the crew, started from his standpoint; and as though not a soul were nigh him resumed his heavy turns upon the deck. With bent head and half-slouched hat he continued to pace, unmindful of the wondering whispering among the men; till Stubb cautiously whispered to Flask, that Ahab must have summoned them there for the purpose of witnessing a pedestrian feat. But this did not last long. Vehemently pausing, he cried:

"What do ye do when ye see a whale, men?"

"Sing out for him!" was the impulsive rejoinder from a score of clubbed voices.

"Good!" cried Ahab, with a wild approval in his tones; observing the hearty animation into which his unexpected question had so magnetically thrown them.

"And what do ye next, men?"

"Lower away, and after him!"

"And what tune is it ye pull to, men?"

"A dead whale or a stove boat!"

More and more strangely and fiercely glad and approving, grew the countenance of the old man at every shout; while the mariners began to gaze curiously at each other, as if marvelling how it was that they themselves became so excited at such seemingly purposeless questions.

But, they were all eagerness again, as Ahab, now half-revolving in his pivot-hole, with one hand reaching high up a shroud, and tightly, almost convulsively grasping it, addressed them thus:

"All ye mast-headers have before now heard me give orders about a white whale. Look ye! d'ye see this Spanish ounce of gold?"—holding up a broad bright coin to the sun—"it is a sixteen-dollar piece, men. D'ye see it? Mr. Starbuck, hand me yon top-maul."

While the mate was getting the hammer, Ahab, without speaking, was slowly rubbing the gold piece against the skirts of his jacket, as if to heighten its lustre, and without using any

Captain Ahab

words was meanwhile lowly humming to himself, producing a sound so strangely muffled and inarticulate that it seemed the mechanical humming of the wheels of his vitality in him.

Receiving the top-maul from Starbuck, he advanced towards the main-mast with the hammer uplifted in one hand, exhibiting the gold with the other, and with a high raised voice exclaiming: "Whosoever of ye raises me a white-headed whale with a wrinkled brow and a crooked jaw; whosoever of ye raises me that white-headed whale, with three holes punctured in his starboard fluke—look ye, whosoever of ye raises me that same white whale, he shall have this gold ounce, my boys!"

"Huzza! huzza!" cried the seamen, as with swinging tarpaulins they hailed the act of nailing the gold to the mast.

"It's a white whale, I say," resumed Ahab, as he threw down the top-maul; "a white whale. Skin your eyes for him, men; look sharp for white water; if ye see but a bubble, sing out."

◆

The sighting of Moby Dick

That night, in the mid-watch, when the old man—as his wont at intervals—stepped forth from the scuttle in which he leaned, and went to his pivot-hole, he suddenly thrust out his face fiercely snuffing up the sea air as a sagacious ship's dog will, in drawing nigh to some barbarous isle. He declared that a whale must be near. Soon that peculiar odour, sometimes to a great distance given forth by the living sperm-whale, was palpable to all the watch; nor was any mariner surprised when, after inspecting the compass, and then the dog-vane, and then ascertaining the precise bearing of the odour as nearly as possible, Ahab rapidly ordered the ship's course to be slightly altered, and the sail to be shortened.

The acute policy dictating these movements was sufficiently vindicated at daybreak, by the sight of a long sleek on the sea directly and lengthwise ahead, smooth as oil, and resembling in the pleated watery wrinkles bordering it, the polished metallic-like marks of some swift tide-rip, at the mouth of a deep, rapid stream.

"Man the mast-heads! Call all hands!"

Thundering with the butts of three clubbed handspikes on the forecastle deck, Daggoo roused the sleepers with such judgment claps that they seemed to exhale from the scuttle, so instantaneously did they appear with their clothes in their hands.

"What d'ye see?" cried Ahab, flattening his face to the sky.

"Nothing, nothing, sir!" was the sound hailing down in reply.

"T'gallant sails!—stunsails! alow and aloft, and on both sides!"

All sail being set, he now cast loose the life-line, reserved for swaying him to the main royal mast-head; and in a few moments they were hoisting him thither, when, while but two thirds of the way aloft, and while peering ahead through the horizontal vacancy between the main-top-sail and top-gallant-sail, he raised a gull-like cry in the air, "There she blows!—there she blows! A hump like a snow-hill! It is Moby Dick!"

Fired by the cry which seemed simultaneously taken up by the three look-outs, the men on deck rushed to the rigging to behold the famous whale they had so long been pursuing. Ahab had now gained his final perch, some feet above the other look-outs, Tashtego standing just beneath him on the cap of the top-gallant-mast, so that the Indian's head was almost on a level with Ahab's heel. From this height the whale was now seen some mile or so ahead, at every roll of the sea revealing his high sparkling hump, and regularly jetting his silent spout into the air. To the credulous mariners it seemed the same silent spout they had so long ago beheld in the moonlit Atlantic and Indian Oceans.

"And did none of ye see it before?" cried Ahab, hailing the perched men all around him.

"I saw him almost that same instant, sir, that Captain Ahab did, and I cried out," said Tashtego.

"Not the same instant; not the same—no, the doubloon is mine, Fate reserved the doubloon for me. *I* only; none of ye could have raised the white whale first. There she blows! there she blows!—there she blows! There again!—there again!" he cried, in long-drawn, lingering, methodic tones, attuned to the gradual prolongings of the whale's visible jets. "He's going to sound! In stunsails! Down top-gallant-sails! Stand by three boats. Mr. Starbuck, remember, stay on board, and keep the ship. Helm there!

Luff, luff a point! So; steady, man, steady! There go flukes! No, no; only black water! All ready the boats there? Stand by, stand by! Lower me, Mr. Starbuck; lower, lower—quick, quicker!" and he slid through the air to the deck.

"He is heading straight to leeward, sir," cried Stubb, "right away from us; cannot have seen the ship yet."

"Be dumb, man! Stand by the braces! Hard down the helm!—brace up! Shiver her!—shiver her!—So; well that! Boats, boats!"

Soon all the boats but Starbuck's were dropped; all the boat-sails set—all the paddles plying; with rippling swiftness, shooting to leeward; and Ahab heading the onset. A pale, death-glimmer lit up Fedallah's sunken eyes; a hideous motion gnawed his mouth.

Like noiseless nautilus shells; their light prows sped through the sea; but only slowly they neared the foe. As they neared him, the ocean grew still more smooth; seemed drawing a carpet over its waves; seemed a noon-meadow, so serenely it spread. At length the breathless hunter came so nigh his seemingly unsuspecting prey, that his entire dazzling hump was distinctly visible, sliding along the sea as if an isolated thing, and continually set in a revolving ring of finest, fleecy, greenish foam. He saw the vast, involved wrinkles of the slightly projecting head beyond. Before it, far out on the soft Turkish-rugged waters, went the glistening white shadow from his broad, milky forehead, a musical rippling playfully accompanying the shade; and behind, the blue waters interchangeably flowed over into the moving valley of his steady wake; and on either hand bright bubbles arose and danced by his side. But these were broken again by the light toes of hundreds of gay fowls softly feathering the sea, alternate with their fitful flight; and like to some flag-staff rising from the painted hull of an argosy, the tall but shattered pole of a recent lance projected from the white whale's back; and at intervals one of the cloud of soft-toed fowls hovering, and to and fro skimming like a canopy over the fish, silently perched and rocked on his pole, the long tail feathers streaming like pennons.

A gentle joyousness—a mighty mildness of repose in swiftness, invested the gliding whale. Not the white bull Jupiter swimming away with ravished Europa clinging to his graceful horns; his lovely, leering eyes sideways intent upon the maid;

with smooth bewitching fleetness, rippling straight for the nuptial bower in Crete; not Jove, not that great majesty Supreme! did surpass the glorified white whale as he so divinely swam.

On each soft side—coincident with the parted swell, that but once leaving him, then flowed so wide away—on each bright side, the whale shed off enticings. No wonder there had been some among the hunters who namelessly transported and allured by all this serenity, had ventured to assail it; but had fatally found that quietude but the vesture of tornadoes. Yet calm, enticing calm, oh, whale! thou glidest on, to all who for the first time eye thee, no matter how many in that same way thou mayst have bejuggled and destroyed before.

And thus, through the serene tranquillities of the tropical sea, among waves whose hand-clappings were suspended by exceeding rapture, Moby Dick moved on, still withholding from sight the full terrors of his submerged trunk, entirely hiding the wrenched hideousness of his jaw. But soon the fore part of him slowly rose from the water; for an instant his whole marbleized body formed a high arch, like Virginia's Natural Bridge, and warningly waving his bannered flukes in the air, the grand god revealed himself, sounded, and went out of sight. Hoveringly halting, and dipping on the wing, the white sea-fowls longingly lingered over the agitated pool that he left.

With oars apeak, and paddles down, the sheets of their sails adrift, the three boats now stilly floated, awaiting Moby Dick's reappearance.

"An hour," said Ahab, standing rooted in his boat's stern; and he gazed beyond the whale's place, towards the dim blue spaces and wide wooing vacancies to leeward. It was only an instant; for again his eyes seemed whirling round in his head as he swept the watery circle. The breeze now freshened; the sea began to swell.

"The birds!—the birds!" cried Tashtego.

In long Indian file, as when herons take wing, the white birds were now all flying towards Ahab's boat; and when within a few yards began fluttering over the water there, wheeling round and round, with joyous, expectant cries. Their vision was keener than man's; Ahab could discover no sign in the sea. But suddenly as he peered down and down into its depths, he profoundly saw a white living spot no bigger than a white weasel, with wonderful celerity uprising, and magnifying as it rose, till it turned, and then there were plainly revealed two long crooked rows of white, glistening teeth, floating up from the undiscoverable bottom. It was Moby Dick's open mouth and scrolled jaw; his vast, shadowed bulk still half blending with the blue of the sea. The glittering mouth yawned beneath the boat like an open-doored marble tomb; and giving one sidelong sweep with his steering oar, Ahab whirled the craft aside from this tremendous apparition. Then, calling upon Fedallah to change places with him, went forward to the bows, and seizing Perth's harpoon, commanded his crew to grasp their oars and stand by to stern.

HERMAN MELVILLE,
Moby Dick

EIGHT BELLS

Four double strokes repeated on the bells,
And then away, away the shufflers go
Aft to the darkness where the ruler dwells,
Where by the rail he sucks his pipe aglow;
Beside him his relief looks down on those below.

There in the dark they answer to their names,
Those dozen men, and one relieves the wheel,
One the look-out, the others sit to games
In moonlight, backed against the bulkhead's steel,
In the lit patch the hands flick, card by card, the deal.

Meanwhile the men relieved are forward all,
Some in their bunks asleep, while others sing
Low-voiced some ditty of the halliard-fall,
The ship impels them on with stooping wing,
Rolling and roaring on with triumph in her swing.

JOHN MASEFIELD

A Descent into the Maelstrom

"It is now within a few days of three years since what I am going to tell you occurred. It was on the 10th of July, 18——, a day which the people of this part of the world will never forget—for it was one in which blew the most terrible hurricane that ever came out of the heavens. And yet all the morning, and indeed until late in the afternoon, there was a gentle and steady breeze from the south-west, while the sun shone brightly, so that the oldest seaman among us could not have foreseen what was to follow.

"The three of us—my two brothers and myself—had crossed over to the islands about two o'clock P.M., and soon nearly loaded the smack with fine fish, which, we all remarked, were more plenty that day than we had ever known them. It was just seven, *by my watch*, when we weighed and started for home, so as to make the worst of the Ström at slack water, which we knew would be at eight.

"We set out with a fresh wind on our starboard quarter, and for some time spanked along at a great rate, never dreaming of danger, for indeed we saw not the slightest reason to apprehend it. All at once we were taken aback by a breeze from over Helseggen. This was most unusual—something that had never happened to us before—and I began to feel a little uneasy, without exactly knowing why. We put the boat on the wind, but could make no headway at all for the eddies, and I was upon the point of proposing to return to the anchorage, when, looking astern, we saw the whole horizon covered with a singular copper-coloured cloud that rose with the most amazing velocity.

"In the meantime the breeze that had headed us off fell away, and we were dead becalmed, drifting about in every direction. This state of things, however, did not last long enough to give us time to think about it. In less than a minute the storm was upon us—in less than two the sky was entirely overcast—and what with this and the driving spray, it became suddenly so dark that we could not see each other in the smack.

"Such a hurricane as then blew it is folly to attempt describing. The oldest seamen in Norway never experienced anything like it. We had let our sails go by the run before it cleverly took us; but, at the first puff, both our masts went by the board as if they had been sawed off—the mainmast taking with it my youngest brother, who had lashed himself to it for safety.

"Our boat was the lightest feather of a thing that ever sat upon water. It had a complete flush deck, with only a small hatch near the bow, and this hatch it had always been our custom to batten down when about to cross the Ström, by way of precaution against the chopping seas. But for this circumstance we should have foundered at once—for we lay entirely buried for some moments. How my elder brother escaped destruction I cannot say, for I never had an opportunity of ascertaining. For my part, as soon as I had let the foresail run, I threw myself flat on deck, with my feet against the narrow gunwale of the bow, and with my hands grasping a ring-bolt near the foot of the foremast. It was mere instinct that prompted me to do this—which was undoubtedly the very best thing I could have done—for I was too much flurried to think.

"For some moments we were completely deluged, as I say, and all this time I held my breath, and clung to the bolt. When I could stand it no longer, I raised myself upon my knees, still keeping hold with my hands, and thus got my head clear. Presently our little boat gave herself a shake, just as a dog does in coming out of the water, and thus rid herself, in some measure, of the seas. I was now trying to get the better of the stupor that had come over me, and to collect my senses, so as to see what was to be done, when I felt somebody grasp my arm. It was my elder brother, and my heart leaped for joy, for I had made sure that he was overboard; but the next moment all this joy was turned into horror, for he put his mouth close to my ear, and screamed out the word '*Moskoe-Ström!*'

"No one ever will know what my feelings were at that moment. I shook from head to foot as if I had the most violent fit of the ague. I knew what he meant by that one word well enough —I knew what he wished to make me understand. With the wind that now drove us on, we were bound for the whirl of the Ström, and nothing could save us!

"You perceive that in crossing the Ström *channel*, we always went a long way up above the whirl, even in the calmest weather, and then had to wait and watch carefully for the slack—but now we were driving right upon the pool itself, and in such a hurricane as this! To be sure, I thought, we shall get there just about the slack—there is some little hope in that—but in the next moment I cursed myself for being so great a fool as to dream of hope at all. I knew very well that we were doomed, had we been ten times a ninety-gun ship.

"By this time the first fury of the tempest had spent itself, or perhaps we did not feel it so much, as we scudded before it, but at all events the seas, which at first had been kept down by the wind and lay flat and frothing, now got up into absolute mountains. A singular change, too, had come over the heavens. Around in every direction it was still as black as pitch, but nearly overhead there burst out, all at once, a circular rift of clear sky—as clear as I ever saw—and of a deep bright blue—and through it there blazed forth the full moon with a lustre that I never before knew her to wear. She lit up everything about us with the greatest distinctness—but, oh, God, what a scene it was to light up!

"I now made one or two attempts to speak to my brother—but in some manner which I could not understand, the din had so increased that I could not make him hear a single word, although I screamed at the top of my voice in his ear. Presently he shook his head, looking as pale as death, and held up one of his fingers, as if to say '*listen!*'

"At first I could not make out what he meant—but soon a hideous thought flashed upon me. I dragged my watch from its fob. It was not going. I glanced at its face by the moonlight, and then burst into tears as I flung it far away into the ocean. *It had run down at seven o'clock! We were behind the time of the slack, and the whirl of the Ström was in full fury!*

"When a boat is well built, properly trimmed, and not deep laden, the waves in a strong gale, when she is going large, seem always to slip from beneath her—which appears very strange to a landsman—and this is what is called *riding*, in sea phrase.

"Well, so far we had ridden the swells very cleverly; but presently a gigantic sea happened to take us right under the counter, and bore us with it as it rose—up—up—as if into the sky. I would not have believed that any wave could rise so high. And then down we came with a sweep, a slide, and a plunge, that made me feel sick and dizzy, as if I was falling from some lofty mountain-top in a dream. But while we were up I had thrown a quick glance around—and that one glance was all sufficient. I saw our exact position in an instant. The Moskoe-Ström whirlpool was about a quarter of a mile dead ahead—but no more like the every-day Moskoe-Ström, than the whirl as you now see it is like a mill-race. If I had not known where we were, and what we had to expect, I should not have recognised the place at all. As it was, I involuntarily closed my eyes in horror. The lids clenched themselves together as if in a spasm.

"It could not have been more than two minutes afterwards until we suddenly felt the waves subside, and were enveloped in foam. The boat made a sharp half-turn to larboard, and then shot off in its new direction like a thunderbolt. At the same moment the roaring noise of the water was completely drowned in a kind of shrill shriek—such a sound as you might imagine given out by the water-pipes of many thousand steam-vessels, letting off their steam all together. We were now in the belt of surf that always surrounds the whirl; and I thought, of course, that another moment would plunge us into the abyss—down which we could only see indistinctly on account of the amazing velocity with which we were borne along. The boat did not seem to sink into the water at all, but to skim like an air bubble upon the surface of the surge. Her starboard side was next the whirl, and on the larboard arose the world of ocean we had left. It stood like a huge writhing wall between us and the horizon.

"It may appear strange, but now, when we were in the very jaws of the gulf, I felt more composed than when we were only approaching it. Having made up my mind to hope no more, I got rid of a great deal of that terror which unmanned me at first. I supposed it was despair that strung my nerves.

"It may look like boasting—but what I tell you is truth—I began to reflect how magnificent a thing it was to die in such a manner, and how foolish it was of me to think of so paltry a consideration as my own individual life, in view of so wonderful a manifestation of God's power. I do believe that I blushed with shame when this idea crossed my mind. After a little while I became possessed with the keenest curiosity about the whirl itself. I positively felt a *wish* to explore its depths, even at the sacrifice I was going to make; and my principal grief was that I should never be able to tell my old companions on shore about the mysteries I should see. These, no doubt, were singular fancies to occupy a man's mind in such extremity—and I have often thought since, that the revolutions of the boat around the pool might have rendered me a little light-headed.

"There was another circumstance which tended to restore my self-possession; and this was the cessation of the wind, which could not reach us in our present situation—for, as you saw yourself, the belt of surf is considerably lower than the general bed of the ocean, and this latter now towered above us, a high, black, mountainous ridge. If you have never been at sea in a heavy gale, you can form no idea of the confusion of mind occasioned by the wind and spray together. They blind, deafen, and strangle you, and take away all power of action or reflection. But we were now, in a great measure, rid of these annoyances—just as death-condemned felons in prison are allowed petty indulgences, forbidden them while their doom is yet uncertain.

"How often we made the circuit of the belt it is impossible to say. We careered round and round for perhaps an hour, flying rather than floating, getting gradually more and more into the middle of the surge, and then nearer and nearer to its horrible inner edge. All this time I had never let go of the ring-bolt. My brother was at the stern, holding on to a small empty water-cask, which had been securely lashed under the coop of the counter, and was the only thing on deck that had not been swept overboard when the gale first took us. As we approached the brink of the pit he let go his hold upon this, and made for the ring, from which, in the agony of his terror, he endeavoured to force my hands, as it was not large enough to afford us both a secure grasp. I never felt deeper grief than when I saw him attempt this act—although I knew he was a madman when he did it—a raving maniac through sheer fright. I did not care, however, to contest the point with him. I knew it could make no difference whether either of us held on at all; so I let him have the bolt, and went astern to the cask. This there was no great difficulty in doing; for the smack flew round steadily enough, and upon an even keel—only swaying to and fro, with the immense sweeps and swelters of the whirl. Scarcely had I secured myself in my new position, when we gave a wild lurch to starboard, and rushed headlong into the abyss. I muttered a hurried prayer to God, and thought all was over.

"As I felt the sickening sweep of the descent, I had instinctively tightened my hold upon the barrel, and closed my eyes. For some seconds I dared not open them—while I expected instant destruction, and wondered that I was not already in my death-struggles with the water. But moment after moment elapsed. I still lived. The sense of falling had ceased; and the motion of the vessel seemed much as it had been before, while in the belt of foam, with the exception that she now lay more along. I took courage and looked once again upon the scene.

"Never shall I forget the sensations of awe, horror, and admiration with which I gazed about me. The boat appeared to be hanging, as if by magic, midway down, upon the interior surface of a funnel, vast in circumference, prodigious in depth, and whose perfectly smooth sides might have been mistaken for ebony, but for the bewildering rapidity with which they spun around, and for the gleaming and ghastly radiance they shot forth, as the rays of the full moon, from that circular rift amid the clouds which I have already described, streamed in a flood of golden glory along the black walls, and far away down into the inmost recesses of the abyss.

"At first I was too much confused to observe anything accurately. The general burst of terrific grandeur was all that I beheld. When I recovered myself a little, however, my gaze fell instinctively downward. In this direction I was able to obtain an unobstructed view, from the manner in which the smack hung on the inclined surface of the pool. She was quite upon an even keel —that is to say, her deck lay in a plane parallel with that of the water—but this latter sloped at an angle of more than forty-five degrees, so that we seemed to be lying upon our beam-ends. I could not help observing, nevertheless, that I had scarcely more difficulty in maintaining my hold and footing in this situation, than if we had been upon a dead level; and this, I suppose, was owing to the speed at which we revolved.

"The rays of the moon seemed to search the very bottom of the profound gulf; but still I could make out nothing distinctly, on account of a thick mist in which everything there was enveloped, and over which there hung a magnificent rainbow, like that narrow and tottering bridge which Mussulmans say is the only pathway between Time and Eternity. This mist, or spray, was no doubt occasioned by the clashing of the great walls of the funnel, as they all met together at the bottom—but the yell that went up to the heavens from out of that mist, I dare not attempt to describe.

"Our first slide into the abyss itself, from the belt of foam above, had carried us to a great distance down the slope; but our farther descent was by no means proportionate. Round and round we swept—not with any uniform movement—but in dizzying swings and jerks, that sent us sometimes only a few hundred yards—sometimes nearly the complete circuit of the whirl. Our progress downward, at each revolution, was slow, but very perceptible.

"Looking about me upon the wide waste of liquid ebony on which we were thus borne, I perceived that our boat was not the only object in the embrace of the whirl. Both above and below us were visible fragments of vessels, large masses of building timber and trunks of trees, with many smaller articles, such as pieces of house furniture, broken boxes, barrels and staves. I have already described the unnatural curiosity which had taken the place of my original terrors. It appeared to grow upon me as I drew nearer and nearer to my dreadful doom. I now began to watch, with a strange interest, the numerous things that floated in our company. I must have been delirious—for I even sought *amusement* in speculating upon the relative velocities of their several descents toward the foam below. 'This fir tree,' I found myself at one time saying, 'will certainly be the next thing that takes the awful plunge and disappears,' and then I was disappointed to find that the wreck of a Dutch merchant ship overtook it and went down before. At length, after making several guesses of this nature, and being deceived in all—this fact—the fact of my invariable miscalculation, set me upon a train of reflection that made my limbs again tremble, and my heart beat heavily once more.

"It was not a new terror that thus affected me, but the dawn of a more exciting *hope*. This hope arose partly from memory and partly from present observation. I called to mind the great variety of buoyant matter that strewed the coast of Lofoden, having been absorbed and then thrown forth by the Moskoe-Ström. By far the greater number of the articles were shattered in the most extraordinary way—so chafed and roughened as to have the appearance of being stuck full of splinters—but then I distinctly recollected that there were *some* of them which were not disfigured at all. Now I could not account for the difference except by supposing that the roughened fragments were the only ones which had been *completely absorbed*—that the others had entered the whirl at so late a period of the tide, or, from some reason, had descended so slowly after entering, that they did not reach the bottom before the turn of the flood came, or of the ebb as the case might be. I conceived it possible, in either instance, that they might thus be whirled up again to the level of the ocean, without undergoing the fate of those which had been drawn in more early or absorbed more rapidly. I made, also, three important observations. The first was, that as a general rule, the larger the bodies were, the more rapid their descent—the second, that, between two masses of equal extent, the one spherical, and the other *of any other shape*, the superiority in speed of descent was with the sphere—the third, that, between two masses of equal size, the one cylindrical, and the other of any other shape, the cylinder was absorbed the more slowly. Since my escape, I have had several conversations on this subject with an old schoolmaster of the district; and it was from him that I learned the use of the words 'cylinder' and 'sphere.' He explained to me—although I have forgotten the explanation—how what I observed was, in fact, the natural consequence of the forms of the floating fragments—and showed me how it happened that a cylinder, swimming in a vortex, offered more resistance to its suction, and was drawn in with greater difficulty than an equally bulky body of any form whatever.

"There was one startling circumstance which went a great way in enforcing these observations, and rendering me anxious to turn them to account, and this was that, at every revolution, we passed something like a barrel, or else the yard or the mast of a vessel, while many of these things, which had been on our level when I first opened my eyes upon the wonders of the whirl-pool, were now high up above us, and seemed to have moved but little from their original station.

"I no longer hesitated what to do. I resolved to lash myself securely to the water-cask upon which I now held, to cut it loose from the counter, and to throw myself with it into the water. I attracted my brother's attention by signs, pointed to the floating barrels that came near us, and did everything in my power to make him understand what I was about to do. I thought at length that he comprehended my design—but whether this was the case or not, he shook his head despairingly, and refused to move from his station by the ring-bolt. It was impossible to reach him; the emergency admitted of no delay; and so, with a bitter struggle, I resigned him to his fate, fastened myself to the cask by means of the lashings which secured it to the counter, and precipitated myself with it into the sea, without another moment's hesitation.

"The result was precisely what I had hoped it might be. As it is myself who now tell you this tale—as you see that I *did* escape—and as you are already in possession of the mode in which this escape was effected, and must therefore anticipate all that I have further to say—I will bring my story quickly to conclusion. It might have been an hour, or thereabout, after my quitting the smack, when, having descended to a vast distance beneath me, it made three or four wild gyrations in rapid succession, and, bearing my loved brother with it, plunged headlong, at once and for ever, into the chaos of foam below. The barrel to which I was attached sunk very little farther than half the distance between the bottom of the gulf and the spot at which I leaped overboard, before a great change took place in the character of the whirlpool. The slope of the sides of the vast funnel became momentarily less and less steep, the gyrations of the whirl grew gradually less and less violent. By degrees, the froth and the rainbow disappeared, and the bottom of the gulf seemed slowly to uprise. The sky was clear, the winds had gone down, and the full moon was setting radiantly in the west, when I found myself on the surface of the ocean, in full view of the shores of Lofoden, and above the spot where the pool of the Moskoe-Ström *had been*. It was the hour of the slack—but the sea still heaved in mountainous waves from the effects of the hurricane. I was borne violently into the channel of the Ström, and in a few minutes, was hurried down the coast into the 'grounds' of the fishermen. A boat picked me up—exhausted from fatigue—and (now that the danger was removed)

—speechless from the memory of its horror. Those who drew me on board were my old mates and daily companions—but they knew me no more than they would have known a traveller from the spirit-land. My hair, which had been raven-black the day before, was as white as you see it now. They say, too, that the whole expression of my countenance had changed. I told them my story—they did not believe it. I now tell it to *you*—and I can scarcely expect you to put more faith in it than did the merry fishermen of Lofoden."

EDGAR ALLAN POE,
"A Descent into the Maelstrom"

*from The Narrative of
Arthur Gordon Pym*

———◆———

The *Narcissus* comes home

In all of sea literature there can be few descriptions of the homecoming of a great sailing ship to rival this one.

A week afterwards the *Narcissus* entered the chops of the Channel. Under white wings she skimmed low over the blue sea like a great tired bird speeding to its nest. The clouds raced with her mastheads; they rose astern enormous and white, soared to the zenith, flew past, and falling down the wide curve of the sky seemed to dash headlong into the sea—the clouds swifter than the ship, more free, but without a home. The coast to welcome her stepped out of space into the sunshine. The lofty headlands trod masterfully into the sea; the wide bays smiled in the light; the shadows of homeless clouds ran along the sunny plains, leaped over valleys, without a check darted up the hills, rolled down the slopes; and the sunshine pursued them with patches of running brightness. On the brows of dark cliffs white lighthouses shone in pillars of light. The Channel glittered like a blue mantle shot with gold and starred by the silver of the capping seas. The

Narcissus rushed past the headlands and the bays. Outward-bound vessels crossed her track, lying over, and with their masts stripped for a slogging fight with the hard sou'wester. And, in shore, a string of smoking steam-boats waddled, hugging the coast, like migrating and amphibious monsters, distrustful of the restless waves.

At night the headlands retreated, the bays advanced into one unbroken line of gloom. The lights of the earth mingled with the lights of heaven; and above the tossing lanterns of a trawling fleet a great lighthouse shone steadily, such as an enormous riding light burning above a vessel of fabulous dimensions. Below its steady glow, the coast, stretching away, straight and black, re-sembled the high side of an indestructible craft riding motionless upon the immortal and unresting sea. The dark land lay alone in the midst of waters, like a mighty ship bestarred with vigilant lights—a ship carrying the burden of millions of lives—a ship freighted with dross and with jewels, with gold and with steel. She towered up immense and strong, guarding priceless tradi-tions and untold suffering, sheltering glorious memories and base forgetfulness, ignoble virtues and splendid transgressions. A great ship! For ages had the ocean battered in vain her enduring sides; she was there when the world was vaster and darker, when the sea was great and mysterious, and ready to surrender the prize of fame to audacious men. A ship mother of fleets and nations! The great flagship of the race; stronger than the storms! and anchored in the open sea.

The *Narcissus*, heeling over to off-shore gusts, rounded the South Foreland, passed through the Downs, and, in tow, entered the river. Shorn of the glory of her white wings, she wound obe-diently after the tug through the maze of invisible channels. As she passed them the red-painted light-vessels, swung at their moorings, seemed for an instant to sail with great speed in the rush of tide, and the next moment were left hopelessly behind. The big buoys on the tails of the banks slipped past her sides very low, and, dropping in her wake, tugged at their chains like fierce watch dogs. The reach narrowed; from both sides the land approached the ship. She went steadily up the river. On the river-side slopes the houses appeared in groups—seemed to stream down the declivities at a run to see her pass, and, checked by the

mud of the foreshore, crowded on the banks. Further on, the tall
factory chimneys appeared in insolent bands and watched her go
by, like a straggling crowd of slim giants, swaggering and upright under the black plummets of smoke, cavalierly aslant. She
swept round the bends; an impure breeze shrieked a welcome
between her stripped spars; and the land, closing in, stepped
between the ship and the sea.

A low cloud hung before her—a great opalescent and tremulous cloud, that seemed to rise from the steaming brows of millions
of men. Long drifts of smoky vapours soiled it with livid trails; it
throbbed to the beat of millions of hearts, and from it came an
immense and lamentable murmur—the murmur of millions of lips
praying, cursing, sighing, jeering—the undying murmur of folly,
regret, and hope exalted by the crowds of the anxious earth. The
Narcissus entered the cloud; the shadows deepened; on all sides
there was the clang of iron, the sound of mighty blows, shrieks,
yells. Black barges drifted stealthily on the murky stream. A
mad jumble of begrimed walls loomed up vaguely in the smoke,
bewildering and mournful, like a vision of disaster. The tugs,
panting furiously, backed and filled in the stream, to hold the
ship steady at the dock-gates; from her bows two lines went
through the air whistling, and struck at the land viciously, like
a pair of snakes. A bridge broke in two before her, as if by
enchantment; big hydraulic capstans began to turn all by themselves, as though animated by a mysterious and unholy spell. She
moved through a narrow lane of water between two low walls of
granite, and men with check-ropes in their hands kept pace with
her, walking on the broad flagstones. A group waited impatiently
on each side of the vanished bridge: rough heavy men in caps;
sallow-faced men in high hats; two bareheaded women; ragged
children, fascinated and with wide eyes. A cart coming at a jerky
trot pulled up sharply. One of the women screamed at the silent
ship—"Hallo, Jack!" without looking at any one in particular
and all the hands looked at her from the forecastle head. "Stand
clear! Stand clear of that rope!" cried the dockmen, bending over
stone posts. The crowd murmured, stamped where they stood.
—"Let go your quarter-checks! Let go!" sang out a ruddy-faced
old man on the quay. The ropes splashed heavily falling in the
water, and the *Narcissus* entered the dock.

The stony shores ran away right and left in straight lines, enclosing a sombre and rectangular pool. Brick walls rose high above the water—soulless walls, staring through hundreds of windows as troubled and dull as the eyes of overfed brutes. At their base monstrous iron cranes crouched, with chains hanging from their long necks, balancing cruel-looking hooks over the decks of lifeless ships. A noise of wheels rolling over stones, the thump of heavy things falling, the racket of feverish winches, the grinding of strained chains, floated on the air. Between high buildings the dust of all the continents soared in short flights; and a penetrating smell of perfumes and dirt, of spices and hides, of things costly and of things filthy, pervaded the space, made for it an atmosphere precious and disgusting. The *Narcissus* came gently into her berth; the shadows of the soulless walls fell upon her, the dust of all the continents leaped upon her deck, and a swarm of strange men clambered up her sides, took possession of her in the name of the sordid earth. She had ceased to live.

JOSEPH CONRAD,
The Nigger of the Narcissus

THE LEADSMAN'S SONG

For England when, with favouring gale,
  Our gallant ship up Channel steered;
And, scudding under easy sail,
  The high blue western land appeared,—
To heave the lead the seaman sprung,
And to the pilot cheerly sung:
  "By the deep—*Nine!*"

And, bearing up to gain the port,
  Some well-known object kept in view,—
An Abbey-tower, a harbour-fort,
  Or beacon to the vessel true;
While oft his lead the seaman flung,
And to the pilot cheerly sung:
  "By the mark—*Seven!*"

And, as the much-loved shore drew near,
  With transport we beheld the roof
Where dwelt a friend or partner dear,
  Of faith and love a matchless proof,—
His lead once more the seaman flung,
And to the watchful pilot sung:
  "Quarter less *Five!*"

Now to the berth the ship draws nigh;
  We shorten sail,—she feels the tide.
"Stand clear the cable!" is the cry:
  The anchor's gone . . . we safely ride.
The watch is set, and through the night
We hear the seaman, with delight,
  Proclaim: "All's well!"

WILLIAM PEARCE
(from the operatic farce *Thetford Bridge*, 1793)

———◆———

The last lap

Phileas Fogg has made a bet that he will circumnavigate the
world in eighty days. He is now nearing the coast of Ireland
with only five days to go. With him in the ship *Henrietta* are
his valet Passepartout and the detective Mr. Fix, who is waiting only for an opportunity to arrest him.

The 16th of December was the seventy-fifth day since Phileas
Fogg's departure from London, and the *Henrietta* had not yet
been seriously delayed. Half of the voyage was almost accomplished, and the worst localities had been passed. In summer,
success would have been well-nigh certain. In winter, they were
at the mercy of the bad season. Passepartout said nothing; but
he cherished hope, in secret, and comforted himself with the

reflection that, if the wind failed them, they might still count on the steam.

On this day the engineer came on deck, went up to Mr. Fogg, and began to speak earnestly with him. Without knowing why— it was a presentiment, perhaps—Passepartout became vaguely uneasy. He would have given one of his ears to hear with the other what the engineer was saying. He finally managed to catch a few words, and was sure he heard his master say, "You are certain of what you tell me?"

"Certain, sir," replied the engineer. "You must remember that, since we started, we have kept up hot fires in all our furnaces, and though we had enough coal to go on short steam from New York to Bordeaux, we haven't enough to go with all steam from New York to Liverpool."

"I will consider," replied Mr. Fogg.

Passepartout understood it all; he was seized with mortal anxiety. The coal was giving out! "Ah, if my master can get over that," muttered he, "he'll be a famous man!" He could not help imparting to Fix what he had overheard.

"Then you believe that we really are going to Liverpool?"

"Of course."

"Ass!" replied the detective, shrugging his shoulders, and turning on his heel.

Passepartout was on the point of vigorously resenting the epithet, the reason of which he could not for the life of him comprehend; but he reflected that the unfortunate Fix was probably very much disappointed and humiliated in his self-esteem, after having so awkwardly followed a false scent around the world, and refrained.

And now what course would Phileas Fogg adopt? It was difficult to imagine. Nevertheless he seemed to have decided on one, for that evening he sent for the engineer, and said to him, "Feed all the fires until the coal is exhausted."

A few moments after, the funnel of the *Henrietta* vomited forth torrents of smoke. The vessel continued to proceed with all steam on; but on the 18th, the engineer, as he had predicted, announced that the coal would give out in the course of the day.

"Do not let the fires go down," replied Mr. Fogg. "Keep them up to the last. Let the valves be filled."

Towards noon Phileas Fogg, having ascertained their position, called Passepartout, and ordered him to go for Captain Speedy. It was as if the honest fellow had been commanded to unchain a tiger. He went to the poop, saying to himself, "He will be like a madman!"

In a few moments, with cries and oaths, a bomb appeared on the poop-deck. The bomb was Captain Speedy. It was clear that he was on the point of bursting.

"Where are we?" were the first words his anger permitted him to utter. Had the poor man been apoplectic, he would never have recovered from his paroxysm of wrath.

"Where are we?" he repeated, with purple face.

"Seven hundred and seven miles from Liverpool," replied Mr. Fogg, with imperturbable calmness.

"Pirate!" cried Captain Speedy.

"I have sent for you, sir—"

"Pickaroon!"

"—sir," continued Mr. Fogg, "to ask you to sell me your vessel."

"No! By all the devils, no!"

"But I shall be obliged to burn her."

"Burn the *Henrietta!*"

"Yes; at least the upper part of her. The coal has given out."

"Burn my vessel!" cried Captain Speedy, who could scarcely pronounce the words. "A vessel worth fifty thousand dollars!"

"Here are sixty thousand," replied Phileas Fogg, handing the captain a roll of bank-bills.

This had a prodigious effect on Andrew Speedy. An American can scarcely remain unmoved at the sight of sixty thousand dollars. The captain forgot in an instant his anger, his imprisonment, and all his grudges against his passenger. The *Henrietta* was twenty years old; it was a great bargain. The bomb would not go off, after all. Mr. Fogg had taken away the match.

"And I shall still have the iron hull," said the captain in a softer tone.

"The iron hull and the engine. Is it agreed?"

"Agreed."

And Andrew Speedy, seizing the banknotes, counted them and consigned them to his pocket.

During this colloquy, Passepartout was as white as a sheet, and Fix seemed on the point of having an apoplectic fit. Nearly twenty thousand pounds had been expended, and Fogg left the hull and engine to the captain, that is, near the whole value of the craft! It was true, however, that fifty-five thousand pounds had been stolen from the bank.

When Andrew Speedy had pocketed the money, Mr. Fogg said to him, "Don't let this astonish you, sir. You must know that I shall lose twenty thousand pounds, unless I arrive in London by a quarter before nine on the evening of the 21st of December. I missed the steamer at New York, and as you refused to take me to Liverpool—"

"And I did well," cried Andrew Speedy; "for I have gained at least forty thousand dollars by it!" He added, more sedately, "Do you know one thing, Captain—?"

"Fogg."

"Captain Fogg, you've got something of the Yankee about you."

And, having paid his passenger what he considered a high compliment, he was going away, when Mr. Fogg said, "The vessel now belongs to me?"

"Certainly, from the keel to the truck of the masts—all the wood, that is."

"Very well. Have the interior seats, bunks, and frames pulled down, and burn them."

It was necessary to have dry wood to keep the steam up to the adequate pressure, and on that day the poop, cabins, bunks, and the spare deck were sacrificed. On the next day, the 19th of December, the masts, rafts, and spars were burned; the crew worked lustily, keeping up the fires. Passepartout hewed, cut, and sawed away with all his might. There was a perfect rage for demolition.

The railings, fittings, the greater part of the deck, and top sides, disappeared on the 20th, and the *Henrietta* was now only a flat hulk. But on this day they sighted the Irish coast and Fastnet Light. By ten in the evening they were passing Queenstown. Phileas Fogg had only twenty-four hours more in which to get to London; that length of time was necessary to reach Liverpool, with all steam on. And the steam was about to give out altogether!

"Sir," said Captain Speedy, who was now deeply interested in Mr. Fogg's project, "I really commiserate you. Everything is against you. We are only opposite Queenstown."

"Ah," said Mr. Fogg, "is that place where we see the lights Queenstown?"

"Yes."

"Can we enter the harbour?"

"Not under three hours. Only at high tide."

"Stay," replied Mr. Fogg calmly, without betraying in his features that by a supreme inspiration he was about to attempt once more to conquer ill-fortune.

Queenstown is the Irish port at which the transatlantic steamers stop to put off the mails. These mails are carried to Dublin by express trains always held in readiness to start; from Dublin they are sent on to Liverpool by the most rapid boats, and thus gain twelve hours on the Atlantic steamers.

Phileas Fogg counted on gaining twelve hours in the same way. Instead of arriving at Liverpool the next evening by the *Henrietta*, he would be there by noon, and would therefore have time to reach London before a quarter before nine in the evening.

The *Henrietta* entered Queenstown Harbour at one o'clock in the morning, it then being high tide; and Phileas Fogg, after being grasped heartily by the hand of Captain Speedy, left that gentleman on the levelled hulk of his craft, which was still worth half what he had sold it for.

The party went on shore at once. Fix was greatly tempted to arrest Mr. Fogg on the spot; but he did not. Why? What struggle was going on within him? Had he changed his mind about "his man"? Did he understand that he had made a grave mistake? He did not, however, abandon Mr. Fogg. They all got upon the train, which was just ready to start, at half-past one; at dawn of day they were in Dublin; and they lost no time in embarking on a steamer which, disdaining to rise upon the waves, invariably cut through them.

Phileas Fogg at last disembarked on the Liverpool quay, at twenty minutes before twelve, December 21st. He was only six hours distant from London.

But at this moment Fix came up, put his hand upon Mr. Fogg's shoulder, and, showing his warrant, said, "You are really Phileas Fogg?"

"I am."

"I arrest you in the Queen's name!"

JULES VERNE,
Around the World in Eighty Days

———◆———

Land in sight

The American writer Stephen Crane is most famous for his novel of the American Civil War, *The Red Badge of Courage*. But in his brief life (he was only twenty-nine when he died) he wrote many other shorter pieces. Readers of *A Book of Railway Journeys* will remember his graphic account of a journey on the footplate of the London to Glasgow express. He was living in England at this time and had become a close friend of Joseph Conrad. His short story "The Open Boat" from which this extract is taken, was based on his experiences when shipwrecked off Cuba during the Spanish-American War.

It would be difficult to describe the subtle brotherhood of men that was here established on the seas. No one said that it was so. No one mentioned it. But it dwelt in the boat, and each man felt it warm him. They were a captain, an oiler, a cook, and a correspondent, and they were friends, friends in a more curiously ironbound degree than may be common. The hurt captain, lying against the water-jar in the bow, spoke always in a low voice and calmly, but he could never command a more ready and swiftly obedient crew than the motley three of the dingey. It was more than a mere recognition of what was best for the common safety. There was surely in it a quality that was personal and heartfelt. And after this devotion to the commander of the boat there was this comradeship that the correspondent, for instance, who had been taught to be cynical of men, knew even at the time was the best experience of his life. But no one said that it was so. No one mentioned it.

"I wish we had a sail," remarked the captain. "We might try my overcoat on the end of an oar and give you two boys a chance to rest." So the cook and the correspondent held the mast and spread wide the overcoat. The oiler steered, and the little boat made good way with her new rig. Sometimes the oiler had to scull sharply to keep a sea from breaking into the boat, but otherwise sailing was a success.

Meanwhile the lighthouse had been growing slowly larger. It had now almost assumed colour, and appeared like a little grey shadow on the sky. The man at the oars could not be prevented from turning his head rather often to try for a glimpse of this little grey shadow.

At last, from the top of each wave the men in the tossing boat could see land. Even as the lighthouse was an upright shadow on the sky, this land seemed but a long black shadow on the sea. It certainly was thinner than paper. "We must be about opposite New Smyrna," said the cook, who had coasted this shore often in schooners. "Captain, by the way, I believe they abandoned that life-saving station there about a year ago."

"Did they?" said the captain.

The wind slowly died away. The cook and the correspondent were not now obliged to slave in order to hold high the oar. But the waves continued their old impetuous swooping at the dingey, and the little craft, no longer under way, struggled woundily over them. The oiler or the correspondent took the oars again.

Shipwrecks are à propos of nothing. If men could only train for them and have them occur when the men had reached pink condition, there would be less drowning at sea. Of the four in the dingey none had slept any time worth mentioning for two days and two nights previous to embarking in the dingey, and in the excitement of clambering about the deck of a foundering ship they had also forgotten to eat heartily.

For these reasons, and for others, neither the oiler nor the correspondent was fond of rowing at this time. The correspondent wondered ingenuously how in the name of all that was sane could there be people who thought it amusing to row a boat. It was not an amusement; it was a diabolical punishment, and even a genius of mental aberrations could never conclude that it was anything but a horror to the muscles and a crime against the back. He mentioned to the boat in general how the amusement of rowing struck him, and the weary-faced oiler smiled in full sympathy. Previously to the foundering, by the way, the oiler had worked double-watch in the engine-room of the ship.

"Take her easy, now, boys," said the captain. "Don't spend yourselves. If we have to run a surf you'll need all your strength, because we'll sure have to swim for it. Take your time."

Slowly the land arose from the sea. From a black line it became a line of black and a line of white, trees and sand. Finally, the captain said that he could make out a house on the shore. "That's the house of refuge, sure," said the cook. "They'll see us before long, and come out after us."

The distant lighthouse reared high. "The keeper ought to be able to make us out now, if he's looking through a glass," said the captain. "He'll notify the life-saving people."

"None of those other boats could have got ashore to give word of the wreck," said the oiler, in a low voice. "Else the lifeboat would be out hunting us."

Slowly and beautifully the land loomed out of the sea. The wind came again. It had veered from the north-east to the south-east. Finally, a new sound struck the ears of the men in the boat. It was the low thunder of the surf on the shore. "We'll never be able to make the lighthouse now," said the captain. "Swing her head a little more north, Billie," said he.

" 'A little more north,' sir," said the oiler.

Whereupon the little boat turned her nose once more down the wind, and all but the oarsman watched the shore grow. Under the influence of this expansion doubt and direful apprehension was leaving the minds of the men. The management of the boat was still most absorbing, but it could not prevent a quiet cheerfulness. In an hour, perhaps, they would be ashore.

Their backbones had become thoroughly used to balancing in the boat, and they now rode this wild colt of a dingey like circus men. The correspondent thought that he had been drenched to the skin, but happening to feel in the top pocket of his coat, he found therein eight cigars. Four of them were soaked with sea-water; four were perfectly scatheless. After a search, somebody produced three dry matches, and thereupon the four waifs rode impudently in their little boat, and with an assurance of an impending rescue shining in their eyes, puffed at the big cigars and judged well and ill of all men. Everybody took a drink of water.

STEPHEN CRANE,
The Open Boat

WHERE LIES THE LAND TO WHICH THE SHIP WOULD GO?

Where lies the land to which the ship would go?
Far, far ahead, is all her seamen know,
And where the land she travels from? Away,
Far, far behind, is all that they can say.

On sunny noons upon the deck's smooth face,
Linked arm in arm, how pleasant here to pace!
Or, o'er the stern reclining, watch below
The foaming wake far widening as we go.

On stormy nights when wild Northwesters rave,
How proud a thing to fight with wind and wave!
The dripping sailor on the reeling mast
Exults to bear, and scorns to wish it past.

Where lies the land to which the ship would go?
Far, far ahead, is all her seamen know.
And where the land she travels from? Away,
Far, far behind, is all that they can say.

ARTHUR HUGH CLOUGH

Man overboard!

An Episode of the Red Sea

This piece has been included for its curiosity rather than its
literary value.

It was a little after half-past nine when the man fell overboard.
The mail steamer was hurrying through the Red Sea in the hope
of making up the time which the currents of the Indian Ocean
had stolen. The night was clear, though the moon was hidden behind clouds. The warm air was laden with moisture. The still
surface of the waters was only broken by the movement of the
great ship, from whose quarter the long, slanting undulations
struck out, like the feathers from an arrow shaft, and in whose
wake the froth and air bubbles churned up by the propeller trailed
in a narrowing line to the darkness of the horizon.

There was a concert on board. All the passengers were glad
to break the monotony of the voyage, and gathered around the
piano in the companion-house. The decks were deserted. The man
had been listening to the music and joining in the songs. But the
room was hot, and he came out to smoke a cigarette and enjoy a
breath of the wind which the speedy passage of the liner created.
It was the only wind in the Red Sea that night.

The accommodation-ladder had not been unshipped since leaving Aden, and the man walked out on to the platform, as on to a
balcony. He leaned his back against the rail and blew a puff of
smoke into the air reflectively. The piano struck up a lively tune,
and a voice began to sing the first verse of "The Rowdy Dowdy
Boys." The measured pulsations of the screw were a subdued but
additional accompaniment. The man knew the song. It had been
the rage at all the music halls, when he had started for India seven
years before. It reminded him of the brilliant and busy streets he
had not seen for so long, but was soon to see again. He was just
going to join in the chorus, when the railing, which had been in-
securely fastened, gave way suddenly with a snap, and he fell
backwards into the warm water of the sea amid a great splash.

For a moment he was physically too much astonished to think.
Then he realised that he must shout. He began to do this even
before he rose to the surface. He achieved a hoarse, inarticulate,
half-choked scream. A startled brain suggested the word "Help!"
and he bawled this out lustily and with frantic effort six or seven
times without stopping. Then he listened.

> Hi! hi! clear the way
> For the Rowdy Dowdy Boys.

The chorus floated back to him across the smooth water, for
the ship had already passed completely by. And as he heard the
music a long stab of terror drove through his heart. The possibility that he would not be picked up dawned for the first time on
his consciousness. The chorus started again—

> Then—I—say—boys,
> Who's for a jolly spree?
> Rum—tum—tiddley—um,
> Who'll have a drink with me?

"Help! help! help!" shrieked the man, in desperate fear.

> Fond of a glass now and then,
> Fond of a row or noise;
> Hi! hi! clear the way
> For the Rowdy Dowdy Boys!

The last words drawled out faint and fainter. The vessel was
steaming fast. The beginning of the second verse was confused
and broken by the ever-growing distance. The dark outline of the
great hull was getting blurred. The stern light dwindled.

Then he set out to swim after it with furious energy, pausing
every dozen strokes to shout long wild shouts. The disturbed
waters of the sea began to settle again to their rest. The widening
undulations became ripples. The aerated confusion of the screw
fizzed itself upwards and out. The noise of motion and the sounds
of life and music died away.

The liner was but a single fading light on the blackness of the
waters and a dark shadow against the paler sky.

At length full realisation came to the man, and he stopped
swimming. He was alone—abandoned. With the understanding
his brain reeled. He began again to swim, only now instead of

shouting he prayed—mad, incoherent prayers, the words stumbling into one another.

Suddenly a distant light seemed to flicker and brighten. A
surge of joy and hope rushed through his mind. They were going
to stop—to turn the ship and come back. And with the hope came
gratitude. His prayer was answered. Broken words of thanksgiving rose to his lips. He stopped and stared after the light—his
soul in his eyes. As he watched it, it grew gradually but steadily
smaller. Then the man knew that his fate was certain. Despair
succeeded hope. Gratitude gave place to curses. Beating the water
with his arms, he raved impotently. Foul oaths burst from him, as
broken as his prayers—and as unheeded.

The fit of passion passed, hurried by increasing fatigue. He
became silent—silent as was the sea, for even the ripples were
subsiding into the glassy smoothness of the surface. He swam on
mechanically along the track of the ship, sobbing quietly to himself, in the misery of fear. And the stern light became a tiny speck,
yellower but scarcely bigger than some of the stars, which here
and there shone between the clouds.

Nearly twenty minutes passed, and the man's fatigue began to
change to exhaustion. The overpowering sense of the inevitable
pressed upon him. With the weariness came a strange comfort.
He need not swim all the long way to Suez. There was another
course. He would die. He would resign his existence since he was
thus abandoned. He threw up his hands impulsively and sank.
Down, down he went through the warm water. The physical
death took hold of him and he began to drown. The pain of that
savage grip recalled his anger. He fought with it furiously. Striking out with arms and legs he sought to get back to the air. It
was a hard struggle, but he escaped victorious and gasping to the
surface. Despair awaited him. Feebly splashing with his hands
he moaned in bitter misery—

"I can't—I must. O God! let me die."

The moon, then in her third quarter, pushed out from behind
the concealing clouds and shed a pale, soft glitter upon the sea.
Upright in the water, fifty yards away, was a black triangular object. It was a fin. It approached him slowly.

His last appeal had been heard.

WINSTON SPENCER CHURCHILL, in
The Harmsworth Magazine, 1899

THE SHIP

The streets are brightly lit; our city is kept clean:
The third class have the greasiest cards, the first play high;
The beggars sleeping in the bows have never seen
What can be done in staterooms; no one asks why.

Lovers are writing letters, sportsmen playing ball;
One doubts the honour, one the beauty, of his wife;
A boy's ambitious; perhaps the captain hates us all;
Someone perhaps is leading the civilized life.

It is our culture that with such calm progresses
Over the barren plains of a sea; somewhere ahead
The septic East, a war, new flowers and new dresses.

Somewhere a strange and shrewd Tomorrow goes to bed
Planning the test for men from Europe; no one guesses
Who will be most ashamed, who richer, and who dead.

W. H. AUDEN

Mr. Know-All

I was prepared to dislike Max Kelada even before I knew him. The war had just finished and the passenger traffic in the ocean-going liners was heavy. Accommodation was very hard to get and you had to put up with whatever the agents chose to offer you. You could not hope for a cabin to yourself and I was thankful to be given one in which there were only two berths. But when I was told the name of my companion my heart sank. It suggested closed port-holes and the night air rigidly excluded. It was bad enough to share a cabin for fourteen days with anyone (I was going from San Francisco to Yokohama), but I should have looked upon it with less dismay if my fellow-passenger's name had been Smith or Brown.

When I went on board I found Mr. Kelada's luggage already below. I did not like the look of it; there were too many labels on the suitcases, and the wardrobe trunk was too big. He had unpacked his toilet things, and I observed that he was a patron of the excellent Monsieur Coty; for I saw on the washing-stand his scent, his hair-wash and his brilliantine. Mr. Kelada's brushes, ebony with his monogram in gold, would have been all the better for a scrub. I did not at all like Mr. Kelada. I made my way into the smoking-room. I called for a pack of cards and began to play patience. I had scarcely started before a man came up to me and asked me if he was right in thinking my name was so-and-so.

"I am Mr. Kelada," he added, with a smile that showed a row of flashing teeth, and sat down.

"Oh, yes, we're sharing a cabin, I think."

"Bit of luck, I call it. You never know who you're going to be put in with. I was jolly glad when I heard you were English. I'm all for us English sticking together when we're abroad, if you understand what I mean."

I blinked.

"Are you English?" I asked, perhaps tactlessly.

"Rather. You don't think I look like an American, do you? British to the backbone, that's what I am."

To prove it, Mr. Kelada took out of his pocket a passport and airily waved it under my nose.

King George has many strange subjects. Mr. Kelada was short and of a sturdy build, clean-shaven and dark-skinned, with a fleshy, hooked nose and very large, lustrous and liquid eyes. His long black hair was sleek and curly. He spoke with a fluency in which there was nothing English and his gestures were exuberant. I felt pretty sure that a closer inspection of that British passport would have betrayed the fact that Mr. Kelada was born under a bluer sky than is generally seen in England.

"What will you have?" he asked me.

I looked at him doubtfully. Prohibition was in force and to all appearances the ship was bone-dry. When I am not thirsty I do not know which I dislike more, ginger-ale or lemon-squash. But Mr. Kelada flashed an oriental smile at me.

"Whisky and soda or a dry Martini, you have only to say the word."

From each of his hip-pockets he fished a flask and laid them on the table before me. I chose the Martini, and calling the steward he ordered a tumbler of ice and a couple of glasses.

"A very good cocktail," I said.

"Well, there are plenty more where that came from, and if you've got any friends on board, you tell them you've got a pal who's got all the liquor in the world."

Mr. Kelada was chatty. He talked of New York and of San Francisco. He discussed plays, pictures, and politics. He was patriotic. The Union Jack is an impressive piece of drapery, but when it is flourished by a gentleman from Alexandria or Beirut, I cannot but feel that it loses somewhat in dignity. Mr. Kelada was familiar. I do not wish to put on airs, but I cannot help feeling that it is seemly in a total stranger to put mister before my name when he addresses me. Mr. Kelada, doubtless to set me at my ease, used no such formality. I did not like Mr. Kelada. I had put aside the cards when he sat down, but now, thinking that for this first occasion our conversation had lasted long enough, I went on with my game.

Conversation piece

"The three on the four," said Mr. Kelada.

There is nothing more exasperating when you are playing patience than to be told where to put the card you have turned up before you have had a chance to look for yourself.

"It's coming out, it's coming out," he cried. "The ten on the knave."

With rage and hatred in my heart I finished. Then he seized the pack.

"Do you like card tricks?"

"No, I hate card tricks," I answered.

"Well, I'll just show you this one."

He showed me three. Then I said I would go down to the dining-room and get my seat at table.

"Oh, that's all right," he said. "I've already taken a seat for you. I thought that as we were in the same state-room we might just as well sit at the same table."

I did not like Mr. Kelada.

I not only shared a cabin with him and ate three meals a day at the same table, but I could not walk round the deck without his joining me. It was impossible to snub him. It never occurred to him that he was not wanted. He was certain that you were as glad to see him as he was to see you. In your own house you might have kicked him downstairs and slammed the door in his face without the suspicion dawning on him that he was not a welcome visitor. He was a good mixer, and in three days knew everyone on board. He ran everything. He managed the sweeps, conducted the auctions, collected money for prizes at the sports, got up quoit and golf matches, organised the concert and arranged the fancy dress ball. He was everywhere and always. He was certainly the best-hated man in the ship. We called him Mr. Know-All, even to his face. He took it as a compliment. But it was at meal times that he was most intolerable. For the better part of an hour then he had us at his mercy. He was hearty, jovial, loquacious and argumentative. He knew everything better than anybody else, and it was an affront to his overweening vanity that you should disagree with him. He would not drop a subject, however unimportant, till he had brought you round to his way of thinking. The possibility that he could be mistaken never occurred to him. He was the chap who knew. We sat at the doctor's table. Mr. Kelada would certainly

have had it all his own way, for the doctor was lazy and I was
frigidly indifferent, except for a man called Ramsay who sat there
also. He was as dogmatic as Mr. Kelada and resented bitterly the
Levantine's cocksureness. The discussions they had were acrimo-
nious and interminable.

Ramsay was in the American Consular Service, and was stationed at Kobe. He was a great heavy fellow from the Middle
West, with loose fat under a tight skin, and he bulged out of his
ready-made clothes. He was on his way back to resume his post,
having been on a flying visit to New York to fetch his wife, who
had been spending a year at home. Mrs. Ramsay was a very pretty
little thing, with pleasant manners and a sense of humour. The
Consular Service is ill paid, and she was dressed always very
simply; but she knew how to wear her clothes. She achieved an
effect of quiet distinction. I should not have paid any particular
attention to her but that she possessed a quality that may be common enough in women, but nowadays is not obvious in their de-
meanour. You could not look at her without being struck by her
modesty. It shone in her like a flower on a coat.

One evening at dinner the conversation by chance drifted to
the subject of pearls. There had been in the papers a good deal of
talk about the culture pearls which the cunning Japanese were
making, and the doctor remarked that they must inevitably diminish the value of real ones. They were very good already; they
would soon be perfect. Mr. Kelada, as was his habit, rushed the
new topic. He told us all that was to be known about pearls. I do
not believe Ramsay knew anything about them at all, but he could
not resist the opportunity to have a fling at the Levantine, and in
five mintues we were in the middle of a heated argument. I had
seen Mr. Kelada vehement and voluble before, but never so voluble
and vehement as now. At last something that Ramsay said stung
him, for he thumped the table and shouted:

"Well, I ought to know what I am talking about. I'm going to
Japan just to look into this Japanese pearl business. I'm in the
trade and there's not a man in it who won't tell you that what I say
about pearls goes. I know all the best pearls in the world, and
what I don't know about pearls isn't worth knowing."

Here was news for us, for Mr. Kelada, with all his loquacity,
had never told anyone what his business was. We only knew

vaguely that he was going to Japan on some commercial errand. He looked round the table triumphantly.

"They'll never be able to get a culture pearl that an expert like me can't tell with half an eye." He pointed to a chain that Mrs. Ramsay wore. "You take my word for it, Mrs. Ramsay, that chain you're wearing will never be worth a cent less than it is now."

Mrs. Ramsay in her modest way flushed a little and slipped the chain inside her dress. Ramsay leaned forward. He gave us all a look and a smile flickered in his eyes.

"That's a pretty chain of Mrs. Ramsay's, isn't it?"

"I noticed it at once," answered Mr. Kelada. "Gee, I said to myself, those are pearls all right."

"I didn't buy it myself, of course. I'd be interested to know how much you think it cost."

"Oh, in the trade somewhere round fifteen thousand dollars. But if it was bought on Fifth Avenue I shouldn't be surprised to hear that anything up to thirty thousand was paid for it."

Ramsay smiled grimly.

"You'll be surprised to hear that Mrs. Ramsay bought that string at a department store the day before we left New York, for eighteen dollars."

Mr. Kelada flushed.

"Rot. It's not only real, but it's as fine a string for its size as I've ever seen."

"Will you bet on it? I'll bet you a hundred dollars it's imitation."

"Done."

"Oh, Elmer, you can't bet on a certainty," said Mrs. Ramsay.

She had a little smile on her lips and her tone was gently deprecating.

"Can't I? If I get a chance of easy money like that I should be all sorts of a fool not to take it."

"But how can it be proved?" she continued. "It's only my word against Mr. Kelada's."

"Let me look at the chain, and if it's imitation I'll tell you quickly enough. I can afford to lose a hundred dollars," said Mr. Kelada.

"Take it off, dear. Let the gentleman look at it as much as he wants."

Mrs. Ramsay hesitated a moment. She put her hands to the clasp.

"I can't undo it," she said. "Mr. Kelada will just have to take my word for it."

I had a sudden suspicion that something unfortunate was about to occur, but I could think of nothing to say.

Ramsay jumped up.

"I'll undo it."

He handed the chain to Mr. Kelada. The Levantine took a magnifying glass from his pocket and closely examined it. A smile of triumph spread over his smooth and swarthy face. He handed back the chain. He was about to speak. Suddenly he caught sight of Mrs. Ramsay's face. It was so white that she looked as though she were about to faint. She was staring at him with wide and terrified eyes. They held a desperate appeal; it was so clear that I wondered why her husband did not see it.

Mr. Kelada stopped with his mouth open. He flushed deeply. You could almost *see* the effort he was making over himself.

"I was mistaken," he said. "It's a very good imitation, but of course as soon as I looked through my glass I saw that it wasn't real. I think eighteen dollars is just about as much as the damned thing's worth."

He took out his pocket-book and from it a hundred-dollar note. He handed it to Ramsay without a word.

"Perhaps that'll teach you not to be so cocksure another time, my young friend," said Ramsay as he took the note.

I noticed that Mr. Kelada's hands were trembling.

The story spread over the ship as stories do, and he had to put up with a good deal of chaff that evening. It was a fine joke that Mr. Know-All had been caught out. But Mrs. Ramsay retired to her state-room with a headache.

Next morning I got up and began to shave. Mr. Kelada lay on his bed smoking a cigarette. Suddenly there was a small scraping sound and I saw a letter pushed under the door. I opened the door and looked out. There was nobody there. I picked up the letter and saw that it was addressed to Max Kelada. The name was written in block letters. I handed it to him.

"Who's this from?" He opened it. "Oh!"

He took out of the envelope, not a letter, but a hundred-dollar note. He looked at me and again he reddened. He tore the envelope into little bits and gave them to me.

"Do you mind just throwing them out of the port-hole?"

I did as he asked, and then I looked at him with a smile.

"No one likes being made to look a perfect damned fool," he said.

"Were the pearls real?"

"If I had a pretty little wife I shouldn't let her spend a year in New York while I stayed at Kobe," said he.

At that moment I did not entirely dislike Mr. Kelada. He reached out for his pocket-book and carefully put in it the hundred-dollar note.

W. Somerset Maugham,
Mr. Know-All

ON SUCH A NIGHT

On such a night as this the ships of Rome
Sailed out and out on such a darkling sea,
And many a Roman sailor dreamed of home—
Of love and life in far-off Italy.
On such a night, my dear, some Portuguese
Has leaned his sunburned shoulders on the rail,
Has heard the soothing rustle of the breeze,
Looked up, and seen, above the soft-curved sail,
The pointed mast trace missives in the sky;
Then, humming low in liquid latin tone,
Enchanted by the world's tranquillity,
Has thought of one who lived for him alone.
The sky above so deep, the stars so bright!
Oh for my love, close-held, on such a night.

Thomas Johnston

Orphans of the storm

Next day the wind had again dropped, and again we were wallowing in the swell. The talk was less of sea-sickness now than of broken bones; people had been thrown about in the night, and there had been many nasty accidents on bathroom floors.

That day, because we had talked so much the day before and because what we had to say needed few words, we spoke little. We had books; Julia found a game she liked. When after long silences we spoke, our thoughts, we found, had kept pace together side by side.

Once I said, "You are standing guard over your sadness."

"It's all I have earned. You said yesterday. My wages."

"An I.O.U. from life. A promise to pay on demand."

Rain ceased at midday; at evening the clouds dispersed and the sun, astern of us, suddenly broke into the lounge where we sat, putting all the lights to shame.

"Sunset," said Julia, "the end of our day."

She rose and, though the roll and pitch of the ship seemed unabated, led me up to the boat-deck. She put her arm through mine and her hand into mine, in my great-coat pocket. The deck was dry and empty, swept only by the wind of the ship's speed. As we made our halting, laborious way forward, away from the flying smuts of the smoke stack, we were alternately jostled together, then strained, nearly sundered, arms and fingers interlocked as I held the rail and Julia clung to me, thrust together again, drawn apart; then, in a plunge deeper than the rest, I found myself flung across her, pressing her against the rail, warding myself off her with the arms that held her prisoner on either side, and as the ship paused at the end of its drop as though gathering strength for the ascent, we stood thus embraced, in the open, cheek against cheek, her hair blowing across my eyes; the dark horizon of tumbling water, flashing now with gold, stood still above us, then came sweeping down till I was staring through Julia's dark hair into a wide and golden sky, and she was thrown forward on my heart, held up by my hands on the rail, her face still pressed to mine.

In that minute, with her lips to my ear and her breath warm in the salt wind, Julia said, though I had not spoken, "Yes, now," and as the ship righted herself and for the moment ran into calmer waters, Julia led me below.

So at sunset I took formal possession of her as her lover. It was no time for the sweets of luxury; they would come, in their season, with the swallow and the lime flowers. Now on the rough water, as I was made free of her narrow loins and, it seemed now, in assuaging that fierce appetite, cast a burden which I had borne all my life, toiled under, not knowing its nature—now, while the waves still broke and thundered on the prow, the act of possession was a symbol, a rite of ancient origin and solemn meaning.

We dined that night high up in the ship, in the restaurant, and saw through the bow windows the stars come out and sweep across the sky as once, I remembered, I had seen them sweep above the towers and gables of Oxford. The stewards promised that to-morrow night the band would play again and the place be full. We had better book now, they said, if we wanted a good table.

"Oh dear," said Julia, "where can we hide in fair weather, we orphans of the storm?"

I could not leave her that night, but early next morning, as once again I made my way back along the corridor, I found I could walk without difficulty; the ship rode easily on a smooth sea, and I knew that our solitude was broken.

My wife called joyously from her cabin: "Charles, Charles, I feel so well. What do you think I am having for breakfast?"

I went to see. She was eating a beef steak.

"I've fixed up for a visit to the hairdresser—do you know they couldn't take me till four o'clock this afternoon, they're so busy suddenly? So I shan't appear till the evening, but lots of people are coming in to see us this morning, and I've asked Miles and Janet to lunch with us in our sitting-room. I'm afraid I've been a worthless wife to you the last two days. What have you been up to?"

"One gay evening," I said, "we played roulette till two o'clock, next door in the sitting-room, and our host passed out."

"Goodness. It sounds very disreputable. Have you been behaving, Charles? You haven't been picking up sirens?"

"There was scarcely a woman about. I spent most of the time with Julia."

"Oh, good. I always wanted to bring you together. She's one of my friends I knew you'd like. I expect you were a godsend to her. She's had rather a gloomy time lately. I don't expect she mentioned it, but . . . " my wife proceeded to relate a current version of Julia's journey to New York. "I'll ask her to cocktails this morning," she concluded.

Julia came, and it was happiness enough, now, merely to be near her.

"I hear you've been looking after my husband for me," my wife said.

"Yes, we've become very matey. He and I and a man whose name we don't know."

"Mr. Kramm, what have you done to your arm?"

"It was the bathroom floor," said Mr. Kramm, and explained at length how he had fallen.

Dancing on board the *France*

That night the captain dined at his table and the circle was complete, for claimants came to the chairs on the Bishop's right, two Japanese who expressed deep interest in his projects for world-brotherhood. The captain was full of chaff at Julia's endurance in the storm, offering to engage her as a seaman; years of sea-going had given him jokes for every occasion. My wife, fresh from the beauty parlour, was unravaged by her three days of distress, and in the eyes of many seemed to outshine Julia, whose sadness had gone and been replaced by an incommunicable content and tranquility; incommunicable save to me; she and I, separated by the crowd, sat alone together close enwrapped, as we had lain in each other's arms the night before.

There was a gala spirit in the ship that night. Though it meant rising at dawn to pack, everyone was determined that for this one night he would enjoy the luxury the storm had denied him. There was no solitude. Every corner of the ship was thronged; dance music and high, excited chatter, stewards darting everywhere with trays of glasses, the voice of the officer in charge of tombola —"Kelly's eye—number one; legs, eleven; and we'll Shake the Bag"—Mrs. Stuyvesant Oglander in a paper cap, Mr. Kramm and his bandages, the two Japanese decorously throwing paper streamers and hissing like geese.

I did not speak to Julia, alone, all that evening.

We met for a minute next day on the starboard side of the ship while everyone else crowded to port to see the officials come aboard and to gaze at the green coastline of Devon.

"What are your plans?"

"London for a bit," she said.

"Celia's going straight home. She wants to see the children."

"You, too?"

"No."

"In London then."

EVELYN WAUGH,
Brideshead Revisited

CROSSING THE BAR

Lord Tennyson wrote this famous poem in 1849 while crossing in the ferry to the Isle of Wight. It took him, he said, no more than twenty minutes, though he admitted the idea had been in his mind for some time. He left instructions that in any future collection of his verse, it was to be placed at the end. It seems a fitting end to this book.

Sunset and evening star,
    And one clear call for me!
And may there be no moaning of the bar,
    When I put out to sea,

But such a tide as moving seems asleep,
    Too full for sound and foam,
When that which drew from out the boundless deep
    Turns again home.

Twilight and evening bell,
    And after that the dark!
And may there be no sadness of farewell,
    When I embark;

For though from out our bourne of Time and Place
    The flood may bear me far,
I hope to see my Pilot face to face
    When I have crost the bar.

ALFRED, LORD TENNYSON